HOME FRONT HEROES

HOME FRONT HEROES

A Biographical Dictionary of Americans during Wartime

Volume 3
O–Z

Edited by
Benjamin F. Shearer

GREENWOOD PRESS
Westport, Connecticut • London

Library of Congress Cataloging-in-Publication Data

Home front heroes : a biographical dictionary of Americans during wartime /
edited by Benjamin F. Shearer.
  p. cm.
  Includes bibliographical references and index.
  ISBN 0–313–33420–X (set : alk. paper)—ISBN 0–313–33421–8
(vol. 1 : alk. paper)—ISBN 0–313–33422–6 (vol. 2 : alk. paper)—
ISBN 0–313–33423–4 (vol. 3 : alk. paper)
  1. United States—History, Military—Miscellanea. 2. United States—
Biography—Dictionaries. 3. Heroes—United States—Biography—Dictionaries.
4. United States—Social conditions—Miscellanea. I. Shearer, Benjamin F.
E181.H755 2007
973.09'9—dc22
  [B]   2006014783

British Library Cataloguing in Publication Data is available.

Library of Congress Catalog Card Number: 2006014783
ISBN: 0–313–33420–X (set)
     0–313–33421–8 (vol. 1)
     0–313–33422–6 (vol. 2)
     0–313–33423–4 (vol. 3)

First published in 2007

Greenwood Press, 88 Post Road West, Westport, CT 06881
An imprint of Greenwood Publishing Group, Inc.
www.greenwood.com

Printed in the United States of America

The paper used in this book complies with the
Permanent Paper Standard issued by the National
Information Standards Organization (Z39.48–1984).

10 9 8 7 6 5 4 3 2 1

Contents

Alphabetical List of Biographical Entries

Fisher, Harrison
Fiske, Bradley Allen
Fitch, John
Fitzgerald, Frances
Flagg, James Montgomery
Flanner, Janet
Fleet, Reuben Hollis
Flint, Grover
Flint, Joseph Marshall
Fonda, Jane Seymour
Ford, Henry
Ford, John
Forrestal, James Vincent
Forrester, Jay Wright
Fosdick, Harry Emerson
Franken, Al
Frankfurter, Felix
Franti, Michael
Fraser, Harry W.
Frayne, Hugh
Freneau, Philip
Friedman, William Frederick
Frissell, Antonette "Toni"
Fruehauf, August Charles
Fulton, Robert
Furrer, Rudolph
Fuson, Reynold Charles
Gable, William Clark
Galloway, Joseph
Galloway, Joseph L.
Galston, Arthur William
Garand, John Cantius
Gardiner, Samuel Jr.
Garfield, Harry Augustus
Garofalo, Janeane
Garrett, Edwin Clarkson
Garson, Barbara
Garvey, Marcus
Garwin, Richard Lawrence
Gaston, Charles A.
Gatling, Richard Jordan
Gay, Edwin Francis
Gaye, Marvin
Gellhorn, Martha "Marty" Ellis
George, Daniel

Getting, Ivan A.
Gibbs, William Francis
Gifford, Walter Sherman
Giles, Nell
Gill, John
Ginsberg, Allen
Gladden, Washington
Glidden, Joseph Farwell
Glover, Danny Lebern
Goddard, Robert Hutchings
Goddard, William
Godfrey, Hollis
Godkin, Edwin Lawrence
Goldmark, Peter Carl
Gompers, Samuel
Goodman, Benjamin "Benny" David
Goodrich, Annie Warburton
Gordon, Eleanor "Nellie" Kinzie
Gorman, Carl Nelson
Gottler, Archie
Gottschalk, Louis Moreau
Gould, Beatrice Blackmar
Gould, Richard Gordon
Grable, Ruth Elizabeth "Betty"
Greeley, Horace
Green, William L.
Gregory, Dick
Griffith, David Wark
Gropper, William
Gross, Al
Gross, Frank G.
Grumman, Leroy "Roy" Randle
Guedel, Arthur Ernest
Guenther, Dan
Guthrie, Robert Chilton
Guthrie, Samuel Jr.
Guthrie, Woodrow "Woody" Wilson
Haas, Francis Joseph
Hait, James M.
Halberstam, David
Haldeman, Joe
Hale, George C.
Hall, Elbert John
Hall, John H.
Halpine, Charles Graham

List of Biographical Entries by War

REVOLUTIONARY WAR

Bard, Samuel (physician/surgeon)
Billings, William (musician)
Bingham, William (banker)
Brown, William (physician)
Bushnell, David (shipbuilder)
Butler, Thomas (gun/munitions designer)
Caldwell, James (clergy)
Chalmers, James (writer)
Church, Benjamin (physician/surgeon)
Clymer, George (financier)
Cochran, John (physician)
Craik, James (physician/surgeon)
Deane, Silas (lawyer)
De Haven, Peter (manufacturer)
Duché, Jacob (clergy)
Dwight, Timothy (writer)
Edes, Benjamin (journalist)
Evans, Israel (clergy)
Freneau, Philip (poet)
Galloway, Joseph (lawyer)
George, Daniel (writer)
Gill, John (writer)

Goddard, William (journalist)
Hopkinson, Joseph (songwriter)
Humphreys, Joshua (shipbuilder)
Johnson, William Samuel (lawyer)
Jones, John (physician/surgeon)
Keteltas, Abraham (clergy)
Leutze, Emanuel (artist)
Morgan, John (physician/surgeon)
Muhlenberg, John Peter Gabriel (clergy)
Odell, Jonathan (clergy)
Paine, Thomas (writer)
Peale, Charles Willson (artist)
Pollock, Oliver (businessman)
Revere, Paul (artist)
Rivington, James (journalist)
Robertson, James (journalist)
Rush, Benjamin (physician)
Shippen, William Jr. (physician)
Thomas, Isaiah (journalist)
Tilton, James (physician/surgeon)
Trumbull, John (artist)
Trumbull, Joseph (businessman)
Tyler, Royall (William) (writer)
Warren, Joseph (physician/surgeon)

Warren, Mercy Otis (playwright)
White, William (clergy)
Willard, Archibald McNeal (artist)
Witherspoon, John (clergy)

WAR OF 1812

Barton, William Paul Crillon
    (physician/surgeon)
Bradford, James M. (journalist)
Brander, Martin (manufacturer)
Carey, Mathew (writer)
Deringer, Henry (manufacturer)
Fitch, John (inventor)
Key, Francis Scott (songwriter)
Lingan, James McCubbin (journalist)
North, Simeon (manufacturer)
Parsons, Usher (physician/surgeon)
Stevens, John (shipbuilder)
Whitney, Eli (manufacturer)

MEXICAN WAR

Ballou, Adin Augustus (clergy)
Blanchard, Thomas (engineer)
Currier, Nathaniel (artist)
Elliott, Richard Smith (journalist)
Fulton, Robert (inventor)
Hall, John H. (gun/munitions designer)
Kendall, George Wilkins (journalist)
Lowell, James Russell (writer)
O'Sullivan, John L. (journalist)
Thoreau, Henry David (writer)

CIVIL WAR

Adams, Henry Brooks (writer)
Ager, Wilson (gun/munitions designer)
Alcott, Louisa May (novelist)
Alexander, Peter W. (journalist)
Allin, Erskine S. (gun/munitions
    designer)
Arick, Clifford (gun/munitions
    designer)
Barton, Clarissa Harlowe (nurse)

Bates, David Homer (telegrapher)
Bean, James Baxter (physician/dentist)
Bellows, Henry Whitney (clergy)
Benét, Stephen Vincent (poet)
Bennett, James Gordon (journalist)
Bethune, Thomas Greene Wiggins
    (musician)
Bickerdyke, Mary Ann Ball (nurse)
Bierce, Ambrose Gwinnett (writer)
Bierstadt, Albert (artist)
Billings, John Shaw (physician/surgeon)
Brady, Mathew B. (photographer)
Brinton, John Hill (physician/surgeon)
Brooke, John Mercer (gun/munitions
    designer)
Broun, William LeRoy (gun/munitions
    designer)
Bryant, William Cullen (journalist)
Burr, David Judson (manufacturer)
Bushnell, Horace (clergy)
Butterfield, Daniel (songwriter)
Cadwallader, Sylvanus (journalist)
Chandler, Albert Brown (telegrapher)
Chesnut, Mary Boykin (writer)
Chester, Thomas Morris (journalist)
Chisolm, John Julian (physician/surgeon)
Coffin, Charles Carleton (journalist)
Colt, Samuel (gun/munitions designer)
Conway, Moncure Daniel (writer)
Cooke, Jay (financier)
de Fontaine, Felix Gregory (journalist)
De Forest, John William (novelist)
Dix, Dorothea Lynde (nurse)
Douglass, Frederick (civil rights leader)
Ellet, Charles (shipbuilder)
Emmett, Daniel Decatur (songwriter)
Ericsson, John (inventor)
Etheridge, Anna Blair (nurse)
Gardiner, Samuel Jr. (gun/munitions
    designer)
Gaston, Charles A. (telegrapher)
Gatling, Richard Jordan (gun/munitions
    designer)
Gottschalk, Louis Moreau (musician)
Greeley, Horace (journalist)

Guthrie, Samuel Jr. (chemist)
Halpine, Charles Graham (journalist)
Hammond, William Alexander (physician/neurologist)
Haupt, Herman (engineer)
Hays, William Shakespeare (songwriter)
Henry, Benjamin Tyler (gun/munitions designer)
Henry, Edward Lamson (artist)
Henry, Joseph (inventor)
Holmes, Oliver Wendell Sr. (poet)
Homer, Winslow (artist)
Howe, Frederick Webster (gun/munitions designer)
Howe, Julia Ward (lyricist)
Hunley, Horace Lawson (shipbuilder/financier)
Knox, Thomas Wallace (journalist)
Lanier, Sydney Clopton (writer)
Lawrence, Catherine S. (nurse)
Leech, Thomas H. (manufacturer)
Leland, Henry Martyn (gun/munitions designer)
Letterman, Jonathan (physician/surgeon)
Lieber, Francis (lawyer)
Love, Alfred Henry (war protester)
Lowe, Thaddeus Sobieski Constantine (engineer)
Macarthy, Harry (actor)
Maynard, Edward (gun/munitions designer)
McClellan, George Brinton (inventor)
McClintock, James (financier/engineer)
McCulloh, Richard Sears (chemist)
McGuire, Hunter Holmes (physician/surgeon)
Melville, Herman (poet)
Mitchell, Silas Weir (neurologist)
Moore, Samuel Preston (physician/surgeon)
Morse, Samuel Finley Breese (inventor)
Mott, Lucretia Coffin (war protester)
Nast, Thomas (cartoonist)
Norton, Charles Eliot (writer)
O'Hara, Theodore (poet)
Olmsted, Frederick Law (architect)
Page, Charles A. (journalist)

Parrott, Robert Parker (gun/munitions designer)
Porcher, Francis Peyre (physician/surgeon)
Raymond, Henry Jarvis (journalist)
Read, John Braham (physician/surgeon)
Reid, Whitelaw (journalist)
Richardson, Albert Deane (journalist)
Rigdon, Charles (manufacturer)
Rodman, Thomas Jackson (gun/munitions designer)
Roebling, Washington Augustus (engineer)
Root, Elisha (gun/munitions designer)
Root, George Frederick (songwriter)
Ross, John (social activist)
Safford, Mary Jane (nurse)
Sanford, E. S. (businessman)
Sharps, Christian (gun/munitions designer)
Sheeran, James B. (clergy)
Simms, William Gilmore (poet)
Smith, Horace (manufacturer)
Spencer, Christopher M. (gun/munitions designer)
Spiller, Edward N. (manufacturer)
Starr, Ebenezer "Eban" Townsend (manufacturer)
Stedman, Edmund Clarence (poet)
Stillé, Charles Janeway (lawyer)
Stout, Samuel Hollingsworth (physician)
Strong, George Templeton (lawyer)
Taylor, Susie Baker King (nurse)
Tinker, Charles Almerin (telegrapher)
Tompkins, Sally Louise (nurse)
Villard, Henry (journalist)
Walker, Mary Edwards (physician/surgeon)
Watson, Baxter (financier/engineer)
Wesson, Daniel (manufacturer)
Whitman, Walt (poet)
Whitney, Eli Jr. (gun/munitions designer)
Williams, R. S. (gun/munitions designer)
Winchester, Oliver (manufacturer)
Wing, Henry Ebenezer (journalist)
Winner, Septimus (songwriter)
Winthrop, Theodore (novelist)

SPANISH-AMERICAN WAR

Ade, George (playwright)
Adler, Julius (songwriter)
Atherton, Gertrude (writer/novelist)
Bates, Katharine Lee (poet)
Bell, Alexander Graham (inventor)
Benjamin, Anna (photojournalist)
Bradford, Gamaliel (social activist)
Bridgman, Raymond L. (writer/novelist)
Carroll, James (microbiologist)
Crane, Stephen (writer/journalist)
Creelman, James (journalist)
Crosby, Ernest Howard (writer/novelist)
Davenport, Homer Calvin (cartoonist)
Davis, Richard Harding (journalist)
Decker, Karl (journalist)
Edison, Thomas Alva (film director)
Fiske, Bradley Allen (gun/munitions designer)
Flint, Grover (journalist)
Garrett, Edwin Clarkson (poet)
Gladden, Washington (clergy)
Godkin, Edwin Lawrence (journalist)
Gordon, Eleanor "Nellie" Kinzie (nurse)
Hattersley, Charles M. (songwriter)
Hearst, William Randolph (journalist)
Holland, John Philip (shipbuilder)
Holzmann, Abe (songwriter)
Howells, William Dean (writer/novelist)
Kinney, Dita Hopkins (nurse)
Mahan, Alfred Thayer (writer/military theorist)
McCutcheon, John Tinney (journalist)
McGee, Anita Newcomb (physician)
Mead, Lucia Ames (journalist)
Moody, William Vaughn (poet)
Morrison, Harry Steele (writer)
Munroe, Charles Edward (gun/munitions designer)
Nelan, Charles (cartoonist)
Oakley, Annie (actor/shootist)
Porter, William Sydney (a.k.a. O. Henry) (writer)
Pulitzer, Joseph (journalist)

Rea, George Bronson (journalist)
Remington, Frederic (artist)
Scovel, (Henry) Sylvester (journalist)
Senn, Nicholas (physician/surgeon)
Shakespeare, Edward Oram (physician/surgeon)
Sousa, John Philip (musician/composer)
Stickney, Joseph L. (journalist)
Vaughan, Victor Clarence (physician/surgeon)
Wood, Charles Erskine Scott (poet)

WORLD WAR I

Abrams, Ray Hamilton "Harry" (clergy)
Adams, Roger (chemist)
Addams, (Laura) Jane (war protester)
Armstrong, Edwin Howard (engineer)
Aylward, William James (artist)
Ayres, Leonard Porter (economist)
Bailey, Pearce (neurologist)
Balch, Emily Greene (war protester)
Baldwin, Roger Nash (lawyer)
Baldwin, Thomas Scott (aircraft designer)
Banker, Grace D. (women and the military)
Barsness, Nellie (physician)
Bartow, Edward (chemist)
Baruch, Bernard Mannes (financier)
Baskette, Billy (songwriter)
Becker, Maurice (cartoonist)
Bellows, George (artist)
Berlin, Irving (songwriter)
Blair, Vilray Papin (physician/surgeon)
Blunt, Katherine (chemist)
Boeing, William Edward (aircraft designer)
Booth, Evangeline Cory (clergy)
Boring, Edwin Garrigues (psychologist)
Breithut, Frederick Earnest (chemist)
Brinkley, Nell (artist/illustrator)
Brookings, Robert Somers (businessman)
Browning, John Moses (gun/munitions designer)
Bush, Samuel Prescott (businessman)

WORLD WAR II

Johnson, Clarence Leonard "Kelly" (aircraft designer)

Johnson, J. Monroe (businessman)

Jones, Frederick McKinley (inventor)

Jones, James (writer/novelist)

Julian, Percy Lavon (chemist)

Kahn, Albert (architect)

Kaiser, Henry J. (shipbuilder)

Kane, Jasper H. (chemist)

Katz, Daniel (psychologist)

Kellems, Vivien (gun/munitions designer)

Kent, Robert Harrington (engineer)

Kerkam, Earl Cavis (artist)

Keys, Ancel Benjamin (nutritionist)

Kharasch, Morris Selig (chemist)

Knudsen, William S. (industrialist)

Kollsman, Paul (inventor)

Kolthoff, Izaak Maurits (chemist)

Korematsu, Fred Toyosaburo (social activist)

Kroeger, William K. (gun/munitions designer)

Krug, Julius Albert (businessman)

Kuiper, Henry J. (religious journalist)

Kuznets, Simon (economist)

Lamarr, Hedy (actor)

Lamb, Willis Eugene Jr. (physicist)

Lange, Dorothea (photographer)

Langford, Frances (singer/actor)

Langmuir, Irving (chemist)

Lawrence, Ernest Orlando (physicist)

Lea, Tom (artist)

Leonard, Adna Wright (clergy)

Lewis, John Llewellyn (labor leader)

Lewisohn, Richard (physician/surgeon)

Liebling, Abbott Joseph (journalist)

Likert, Rensis (psychologist)

Lindbergh, Charles Augustus (social activist)

Lindner, Victor (gun/munitions designer)

Link, Edwin A. Jr. (businessman)

Linschitz, Henry (chemist)

Loesser, Francis Henry (songwriter)

Lombard, Carole (actor)

Loomis, Alfred Lee (physicist)

Loomis, Francis Wheeler (physicist)

Lorenzen, Howard Otto (engineer)

Loughead, Allan (aircraft designer)

Luce, Clare Boothe (playwright)

Maccuddam, Pi (One without a Grindstone; a.k.a. Pia Machita) (social activist)

MacLeish, Archibald (poet)

Madigan, Michael J. (industrialist)

Mainbocher (clothing designer)

Mallinckrodt, Edward Jr. (industrialist)

Mangone, Philip (clothing designer)

Manning, Reginald "Reg" West (cartoonist)

Marquand, John P. (writer/novelist)

Marshall, Peter (clergy)

Marshall, Sarah Catherine Wood (writer)

Martin, Glenn Luther (aircraft designer)

Marvel, Carl Shipp (chemist)

Masaoka, Mike Masaru (social activist)

Mauchly, John William (engineer)

Mauldin, William Henry (cartoonist)

McNutt, Paul Vories (lawyer)

Mead, George Houk (industrialist)

Mead, George Jackson (engineer)

Mead, Margaret (sociologist/ archaeologist)

Meany, George (labor leader)

Meigs, Merrill C. (journalist)

Merck, George W. (manufacturer)

Michener, James (writer/novelist)

Midgley, Thomas Jr. (chemist)

Miller, Alton Glenn (musician/bandleader)

Momaday, Navarre Scott (writer/novelist)

Morrison, Charles Clayton (clergy)

Morrison, Philip (physicist)

Moss, Sanford Alexander (engineer)

Moyer, Andrew J. (mycologist)

Mulliken, Robert Sanderson (chemist)

Murphy, Audie Leon (poet)

Murray, Henry Alexander (psychologist)

Murray, John Courtney (clergy)

Murray, Philip (labor leader)

Murrow, Edward Roscoe (journalist)

VIETNAM WAR

Jackson, Jesse Louis (civil rights leader)
Joel, Billy (singer/songwriter)
Kaman, Charles Huron (aircraft designer)
Kao, Charles Kuen (engineer)
Kerry, John Forbes (social activist)
Kilby, Jack St. Clair (engineer)
King, Martin Luther Jr. (civil rights leader)
Kistiakowsky, George Bogdan (chemist)
Komunyakaa, Yusef (poet)
Kubrick, Stanley (film director)
Kwolek, Stephanie Louise (chemist)
Laurie, James Andrew (journalist)
Levertov, Denise (poet)
Lippmann, Walter (journalist)
Lynd, Staughton (lawyer/historian)
Mailer, Norman Kingsley (writer/novelist)
McDaniel, John Lester (engineer)
McDonald, "Country" Joe (singer)
McDonald, Walter (poet)
McGuire, Barry (singer)
Mills, Charles Wright (writer)
Moody, Burdell (artist)
Moore, Robin (writer)
Morrison, Norman (social activist)
Newton, Huey P. (civil rights leader)
O'Brien, Tim (novelist/poet)
Paley, Grace (social activist)
Pardue, Kerry "Doc" (poet)
Pinsky, Robert (poet)
Pollock, Jim (artist)
Pulitzer, Joseph Jr. (journalist)
Ramsey, Paul (theologian)
Rickard, Clinton (social activist)
Rorem, Ned (musician/composer)
Rubin, Jerry C. (social activist)
Russo, Anthony "Tony" Joseph (social activist)
Salisbury, Harrison Evans (journalist)
Schairer, George Swift (aircraft designer)
Seale, Robert "Bobby" George (civil rights leader)
Seeger, Pete (singer/songwriter)
Sheehan, John Clark (chemist)

Shockley, William Bradford (physicist)
Spock, Benjamin McLane (physician)
Stafford, Patrick P. (poet)
Stone, Isidor Feinstein (journalist)
Stone, Robert Anthony (writer/novelist)
Stoner, Eugene Morrison (gun/munitions designer)
Trudeau, Garretson Beekman (cartoonist)
Tuohy, William Klaus (journalist)
Vonnegut, Kurt Jr. (writer/novelist)
Wayne, John "Duke" (actor)
Weigl, Bruce (poet)
Wells, Edward C. (aircraft designer)
Wheeler, (John) Harvey (writer/novelist)
Wiesner, Jerome Bert (engineer)
Williams, Sam B. (engineer)
Wolff, Tobias (writer/novelist)
Yarmolinsky, Adam (educator)

GULF WAR I

Amanpour, Christiane (journalist)
Arnett, Peter (journalist)
Blitzer, Wolf (journalist)
Boggs, David R. (engineer)
Buncke, Harry J. (physician/surgeon)
Coulter, Ann (writer)
Earle, Stephen "Steve" Fain (singer/songwriter)
Falwell, Jerry (clergy)
Getting, Ivan A. (engineer)
Heston, Charlton (actor)
Holliman, John (journalist)
Jackson, Jesse Louis (civil rights leader)
Kent, Arthur (journalist)
Limbaugh, Rush (journalist)
Looking Horse, Arvol (social activist)
Metcalfe, Robert M. (engineer)
Parkinson, Bradford W. (engineer)
Robertson, Pat (cleric)
Shaw, Bernard (journalist)
Simon, Bob (journalist)

List of Biographical Entries by Categories/Occupations

ARTS AND CULTURE

Actors

Ayres, Lew (WW II)
Day, Doris (WW II)
Douglas, Melvin (WW II)
Fonda, Jane Seymour (Vietnam War)
Franken, Al (Gulf War II)
Gable, William Clark (WW II)
Garofalo, Janeane (Gulf War II)
Glover, Danny Lebern (Gulf War II)
Grable, Ruth Elizabeth "Betty" (WW II)
Heston, Charlton (Vietnam War and Gulf War I)
Hope, Leslie Townes "Bob" (WW II and Vietnam War)
Lamarr, Hedy (WW II)
Lombard, Carole (WW II)
Macarthy, Harry (Civil War)
Oakley, Annie (Sp.-Am. War)
Penn, Sean (Gulf War II)
Russell, Jane (WW II)
Sarandon, Susan (Gulf War II)
Sheen, Martin (Gulf War II)
Sinatra, Francis Albert (WW II)
Stewart, James Maitland (WW II)
Wayne, John "Duke" (Vietnam War)
Young, Loretta (WW II)

Architects

Kahn, Albert (WW II)
Olmsted, Frederick Law (Civil War)

Artists

Angus, Charlotte (WW II)
Aylward, William James (WW I)
Bayer, Herbert (WW II)
Bellows, George (WW I)
Biddle, George (WW II)
Bierstadt, Albert (Civil War)
Boggs, Franklin (WW II)
Bohrod, Aaron (WW II)
Brinkley, Nell (WW I)
Brodie, Howard Joseph (WW II)

Christy, Howard Chandler (WW I)
Currier, Nathaniel (Mexican War)
Duncan, Walter Jack (WW I)
Dunn, Harvey Thomas (WW I)
Finley, William B. (WW II)
Fisher, Harrison (WW I)
Flagg, James Montgomery (WW I)
Gorman, Carl Nelson (WW II)
Harding, George Matthews (WW I)
Henry, Edward Lamson (Civil War)
Homer, Winslow (Civil War)
Kerkam, Earl Cavis (WW II)
Ladd, Anna Coleman (WW I)
Lea, Tom (WW II)
Leutze, Emanuel (Rev. War)
Leyendecker, Joseph Christian (WW I)
Moody, Burdell (Vietnam War)
Morgan, Wallace (WW I)
Peale, Charles Willson (Rev. War)
Peixotto, Ernest Clifford (WW I)
Penfield, Edward (WW I)
Pennell, Joseph (WW I)
Pollock, Jim (Vietnam War)
Remington, Frederic (Sp.-Am. War)
Revere, Paul (Rev. War)
Rockwell, Norman Percevel (WW II)
Shahn, Ben (WW II)
Smith, J. Andre (WW I)
Thayer, Abbott Handerson (WW I)
Townsend, Harry Everett (WW I)
Trumbull, John (Rev. War)
Vargas y Chávez, Joaquín Alberto
  (WW II)
Willard, Archibald McNeal (Rev. War)

Cartoonists

Becker, Maurice (WW I and II)
Davenport, Homer Calvin (Sp.-Am. War)
Gropper, William (WW I and II)
Manning, Reginald "Reg" West (WW II)
Mauldin, William Henry (WW II)
Nast, Thomas (Civil War)
Nelan, Charles (Sp.-Am. War)
Rees, David (Gulf War II)

Robinson, Boardman (WW I)
Trudeau, Garretson Beekman (Vietnam
  War)
Young, Arthur Henry (WW I)

Civil Rights Leaders

Baker, Josephine (WW II)
Bethune, Mary McLeod (WW II)
Douglass, Frederick (Civil War)
Garvey, Marcus (WW I)
Hill, T. Arnold (WW II)
Jackson, Jesse Louis (Vietnam War and
  Gulf Wars I and II)
King, Martin Luther Jr. (Vietnam
  War)
Newton, Huey P. (Vietnam War)
Randolph, Asa Philip (WW II)
Seale, Robert "Bobby" George
  (Vietnam War)
White, Walter Francis (WW II)

Clergy and Religious Leaders

Abrams, Ray Hamilton "Harry"
  (WW I)
Ballou, Adin Augustus (Mexican War)
Beers, George Pitt (WW II)
Bellows, Henry Whitney (Civil War)
Berrigan, Daniel (Vietnam War)
Berrigan, Philip (Vietnam War)
Blair, Mrs. Roswell (WW II)
Booth, Evangeline Cory (WW I)
Bushnell, Horace (Civil War)
Caldwell, James (Rev. War)
Coffin, William Sloane (Vietnam War)
Coughlin, Charles Edward (WW II)
Duché, Jacob (Rev. War)
Evans, Israel (Rev. War)
Falwell, Jerry (Gulf Wars I and II)
Fosdick, Harry Emerson (WW I)
Gladden, Washington (Sp.-Am. War)
Harkness, Georgia Elma (WW II)
Hartman, Lewis Oliver (WW II)
Holmes, John Haynes (WW I)
Keteltas, Abraham (Rev. War)

Kuiper, Henry J. (WW II)
Leonard, Adna Wright (WW II)
Looking Horse, Arvol (Gulf Wars I
and II)
Marshall, Peter (WW II)
Morrison, Charles Clayton (WW II)
Muhlenberg, John Peter Gabriel
(Rev. War)
Murray, John Courtney (WW II)
Muste, Abraham Johannes (WW II)
Niebuhr, Karl Paul Reinhold (WW II)
Odell, Jonathan (Rev. War)
Pepper, Almon R. (WW II)
Poling, Daniel Alfred (WW II)
Ramsey, Paul (WW II and
Vietnam War)
Rauschenbusch, Walter (WW I)
Robertson, Pat (Gulf Wars I and II)
Sayre, John Nevin (WW I)
Sharpton, Alfred Charles Jr.
(Gulf War II)
Sheeran, James B. (Civil War)
Skinner, Clarence Russell (WW I)
Smith, Roy Lemon (WW II)
Talbot, Francis Xavier (WW II)
Tittle, Ernest Fremont (WW II)
Weigle, Luther Allan (WW II)
White, William (Rev. War)
Witherspoon, John (Rev. War)

Clothing Designers

Cookman, Helen Cramp (WW II)
Mainbocher (WW II)
Mangone, Philip (WW II)
Patterson, Russell (WW II)

Educators

Butler, Nicholas Murray (WW I)
Compton, Karl Taylor (WW II)
Eisenhower, Milton Stover (WW II)
Gay, Edwin Francis (WW I)
Godfrey, Hollis (WW I)
Haas, Francis Joseph (WW II)
Yarmolinsky, Adam (Vietnam War)

Film Directors

Capra, Frank Rosario (WW II)
Cimino, Michael (Vietnam War)
Coppola, Francis Ford (Vietnam
War)
Edison, Thomas Alva (Sp.-Am. War)
Ford, John (WW II)
Griffith, David Wark (WW I)
Ingram, Rex (WW I)
Kubrick, Stanley (Vietnam War)
Moore, Michael (Gulf War II)

Lawyers

Baldwin, Roger Nash (WW I)
Clark, Grenville (WW II)
Davis, William Hammatt (WW II)
Deane, Silas (Rev. War)
Donovan, William Joseph (WW II)
Frankfurter, Felix (WW I)
Galloway, Joseph (Rev. War)
Garfield, Harry Augustus (WW I)
Hickey, Margaret A. (WW II)
Johnson, William Samuel (Rev. War)
Lieber, Francis (Civil War)
Lynd, Staughton (Vietnam War)
McNutt, Paul Vories (WW II)
Parker, Edwin Brewington (WW I)
Patterson, Robert Porter (WW II)
Riter, Benjamin Franklin Jr. (WW II)
Stillé, Charles Janeway (Civil War)
Strong, George Templeton (Civil War)
Wheeler, Burton K. (WW II)

Musicians, Singers, and Songwriters

Adler, Julius (Sp.-Am. War)
Baez, Joan Chandos (Vietnam War)
Barber, Samuel (WW II)
Baskette, Billy (WW I)
Berlin, Irving (WW I)
Bethune, Thomas Greene Wiggins
(Civil War)
Billings, William (Rev. War)
Brooke, Jonatha (Gulf War II)

Bukvich, Daniel J. (WW II)
Butterfield, Daniel (Civil War)
Byrne, David (Gulf War II)
Cohan, George Michael (WW I)
Collins, Judy Marjorie (Vietnam War)
Crumb, George Henry (Vietnam War)
Daniels, Charlie (Vietnam War and Gulf
  War II)
Dylan, Bob (Vietnam War)
Earle, Stephen "Steve" Fain
  (Gulf Wars I and II)
Emmett, Daniel Decatur (Civil War)
Europe, William James Reese (WW I)
Franti, Michael (Gulf War II)
Gaye, Marvin (Vietnam War)
Goodman, Benjamin "Benny" David
  (WW II)
Gottler, Archie (WW I)
Gottschalk, Louis Moreau (Civil War)
Guthrie, Woodrow "Woody" Wilson
  (WW II)
Hattersley, Charles M. (Sp.-Am. War)
Hays, William Shakespeare (Civil War)
Henderson, Ray (WW II)
Holzmann, Abe (Sp.-Am. War)
Hopkinson, Joseph (Rev. War)
Howe, Julia Ward (Civil War)
Ives, Charles Edward (WW I
  and WW II)
Joel, Billy (Vietnam War)
Keith, Toby (Gulf War II)
Key, Francis Scott (War of 1812)
Langford, Frances (WW II)
Loesser, Francis Henry (WW II)
McDonald, "Country" Joe
  (Vietnam War)
McGuire, Barry (Vietnam War)
Miller, Alton Glenn (WW II)
Pastor, Tony (WW II)
Porter, Cole Albert (WW II)
Root, George Frederick (Civil War)
Rorem, Ned (Vietnam War)
Seeger, Pete (WW II and Vietnam War)
Simmons, Russell (Gulf War II)
Smith (Said), Stephan (Gulf War II)

Sousa, John Philip (Sp.-Am. War)
Tillman, Floyd (WW II)
Wallace, Oliver (WW II)
Whiting Richard Armstrong (WW I)
Willson, Meredith (WW II)
Winner, Septimus (Civil War)
Wrubel, Allie (WW II)

Newspaper, Radio, and Television Journalists

Alexander, Peter W. (Civil War)
Alsop, Joseph Wright (Vietnam War)
Amanpour, Christiane (Gulf Wars I
  and II)
Arnett, Peter (Gulf War)
Ashmore, Harry Scott (Vietnam War)
Baggs, William "Bill" Calhoun
  (Vietnam War)
Beech, Keyes (Korean War)
Bennett, James Gordon (Civil War)
Bigart, Homer (Korean War)
Blitzer, Wolf (Gulf War I)
Bloom, David (Gulf War II)
Bradford, James M. (War of 1812)
Browne, Malcolm Wilde (Vietnam War)
Bryant, William Cullen (Civil War)
Buchwald, Art (Vietnam War)
Butterfield, Fox (Vietnam War)
Cadwallader, Sylvanus (Civil War)
Chester, Thomas Morris (Civil War)
Chodorov, Frank (WW II)
Coffin, Charles Carleton (Civil War)
Craig, May Adams (WW II)
Creel, George (WW I)
Creelman, James (Sp.-Am. War)
Cronkite, Walter Leland (Vietnam
  War)
Davis, Elmer Holmes (WW II)
Davis, Richard Harding (Sp.-Am. War)
Day, Dorothy (WW II)
Decker, Karl (Sp.-Am. War)
de Fontaine, Felix Gregory (Civil War)
Deming, Barbara (Vietnam War)
Donovan, Hedley (Vietnam War)

Dunn, William J. (WW II)
Eastman, Max Forrester (WW I)
Edes, Benjamin (Rev. War)
Elliott, Richard Smith (Mexican War)
Ethridge, Mark Foster (WW II)
Fitzgerald, Frances (Vietnam War)
Flanner, Janet (WW II)
Flint, Grover (Sp.-Am. War)
Galloway, Joseph L. (Vietnam War)
Gellhorn, Martha "Marty" Ellis
  (WW II and Vietnam War)
Giles, Nell (WW II)
Goddard, William (Rev. War)
Godkin, Edwin Lawrence (Sp.-Am. War)
Gould, Beatrice Blackmar (WW II)
Greeley, Horace (Civil War)
Halberstam, David (Vietnam War)
Halpine, Charles Graham (Civil War)
Hard, William (WW I)
Hearst, William Randolph
  (Sp.-Am. War)
Herrick, Genevieve Forbes (WW II)
Hersh, Seymour Myron (Vietnam War)
Higgins, Marguerite (Korean War)
Hobby, Oveta Culp (WW II)
Holliman, John (Gulf War I)
Hughes, Langston (WW II)
Kendall, George Wilkins
  (Mexican War)
Kent, Arthur (Gulf War I)
Knox, Thomas Wallace (Civil War)
Laurie, James Andrew (Vietnam War)
Ledeen, Michael Arthur (Gulf War II)
Liebling, Abbott Joseph (WW II)
Limbaugh, Rush (Gulf Wars I and II)
Lingan, James McCubbin (War of 1812)
Lippmann, Walter (Vietnam War)
McCutcheon, John Tinney
  (Sp.-Am. War)
Mead, Lucia Ames (Sp.-Am. War)
Meigs, Merrill C. (WW II)
Murrow, Edward Roscoe (WW II)
O'Sullivan, John L. (Mexican War)
Page, Charles A. (Civil War)
Palmer, Frederick (WW I)

Patterson, Joseph Medill (WW I)
Pinchot, Amos Richards Eno
  (WW II)
Price, Byron (WW II)
Pulitzer, Joseph (Sp.-Am. War)
Pulitzer, Joseph Jr. (Vietnam War)
Pyle, Ernest Taylor (WW II)
Raymond, Henry Jarvis (Civil War)
Rea, George Bronson (Sp.-Am. War)
Reed, John Silas (WW I)
Reid, Whitelaw (Civil War)
Richardson, Albert Deane (Civil War)
Rinehart, Mary Roberts (WW II)
Rivera, Geraldo (Gulf War II)
Rivington, James (Rev. War)
Robertson, James (Rev. War)
Rodgers, Walter C. (Gulf War II)
Salisbury, Harrison Evans (Vietnam
  War)
Schuyler, George Samuel (WW II)
Scovel, (Henry) Sylvester
  (Sp.-Am. War)
Shaw, Bernard (Gulf War I)
Sherrod, Robert Lee (WW II)
Simon, Bob (Gulf War I)
Skillin, Edward Jr. (WW II)
Stickney, Joseph L. (Sp.-Am. War)
Stone, Isidor Feinstein (Korean
  War and Vietnam War)
Swope, Herbert Bayard (WW I)
Thomas, Isaiah (Rev. War)
Tuohy, William Klaus (Vietnam
  War)
Villard, Henry (Civil War)
White, William Allen (WW II)
Wing, Henry Ebenezzer (Civil War)

Photographers and Photojournalists

Adams, Ansel (WW II)
Adams, Edward "Eddie" Thomas
  (Vietnam War)
Benjamin, Anna (Sp.-Am. War)
Bonney, Thérèse (WW II)
Bourke-White, Margaret (WW II)

Brady, Mathew B. (Civil War)
Bubbly, Esther (WW II)
Capa, Robert (Vietnam War)
Frissell, Antonette "Toni" (WW II)
Lange, Dorothea (WW II)
Patterson, Mary Marvin Breckinridge
  (WW II)
Stryker, Roy Emerson (WW II)

Poets

Bates, Katharine Lee (Sp.-Am. War)
Benét, Stephen Vincent (Civil War)
Bly, Robert Elwood (Vietnam War)
Butler, Robert Olen (Vietnam War)
Durden, Charles (Vietnam War)
Ehrhart, William Daniel (Vietnam War)
Freneau, Philip (Rev. War)
Garrett, Edwin Clarkson (Sp.-Am. War)
Ginsberg, Allen (Vietnam War)
Gross, Frank G. (Korean War)
Guenther, Dan (Vietnam War)
Haldeman, Joe (Vietnam War)
Hamill, Sam (Gulf War II)
Heinemann, Larry (Vietnam War)
Holmes, Oliver Wendell Sr. (Civil War)
Komunyakaa, Yusef (Vietnam War)
Levertov, Denise (Vietnam War)
MacLeish, Archibald (WW II)
McDonald, Walter (Vietnam War)
Melville, Herman (Civil War)
Moody, William Vaughn (Sp.-Am.
  War)
Murphy, Audie Leon (WW II)
O'Hara, Theodore (Civil War)
Pardue, Kerry "Doc" (Vietnam War)
Pinsky, Robert (Vietnam War)
Simms, William Gilmore (Civil War)
Stafford, Patrick P. (Vietnam War)
Stedman, Edmund Clarence (Civil
  War)
Weigl, Bruce (Vietnam War)
Whitman, Walt (Civil War)
Wood, Charles Erskine Scott (Sp.-Am.
  War)

Psychologists

Allport, Floyd Henry (WW II)
Boring, Edwin Garrigues (WW I)
Hovland, Carl (WW II)
Katz, Daniel (WW II)
Likert, Rensis (WW II)
Murray, Henry Alexander (WW II)
Myers, Isabel Briggs (WW II)
Terman, Lewis Madison (WW I)
Wechsler, David (WW I)
Yerkes, Robert Mearns (WW I)

Social Activists and War Protesters

Addams, (Laura) Jane (WW I)
Ali, Muhammad (Vietnam War)
Andrews, Thomas Hiram (Gulf War II)
Balch, Emily Greene (WW I)
Banyacya, Thomas (WW II)
Bennett, William John (Gulf War II)
Bradford, Gamaliel (Sp.-Am. War)
Browder, Earl Russell (WW II)
Brown, Catherine Veronica (WW II)
Catt, Carrie Chapman (WW I)
Curtis, Cathrine (WW II)
Davis, Rennie (Vietnam War)
Dellinger, David T. (Vietnam War)
Deloria, Victor "Vine" Jr. (Vietnam
  War)
Detzer, Dorothy (WW II)
Dilling, Elizabeth (WW II)
Dixon, Joseph Kossuth (WW I)
Eastman, Crystal (WW I)
Ellsberg, Daniel (Vietnam War)
Fisher, Carl G. (WW I)
Fisher, Galen Merriam (WW II)
Gregory, Dick (Vietnam War)
Harris, David Victor (Vietnam War)
Hayden, Thomas Emmett (Vietnam
  War)
Hughan, Jessie Wallace (WW I)
Jordan, David Starr (WW I)
Kerry, John Forbes (Vietnam War)
Korematsu, Fred Toyosaburo (WW II)
Laduke, Winona (Gulf War II)

Lindbergh, Charles Augustus (WW II)
Love, Alfred Henry (Civil War)
Maccuddam, Pi (One without a
  Grindstone; a.k.a. Pia Machita)
  (WW II)
Masaoka, Mike Masaru (WW II)
Montezuma, Carlos (a.k.a. Wassaja)
  (WW I)
Morgan, Anne Tracy (WW I)
Morrison, Norman (Vietnam War)
Mott, Lucretia Coffin (Civil War)
Mygatt, Tracy (WW I)
Nusbaumer, Stewart (Gulf War II)
Olmsted, Mildred Scott (WW II)
Paley, Grace (Vietnam War)
Pariser, Eli (Gulf War II)
Rickard, Clinton (WW II and
  Vietnam War)
Ross, John (Civil War)
Rubin, Jerry C. (Vietnam War)
Russo, Anthony "Tony" Joseph
  (Vietnam War)
Ryerson, Donald M. (WW I)
Schenck, Charles T. (WW I)
Schneiderman, William (WW II)
Sheehan, Cindy (Gulf War II)
Smith, Gerald Lyman Kenneth
  (WW II)
Summers, Clyde Wilson (WW II)
Thomas, Norman Mattoon
  (WW I and WW II)
Van Hyning, Lyrl Clark (WW II)
Viguerie, Richard A. (Gulf
  War I)
Villard, Helen Frances "Fanny"
  Garrison (WW I)
Walsh, Francis Patrick (WW I)
Waters, Agnes (WW II)
Winrod, Gerald Burton (WW II)
Witherspoon, Frances (WW I)

Sociologists

Mead, Margaret (WW II)
Stouffer, Samuel Andrew (WW II)

Writers, Novelists, and Playwrights

Adams, Henry Brooks (Civil War)
Adams, Samuel Hopkins (WW II)
Ade, George (Sp.-Am. War)
Alcott, Louisa May (Civil War)
Atherton, Gertrude (Sp.-Am. War)
Bierce, Ambrose Gwinnett (Civil War)
Blume, Kathryn (Gulf War II)
Bridgman, Raymond L. (Sp.-Am. War)
Buck, Pearl Sydenstricker (WW II)
Burdick, Eugene Leonard (Vietnam War)
Carey, Mathew (War of 1812)
Cather, Willa (WW I)
Chalmers, James (Rev. War)
Chesnut, Mary Boykin (Civil War)
Conway, Moncure Daniel (Civil War)
Coulter, Ann (Gulf Wars I and II)
Cozzens, James Gould (WW II)
Crane, Stephen (Civil War and
  Sp.-Am. War)
Crosby, Ernest Howard (Sp.-Am. War)
De Forest, John William (Civil War)
de Mare, Anne Catherine (Gulf War II)
Dwight, Timothy (Rev. War)
Emerson, Gloria (Vietnam War)
Garson, Barbara (Vietnam War)
George, Daniel (Rev. War)
Gill, John (Rev. War)
Hemingway, Ernest (WW I and WW II)
Hersey, John (WW II)
Hornberger, H. Richard (a.k.a. Richard
  Hooker) (Korean War and
  Vietnam War)
Howells, William Dean (Sp.-Am. War)
Jones, James (WW II)
Lanier, Sydney Clopton (Civil War)
Lowell, James Russell (Mexican War)
Luce, Clare Boothe (WW II)
Mahan, Alfred Thayer (Sp.-Am. War)
Mailer, Norman Kingsley (Vietnam War)
Marquand, John P. (WW II)
Marshall, Sarah Catherine Wood (WW II)
Michener, James (WW II)
Mills, Charles Wright (Vietnam War)

Momaday, Navarre Scott (WW II)
Moore, Robin (Vietnam War)
Morrison, Harry Steele (Sp.-Am. War)
Norton, Charles Eliot (Civil War)
O'Brien, Tim (Vietnam War)
Paine, Thomas (Rev. War)
Porter, William Sydney (a.k.a. O. Henry) (Sp.-Am. War)
Shaw, Irwin (WW II)
Sherwood, Robert Emmet (WW II)
Silko, Leslie Marmon (WW II)
Sinclair, Upton Beall (WW I)
Steinbeck, John (WW II)
Stone, Robert Anthony (Vietnam War)
Stout, Rex Todhunter (WW II)
Thoreau, Henry David (Mexican War)
Tyler, Royall (William) (Rev. War)
Vonnegut, Kurt Jr. (Vietnam War)
Warren, Mercy Otis (Rev. War)
Wharton, Edith (WW I)
Wheeler, (John) Harvey (Vietnam War)
Winthrop, Theodore (Civil War)
Wolff, Tobias (Vietnam War)
Wouk, Herman (WW II)
Ylvisaker, Nils Martin (WW II)

Women and the Military

Bandel, Betty (WW II)
Banker, Grace D. (WW I)
Cockett, Marguerite Standish (WW I)
Knowlton, Ada (a.k.a. Mrs. Oswald Chew) (WW I)
Phipps, Anita Evans (WW II)
West (Waddy), Harriet M. (WW II)
Woods, Helen Hamilton (WW II)

BUSINESS, INDUSTRY, AND LABOR

Bankers

Bingham, William (Rev. War)
Myer, Dillon Seymour (WW II)

Businessmen and -women, Industrialists, Manufacturers

Avery, Sewell Lee (WW II)
Barton, Bruce (WW II)
Behn, Sosthenes (WW II)
Brander, Martin (War of 1812)
Brookings, Robert Somers (WW I)
Budd, Ralph (WW II)
Burr, David Judson (Civil War)
Bush, Samuel Prescott (WW I)
Coffin, Howard E. (WW I)
Cole, Edward Nicholas (Korean War)
Davis, Chester Charles (WW II)
Deeds, Edward Andrew (WW I)
De Haven, Peter (Rev. War)
Denny, Reginald (WW II)
Deringer, Henry (War of 1812)
Fleet, Reuben Hollis (WW II)
Ford, Henry (WW II)
Forrestal, James Vincent (WW II)
Fruehauf, August Charles (WW I)
Furrer, Rudolph (WW II)
Gifford, Walter Sherman (WW I)
Harrison, William Henry (WW II)
Hurley, Edward Nash (WW I)
Jeffers, William Martin (WW II)
Johnson, J. Monroe (WW II)
Keller, Kaufman Thuma (WW II)
Knudsen, William S. (WW II)
Krug, Julius Albert (WW II)
Land, Edwin Herbert (Cold War)
Leech, Thomas H. (Civil War)
Legge, Alexander (WW I)
Link, Edwin A. Jr. (WW II)
Lovett, Robert Scott (WW I)
Madigan, Michael J. (WW II)
Mallinckrodt, Edward Jr. (WW II)
McCormick, Vance Criswell (WW I)
Mead, George Houk (WW II)
Merck, George W. (WW II)
Nelson, Donald M. (WW II)
North, Simeon (War of 1812)
Olin, John Merrill (WW II)
Peek, George N. (WW I)

Pollock, Oliver (Rev. War)
Rickenbacker, Edward Vernon
    (WW II)
Rigdon, Charles (Civil War)
Rosenwald, Julius (WW I)
Ryan, John Dennis (WW I)
Sanford, E. S. (Civil War)
Sarnoff, David (WW II)
Smith, Horace (Civil War)
Spiller, Edward N. (Civil War)
Starr, Ebenezer "Eban" Townsend
    (Civil War)
Stettinius, Edward Reilly Jr. (WW II)
Stevens, O. Nelson (World War II)
Trumbull, Joseph (Rev. War)
Vauclain, Samuel Matthews (WW I)
Vincent, Jessie G. (WW I)
Wesson, Daniel (Civil War)
Whitney, Eli (War of 1812)
Willard, Daniel (WW I)
Wilson, Charles Edward (WW II)
Winchester, Oliver (Civil War)
Wood, Robert Elkington (WW II)
Young, Robert Ralph (WW II)

Economists

Ayres, Leonard Porter (WW I)
Bowles, Chester (WW II)
Henderson, Leon (WW II)
Kuznets, Simon (WW II)
Mitchell, Wesley Clair
    (WW I)
Nathan, Robert Roy (WW II)
Ruml, Beardsley (WW II)

Financiers

Baruch, Bernard Mannes (WW I)
Clymer, George (Rev. War)
Cooke, Jay (Civil War)
Dillon, Clarence (WW I)
Eberstadt, Ferdinand (WW II)
McClintock, James (Civil War)
Sachs, Alexander (WW II)
Watson, Baxter (Civil War)

Labor Leaders

Bellanca, Dorothy Jacobs (WW II)
Debs, Eugene Victor (WW I)
Easley, Ralph Montgomery
    (WW I)
Fraser, Harry W. (WW II)
Frayne, Hugh (WW I)
Gompers, Samuel (WW I)
Green, William L. (WW II)
Haywood, William Dudley (WW I)
Hillman, Sidney (WW II)
Lewis, John Llewellyn (WW II)
Little, Frank (WW I)
Maisel, Robert (WW I)
Meany, George (WW II)
Murray, Philip (WW II)
Patton, James George (WW II)
Reuther, Walter (WW II)

Shipbuilders

Bushnell, David (Rev. War)
Ellet, Charles (Civil War)
Ericsson, John (Civil War)
Fitch, John (War of 1812)
Fulton, Robert (Mexican War)
Gibbs, William Francis (WW II)
Holland, John Philip (Sp.-Am.
    War and WW I)
Humphreys, Joshua (Rev. War)
Hunley, Horace Lawson
    (Civil War)
Kaiser, Henry J. (WW II)
Lake, Simon (WW I)
Stevens, John (War of 1812)

NURSING AND MEDICINE

Bacteriologists

Bayne-Jones, Stanhope (WW II)

Immunologists

Kahn, Reuben Leon (WW I)

Microbiologists

Carroll, James (Sp.-Am. War)

Neurologists

Bailey, Pearce (WW I)
Hammond, William Alexander
  (Civil War)
Mitchell, Silas Weir (Civil War)

Nurses

Barton, Clarissa Harlowe (Civil War)
Bickerdyke, Mary Ann Ball
  (Civil War)
Dix, Dorothea Lynde (Civil War)
Etheridge, Anna Blair (Civil War)
Goodrich, Annie Warburton
  (WW I)
Gordon, Eleanor "Nellie" Kinzie
  (Sp.-Am. War)
Hodgins, Agatha Cobourg (WW I)
Kinney, Dita Hopkins (Sp.-Am. War)
Lawrence, Catherine S. (Civil War)
Safford, Mary Jane (Civil War)
Taylor, Susie Baker King (Civil War)
Tompkins, Sally Louise (Civil War)
Wald, Lillian D. (WW I)

Physicians and Surgeons

Bard, Samuel (Rev. War)
Barsness, Nellie (WW I)
Barton, William Paul Crillon
  (War of 1812)
Bean, James Baxter (Civil War)
Billings, John Shaw (Civil War)
Blair, Vilray Papin (WW I)
Blalock, Alfred (WW II)
Brinton, John Hill (Civil War)
Brown, William (Rev. War)
Buncke, Harry J. (Gulf War I)
Bunnell, Sterling (WW II)
Chisolm, John Julian (Civil War)
Church, Benjamin (Rev. War)
Cochran, John (Rev. War)

Craik, James (Rev. War)
Crile, George Washington
  (WW I)
Cushing, Harvey Williams (WW I)
Davis, John Staige (WW I)
Drew, Charles Richard (WW II)
Flint, Joseph Marshall (WW I)
Guedel, Arthur Ernest (WW I)
Hench, Philip Showalter
  (Korean War)
Ivy, Robert Henry (WW I)
Jones, John (Rev. War)
Landsteiner, Karl (WW I)
Letterman, Jonathan (Civil War)
Lewisohn, Richard (WW II)
Martin, Franklin Henry (WW I)
McGee, Anita Newcomb
  (Sp.-Am. War)
McGuire, Hunter Holmes (Civil
  War)
Moore, Samuel Preston (Civil War)
Morgan, John (Rev. War)
Parsons, Usher (War of 1812)
Porcher, Francis Peyre (Civil War)
Read, John Braham (Civil War)
Richards, Alfred Newton (WW II)
Rush, Benjamin (Rev. War)
Rusk, Howard A. (WW II)
Salmon, Thomas W. (WW I)
Senn, Nicholas (Sp.-Am. War)
Shakespeare, Edward Oram
  (Sp.-Am. War)
Shippen, William Jr. (Rev. War)
Spock, Benjamin McLane (Vietnam
  War)
Stout, Samuel Hollingsworth (Civil
  War)
Tallant, Alice Weld (WW I)
Tilton, James (Rev. War)
Vaughan, Victor Clarence (Sp.-Am.
  War)
Walker, Mary Edwards
  (Civil War)
Warren, Joseph (Rev. War)
Weed, Lewis Hill (WW II)

SCIENCE, ENGINEERING, AND INVENTIONS

Aircraft Designers

Atwood, John Leland "Lee" (WW II)
Baldwin, Thomas Scott (WW I)
Bell, Lawrence Dale (WW II)
Bertelsen, William Robert (Vietnam War)
Boeing, William Edward (WW I)
Cessna, Clyde Vernon (WW II)
Curtiss, Glenn Hammond (WW I)
Douglas, Donald Wills (WW I)
Egtvedt, Clairmont "Claire" Leroy (WW I)
Grumman, Leroy "Roy" Randle (WW II)
Hughes, Howard Robard Jr. (WW II)
Hunsaker, Jerome Clark (WW I)
Johnson, Clarence Leonard "Kelly" (WW II)
Johnson, Philip Gustav (WW I)
Kaman, Charles Huron (Vietnam War)
Lawrance, Charles Lanier (WW I)
Loening, Grover Cleveland (WW I)
Loughead, Allan (WW II)
Martin, Glenn Luther (WW II)
McDonnell, James Smith (Korean War)
Northrop, John Knudsen (WW II)
Piasecki, Frank (WW II)
Schairer, George Swift (Vietnam War)
Sikorsky, Igor Ivanovich (WW II)
Wells, Edward C. (Vietnam War)
Whitcomb, Richard (WW II)
Wright, Orville and Wilbur (WW I)
Wright, Theodore Paul (WW II)

Astronomers

Baker, James Gilbert (Cold War)

Chemists

Adams, Roger (WW I)
Adkins, Homer Burton (WW II)

Bachmann, Werner Emmanuel (WW II)
Baker, William Oliver (Cold War)
Bartow, Edward (WW I)
Blunt, Katherine (WW I)
Breithut, Frederick Earnest (WW I)
Burt, William Irving (WW II)
Carothers, Wallace Hume (WW II)
Clark, William Mansfield (WW II)
Cohn, Edwin J. (WW II)
Conant, James Bryant (WW II)
Daniels, Farrington (WW II)
Dewey, Bradley (WW II)
Dow, Herbert Henry (WW II)
Elder, Albert Lawrence (WW II)
Ellis, Carleton (WW I)
Fieser, Louis Frederick (WW II)
Fuson, Reynold Charles (WW II)
Galston, Arthur William (Vietnam War)
Guthrie, Samuel Jr. (Civil War)
Hale, George C. (WW II)
Harkins, William Draper (WW II)
Hornig, Donald Frederick (WW II)
Kane, Jasper H. (WW II)
Kendall, Edward Calvin (Korean War)
Kharasch, Morris Selig (WW II)
Kistiakowsky, George Bogdan (Vietnam War)
Kolthoff, Izaak Maurits (WW II)
Kwolek, Stephanie Louise (Vietnam War)
Langmuir, Irving (WW II)
Lewis, Winford Lee (WW I)
Linschitz, Henry (WW II)
Marvel, Carl Shipp (WW II)
McCulloh, Richard Sears (Civil War)
Midgley, Thomas Jr. (WW II)
Mulliken, Robert Sanderson (WW II)
Nichols, William Henry (WW I)
Noyes, William Albert Jr. (WW II)
Parsons, Charles Lathrop (WW I)
Pauling, Linus Carl (WW II)
Schaefer, Vincent Joseph (WW II)
Seaborg, Glenn Theodore (WW II)
Sheehan, John Clark (Vietnam War)

Simmons, Hezzleton Erastus (WW II)
Small, Lyndon Frederick (WW II)
Sparks, William Joseph (WW II)
Spedding, Frank Harold (WW II)
Spence, David (WW I)
Stanley, Wendell Meredith (WW II)
Stevenson, Earl Place (WW II)
Stieglitz, Julius Oscar (WW I)
Thomas, Charles Allen (WW II)
Toch, Maximilian (WW I)
Turrentine, John William (WW I)
Veazey, William Reed (WW I)
Woodbridge, Richard George Jr.
  (WW I)

Cryptographers

Friedman, William Frederick (WW II)
Shannon, Claude Elwood (WW II)
Yardley, Herbert Osborne (WW I)

Defense Theorists

Arquilla, John (Future War)
Kahn, Herman (Cold War)
Ronfeldt, David (Future War)

Engineers

Alexanderson, Ernst Frederik Werner
  (WW II)
Armstrong, Edwin Howard (WW I)
Batt, William Loren Jr. (WW II)
Blanchard, Thomas (Mexican War)
Bode, Hendrick Wade (WW II)
Boggs, David R. (Gulf War I)
Bowles, Edward Lindley (WW II)
Bush, Vannevar (WW II)
Chu, Lan Jen (WW II)
Cray, Seymour Roger (Gulf War I)
Davies, Merton Edward (Cold War)
Draper, Charles Stark (WW II)
Dryden, Hugh Latimer (WW II)
Eckert, John Presper Jr. (WW II)
Edgerton, Harold Eugene (WW II)
Emmet, William LeRoy (WW I)

Engelbart, Douglas Carl (Vietnam War)
English, William "Bill" (Vietnam War)
Farber, Edward Rolke (WW II)
Fisher, Chester Garfield (WW I)
Forrester, Jay Wright (Cold War)
Getting, Ivan A. (Gulf War)
Goldmark, Peter Carl (WW II)
Hait, James M. (WW II)
Hall, Elbert John (WW I)
Hander, O. Benjamin (Korean War)
Haupt, Herman (Civil War)
Hazeltine, Louis Alan (WW I)
Herr, Herbert Thacker (WW I)
Herrington, Arthur William
  Sidney (WW II)
Hewlett, William R. (WW II)
Hoff, Marcian Edward "Ted" (Vietnam
  War)
Hoover, Herbert (WW I)
Hopper, Grace Brewster Murray (WW II)
Hunt, Frederick Vinton "Ted" (WW II)
Hursey, Francis X. (Gulf War II)
Hyland, Lawrence Avison (WW II)
Julian, Percy Lavon (WW II)
Kao, Charles Kuen (Vietnam War)
Kent, Robert Harrington (WW II)
Kilby, Jack St. Clair (Vietnam War)
Killian, James Rhyne Jr. (Cold War)
Lorenzen, Howard Otto (WW II)
Lowe, Thaddeus Sobieski Constantine
  (Civil War)
Mauchly, John William (WW II)
McDaniel, John Lester (Vietnam War)
Mead, George Jackson (WW II)
Metcalfe, Robert M. (Gulf War I)
Moss, Sanford Alexander (WW II)
Noble, Daniel Earl (WW II)
Norden, Carl Lukas (WW II)
Page, Robert Morris (WW II)
Parkinson, Bradford W. (Gulf War I)
Parsons, John Thoren (Cold War)
Pierce, John Robinson (WW II)
Ramo, Simon (Cold War)
Roebling, Washington Augustus (Civil
  War)

Ross, Mary G. (WW II and Cold War)
Russell, Robert Price (WW II)
Sperry, Elmer Ambrose (WW I)
Taylor, Albert Hoyt (WW II)
Terman, Frederick Emmons (WW II)
Trump, John George (WW II)
Villard, Oswald Garrison Jr.
    (WW II and Cold War)
Walker, Eric Arthur (WW II)
Walker, Hildreth "Hal" Jr.
    (Gulf War I)
Wiesner, Jerome Bert (Vietnam War)
Williams, Joseph (WW II)
Williams, Sam B. (Vietnam War)
Young, Leo Clifford (WW II)
Zworykin, Vladimir (WW II)

Geophysicists

Berkner, Lloyd Viel (WW II)

Gun and Munitions Designers

Ager, Wilson (Civil War)
Allin, Erskine S. (Civil War)
Arick, Clifford (Civil War)
Barr, Irwin R. (WW II and
    Cold War)
Brooke, John Mercer (Civil War)
Broun, William LeRoy (Civil War)
Browning, John Moses (WW I)
Butler, Thomas (Rev. War)
Colt, Samuel (Civil War)
DeWitt, John Hibbett Jr. (WW II)
Diamond, Harry (WW II)
Eichelberger, Robert John (Cold War)
Feltman, Samuel (WW II)
Fiske, Bradley Allen (Sp.-Am. War)
Garand, John Cantius (WW II)
Gardiner, Samuel Jr. (Civil War)
Gatling, Richard Jordan (Civil War)
Hall, John H. (Mexican War)
Henry, Benjamin Tyler (Civil War)
Hotchkiss, Benjamin Berkeley (WW I)
Howe, Frederick Webster (Civil War)
Kellems, Vivien (WW II)

Kroeger, William K. (WW II)
Leland, Henry Martyn (Civil War)
Lewis, Isaac Newton (WW I)
Lindner, Victor (WW II and
    Cold War)
Maxim, Hiram Stevens (WW I)
Maxim, Hudson (WW I)
Maynard, Edward (Civil War)
Moulton, Forest Ray (WW I)
Munroe, Charles Edward (Sp.-Am. War)
Musser, C. Walton (WW II)
Norris, Kenneth T. Sr. (Cold War)
Parrott, Robert Parker (Civil War)
Rabinow, Jacob (WW II)
Rodman, Thomas Jackson (Civil War)
Root, Elisha (Civil War)
Sharps, Christian (Civil War)
Spencer, Christopher M. (Civil War)
Stoner, Eugene Morrison
    (Vietnam War)
Thompson, John Taliaferro (WW II)
Tuve, Merle Antony (WW II)
Whitney, Eli Jr. (Civil War)
Williams, R. S. (Civil War)

Inventors

Bell, Alexander Graham (Sp.-Am.
    War)
Christie, John Walter (WW I)
Coover, Harry W. (Vietnam War)
De Forest, Lee (WW I and WW II)
Farnsworth, Philo Taylor (WW II)
Fessenden, Reginald Aubrey (WW I)
Glidden, Joseph Farwell (WW I)
Gross, Al (WW II)
Hammond, John Hays Jr. (WW I)
Hammond, Laurens (WW II)
Henry, Joseph (Civil War)
Higgins, Andrew Jackson (WW II)
Holt, Benjamin (WW I)
Jones, Frederick McKinley (WW II)
Kettering, Charles Francis (WW I)
Kollsman, Paul (WW II)
McClellan, George Brinton (Civil War)

Morgan, Garrett Augustus (WW I)
Morse, Samuel Finley Breese
(Civil War)

Marine Scientists

Iselin, Columbus O'Donnell
(WW II)

Mathematicians

Bucy, Richard Snowden (Cold War)
Dantzig, George Bernard (Cold War)
Kalman, Rudolph Emil (Cold War)
Nash, John Forbes (Future War)
Perry, William James (Cold War)
von Kármán, Theodore (WW II)
von Neumann, John Louis
(WW II)

Meteorologists

Spilhaus, Athelstan Frederick (WW II)

Mycologists

Moyer, Andrew J. (WW II)
Raper, Kenneth Bryan (WW II)

Nutritionists

Keys, Ancel Benjamin (WW II)

Physicists

Abelson, Philip Hauge (WW II)
Aiken, Howard (WW II)
Alvarez, Luis Walter (WW II)
Anderson, Herbert L. (WW II)
Avery, William Hinckley (WW II)
Bainbridge, Kenneth T. (WW II)
Bardeen, John (Cold War)
Bethe, Hans (WW II)
Brattain, Walter Houser (Vietnam
War)
Breit, Gregory (WW II)
Compton, Arthur Holly (WW II)
Condon, Edward Uhler (WW II)

Coolidge, William David (WW I)
Davenport, Lee Losee (WW II)
Dempster, Arthur Jeffrey (WW II)
Dicke, Robert Henry (WW II)
Drell, Sidney David (Cold War)
DuBridge, Lee Alvin (WW II)
Einstein, Albert (WW II)
Fermi, Enrico (WW II)
Feynman, Richard Phillips (WW II)
Garwin, Richard Lawrence
(Cold War)
Goddard, Robert Hutchings
(WW II)
Gould, Richard Gordon (WW II)
Guthrie, Robert Chilton (WW II)
Hansen, William Webster
(WW II)
Jewett, Frank Baldwin (WW II)
Katz, Amrom Harry (Cold War)
Kroemer, Herbert (Cold War)
Kusch, Polykarp (Cold War)
Lamb, Willis Eugene Jr. (WW II
and Cold War)
Lawrence, Ernest Orlando (WW II)
Loomis, Alfred Lee (WW II)
Loomis, Francis Wheeler (WW II)
Millikan, Robert Andrews (WW I)
Morrison, Philip (WW II)
Noyce, Robert Norton (Cold War)
Oppenheimer, Julius Robert
(WW II)
Purcell, Edward Mills (Cold War)
Rabi, Isidor Isaac (WW II)
Ramsey, Norman Foster Jr.
(WW II)
Ridenour, Louis Nicot Jr. (WW II)
Rines, Robert H. (WW II)
Schawlow, Arthur L. (Cold War)
Serber, Robert (WW II)
Shockley, William Bradford
(Vietnam War)
Szilard, Leo (WW II)
Teller, Edward (WW II and
Cold War)
Tolman, Richard Chace (WW II)

Townes, Charles Hard (Cold War)
Tsui, Daniel Chee (Cold War)
Urey, Harold Clayton (WW II)
Valley, George Edward Jr. (WW II)
Wattenberg, Albert (WW II)
Wheeler, John Archibald (WW II)
Wigner, Eugene Paul (WW II)
Wilson, Robert Rathbun (WW II)
Wolff, Irving (WW II)
Zinn, Walter Henry (WW II)

Pilots

Anderson, Charles Alfred (WW II)
Ely, Eugene (WW I)

Telegraphers

Bates, David Homer (Civil War)
Chandler, Albert Brown (Civil War)
Gaston, Charles A. (Civil War)
Tinker, Charles Almerin (Civil War)

O

OAKLEY, ANNIE (1860–1926)

Annie Oakley, "The Rifle Queen," was born Phoebe Anne Moses (Mosey) on August 13, 1860, to a poor family in Darke County, Ohio. At a young age, she became a market hunter to supplement her family's income. In the 1870s, Oakley met her husband, Frank Butler, at a shooting match, beat him by a shot, and they were married in 1876. When Butler's partner fell ill before a performance in 1882, Oakley took his place and thus began her legendary career. Oakley became her stage name. The pair performed at circuses, and in 1885, they joined Buffalo Bill's Wild West Show, where she was billed second for half of her sixteen seasons with the show. Oakley became a symbol of the capability of women while remaining traditionally feminine.

In the 1890s, Oakley's popularity surged. In 1898, with America on the verge of war with Spain, Oakley made a bold move. In April, she wrote President William McKinley and offered a company of fifty women sharpshooters in case war broke out. The president, however, was not

Annie Oakley. Courtesy of the Library of Congress.

643

impressed with her offer. In 1918, Oakley again offered a women's regiment for World War I. President Woodrow Wilson was against her plan. Instead of leading a regiment, she performed at army posts and camps for the war effort. Oakley continued shooting throughout her life. She died on November 3, 1926.

Further Reading: Riley, Glenda. *The Life and Legacy of Annie Oakley*. Norman: University of Oklahoma Press, 1994.

Kelly J. Baker

O'BRIEN, TIM (1946–)

Tim O'Brien, one of America's foremost writers about the Vietnam War, won the National Book Award in 1979 for *Going after Cacciato*. O'Brien was born on October 1, 1946, in Austin, Minnesota, and served in the infantry in Vietnam from 1969 to 1970. While there, he began writing a book that would become *If I Die in a Combat Zone Box Me Up and Ship Me Home*, a memoir of his Vietnam experiences published in 1973.

Going after Cacciato (1978) remains O'Brien's masterpiece and one of the finest novels to be published about the Vietnam War. The novel combines realism and fantasy in a three-part structure (past incidents, a night spent standing guard in an observation post, and pursuit of Cacciato, who has deserted and is attempting to walk to Paris) while exploring the nature of duty. The novel also demonstrates O'Brien's connection to **Ernest Hemingway**, especially in the "Lake Country" chapters.

O'Brien's *The Things They Carried* (1990), a hybrid of memoir and novel, consists of stories about a platoon of grunts. It was a finalist for both the Pulitzer Prize and the National Book Critics Circle Award. Vietnam veterans appear in other novels—*Northern Lights* (1975), *Tomcat in Love* (1998), and, most significantly, *In the Lake of the Woods* (1994), whose protagonist participated in the My Lai massacre.

Further Reading: Herzog, Tobey C. *Tim O'Brien*. New York: Twayne, 1997; Kaplan, Steven. *Understanding Tim O'Brien*. Columbia: University of South Carolina Press, 1995.

Edward J. Rielly

ODELL, JONATHAN (1737–1818)

Along with Joseph Stansbury, Anglican priest Jonathan Odell was one of the most important satirists to support the British cause in the American Revolution. The grandson of Reverend Jonathan Dickinson, first president of the College of New Jersey (now Princeton), Odell was born on September 25, 1737, in Newark, New Jersey. After graduating from that college in 1757, Odell became a surgeon with the British Army, served in the West Indies, then went to England to study for the ministry. He was ordained in 1767 and became the rector at St. Ann's Church in Burlington, New Jersey.

A British loyalist, Odell found himself on parole to remain within Burlington after his verses in honor of the king's birthday were sung by prisoners in the Burlington jail on July 4, 1776. He fled to New York City in December, followed in 1778 by a treason charge, and provided various support services for the British army. In 1779, Odell served as go-between in Benedict Arnold's negotiations to change sides from the Revolutionaries to the British.

Of his essays and satiric verses published during the Revolutionary War, the best known is *The American Times*, printed in 1780 under the pseudonym Camillo Querno. This three-part, 450-line satiric poem attacked all of the major Revolutionary leaders, with special venom for fellow clergy.

After the British defeat, Odell immigrated to the Canadian province of New Brunswick, where he served as registrar and clerk until 1812. He died on November 25, 1818.

Wende Vyborney Feller

O'HARA, THEODORE (1820–1867)

Theodore O'Hara was born in Danville, Kentucky, on February 11, 1820, to Kane O'Hara, a political exile from Ireland. As a young boy, he spent much of his time in nearby Frankfort. He later attended St. Joseph's College in Bardstown, Kentucky. O'Hara practiced law for several years after graduating from college, but he chose to enter the army, serving in the Mexican War. *Bivouac of the Dead*, perhaps his most well known poem, was written in memory of the Kentucky soldiers who died at Buena Vista during the Mexican War. At the end of the war, O'Hara returned to practicing law.

When the Civil War began, O'Hara was again a soldier, this time for the Confederate Army. He was appointed colonel of the Twelfth Alabama Regiment. He later served as an aide to General Albert Sidney Johnston and General John C. Breckinridge, a former classmate of O'Hara's at St. Joseph's.

At the close of the Civil War, O'Hara journeyed to Columbus, Georgia, where he began a cotton business. He eventually retired to his plantation in Alabama. He died of bilious fever on June 6, 1867. Though he was buried in Columbus, his remains were reinterred in the Kentucky State Cemetery in 1874.

Further Reading: Hughes, Nathan Cheairs, and Thomas Clayton Ware. *Theodore O'Hara: Poet-Soldier of the Old South*. Knoxville: University of Tennessee Press, 1998; Ranck, George W. *The Bivouac of the Dead and Its Author*. Cincinnati: R. Clarke Co., 1898; Ranck, George W. *O'Hara and His Elegies*. Baltimore: Turnbull Brothers, 1875.

Nicole Mitchell

OLIN, JOHN MERRILL (1892–1982)

John M. Olin was born on November 10, 1892, in East Alton, Illinois. His father, Franklin Olin, produced blasting powder for coal mines in the 1890s, and also began manufacturing ammunition. After designing a machine that loaded ammunition, Franklin founded the Western Cartridge Company in 1898, and added a plant that manufactured a primer and .22 caliber ammunition in 1903. A plant to manufacture empty ammunition shells was purchased in 1907.

During World War I, Western Cartridge Company, largely run now by John Olin, supplied ammunition to the army, but the company had difficulty obtaining high-quality brass cups for cartridge cases, so John purchased a brass casting and rolling mill as well as primer, loading, and smokeless gunpowder plants to meet the growing wartime needs of the army.

In 1931, John risked his family fortune by acquiring the bankrupt Winchester Repeating Arms Company. During World War II, Olin's Winchester Company sold more than 15 billion rounds of ammunition and millions of rifles to the U.S military and its allies. Winchester was able to design a model of the M-1 carbine in only thirteen days in 1941. By the end of the war, the company had manufactured more than one million of these rifles.

In the 1950s and 1960s, Olin's various companies developed rocket fuel for the Military, and continued to design various new types of ammunition. At the time of his death on September 8, 1982, Olin held over twenty patents in ammunition development.

Gene C. Gerard

OLMSTED, FREDERICK LAW (1822–1903)

Frederick Law Olmsted was a landscape artist, journalist, and proponent of city beautification. Born in Hartford, Connecticut, on April 26, 1822, he began his career as a farmer but ultimately failed. Then, he toured Europe, became a seaman, and eventually entered journalism by publishing articles on life in the South. He was also associated with the *New York Times* and *Putnam's Magazine*. In 1857, he was appointed the chief architect of New York City's Central Park. He later founded a landscape architecture firm, which remained in operation until 1980.

In 1861, Olmsted took leave of the Central Park project to become the general secretary of the U.S. Sanitary Commission, which inspected the conditions of the Union Army during the Civil War. The Sanitary Commission paid investigators to inspect camps, and they overwhelmingly found unsanitary conditions. The commission aided in the sanitation of the camps. After the war, Olmsted and his firm worked on various park projects, including the Golden Gate Park; Niagara Reservation; a series of parks in New York, Wisconsin, and Kentucky; and the design of the World's Columbian Exposition in 1893. A series of parks in Boston and his work on the exposition were the last of Olmsted's landscape artistry. He turned over leadership of his firm to his partners in 1895. Tragically, he had to be institutionalized for senility at McLean Hospital in Massachusetts, where he had designed the landscape. Olmsted died on August 28, 1903.

Further Reading: Rybcznski, Witold. *A Clearing in the Distance: Frederick Law Olmsted and America in the Nineteenth Century.* New York: Scribner, 1999.

Kelly J. Baker

OLMSTED, MILDRED SCOTT (1890–1990)

Mildred Scott Olmsted was an anti-war activist with a flair for organization. She was born on December 5, 1890, in Philadelphia, Pennsylvania, attended Smith College, and went into social work on graduating in 1912. During World War I, she worked for the Girls' Protective League at Camp Meade in Maryland, organizing social events that would entertain the soldiers and protect single girls from immoral behavior. She then worked in Europe on relief efforts, where she met activists who were active with the Women's International League for Peace and Freedom (WILPF).

Olmsted became active in the WILPF upon her return home. She married Allen Olmsted in 1921 and the next year was hired as executive secretary of the Pennsylvania branch of the WILPF, creating regional branches throughout the state. In 1923, Olmsted joined the national board of the WILPF. Following an international conference, she was asked to investigate discreetly the situation of German WILPF members in Nazi Germany in 1934, a dangerous mission. When she returned, Olmsted served as national organization secretary (later titled administrative secretary and executive secretary) from 1935 to 1966, despite fieldwork cutbacks and accusations that she was sympathetic to communism. She favored sanctions and nonviolent civil defense as World War II began to escalate, and formed a committee to advise conscientious objectors. Olmsted advocated nonviolence even after her retirement from the WILPF until her death on July 2, 1990.

Further Reading: Hope, Margaret Beacon. *One Woman's Passion for Peace and Freedom: The Life of Mildred Scott Olmsted.* Syracuse, NY: Syracuse University Press, 1993.

Ellen Baier

OPPENHEIMER, JULIUS ROBERT (1904–1967)

Though he later faced questions about his loyalty to America during the McCarthy era, J. Robert Oppenheimer was instrumental in the development of the atomic bomb.

Oppenheimer was born on April 22, 1904, in New York City to Julius and Ella (Friedman) Oppenheimer. He attended the Ethical Culture School, then graduated summa cum laude from Harvard College in three years. He pursued graduate studies at the University of Cambridge and Cavendish Laboratory, but received his Ph.D. from the University of Göttingen. He spent the next ten years teaching in the United States and working his way up the academic hierarchy, moving from National Research Council fellow at Harvard University to full professor at both the University of California at Berkeley and the California Institute of Technology (Caltech). Although he was a difficult professor at the beginning of his career, moving too quickly for students to understand and exploding with frustration when they failed to learn, he eventually mellowed to become a much-beloved university figure. It was during this time period that Oppenheimer became, rather naively, politically involved, attending union, communist, and Spanish Loyalist party meetings, under the direction of his girlfriend and his brother, Frank. He severed the ties with these parties (and with the girlfriend) by 1941, though his associations would later resurface to cause him a great deal of trouble.

Under the auspices of the Office of Scientific Research and Development (OSRD), Oppenheimer was recruited to work on the creation of a large-scale weapon derived from the newly emerging possibility of creating chain reactions involving rapid atomic rupture. He served a dual purpose: he worked with **Ernest Orlando Lawrence** on electromagnetic separation, vital in the creation of uranium-235 and plutonium-239, and continued his own personal research on the weapons applications of the new discoveries. His talent for integrating and assimilating large amounts of theoretical data made him a natural leader for the project. In May 1942, Oppenheimer was named coordinator of the fast-fission research after **Gregory Breit** resigned due to ethical concerns. In November, he became the director of Los Alamos Laboratory in Los Alamos, New Mexico, coordinating the weapons research, now known by the code name of the Manhattan Project.

In 1943, already under light surveillance from the FBI because of his previous attachments to the Communist Party, he was approached by intermediaries seeking information on the project to be sent to the Soviet Union. Although Oppenheimer flatly refused to disclose any information, his slowness to report the incident or the name of the man who had contacted him resulted in an investigation. The investigation presumably closed in December 1943, when Oppenheimer provided a name and a plausible explanation.

Oppenheimer headed the lab with remarkable openness and lack of compartmentalization among divisions, heightening military suspicions of security concerns, but allowing for a free flowing of information that only helped the progress of the project. He recruited, in his words, "everyone"—everyone prominent in the physics field at the time—assembling an international team of scientific superstars. Oppenheimer himself was officially ordered not to fly in airplanes or travel unguarded, both for discretion and for safety's sake. The work was dangerous and the accommodations primitive, in many cases, but only one death occurred at the site, a young scientist named Harry Daghlian, whose accident with plutonium led to his death from radiation poisoning. Oppenheimer's charm and optimism made the difference, many felt, between making the project a hardship posting and a difficult but worthwhile job.

In June 1945, when the first atomic bomb detonation test in New Mexico took place, his growing doubts of the ethicality of the development could no longer be denied. Upon witnessing the explosion, he famously quoted the *Bhagavad-Gita*: "I am become death, the destroyer of worlds." Hiroshima, Japan, was bombed on August 6, 1945, and Nagasaki three days later, both devastating strikes that killed over 100,000 people each. The Japanese surrendered on August 14, ending the war. Oppenheimer resigned from the project in October, and returned to teaching at Caltech and Berkeley.

Oppenheimer accepted the position of director of Princeton University's Institute for Advanced Study in April 1947, resigning his professorships from both California universities. Suspicion and surveillance on the part of the national government began to heighten over the next few years as McCarthyism spread, but Oppenheimer nonetheless served as a consultant to the General Advisory Committee of the Atomic Energy Commission, explaining the physics to the politicians and debating the proper and ethical military use of the weapon he had helped to create. He urged openness with the fission discoveries, arguing that scientific sharing of data among countries would only help prevent war by creating an atmosphere of mutual blackmail. He also argued that a fundamental sharing of theoretical work would hasten the efforts toward the possibility of nuclear power, at that point still many years in the future.

Amidst the beginnings of House Un-American Activities Committee (HUAC) investigations, Oppenheimer collected accolades and prizes, among them the Willkie Memorial Building Award and two honorary doctorates. He was brought before the HUAC on June 7, 1949, to testify on his links to the Communist Party and on his actions while at Los Alamos, particularly in reference to the incident of recruitment by the Soviets that had been investigated and dismissed in 1943. He was also asked to provide information on several men he had worked with both before and during the war, and on his brother and sister-in-law, both of whom were active in the Communist Party during the 1930s. His brother lost his job as a result of the hearing.

Oppenheimer continued his theoretical research into isotopes and reactors, but he was dubious of plans to develop an H-bomb, a thermonuclear device using hydrogen and capable of a thousand times the force of the original atomic bomb. He felt that it was not only morally, but also practically, questionable. Anticipating the upcoming arms race, he wrote that, even should such a device be achievable, its existence would do nothing to further the cause of global peace. On December 23, 1953, the Atomic Energy Commission suspended Oppenheimer's security clearance on President Dwight Eisenhower's orders, claiming, among other things, that he had wrongfully withheld information in an attempt to halt the production of the hydrogen bomb. After a hearing that began April 12 and lasted until May 6, 1954, the Atomic Energy Commission voted 4–1 not to restore his clearance. At the time, the proceedings were kept secret, despite public interest in the case, owing to the classified nature of much of the relevant information. Even Oppenheimer's counsel was required to leave the courtroom at several points as testimony from classified documents was entered into the record. After the outcome and transcript of the hearing had been made public, many were outraged and shocked, especially the scientists who had worked with Oppenheimer at Los Alamos, but he declined to pursue any further appeals and retreated to New Jersey and his position at the Institute for Advanced Study.

Oppenheimer continued to lecture and attend conferences, and on December 2, 1963, he received the **Enrico Fermi** Award for "especially meritorious contributions" to the atomic field from the U.S. government. In June

1966, he retired as director of the Institute for Advanced Study, intending to write a history of modern physics. Before he could write it, however, he died of throat cancer on February 18, 1967, in Princeton, New Jersey.

Further Reading: Cassidy, David C. J. *Robert Oppenheimer and the American Century*. New York: Pi Press, 2005.

Ellen Baier

O'SULLIVAN, JOHN L. (1813–1895)

The Irish-American intellectual John L. O'Sullivan coined the term "manifest destiny" in 1845. He believed that the United States was divinely ordained to expand across North America. Born in November 1813 in Gibraltar, where his father was U.S. consul to the Barbary States, O'Sullivan spent his childhood in Europe. After graduating from Columbia in 1834, he began practicing law in New York City. From 1841 to 1846, he was sole editor of the journal he had co-founded, the *United States Magazine and Democratic Review*, which he used to help win the New York vote for James K. Polk, the Democratic presidential candidate in 1844. Polk won on a platform of U.S. expansion into Texas and Oregon. O'Sullivan wrote an editorial in the July–August 1845 issue of the journal denouncing opposition to "the fulfillment of our manifest destiny to overspread the continent allotted by Providence for the free development of our multiplying millions."

O'Sullivan was also the editor of another New York Democratic organ, the *New York Morning News*, from which comes the second appearance of his term in an editorial on December 27, 1845. Manifest destiny, which rationalized the fervor of land-hungry northern Europeans migrating to the United States and heading west, became a motto in the Oregon controversy and the Mexican War. O'Sullivan continued for many years to write editorials arguing that uncivilized Indians and corrupt Mexicans would disappear into the allegedly superior race of Northern Europeans overrunning the continent. He died on February 24, 1895.

David M. Carletta

P

PAGE, CHARLES A. (1838–1873)

Charles A. Page was a clerk in the Treasury Department during the Civil War. He got the job at Treasury as a reward for his activism in Republican politics back in Mount Vernon, Iowa, where he edited the *Mount Vernon News*. Although Page had been born in Palmyra, Illinois, May 22, 1838, he went to Cornell College in Mount Vernon, and remained there after graduating. Page, the former newspaper editor, struck an agreement between Treasury Department officials and **Horace Greeley**'s *New York Tribune* that when he was caught up on his work, he could be a war correspondent.

Page proved to be a sensitive, sometimes humorous feature writer, more interested in writing about soldiers' everyday lives than about the details of battles. With Grant's army, he sent dispatches from the wilderness, Cold Harbor, and Spotsylvania. Page made it to Richmond to see President Abraham Lincoln enter fallen Richmond on April 4, 1865. He noted in a dispatch that thousands rushed to get a look at Lincoln, but the enthusiasm for Lincoln was largely confined "to the Negroes," who enthusiastically whooped, cried, and offered extemporaneous prayers of thanks.

In 1865 President Andrew Johnson appointed Page the U.S. consul in Zurich, Switzerland. The next year, with his brothers Charles and David, Page established the Anglo-Swiss Condensed Milk Company, which was immediately successful. (In 1905 Anglo-Swiss merged with the Nestlé Company.) Page, however, died in May 1873.

Further Reading: Page, Charles A. *Letters of a War Correspondent.* Edited by James R. Gilmore. Boston: L. C. Page, 1899.

Benjamin F. Shearer

PAGE, ROBERT MORRIS (1903–1992)

Physicist Robert Page spent his entire career working at the U.S. Naval Research Laboratory. Starting out as a physicist in 1927, he took over the Radar Research Section in 1938 and held ever increasingly responsible positions, finally becoming director of research from 1957 to 1966. When Page's colleague **Leo Clifford Young** determined, in 1934, that pulsed radio waves would be more effective in detecting and plotting a target than continuous waves, it was Page who actually fabricated the very first pulse radar, which was used extensively during World War II. The XAF radar was installed in ships and the CXAM was installed as the SK set or the "flying bedspring" in planes.

Page was born in St. Paul, Minnesota, on June 2, 1903. He did his undergraduate work at Hamline University, majoring in physics and graduating in 1927. He earned his master's degree in physics at George Washington University while employed at the Naval Research Laboratory. Page continued his pioneering work in radar, developing further systems that could focus on targets and contributing to Cold War systems employed to detect missile attacks. He held seventy-five patents. Page also chronicled his interest in radar in his 1962 book, *The Origin of Radar.*

Page was the recipient of numerous honors, including the navy's Distinguished Civilian Service Award in 1945. A year later he received a Presidential Certificate of Merit. The Institute of Radio Engineers honored him with its **Harry Diamond** Memorial Award in 1953. Page died on May 15, 1992.

Benjamin F. Shearer

PAINE, THOMAS (1737–1809)

Thomas Paine was an international revolutionary whose pamphlet, *Common Sense,* influenced the course of the American Revolution. Paine was born in Thetford, England, on January 29, 1737. His father was a Quaker and his mother a strict Anglican. Paine was educated at the local grammar school but left when he was thirteen to work for his father as a stay-maker's apprentice. Three years later he ran away to sea and served on a privateer for a short time. When he returned he worked as a journeyman for stay-makers in London and Dover before marrying and setting up his own shop in Sandwich in 1759.

His wife died within a year and Paine, unhappy as a stay-maker, decided to prepare for the excise officer's examination. He was appointed to a low-level position with the excise in 1762, but was dismissed in 1765 for filing a report without examining the goods. Paine applied for readmission to the excise three years later and was given a post in Lewes, Sussex, where he remarried and ran a tobacco shop. He spent the winter of 1772–1773 in London, representing excise officers in a campaign for higher wages. The campaign failed, as did Paine's business. He was dismissed from his government post, his shop and effects were sold by public auction, and he was forced to leave Lewes to avoid being imprisoned for debt. Paine's marriage broke up shortly thereafter, and he decided to seek a fresh start in America. After obtaining letters of introduction from Benjamin Franklin, whom he had met while in London, Paine set sail for the New World.

Paine arrived in Philadelphia on November 30, 1774, with the intention of establishing an academy for young women. Instead, his letter of introduction from Franklin earned him a position as co-editor of *Pennsylvania Magazine*. Political change was in the air when Paine arrived in America; the First Continental Congress had assembled in Philadelphia earlier that fall. Paine's experience with

Thomas Paine. Courtesy of the Library of Congress.

Pennsylvania Magazine quickly familiarized him with the issues involved in the colonists' conflict with Britain and introduced him to the literary, philosophical, and political circles of Philadelphia. In addition to editing the periodical, Paine contributed articles on a broad range of topics including the right of the colonists to defend themselves by recourse to arms.

By the end of Paine's first year in America, the situation between Britain and the Colonies had deteriorated considerably. British troops had clashed with the American militia in April 1775, and the Second Continental Congress in May had failed to bring about conciliation. It was in this context that Paine sat down to write *Common Sense*, a pamphlet that transformed the terms of the political debate and significantly influenced the course of the American Revolution. The pamphlet was published in January 1776 and went through twenty-five editions within a year. The exact circulation of *Common Sense* is unknown, but scholars agree that it was unprecedented in eighteenth-century America. Paine's simple and straightforward style made his arguments accessible to a wide audience, reaching hundreds of thousands of readers in 1776 alone. By appealing to a mass readership, Paine extended political discourse beyond the narrow elite to whom political writings were typically addressed. The pamphlet presented a forceful argument both for the independence of the American Colonies from Britain and for the superiority of republican government over hereditary monarchy.

Shortly after the signing of the Declaration of Independence, Paine was appointed aide-de-camp to General Nathanael Greene at Fort Lee on the Hudson River. When Fort Washington fell to the British in the late fall of 1776, Paine joined the continental troops in their long retreat across New Jersey. With American morale severely undermined and British troops steadily advancing, Paine once again turned his pen to bolstering the revolutionary cause. The first number of *The American Crisis*, printed in the *Pennsylvania Journal* on December 19, opened with Paine's most frequently quoted line: "These are the times that try men's souls." As Paine reminded his readers, however, "the harder the conflict, the more glorious the triumph." George Washington reportedly ordered Paine's essay read to his troops before the famous crossing of the Delaware. Paine was appointed secretary to the Congressional Committee on Foreign Affairs in 1777, a post that enabled him to devote nearly all his time to patriotic writings. He published several more *Crisis* essays in support of the war effort. The essays appeared in pamphlet form and were reprinted in newspapers throughout the Colonies. Despite the Colonial army's repeated setbacks, Paine continued to insist upon the feasibility of American victory.

Paine returned to Europe in 1787 to seek financial backing for a single-span bridge he had designed. He expected to be back in America within the year; once in Europe, however, Paine was caught up in revolutionary tide on that side of the ocean as well. It would be another fifteen years before he finally returned to America. While in Paris in the winter of 1789–1790, Paine wrote to Edmund Burke in England about the progress of the French Revolution. Burke had supported the American cause in the 1770s, and Paine probably expected a similar response regarding France. Instead Burke, unconvinced by Paine's characterization of the revolution as beneficial, denounced the events in France and warned his fellow Englishmen about the threat of contagion that the French revolution posed. When Burke published his *Reflections on the Revolution in France* (1790), Paine responded with *The Rights of Man*, in which he both defended the revolutionary cause in France and set out the general principles of republican government.

Like *Common Sense*, *The Rights of Man* appealed to a wide audience—about 100,000 copies were sold in the first two years—and drew the lower orders of society into the political arena. The pamphlet helped to stimulate a broad-based movement for political reform in Britain. Paine was charged with seditious libel after publishing Part 2 of *The Rights of Man* in 1792, and a royal proclamation against seditious writings discouraged the circulation of his work. While awaiting trial, Paine published his *Letter Addressed to the Addressers of the Late Proclamation*, denying the legitimacy of the British political system. Paine left England in September 1792 and was subsequently convicted in abstentia of seditious libel. Throughout Britain, loyalist groups burned Paine in effigy.

In France, Paine was hailed as a hero; the National Assembly made him an honorary French citizen, and he was elected to the National Convention to represent Pays de Calais. The tide turned against Paine shortly thereafter, though, when he argued at the trial and sentencing of Louis XVI that the deposed monarch's life should be spared. He was subsequently arrested by the Jacobins and imprisoned in the Palais de Luxembourg in December 1793, having just completed Part 1 of the *Age of Reason*. Paine narrowly escaped execution and was released on November 4, 1794. He was reinstated in the National Convention and resumed work on Part 2 of the *Age of Reason*, which was published in 1795.

When Paine returned to America on November 1, 1802, he found himself the target of character assassination in the Federalist press for his support of the French Revolution (which Federalists saw as exemplifying the dangers of extreme democracy and social leveling), and for his espousal of deism in the *Age of Reason*. Many Republicans also rejected Paine for his aggressive infidelity. His health began to decline in July 1806, and he died three years later on June 8 with relatively few supporters.

Further Reading: Foner, Eric. *Tom Paine and Revolutionary America*. New York: Oxford University Press, 1976.

Kathleen Ruppert

PALEY, GRACE (1922–)

Grace Paley, an award-winning author, has been a well-known anti-war and anti-nuclear activist since 1961. Born in the Bronx, her parents were Russian immigrants who had been persecuted by the czar. As a result, she grew up in a family that was a living example of what happens to victims of injustice and the abuse of power.

In the late 1950s, married and with children in school, Paley began to protest with fellow Parent-Teacher Association members against nuclear tests that sent radioactivity into the food chain, against the arms race, and against the air raid drills that her children practiced in school. Then, in 1961, the American Friends Service Committee (Quakers) approached a number of Greenwich Village residents—including Paley—to establish a Peace Center to help counsel draft resistors and to organize protests against the Vietnam War. She became the secretary of the Greenwich Village Peace Center and worked to educate the public through theater events, art work, teach-ins, and protests. In 1969 she visited Vietnam and helped to escort home former American POWs. In 1972, she wrote an article for the *New York Times* based on her experience and titled "The Man in the Sky Is a Killer."

Paley has continued to have an impact on society's attitude toward militarism and nuclear weapons through involvement in protests and publishing of nonfiction articles. In 1978, she was arrested for protesting at the White House, and again in 1980 she was arrested at the Pentagon as a participant in a march sponsored by the Coalition for a Non-Nuclear World. An adherent of nonviolent protest, Paley views non-violence as a way to live in a dangerous world.

William P. Toth

PALMER, FREDERICK (1873–1958)

During World War I, Frederick Palmer served a dual role: as a writer and war correspondent, and as General John J. Pershing's censor, whose job was to try to rein in his fellow reporters. Palmer was born on January 29, 1873, in Pleasantville, Pennsylvania. His first war, the Greco-Turkish War in 1896–1897, helped to prepare him for the venture into France in World War I, for which he is best known. At the front in France, Palmer became a good friend of General Pershing, and as of 1917, joined his staff as chief censor. Though he had worked for the Associated Press, he had switched sides in the view of many, and controlled the flow of military reporting from the Military Intelligence Service, which vetted reporters' dispatches. He instituted the policy that facts, even facts observed firsthand by a reporter, could be reported only if they were listed in official press releases. Offenders were charged high fines. Frequently, when battles had been going badly, the facts were altered so that he was forced to lie to bolster the spirits of the general public.

After the heaviest level of the military censorship was lifted, Palmer wrote *My Year of the War* in 1915. He later went on to cover many other wars, including World War II. Over the course of his career, he reported from dozens of countries. Palmer died on September 2, 1958, in Charlottesville, Virginia.

Further Reading: Haverstock, Nathan A. *Fifty Years at the Front; The Life of War Correspondent Frederick Palmer*. New York: Brassey's, 1996.

Ellen Baier

PARDUE, KERRY "DOC" (1948–)

Kerry Pardue came to poetry later in life as a means of healing himself of post-traumatic stress disorder caused by his experience as a medic during the Vietnam War. Pardue was raised in Detroit, Michigan, and Sauk Village, Illinois. He claims a recruiter, upon seeing the results of his tests, told him he could be a medic instead of a foot soldier in Vietnam. Thinking he would be assigned to a hospital, Pardue signed up for an extra year of service, but found himself as a combat medic. In 1968 and 1969 Pardue was a medic with three different units. Finding himself back at home a 100 percent disabled service-connected veteran, Pardue set out on his new life after Vietnam.

While he worked on his associate's degree in police science at Thomas Nelson Community College in Hampton, Virginia, and later his bachelor's degree in political science at Christopher Newport University (1974), Pardue made ends meet working as a detective for the Newport News Police Department. In 1981 he took a job as a postal carrier and was eventually promoted to Director of Postal/Community Relations for the Arizona Post Office. In 1992 he became a recruiter for a private technical college, retiring in 2003.

Retirement gave Pardue time to deal with his demons by writing poetry about his war experiences. *Poems in the Keys of Life: Reflections of a Combat Medic* was published in 2005. Pardue found in these poems a road back home.

Benjamin F. Shearer

PARISER, ELI (1981–)

Eli Pariser used his computer skills to coordinate the MoveOn organization's campaign against the war in Iraq and to promote other progressive causes. He was born in 1981 in Camden, Maine. A precocious and intelligent young man, Pariser graduated from Simon's Rock College of Bard at age nineteen. He deferred his acceptance to the University of Chicago's law school to work as a web designer. Pariser was also active in protests against globalization, but in 2000 he began to despair of confrontational politics.

Any sense of Pariser's political apathy was shattered by the terrorist attacks of September 11, 2001, and concern that President George W. Bush might respond to the attacks in a violent fashion. He created 9-11peace.org, an online petition calling for military restraint. His petition garnered over 500,000 signatures, bringing Pariser to the attention of Wes Boyd, who founded the MoveOn organization during the impeachment of President Bill Clinton.

Boyd invited Pariser to unite their web sites, and membership doubled after Pariser joined MoveOn in 2002. Boyd tapped Pariser to head the organization's opposition to military intervention in Iraq. Before he spoke at a February 2003 New York City anti-war rally, Pariser sought the online collective wisdom of MoveOn supporters. The result was Pariser's pragmatic message than an invasion of Iraq would not make America safer. His labors raised over $400,000 for anti-war advertising.

The war, however, did not disillusion Pariser, who assumed leadership of MoveOn's progressive political action committee, which he runs from his New York City apartment.

Ron Briley

PARKER, EDWIN BREWINGTON (1868–1929)

Edwin Brewington Parker arbitrated over $1 billion in international claims related to World War I. Born in Missouri on September 7, 1868, Parker earned an LL.B. from the University of Texas in 1889. He joined the firm of Baker, Botts, Baker & Lovett in 1893. By 1903, he had become a partner in the firm and prominent in the legal community.

In September 1917, Parker was appointed Priorities Commissioner for the War Industries Board. The priorities commissioner headed a division that apportioned materials to various war functions, work that included arbitrating the claims of multiple industries and government agencies. Following the war,

Parker became chair of the Liquidation Commission, which was responsible for shipping home or selling the $3 billion of U.S. Army munitions and supplies still in France.

After a brief return to law practice, in 1923 Parker was appointed umpire of the Mixed Claims Commission, United States and Germany. This commission was responsible for arbitrating legal claims related to the war, including novel issues such as legal obligations related to airplanes, submarines, and poison gas. The commission processed over 12,000 claims worth almost $1.5 billion. So successful was Parker's leadership that the Tripartite Claims Commission—United States, Austria, and Hungary—was designed for him to head. In 1928, he also arbitrated Austrian and German claims against the United States for seizure of ships.

Parker's awards included the Distinguished Service Medal, the French Legion of Honor, and the Polish Order of Polonia Restituta. He is also credited with inventing the modern law firm. He died on October 30, 1929.

Wende Vyborney Feller

PARKINSON, BRADFORD W. (1935–)

Former Air Force colonel and Stanford engineering professor Bradford Parkinson was the chief architect of the Global Positioning System (GPS) used for navigation and precision weapon delivery.

Parkinson was born in Wisconsin in 1935. He joined the air force in 1957, having received his bachelor's degree that year from the U.S. Naval Academy. During his years in the air force, he earned a master's degree from Massachusetts Institute of Technology and a doctorate from Stanford, completed in 1966. In 1972, Parkinson created the NAVSTAR GPS (Navigation Signal Timing and Ranging Global Positioning System) Joint Program Office, which was charged with developing the next-generation navigation tool to follow LORAN. He headed this project until his retirement in 1978.

The GPS developed by this team works by having a number of satellites, each bearing a highly accurate atomic clock, send regular signals broadcasting their time and orbit data. A receiver on the ground compares the signals from at least four satellites to determine its own position. The system can be made accurate to very small distances, making it useful for navigating as well as for aiming missiles.

After holding leadership positions at Rockwell International and Intermetrics, in 1984 Parkinson became a professor at Stanford, where he led development of differential GPS, which incorporates ground stations. This system makes possible "blind" plane landings and automatic space vehicle guidance.

Parkinson's numerous awards include induction into the NASA Hall of Fame. He retired from Stanford in 2002 but continues to pursue research.

Wende Vyborney Feller

PARROTT, ROBERT PARKER (1804–1877)

Robert P. Parrott invented the Parrot muzzle-loading rifled cannon used during the Civil War. Born on October 5, 1804, in Lee, New Hampshire, Parrott attended West Point Military Academy and graduated third in his class in 1824. He married Mary Kemble in 1839. The Parrotts adopted one child.

Parrott served in the army until convinced to resign his commission and become the superintendent of the West Point Foundry in Cold Springs, New York. After three years he leased the foundry from its owner, and, with his brother, purchased the Greenwood Iron Furnace. Parrott spent the next forty years doing ordnance experimentation and research. Upon hearing that the Germans had developed a rifled cannon, Parrott began his own experiments that led him to develop the Parrot rifled cannon. The design had a band around the breech for reinforcement, and was patented on October 1, 1861.

The army and the navy both used Parrott's guns during the war. Early in the war the guns experienced problems that caused them to explode at the breech or blow off the muzzle. The problem was remedied by using less powder and the introduction of improved casings developed by **Thomas Jackson Rodman**. By the end of the war more than half the rifled guns in use by the Union Army were Parrotts.

In 1875, Parrott and his brother pioneered the production of slag wool. Parrott retired from business in 1877 and died in Cold Springs, New York, on December 24, 1877.

Dallace W. Unger Jr.

PARSONS, CHARLES LATHROP (1867–1954)

As World War I stagnated in European trenches and United States entry into the war seemed nearly inevitable, some government officials, including **Bernard Mannes Baruch**, became concerned about the lack of nitrate supplies. Nitrates were basic components of TNT and most other high explosives and propellants as well as fertilizers. The search for domestic nitrates by the U.S. Geological Survey yielded nothing. Congress even appropriated $20 million to investigate methods of producing nitrates and to build the plants needed to produce them.

The War Department sent Charles Parsons and a colleague to Europe to investigate nitrogen fixation plants in 1917. Parsons had become the chief chemist of the U.S. Bureau of Mines in 1916. Born in Marlboro, Massachusetts, on March 23, 1867, he had obtained his undergraduate degree from Cornell in 1888. Parsons was on the chemistry faculty at the University of New Hampshire until 1911, when he became chief mineralogist at the Bureau of Mines. He also had taken on the half-time duties of secretary of the American Chemical Society in 1907. Parsons left the Bureau in 1919 and remained secretary of the society until retiring in 1946. He died on February 13, 1954.

Parsons' trip to Europe had two effects. Four plants were built to produce nitrates from an ammonia process on his recommendation, but the war ended before any production materialized. More important, Parsons surveyed chemists in America to identify those whose war efforts would be more valuable in labs than in the front lines.

Benjamin F. Shearer

PARSONS, JOHN THOREN (1913–)

John Parsons, the inventor of numerical control, was awarded the National Medal for Technology in 1985. He was born in Detroit on October 11, 1913. Parsons had begun working at his father's auto parts manufacturing company when he was fifteen years old. During World War II, the Parsons Corporation, like all automobile-related industries, turned to war production. Young Parsons, with less than a year of college, was forward-thinking enough to realize that making bomb casings would not be a long-term endeavor. A friend at Ford suggested Parsons get into the helicopter business, which had both military and civilian markets. In 1943 Parsons had his first contract to manufacture rotor blades for helicopters.

In 1946 Parsons hired an engineer to help him perfect the design of the rotor blades. Parsons had the idea to have his engineer program a punch card computer to instruct the machinery how to make accurate blades. This technological innovation not only quickened the manufacturing process, but it also redefined acceptable tolerances to very low levels. In 1948 Parsons applied his revolutionary approach to the design of a new military aircraft wing. In 1952 his system was patented and computer numerical control eventually took over virtually every demanding manufacturing process, turning what had been an art into a science. Parsons sold the family company in 1968 and founded the John T. Parsons Company, where he continued to pioneer in adhesive bonding technologies and the use of polystyrene foam patterns as casts for dies.

Benjamin F. Shearer

PARSONS, USHER (1788–1868)

Born in Alfred, Maine, on August 8, 1778, Usher Parsons distinguished himself as the surgeon with Commodore Oliver Hazard Perry at the Battle of Lake Erie during the War of 1812. Too poor to attend a university, Parsons studied medicine as an apprentice under Dr. Abiel Hall. He then received a background in military medicine working with Dr. John Warren, who had served as a surgeon during the Revolutionary War. After receiving his medical license in 1812, the navy gave Parsons a commission as a Surgeon's Mate aboard the *John Adams*.

In 1813, Parsons was assigned as acting surgeon with Perry's fleet, whose goal was to gain control of Lake Erie from the British and to assist General

William Henry Harrison in the retaking of the Michigan Territory. It is his written recollections that give us the most vivid account of the Battle of Lake Erie on September 10, 1813. While there were two other surgeons for the fleet, both were sick. Parsons was aboard the flagship, *Lawrence*, and helped to treat the entire fleet after the battle. During the battle, some of his patients were killed by cannon balls coming through the ship where he was working. He reported that about one hundred men were wounded, sixty-one aboard the *Lawrence*.

After the war, Parsons had a successful private practice, and taught at Dartmouth and Brown. He also published the *Sailor's Physician* and was the first vice president of the American Medical Association. He died on December 19, 1868.

William P. Toth

PASTOR, TONY (1907–1969)

Big band leader Tony Pastor recorded one of the more didactic pro-war songs of World War II, "Obey Your Air Raid Warden." Born Antonio Pestritto in Middletown, Connecticut, on October 26, 1907, Pastor became a tenor saxophonist, vocalist, and bandleader in the 1920s, touring with a number of big bands before gaining popular notice as a member of Artie Shaw's orchestra. Pastor started his own band in 1940 and throughout the 1940s, Pastor's Orchestra produced at least one major hit each year. Although Pastor and his orchestra appeared in films, playing themselves, the band's popularity was largely attributed to radio.

"Obey Your Air Raid Warden," recorded in 1942, provides a bouncy, two-and-a-half-minute list of instructions on how to respond if the enemy should ever attack the United States. As with much of the pro-war music produced shortly after Pearl Harbor, this song was part of a deliberate attempt to mobilize popular culture in support of the war.

Pastor may be best known for discovering the Clooney Sisters on a trip to Cincinnati in 1945. The first of Rosemary Clooney's many hit songs was recorded with Tony Pastor's Orchestra in 1946. Pastor died in Old Lyme, Connecticut, on October 31, 1969. He was also the father of singer Guy Pastor.

Wende Vyborney Feller

PATTERSON, JOSEPH MEDILL (1879–1946)

After World War I, Joseph Patterson became the founder and publisher of *New York Daily News*, which he used to criticize Franklin Roosevelt's foreign policy at the beginning of World War II. Patterson was born on January 6, 1879, in Chicago, Illinois. His father, the managing editor of the *Chicago Tribune*, sent him to Yale University, from which he graduated in 1901. He joined his father at the *Tribune* on his graduation, rising up the ranks from reporter to assistant editor of the Sunday edition, whereupon he impulsively quit to promote his political goals, briefly endorsing socialism. He could not stay away from publishing for long; in 1910, he returned, becoming the *Tribune*'s co-editor and co-publisher with his conservative cousin, Robert McCormick.

During World War I, Patterson served in the army, leaving as a captain. It was during this time that he and his cousin decided that they could no longer work at the same paper. When Patterson returned from Europe, he left the *Tribune*. He turned his attention to New York in 1919, founding the *Illustrated Daily News* (later just the *Daily News*), a broadsheet tabloid aimed at the basest interests of the public. Needless to say, the paper enjoyed wild success. Though his editorials frequently attacked communism and he was a supporter of President Roosevelt into his third term, Patterson objected to Roosevelt's foreign policies, especially the Lend-Lease Act, which he felt served to draw America into war unnecessarily. He died on May 26, 1946.

Ellen Baier

PATTERSON, MARY MARVIN BRECKINRIDGE (1905–2002)

During the early days of World War II, Mary Marvin Breckinridge Patterson photographed London air-raid shelters and was the first female staff broadcaster in Europe for CBS. Born in New York City to a prominent family, Patterson attended Vassar before embarking on an illustrious career as a freelance journalist and filmmaker. In the early 1930s she studied photography with Clarence White in New York and became established as a photojournalist. Her photographs and illustrated articles appeared in *Life*, *Vogue*, *Harper's Bazaar*, *Town and Country*, and other magazines and metropolitan newspapers.

On assignment in Nuremberg to photograph a Nazi rally for *Life*, she ran into an old friend, **Edward Roscoe Murrow**. He hired her to report on the war's impact on average British families. For her report, Patterson originated and wrote her own broadcast material. Seven months after the outbreak of World War II, Patterson made radio broadcasts from various European capitals for CBS *News of the World* with Edward R. Murrow in London, Tom Grandin in Amsterdam, Eric Severeid in Paris, and William L. Shirer in Berlin. As the war spread across Europe, on several occasions, Patterson was on the last train out as Germany armies advanced.

After her marriage to Jefferson Patterson, in 1940 she served with her husband on foreign-service assignments. Stationed in Berlin before America entered World War II, and until forbidden by the Germans, she and her husband, under the auspices of the Red Cross, visited German camps to interview Allied prisoners of war.

Margaret Denny

PATTERSON, ROBERT PORTER (1891–1952)

As under secretary of war during World War II, Robert P. Patterson was a leader in streamlining procurement of supplies needed for the war. Born on February 12, 1891, in Glens Falls, New York, Patterson graduated in 1912 from nearby Union College, followed by a Harvard law degree in 1915. He joined Elihu Root's law firm in New York. Patterson's World War I service in France earned a Distinguished Service Cross. He returned to law practice and in 1930 was appointed to the U.S. District Court for Southern New York.

In summer 1940, Patterson was appointed assistant secretary of war to support the aging Henry Stimson. By Christmas, this position had become under secretary of war. Patterson's work included representing the military at congressional hearings, streamlining contracts to expand facilities, and coordinating procurement and production of supplies, including the logistical difficulties of maintaining supply lines across France. In *Mobilizing America*, Kenneth Eiler credits Patterson with transforming haphazard preparation into true readiness for war. Eiler argues that building war industries and reorganizing the economy substantially shortened the war.

Patterson also formed a committee to revamp the army's penal system. He was rewarded with a Distinguished Service Medal as well as an appointment in 1946 as secretary of war.

As secretary of war, Patterson unsuccessfully advocated unifying the armed services. He is, however, credited with working to desegregate the military. He resigned in 1947 to return to law, later serving as president of the Council of Foreign Relations. Patterson died in a plane crash on January 22, 1952.

Further Reading: Eiler, Keith E. *Mobilizing America*. Ithaca, NY: Cornell University Press, 1997.

Wende Vyborney Feller

PATTERSON, RUSSELL (1894–1977)

Russell Patterson was perhaps not the most likely person to be called as a consultant to design the uniforms of the new Women's Army Auxiliary Corps (WAAC) from February to May 1942. Women's uniforms had no precedent. It was only after the surprise attack at Pearl Harbor, which brought the United States fully into World War II, and the leadership of **Oveta Culp Hobby** that women would be allowed to serve in order to free men to fight. Patterson was in fact not truly a clothing designer like fellow consultants **Philip Mangone** and **Helen Cramp Cookman**; he was an illustrator and a proven trendsetter. The sophisticated, long-legged, big-eyed, cigarette-smoking "flapper" with patent leather hair was his invention. The "Patterson Girl" became the fashion look of the 1920s.

Patterson was born in Omaha, Nebraska, on December 26, 1894, but his family moved to Canada, where he earned his degree in architecture at McGill University. His first job was as a cartoonist for a Montreal newspaper.

He returned to cartoons again in the 1930s with his syndicated "Mamie," a prototypical dumb blonde. Patterson designed film sets and costumes for Hollywood films as well as for Ziegfield's Follies. He also designed Macy's Christmas windows. In 1931 he advanced the cause of women's emancipation by being the first to illustrate women in fancy evening pajamas. Clear plastic umbrellas and raincoats were also his design concepts. Patterson died in New Jersey on March 17, 1977.

Benjamin F. Shearer

PATTON, JAMES GEORGE (1902–?)

James George Patton was born on November 8, 1902, the same year the Farmers Union was founded by a handful of Texas farmers. After his father's death in 1921, Patton had to discontinue his education and worked at various low-paying jobs.

Patton's father had been a part-time farmer, which made the son sufficiently aware of the hardships faced by small farmers. In 1934, Patton joined the Colorado Farmers Union, and by 1937, he was on the board of the National Farmers Union (NFU), a progressive agricultural organization, particularly oriented toward the welfare of the "family-type" farms.

In 1940, Patton was made the president of the NFU. In 1942, he was appointed a member of the Economic Stabilization Board, and he was also appointed to the War Mobilization and Re-conversion Advisory Board. Patton diligently worked toward the organization of the agricultural sector. He made proposals to improve the mobilization and distribution of food-products during wartime. He stood for fair employment, establishing farm credits, and looking forward to post-war reconstruction.

Patton actively engaged himself with Russian War Relief as well. His hand in the conception of Food and Agricultural Organization of the United Nations cannot be overlooked. Always identifying with the small farmer, Patton claimed in 1943 that manpower was being wasted in agriculture and delivering food to liberated peoples was as important as delivering ammunition. In March 1966 Patton retired as president of the union.

Jitendra Uttam

PAULING, LINUS CARL (1901–1994)

Scientist and political activist Linus Pauling was born on February 28, 1901, in Portland, Oregon. In 1922, he graduated from Oregon State University in chemistry, and he earned his Ph.D. in 1925 at the California Institute of Technology, where he taught chemistry from 1931 to 1963. He then taught at the Center for the Study of Democratic Institutions (1963–1967); University of California—San Diego (1967–1969); and Stanford University (1974–1994). Pauling applied quantum mechanics to the chemistry of molecular bonds, worked on the structure of hemoglobin, and performed early research into the genetic code.

Pauling credited his political activism to his scientific humanism, from which he derived fairly objective ethical principles based upon the traditional "golden rule." During World War II, Pauling helped Jewish refugees fleeing Europe and championed the rights of Japanese Americans. After the war, he advocated world peace, opposed nuclear testing, and criticized the political atmosphere of McCarthyism. Accused of supporting communism, the State Department refused to renew Pauling's passport, but this decision was reversed when the scientist received his first Nobel Prize in 1953.

Pauling continued his opposition to atmospheric nuclear testing, and in 1958 published *No More War!* His efforts for international peace culminated in the 1963 Nobel Peace Prize. During the 1960s and 1970s, Pauling opposed the Vietnam War, while continuing his endeavors on behalf of international peace and nuclear safety. He died from cancer on August 19, 1994.

Linus Pauling. Courtesy of the Library of Congress.

Further Reading: Goertzel, Ted, and Ben Goertzel. *Linus Pauling: A Life in Science and Politics.* New York: Basic Books, 1995.

Ron Briley

PEALE, CHARLES WILLSON (1741–1827)

Charles Willson Peale was an artist, patriot, and patron of the arts. Born on April 15, 1741, in Maryland, he received basic education until he was thirteen years of age, when he was indentured to a saddler. In 1764, following his apprenticeship, Peale joined the Sons of Liberty and painted their banners, which proclaimed the freedom and rights of tradesmen. His involvement with the group caused him to lose his business to Loyalist creditors. However, this loss allowed him to turn to his art full time. He went to London for a year to train as painter of portraits under the guidance of Benjamin West. In the 1760s, Peale turned to themes of liberty in many of his paintings, including portraits in which he alluded to British tyranny.

In early 1776, Peale moved his family to Philadelphia and joined a city militia. He fought at Trenton and Princeton, and eventually became chairman of the Constitutional Society. Peale also produced portraits, especially miniatures, of the Revolutionary War soldiers. He painted sixty paintings of

Washington, his 1781 portrait being the best known. He also portrayed the general in the company of fellow soldiers and generals in *Washington and His Generals at Yorktown* in 1784. Peale opened a public museum that later became the Philadelphia Museum of Art, and he also helped found the Pennsylvania Academy of Fine Arts. He died in Philadelphia on February 22, 1827.

Further Reading: Sellers, Charles Coleman. *Charles Willson Peale.* New York: Charles Scribner's Sons, 1969.

Kelly J. Baker

PEEK, GEORGE N. (1873–1943)

George Peek's public service at the War Industries Board during World War I and at the Industrial Board immediately after the war transformed his life. He left his position as vice president of Deere and Co., never to return, and except for a brief attempt to revive a failing farm-implement manufacturer after the war, he left business for good. Peek went on to lobby unsuccessfully for farm parity—fair prices to farmers through government intervention based on commodity prices in the ten years previous to World War I—and in 1933 became head of the Agricultural Adjustment Administration. This appointment ended after seven months owing to a political dispute, but President Franklin Roosevelt made him a special advisor on foreign trade, a position from which Peek resigned in November 1935 because of disagreement with administration trade policies. He died a critic of the New Deal on December 17, 1943.

Peek was born on November 19, 1873, in Polo, Illinois. With a high school education and a year of work at Northwestern University, he left college in 1893 for a job in a Minneapolis branch of the John Deere Plow Company. By 1901 he had moved to Omaha as a general manager, and ten years later he was vice president with responsibility for Deere and Co. sales at the home office in Moline. He was known in the farm machinery business as a fierce competitor. It was this reputation that took him to Washington, DC, when **Alexander Legge** of International Harvester, who was already there, recommended his former competitor for the War Industries Board.

Having been a frequent visitor to Washington throughout 1917 as a lobbyist for the National Implement and Vehicle Association's War Emergency Committee, Peek was convinced that industry representation in Washington was critical to survival. Military procurement practices were in disarray, and he feared that after the war, quickly built factories and facilities for war production would suddenly become useless and a drag on the economy. Furthermore, government priorities created in the haste to mobilize could very well leave manufacturers without the raw material, particularly steel, they needed to produce their products. Peek was satisfied that he had secured farm implement manufacturers status as an essential industry.

As 1917 progressed, the issue of which industries were considered essential and which non-essential rallied business interests into action, because an industry dubbed as non-essential had little chance of survival. The War

Industries Board decided late in November to create the position of industrial commissioner, whose task would be to meet with manufacturers who might be interested in converting their plants to the production of needed wartime materiel. Peek agreed to take the position if he had enough authority to assure results. He embarked on a Herculean task: to help the government identify factories for its business; to work with industry to assure adequate war and civilian production with as little disruption of the industrial landscape as possible; and to make recommendations for future requirements. Peek became the center of an experiment in business and government cooperation never before attempted in the United States.

Peek began meeting with hundreds of industry representatives as soon as he went to work in December. He believed that the War Industries Board had to become the arbiter between government need and industrial production. The military in particular had to be able to articulate its production requirements and manufacturers had to respond to those needs. Peek quickly became frustrated by the lack of any clear mandate and power to effect his objective. This frustration enveloped all the members of the War Industries Board until it was reorganized in March 1918 with **Bernard Mannes Baruch** as its head. Peek became the commissioner of finished products when the board reorganized, and in this capacity he was finally able to put his ideas for government-industry cooperation into action. First nineteen, and finally twenty-one, industrial regions were created, with a War Industries Board representative on each regional committee. These regional committees had the knowledge of their regions to respond favorably to government needs.

Peek saw himself as a protector of industry. When the war ended in November of 1918, Baruch decided to disband the War Industries Board effective January 1, 1919. Peek, however, believing that a transitional period between war and peace was necessary for industry, agreed to chair the Industrial Board in February. Its aim was to bring wartime prices down voluntarily. The Industrial Board, with no real authority, was a dismal failure and in May 1919, Peek left Washington.

Further Reading: Cuff, Robert D. "A 'Dollar-a-Year Man' in Government: George N. Peek and the War Industries Board." *Business History Review* 41 (Winter 1967): 404–420.

Benjamin F. Shearer

PEIXOTTO, ERNEST CLIFFORD (1869–1940)

Ernest Peixotto was one of eight artists selected to serve with the American Expeditionary Force in France during World War I as an official artistic recorder of the activity at the front. Born in San Francisco on October 15, 1869, he studied art at the School of Fine Arts at the Mark Hopkins Institute. He left in 1888 for the Atelier Julien in Paris, and remained in France for several years. In 1897, he moved to New York City and worked briefly as a commercial illustrator for publications such as *Scribner's*. He returned to

France in 1899 and wrote and illustrated books documenting his extensive travel. He also gained repute as a muralist.

In 1914, when war in France broke out, Peixotto returned to the United States. Though he was too old for active military service, he was chosen for the American Expeditionary Force in 1918. He was the eldest of the eight official artists, and was regarded as the truest artist of the group, six of whom had been illustrators and the seventh an architect. His knowledge of the language and countryside of France informed his paintings, which captured the poignancy of the destruction that modern warfare had wreaked on France.

When the war ended, Peixotto was asked to serve as a co-director of the AEF Art Training Center in Bellevue, France, until he returned to the United States, in 1919. In later life, he was known for his murals in California. He died on December 6, 1940.

Ellen Baier

PENFIELD, EDWARD (1866–1925)

Edward Penfield. Courtesy of the Library of Congress.

As a World War I poster illustrator, Edward Penfield's bold style changed the poster from a propaganda technique into an art form, heralding the beginning of modern advertising. Penfield was born on June 2, 1866, in Brooklyn, New York. Like many other prominent artists of the era, he studied his craft at the Art Students League in New York. He rose quickly in his field, becoming the art editor of *Harper's Magazine* at only twenty-four, and art editor at *Harper's Weekly* and *Harper's Bazaar* soon after that. Until he left *Harper's* in 1901 to pursue his own art, he frequently patronized unknown artists for his publications, giving young and talented illustrators a chance to prove themselves within his magazine's pages.

During World War I, Penfield devoted his energy to creating direct and memorable posters. He pleaded with Americans to "Help the Women of France: Save Wheat!" and told them that when the country was desperate, "The Girl on the Land Serves the Nation's Need," among many other such exhortations to service and sacrifice. His poster of a young woman rowing determinedly, captioned "Every Girl Pulling for Victory," created a rush on the advertised United War Work Campaign.

After the war, Penfield continued to create posters, many of them commercial. He has been credited as the founder of modern advertising techniques in addition to inspiring a great deal of interest in poster art. He died on February 8, 1925, in Beacon, New York, from a spinal injury inflicted during a fall.

Ellen Baier

PENN, SEAN (1960–)

Academy Award winner Sean Penn was born on August 17, 1960, in Santa Monica, California, into the noted show-business family of actress Eileen Ryan and director and actor Leo Penn. Curiosity led Penn into the film world, but he soon found himself a niche. His very first film, *Taps* (1981), won him critical praise, and Penn was recognized as an actor with potential. Penn employs method acting to achieve a commendable versatility in his many roles, from a juvenile law-breaker in *Bad Boys* (1983) to a young marine recruit in *Racing with the Moon* (1984). He has appeared in forty films and written and directed several others.

Sean Penn in *Casualties of War*. Courtesy of Photofest.

In 1989 Penn acted in *Casualties of War*, a film revolving around soldiers who break down during combat in Vietnam. Penn has concerned himself with distinguishing the thin line between humanitarian concerns and unpatriotic conduct. He has steadfastly campaigned against war as a given of the human condition, considering the wars in Afghanistan and Iraq temporary medicine, but no cure. Writing as a father and the son of a veteran, Penn published an open letter in the *Washington Post* in October 2002, beseeching President George W. Bush to halt plans for another war in Iraq and chastising him for a simplistic morality and the unbundling of civil rights at home in the name of a war on terror. Penn then visited Iraq. In June 2005, Penn showed up at a prayer ceremony at Teheran University in Iran as a reporter for the *San Francisco Chronicle*.

Jitendra Uttam

PENNELL, JOSEPH (1857–1926)

Illustrator and art critic Joseph Pennell was born to Quaker parents in Pennsylvania on July 4, 1857. Early in his life, he became interested in drawing, and studied at the Pennsylvania Academy of the Fine Arts. There he established himself as a commercial artist. Pennell worked for a variety of magazines including *The Century*, *McClure's*, and *Harper's*, and established himself as a talented illustrator with subjects ranging from cathedrals and street scenes to architectural and engineering projects like the creation of the Panama Canal. Often described as a great American illustrator, he was able to travel the world and document historic places. Pennell also produced manuals on the techniques of pen drawing and lithography, revived interest in etching, and wrote critiques of art.

World War I had a great impact on this artist, who saw the great cities of Europe, which he had drawn, destroyed. Pennell documented the war efforts of Britain, France, and America in World War I. He also produced posters for the war effort. The most famous poster was his fourth Liberty Loan poster, entitled "That Liberty Shall Not Perish From the Earth" (1918). The poster represented what New York would have looked like if somehow destroyed by an enemy. The artist also organized an exhibition for war relief. Pennell died on April 23, 1926.

Further Reading: Pennell, Joseph. *The Adventures of an Illustrator*. Boston: Little, Brown, and Company, 1925; Rawls, Walton. *Wake Up, America! World War I and the American Poster*. New York: Abbeville Press, 1988.

Kelly J. Baker

PEPPER, ALMON R. (1899–1973)

Almon R. Pepper directed the Episcopal Church's Department of Christian Social Relations from 1936 until his retirement in 1964. Born in Sheboygan Wisconsin, he graduated from Kenyon College in 1921, completed theological studies at Nashotah House and was ordained in 1924. Pepper graduated from Columbia's School of Social Work in 1933 and was a rector in a Cleveland church until 1935.

When President Franklin Roosevelt (FDR) signed Executive Order 9066 in February 1942, authorizing the mass arrest and internment of "enemy aliens," predominantly Japanese Americans, many churches and clergy rose to oppose the forcible relocation of these American citizens even though American public opinion generally favored Roosevelt's policy. The Quaker and Mormon churches on the West Coast were particularly vocal in their support of the Japanese Americans, as were white ministers who were in regular contact with Japanese Americans. Several groups of churches, especially the Council of Churches in California, voiced their disagreement with the internment orders.

Almon Pepper chaired the Commission on Aliens and Prisoners of War, an extra-governmental group opposed to the internment, and signed an April 1942 letter to FDR asking that the Japanese Americans' freedoms be returned. The purpose of the commission, according to the pamphlet it published, "The Churches and Enemy Aliens," was to provide help to the detainees.

A year after the end of World War II, Pepper founded the ecumenical Church World Service. Following his retirement he remained a consultant for the Episcopal Church social action services. He died on September 3, 1973.

Mike Timonin

PERRY, WILLIAM JAMES (1927–)

The National Reconnaissance Organization (NRO) named William Perry along with nine others a Founder of National Reconnaissance. The NRO began as a CIA–Air Force project with President Dwight Eisenhower's support to undertake secret aerial reconnaissance missions over the Soviet Union during the Cold War. The CORONA program, which was in existence from 1960 until 1972, collected intelligence and mapping imagery. Today the NRO is a Department of Defense–CIA joint operation that functions as one of fourteen agencies in the intelligence community.

Perry was born in Vandergrift, Pennsylvania, on October 11, 1927. He graduated from Stanford in 1949, remained there another year for a master's degree, and finished his doctorate in mathematics at Pennsylvania State University in 1957. Perry went to work for HRB-Singer Company as a mathematician in 1952 while he continued to teach math at Penn State. In 1954 he became the director of defense Laboratories for GTE-Sylvania. In 1964 he co-founded ESL, Inc., an electronic surveillance company that worked with the National Security Agency (NSA). He was a consultant to the Department of Defense from 1967 to 1977. Perry divested his interest in ESL when he joined the Jimmy Carter administration in 1977 as under secretary of defense for research and engineering. He returned to the Defense Department as a deputy secretary in 1993 and served as secretary from 1994 to 1997.

In naming him a founder, the NRO cited Perry's role as an advisor to CIA and NSA programs to intercept and analyze Soviet missile telemetry and communications intelligence.

Benjamin F. Shearer

PHIPPS, ANITA EVANS (1886?–1953)

The director of women's relations in the U.S. Army from 1921 to 1931, Anita Phipps laid the critical groundwork for the development of the Women's Corps, though it was not implemented during her tenure with the army. The daughter of a brigadier general, Phipps attended school for social work. In September 1918, she took the position of director of the Motor Corps Service. In 1921, she was appointed the second director of women's relations for the U.S. Army, after the first appointee resigned. The position was created to quell the rising tide of pacifism among the newly minted women voters and assure them that the army after World War I was a kinder, gentler army. Her task was to liaise between the army and several women's groups, such as the Daughters of the American Revolution, the League of Women Voters, American War Mothers, and other important organizations with links to the military, and convince them that the army was not a "ruthless military machine."

Her position was not a military one, and Phipps frequently had difficulties commanding respect from the officers with whom she worked. She had to create a uniform for herself out of odds and ends, which she felt was a source of embarrassment for her in front of army and navy nurses, and worked for nearly a decade to secure official recognition of her status. She objected frequently and volubly when other directors failed to meet with her on matters that she felt directly concerned her office, and flooded the War Department with memoranda of protest. Most of the reports she presented were filed without further consideration. Her advice often went unheard, particularly in reference to a number of speaking engagements. Though she carefully cultivated the women's groups and prepared briefing sheets for the speakers, the staff members who spoke to those groups were patronizing and negative about women's possible war contributions, alienating her base of support and redoubling her workload.

Phipps independently carried out a number of studies, compiling World War I data and administering questionnaires to corps areas, territorial departments, and chiefs of branches. In 1929 she created an extensive plan for integrating women into the army as civilian aides based on women's participation in World War I and the estimated need for nearly 170,000 women during wartime. During World War I, the women aides had no official status, meaning no combat pay, benefits, housing, pensions, or uniforms. Phipps' more generous plan for supporting the civilian aides received the support of the women's groups she addressed. It looked as though the plan was going to move forward, but unfortunately, public protest from the clergy and from male civilian aides when it was announced caused the new secretary of war, James W. Good, to cancel implementation of the plan. Some officers, more suspicious than others, also feared that Phipps wished to infiltrate and take over the army from the inside with her proposed hierarchy of women soldiers and civilian aides, thereby "hampering and embarrassing the War Department." In 1928, Major Everett S. Hughes took the position of planner-in-chief for the Women's Army Corps and created a remarkably similar plan that involved the early military training of women and the integration of men's and women's units for efficiency. He predicted many of the problems that could occur in creating an auxiliary force, and nearly all of them occurred within the corps' first two years, because, like Phipps' many proposals, his plan was put aside for later study.

In 1930, Phipps again attempted to make her position recognized as a military one, but Chief of Staff General Douglas Macarthur refused, stating that he saw her position as serving no military value. Worn down by the decade of struggle, she was forced to resign from her position because of ill health, and the post was eliminated altogether. She left a well-researched, revised plan for what she called a Women's Service Corps, which recommended that women be allowed full military status, with training, housing, uniforms, and all the courtesies that male soldiers were allowed, all on base and under the command of female officers. The Women's Army Auxiliary Corps, based on her plan for civilian aides, was proposed by Congresswoman Edith Nourse Rogers of Massachusetts in 1941, later absorbed into the army proper, and renamed simply the Women's Army Corps, was implemented by necessity in 1942. The Auxiliary was based on her plan, and the official Corps on Hughes' plan. Phipps died on July 17, 1953.

Ellen Baier

PIASECKI, FRANK (1919–)

Philadelphia native Frank Piasecki was born on October 24, 1919, and even as a teenager, he was interested in flight, especially helicopters. With a mechanical engineering degree from the Towne School and a baccalaureate degree in aeronautical engineering from New York University, Piasecki worked for two aeronautical companies until he and his partner, Harold Venzie, formed P-V Engineering Forum in 1943. After Venzie left, Piasecki needed military contracts to make the company viable, so he took his experimental, single-seat helicopter, the PV-2, to National Airport in April 1943 to demonstrate it. As it happened, the navy was in political hot water for not having pursued this new helicopter technology, and in January 1944, Piasecki had his first contract for the PV-3, better known as the XHRP-X Dogship, or the "flying banana" for the shape of the fuselage.

Piasecki's innovation was a tandem twin-rotor design for stability and a lighter structure that allowed space for ten people including the crew. By March 1945 the experimental craft was flying, and it was put into production as the HRP-1. Further improvements led to the HRP-2 and the H-21, which was used extensively in the first years of the Vietnam War.

P-V Engineering Forum became the Piasecki Helicopter Corporation when it went public, but Piasecki left it in 1955 owing to a difficult proxy battle in which he did not have controlling interest. He then formed Piasecki Aircraft Corporation, which continues to design vertical takeoff and landing aircraft.

Benjamin F. Shearer

PIERCE, JOHN ROBINSON (1910–2002)

Electrical engineer John Robinson Pierce's work on improving vacuum tubes was essential to wartime radar. He is better known as the father of unmanned communication satellite technology.

Pierce, born March 27, 1910, in Des Moines, Iowa, attributed his fascination with science to early reading of science fiction. He earned bachelor's, master's, and doctoral degrees from the California Institute of Technology, completing his education in 1936, the same year he joined Bell Laboratories. While at Bell during World War II, his work included making reflex klystrons, a type of oscillator used in radio receivers.

During his first years at Bell, Pierce had worked on improving vacuum tubes and had published several papers on his ideas. His major invention was a device for focusing electron beams within a vacuum tube, which became known as the Pierce Gun. At the same time, he was starting to think about microwaves, which were then seen as the next major communication technology. Pierce expanded on existing work with klystrons to build better amplifiers. The reflex klystron is a vacuum tube that gets its name from the way an electron stream is reflected to pass through the tube twice. An electron gun fires a stream of electrons through the tube. At the far end, an electrode reflects the electrons, so they return the length of the vacuum tube to be collected. On their return trip within the tube, the electrons cause radio frequency oscillations. Klystrons are especially useful in high-power applications that solid-state equipment would not handle well. They also provide better control over signals than do the rival magnetrons.

The goal of Pierce's team was to develop low-voltage klystrons that could be produced inexpensively. One of the first of these, the 723A, would be widely used in American X-band radar during the war. This tube is also called the Pierce-Shepherd tube for inventors Pierce and W. G. Shepherd. The team went on to develop a number of other klystrons for use in wartime technology. Pierce's involvement in wartime technology development also led to his subsequent interest in traveling-wave vacuum tubes. Although he is credited with naming the vacuum tube's successor, the transistor, in 1948, he was not one of its inventors.

The traveling-wave vacuum tube became essential to Pierce's plans for an unmanned communication satellite. Though science fiction writer Arthur C. Clarke had proposed such a satellite as early as 1945, there is probably no connection to Pierce's 1954 proposal, made as part of a speech for the Princeton section of the Institute of Radio Engineers. Pierce's speech included calculations for both a balloon that would only bounce signals and a more active satellite that would transmit signals. However, no adequate launching equipment was then available. While the idea was published in the April 1955 issue of *Jet Propulsion*, it seemed that nothing would come of it.

The 1957 Soviet launch of *Sputnik* galvanized American interest in space. Pierce proposed his ideas more seriously to NASA, which agreed to fund development of *Echo*, a balloon that bounced microwaves from transmitter to receiver from space. On August 12, 1960, *Echo* was launched successfully.

By then Pierce had moved on to develop a full communication satellite, working from plans made by colleague Roy Tillotson in 1959. Although NASA ultimately agreed to launch the planned satellite, its development was primarily the work of AT&T, the parent company of Bell Labs, in conjunction with British and French agencies. On July 10, 1962, the satellite, *Telstar*, was launched from Cape Canaveral into elliptical orbit. Its first international broadcast took place on July 23, 1962.

Less than six weeks later, the United States government created the Communications Satellite Corporation (COMSAT) and granted it a perpetual monopoly on international communication satellite transmission, thus legislating AT&T out of the business. The original *Telstar* became a victim of Cold War experimentation. The satellite's launch had coincided with testing of Starfish Prime, a high-altitude nuclear device that superenergized the Van Allen Belt, the radiation belt that surrounds the planet. *Telstar's* transistors failed from excess radiation in February 1963. A number of subsequent Telstar-type satellites have since been launched, including the first satellite to sit in more stable geosynchronous orbit, *IntelSat 1*, nicknamed "Early Bird," in 1965.

Upon his retirement from Bell Labs in 1971, Pierce returned to Caltech, where he was chief technologist at the Jet Propulsion Laboratory from 1979 to 1982. In 1983, he joined Stanford's Center for Computer Research in Music and Acoustics. He died on April 2, 2002. Pierce also published science fiction under the name J. J. Coupling.

Wende Vyborney Feller

PINCHOT, AMOS RICHARDS ENO (1863–1944)

Amos Pinchot played a central role in the American isolationist movement during World War II. He was born in Paris on December 6, 1863, studied law, married in 1900, divorced, and married again in 1919. He was well known for his work for the liberal magazine, *The Masses*; his efforts in establishing the National Civil Liberties Bureau, which became the American Civil Liberties Union; and his legal defense of the anarchists Nicola Sacco and Bartolomeo Vanzetti.

Pinchot had opposed World War I as a product of a flawed imperial world. He thus spoke out against America's entrance into World War II. In September 1940, he helped to establish the America First Committee (AFC), which was the most prominent isolationist movement of its time. It promoted preparedness for war, argued that America should focus on its own defense, and even suggested that entrance into European hostilities would be detrimental to American democracy. The AFC carried this message to the public through publications and speeches, and within a year, it had grown to 450 local chapters and over 800,000 members only to be dissolved in the wake of Japan's attack on Pearl Harbor on December 7, 1941.

Pinchot's writings included *Big Business in America* and *The History of the Progressive Party*, published after his death. Pinchot suffered from depression, intensified by the progress of the war in Europe, and he attempted suicide in 1942. He remained in poor health until his death from pneumonia on February 18, 1944.

Stacy Dorgan

PINSKY, ROBERT (1940–)

A public critic of the 2003 war in Iraq, Robert Pinsky is a former poet laureate of the United States. Born on October 20, 1940, in Long Beach, New Jersey, he received his M.A. from Rutgers and his Ph.D. from Stanford. Pinsky has taught at Wellesley College, University of California at Berkeley, and Boston University. He has been a regular guest on national public television and has been the poetry critic for the online magazine *Slate*.

In his column for *Slate*, Pinsky has discussed the role of the poet as critic of government war policies and published examples of anti-war poetry written by other poets. Pinsky's strongest example of anti-war criticism came during the run-up to the Iraq war, when he declined to attend a poetry reading sponsored by Laura Bush at the White House. In his letter to Laura Bush declining the offer, he accused President George W. Bush of lying about his reasons for going to war as well as about the reasons for most of his domestic policies. He published his letter of refusal on **Sam Hamill**'s web site, *Poets against War*. Then, on February 12, 2003, Pinsky participated in a protest reading in Boston against the war. The protestors read anti-war poetry and made statements.

Pinsky is the only poet to be elected to the position of poet laureate for three straight years, from 1997 until 2000. He has won many other awards for his poetry and his translations, including the *Los Angeles Times* Book Award in poetry.

William P. Toth

POLING, DANIEL ALFRED (1884–1968)

Methodist minister Daniel Poling gained public attention for his reports on the World War I battlefront before becoming a prominent author, religious advisor to presidents, and editor of the *Christian Herald*. The son of United Evangelical Church (UEC) ministers, Poling was born in Portland, Oregon, on November 30, 1884. He worked his way through Dalles College, married in 1906, and became a UEC minister.

With World War I, Poling became active in organizing a chaplaincy corps in France. His own experiences in a gas attack are featured in his first book, *Huts in Hell*, which was published by the Christian Endeavor Union in 1918. He earned a War Department citation for his war reporting.

After the war, Poling's writing focused on social activism. In 1939, he resigned his position with the Marble Collegiate Church (for which he had become a Methodist) to become owner of the *Christian Herald*, a non-denominational Protestant periodical that he had edited since 1926. The monthly's content reflected Poling's support for U.S. military actions; it advocated universal military training and decried bans on bomb testing.

The bestseller status of Poling's twenty-nine books was a product of World War II. Published in 1944, *Your Daddy Did Not Die* tells the story of the four chaplains on the U.S.S. *Dorchester*, who gave away their life jackets and went down with the ship. One of the four was his son, Clark V. Poling. Daniel Poling retired from the *Christian Herald* in 1965 and died February 7, 1968.

Wende Vyborney Feller

POLLOCK, JIM (1943–)

One of forty-two combat artists deployed during the Vietnam War, Jim Pollock spent two months recording battlefront scenes and other military artwork at the end of 1967. Pollock was born in Pollock, South Dakota. He attended South Dakota State University, and entered the United States Army in 1966. While stationed in Korea with the army, Pollock applied for temporary duty on the Vietnam Combat Art Program, and was selected for Team IV. This was an unusual strategy for the army, which had previously drawn from a pool of professional, civilian artists rather than from within its own ranks, though civilian workers within the army actually instituted the program.

On August 15, 1967, Pollock and the four other members of his team were taken to Vietnam and given free rein to visit units and make notes and sketches. Their task was solely to record the army's operations and functions for history, unlike in previous wars, when combat artists were also expected to provide propagandist materials immediately. Also unlike previous wars, these artists were permitted time on Hawaii, from October 16 through December 31, 1967, to finish their paintings under better conditions. Their war art currently resides at the U.S. Army Center of Military History. At the beginning of 1968, Pollock and the other artists returned to their units.

Pollock is currently living in Pierre, South Dakota, and working as a freelance artist. He maintains a web site chronicling his experience and is happy to answer questions about his art via email.

Ellen Baier

POLLOCK, OLIVER (1737–1823)

Oliver Pollock was born in 1737 in Ireland. He immigrated to America with his father, settling in Cumberland County, Pennsylvania. By 1762, Pollock was a merchant in Havana, Cuba, where he befriended Governor Alejandro O'Reilly, who later was appointed governor of Louisiana by the Spanish government. As a result, Pollock moved to New Orleans, where he became a successful merchant.

When the American Revolution started, Pollock was both wealthy and connected with a number of influential politicians. In 1777, the Secret Committee of the United States appointed him the commercial agent of the American government for New Orleans. As such, he became the personal representative of George Washington. The following year, Pollock borrowed $70,000 from the governor of New Spain, Bernardo de Galvez, to fund General George Rogers Clarke's military campaign to take the Illinois Territory from the British. Pollock also spent large sums of money to supply

Washington's army. He went bankrupt by giving so much support to the military objectives of the American Revolution.

After the war, Pollock was appointed the commercial agent of the United States for Havana, where he was imprisoned for America's debts in 1784. Paroled a year later, he returned to Pennsylvania. In 1791 Congress waived his debt, but never paid him for the money he spent on the Revolutionary War. In 1800 he was confined to a debtor's prison in Philadelphia for several years. Pollock moved to Mississippi in 1815, where he died at eighty-six on December 13, 1823.

Gene C. Gerard

PORCHER, FRANCIS PEYRE (1825–1895)

When the Confederate States of America declared its independence, many of its traditional supply routes were suddenly cut. Medicines came into short supply. Even making soap became difficult because potash had been supplied from New York or Canada. The Confederate surgeon general released physician and surgeon Francis Peyre Porcher from his wartime task of caring for wounded soldiers to bring together what was known about the medicinal and useful qualities of native southern plants and trees so that inexpensive substitutes might be used in place of imported supplies. Porcher's *Resources of the Southern Fields and Forests, Medical, Economical, and Agricultural, Being Also a Medical Botany of the Confederate States* was published in Charleston in 1863.

Porcher, born in St. John's, South Carolina, on December 14, 1825, received his undergraduate degree from South Carolina College in 1844 and his medical degree from the Medical College of the State of South Carolina in 1847. He studied further in Paris. Porcher then began practicing medicine in Charleston where he was active civically as well as in the medical profession. In 1855 he and another physician opened a hospital where slaves could receive medical treatment.

Porcher had done his dissertation on the medicinal values of plants around his hometown and in 1849 enlarged his subject to the entire state, so he was the logical choice to write the *Resources*. His enduring interest, however, was in medical research, especially cardiovascular disease. Internationally respected, Porcher died on November 19, 1895.

Benjamin F. Shearer

PORTER, COLE ALBERT (1891–1964)

Musician and composer Cole Porter was born in Peru, Indiana, on June 9, 1891. By the time he was six years old, Porter was already learning to play both the piano and the violin, though he later gave up the latter. He started composing songs when he was ten. Porter attended both Worcester Academy and Yale University.

In June 1917, near the end of World War I, Porter journeyed to Paris, lying to the American press about his military status and fabricating stories about working with the French Foreign Legion. He did, however, work with the Duryea Relief organization, visiting war-torn towns with supplies for those in need.

By the time America entered World War II, Porter had become very successful composing songs for Broadway and film. He wrote a number of songs to inspire Americans. Songs such as "You'd Be So Nice to Come Home To" echoed the sentiments of many men and women separated by the war. The lyrics of many of Porter's songs made references to the war. His 1943 song "Sailors of the Sky" warns, "So beware you Huns; Whether Japanese or German; 'Cause we've got guns; For exterminatin' vermin." Porter's shows like *Something for the Boys* and songs like "Don't Fence Me In" inspired Americans both at home and abroad. Porter died on October 15, 1964.

Further Reading: Eells, George. *The Life That He Led: A Biography of Cole Porter.* New York: G. P. Putnam's Sons, 1967.

Nicole Mitchell

PORTER, WILLIAM SYDNEY (A.K.A. O. HENRY) (1862–1910)

O. Henry (the pen name of William Sydney Porter) was a prolific short story writer. His popular stories, with plots twisted by irony and coincidence, were noted for their surprise endings. Porter was born on September 11, 1862, in Greensboro, North Carolina. In 1882, Porter went to Texas for health reasons. In 1891, he became a bank teller at the First National Bank in Austin. He was accused of embezzling funds from the bank in 1894. Leaving his wife and young daughter in Austin, Porter fled to New Orleans, then to Honduras, to avoid trial. In 1897, after receiving information that his wife was dying, he returned to Austin. Porter was convicted of embezzlement and sentenced to five years in prison in Columbus, Ohio. While in prison, Porter began writing short stories to earn money to support his daughter. After serving three years of his sentence, Porter changed his name to O. Henry to shield his true identity.

In 1901, he moved to New York City, where he published hundreds of short stories and gained international acclaim as America's favorite short story writer. His stories were filled with realistic detail from his first-hand experiences in Texas, Central America, and New York City. "The Head Hunter" (1902), a short story about an American journalist's return to America after being a war correspondent in the Philippines, convinced many readers that the Filipino people were uncivilized and needed American supervision. Porter died of cirrhosis of the liver in New York City on June 5, 1910.

Michael R. Hall

PRICE, BYRON (1891–1981)

Byron Price was director of the U.S. Office of Censorship during World War II. Born in 1891 in Topeka, Indiana, Price studied at Wabash College and made a career as a journalist for the United Press and the Associated Press, where he rose to the position of executive news editor. He served in the infantry during World War I and married in 1920.

Ten days after the Pearl Harbor bombing, President Franklin Roosevelt asked Price to lead the new Office of Censorship, where he remained until 1945. He was charged with devising the agency's policies. Price decided the agency would recommend rather than impose guidelines—censorship would be voluntary. The news media were required to analyze stories objectively to assure that their content would not abet the enemy's cause. Censors could not cut material or formally punish those who published it, but Price did regulate the release of information. As the chief censor during World War II, Price also sought to monitor foreign communications that passed from, to, or through the United States. The Office soon grew to include the military censorship branches set up within the Navy and War Departments.

After the war Price worked in Germany with occupation forces. He later became vice president of the Motion Picture Association of America, executive editor of the Associated Press, and assistant secretary-general of the United Nations. His awards included the Medal of Merit from President Truman and a 1944 Pulitzer Prize for the development of media censorship codes. Price died on August 6, 1981.

Stacy Dorgan

PULITZER, JOSEPH (1847–1911)

Joseph Pulitzer unwittingly helped to instigate the Spanish-American War through inflammatory journalism. Reports printed in his *New York World* were made all the more effective because he attracted wide readership by using new techniques and strategies for selling to the masses.

Pulitzer was born in Mako, Hungary, (near Budapest) on April 10, 1847, and educated in a private school and by a tutor until his father's death. He sought entrance into the Austrian Army, French Foreign Legion, and British Army before being accepted into the service of the American Union Army, in which he enlisted in New York in 1864 and was released in 1865. He made his way to St. Louis, Missouri, in search of work, studied independently, was admitted to the bar, and became an American citizen. In 1868 Pulitzer was a reporter for the German-language *Westliche Post*. The following year, he was elected to the Missouri state legislature.

In 1872, Pulitzer began his career as a newspaper magnate by purchasing the St. Louis German-language paper, *Staats-Zeitung*, and in 1875 he continued his political involvement with election as a delegate to the Missouri Constitutional

Convention. He eventually became a political correspondent on the Washington staff of the *Sun*.

After his marriage in 1878, Pulitzer formed the St. Louis *Post-Dispatch*. The paper reflected his philosophy that journalism should work in the interest of the people. This made him a "New Journalist." He sought equality of access to information and disdained political or economic loyalties that threatened the integrity of the information he published. He pursued the interests of the poor and middle-class through tax reform and the maintenance of public spaces, including parks and roads. Pulitzer's political influence grew when he was elected as delegate to the National Democratic Convention in 1880. He thus became one of the most respected and powerful American newspaper publishers in the years following the Civil War.

In 1883, Pulitzer bought the *New York World*, to which he brought the same mandate he upheld for the *Post-Dispatch*. Journalism was to be for the public good, but Pulitzer also sought to appeal to a mass audience through broad coverage, sensational stories, the acquisition of top journalists, and low prices. The use of "yellow" journalism, or the inclusion of scandalous stories in order to sell papers, not only increased his papers' circulation and profits, but it also increased the audience for his social causes. Pulitzer continued to be political, but abstained from political involvement. He was elected to Congress in 1885, but he resigned in the spring of 1886 to maintain the political independence he felt was necessary to pursue his social reforms and journalistic integrity.

Though Pulitzer's declining health kept him from the office in the years following 1890, he retained control over operations. The competition with **William Randolph Hearst** beginning in 1895 was indicative of his continued involvement in the paper. Hearst worked to hire *New York World* staff away from the *World* and imitated several of Pulitzer's techniques for increasing readership, including reducing the price of his paper. Their circulation battle was instrumental to the start of the Spanish-American War in 1898. Following the outbreak of the Cuban Revolution, many American journalists looked to the island for stories, but often got their information in the form of propaganda from the Cuban Junta, a pro-revolution U.S. group. Sensationalized stories of the Cuban struggle against the Spanish oppressor appeared in Pulitzer's and Hearst's papers, including eye-catching headlines and graphic accounts of atrocities that played on the emotions of readers. The publications' reports on the explosion of the U.S. battleship, *Maine*, in Havana's harbor in 1898 incited the American public to push the president and Congress for war. Wartime reports employed similar tactics to win over readers, but ultimately also undermined Pulitzer's journalistic philosophy.

In the years following the war, Pulitzer renewed his journalistic efforts in the name of social causes. He exposed corruption in the building of the Panama Canal, maintaining that political payoffs influenced decisions, accusations for which President Theodore Roosevelt sought to have him indicted for criminal libel. Pulitzer also busied himself with creating the Pulitzer Prizes and developing the Columbia School of Journalism. He campaigned for the recognition of journalism as a profession requiring distinct expertise and a responsibility to serve the public good. Pulitzer died on October 19, 1911.

Further Reading: Barrett, James Wyman. *Joseph Pulitzer and His World*. New York: Vanguard Press, 1941; Juergens, George. *Joseph Pulitzer and the New York World*. Princeton, NJ: Princeton University Press, 1966.

Stacy Dorgan

PULITZER, JOSEPH JR. (1885–1955)

Joseph Pulitzer Jr., played a seminal role in educating the American public about Nazi atrocities during World War II. He was born in New York City on March 21, 1885, attended Harvard University, and married in 1910. In 1916, Pulitzer served in the Aviation Corps, then in 1926, a year after his wife's death, remarried.

Pulitzer followed in the footsteps of his father, **Joseph Pulitzer**, and became a prominent newspaper publisher. He headed the St. Louis *Post-Dispatch* for 43 years. His high sense of ethics led him to consider the credibility and honesty of advertisers above advertising revenue, thus finally assuring the paper's reputation for high integrity. The *Post-Dispatch* strove to serve the public good through investigative reports that held leaders accountable for corruption.

After the onset of the war in Europe in 1939, Pulitzer created a news analysis page, "The War" page, to inform the public of events in Europe. In 1945, Pulitzer was among the journalists General Dwight D. Eisenhower invited to visit the concentration camps. He arrived at Buchenwald only twelve days after its liberation by American troops. The series of articles he wrote were published in *A Report to the American People* (1945), his effort to inform the public that Nazi atrocities against Jewish, Polish, and Russian prisoners were not just propaganda. Pulitzer tried to have the Signal Corps' classified photographs released to the public, arranged for public viewings of films made in postwar Germany, and spoke out publicly against German militarism and Nazism. He died on March 30, 1955.

Stacy Dorgan

PURCELL, EDWARD MILLS (1912–1997)

Edward Purcell of Harvard University won the Nobel Prize in physics in 1952 with Felix Bloch of Stanford University for discovering a way of detecting the extremely weak magnetism of atomic nuclei. Another of his many achievements was the discovery in 1945 with Henry C. Torrey and Robert V. Pound of nuclear magnetic resonant absorption (NMR), which has become an important research tool in many other areas including materials sciences, chemistry and medicine.

Born August 30, 1912, in Taylorville, Illinois, Purcell's father was the general manager of an independent telephone company and his mother a high school teacher. Purcell attended Purdue University, receiving a bachelor's degree in electrical engineering in 1933. After a short time at the Technische Hochschule in Karlsruhe, Germany, he returned to the United States and went to Harvard University where he obtained a master's degree in physics in 1935 and a Ph.D. in 1938. He stayed on the faculty of Harvard University until his retirement in 1977 as the Gerhard Gade University professor.

After initially serving two years as an instructor at Harvard, Purcell was asked in fall 1940 to join the Radiation Laboratory at the Massachusetts Institute of Technology to do emergency research for the war effort. The Rad Lab was organized for the military with the purpose of conducting research and development in the field of microwaves. Purcell was head of the Fundamental Developments Group. This group was responsible for the study of radar frequencies and systems on the X-band and K-band projects, which involved the development of magnetrons. There, he had the opportunity of associating with **Isidor Isaac Rabi** and others who had done research on the study of molecular and nuclear properties by using radio methods. After World War II ended in 1945, Purcell and other members of his team were asked to stay on with the Office of Publications of the Radiation Laboratory in order to write the Radiation Laboratory Technical Series, which represented the technological developments produced by the laboratory under military secrecy during the World War II period.

It was during this time in 1945 that Purcell and his colleagues, using improvised equipment, discovered NMR. By mounting the equipment at the top of a Harvard's Research Laboratory of Physics building, NMR was detected for the first time. It was detected by the absorption of radio-frequency energy; the radio emissions came from clouds of hydrogen in space. Further, since hydrogen is the dominant element of the universe, this method became a major tool in astronomical observations. NMR also provides a precise way to determine chemical structures and properties of materials. NMR is also the basis of magnetic resonance imaging (MRI), one of the most important medical exploratory techniques of modern medicine.

Purcell was also influential in the development of radio astronomy. He and Harold I. Ewen detected the astronomical spectral line of the interstellar atomic hydrogen in the galaxy. Astronomers at that time successfully corroborated this technique. The seminal work of Purcell and Ewen in this area made atomic and molecular spectroscopy a major field of study in radio astronomy.

Purcell was elected president of the American Physical Society in 1970. He was a member of the National Academy of Sciences, the American Philosophical Society and the American Academy of Arts and Sciences. In 1968 he won the Oersted Medal of the American Association of Physics Teachers, and in 1979 he received the National Medal of Science. A member of the President's Science Advisory Committee under President Dwight D. Eisenhower from 1957 to 1960, he chaired a subcommittee on space and was responsible for publishing materials to educate the public about space explorations. He also served under presidents John F. Kennedy and Lyndon B. Johnson, from

1960 to 1965. His committee was influential in the organization of the National Aeronautics and Space Administration (NASA) and the planning for the Apollo mission. He was also a consultant throughout his career to several agencies of the federal government. Purcell died on March 7, 1997.

Further Reading: Crane, H. R. "Edward M. Purcell: Oersted Medalist for 1967." *American Journal of Physics* 65 (August 1997): 691; Pound, Robert V. "Edward Mills Purcell, August 30, 1912–March 7, 1997." *Biographical Memoirs of the National Academy of Sciences* 78 (2000): 183–204.

Nestor L. Osorio

PYLE, ERNEST TAYLOR (1900–1945)

Born on a farm southwest of Dana, Indiana, on August 3, 1900, Ernie Pyle grew up in rural Indiana. He attended Indiana University, majoring in journalism. His career began with the *LaPorte Herald* as a cub reporter. Four months later, he moved to the *Washington Daily News*. For four years he wrote a daily column on aviation and then became the managing editor of the paper. Recovering from influenza in December 1934, Ernie and his wife took an extended motor trip to the West and Southwest. He wrote eleven articles about his trip for his employer, Scripps Howard Newspapers. Saying the columns had a Mark Twain quality, Scripps yielded to Pyle's idea of a series of travelogue articles. He was expected to produce six pieces a week. He could go wherever and write whatever he pleased.

Pyle's talent for description and his familiarity with people soon earned him a wide following in all twenty-four Scripps Howard papers. Pyle provided glimpses of a world that, in the Depression years, most would never visit personally. For seven years, Ernie Pyle was the eyes and ears of Americans in and around the world. In 1940, he went to London to cover the Battle of Britain. His skills made the war real for his followers as he covered England, North Africa, Italy and Normandy. Covering the Pacific advance, he was killed on the island of le Shima by machine gun fire on April 18, 1945.

Further Reading: Nichols, David. *Ernie's America.* New York: Random House, 1989.

Jerry L. Parker

R

RABI, ISIDOR ISAAC (1898–1988)

Isidor Rabi was instrumental in developing radar during World War II. Born in Rymanow, Austria-Hungary on July 29, 1898, his family immigrated to America in 1899. Rabi earned his Ph.D. in physics at Columbia University in 1927 and went on to earn the Nobel Prize in 1944. As associate director of the Radiation Laboratory during World War II, Rabi made vital contributions to the Allied war effort.

Between 1940 and 1945, the Massachusetts Institute of Technology's Radiation Laboratory, commonly called the Rad Lab, operated as part of the National Defense Research Committee, a commission under the leadership of MIT President **Karl Taylor Compton** and dean of engineering **Vannevar Bush**. **Lee Alvin DuBridge** was its director. In addition to this Cambridge facility, another radiation laboratory was set up at Columbia University in New York under Rabi's direction. The technology that emerged from these labs was remarkable and gave the upper hand to the Allies during the war. Radar, the acronym of radio detection and ranging, was an electronic device that could see through fog and the blackness of night. From radar gun-control equipment to radar variable-time fuses used against the Japanese kamikaze attacks, this non-weapon saved lives and won the war. For his work during the war on radar, Rabi earned the prestigious Medal for Merit, the highest civilian award.

After the war, Rabi served as chairman of the Atomic Energy Commission's General Advisory Committee from 1952 through 1956. He died in New York City on January 11, 1988.

Valerie L. Adams

RABINOW, JACOB (1910–1999)

Jacob Rabinow was one of America's most prolific and honored inventors, with 230 patents to his name. Born in Kharkov in the Ukraine in 1910, he came to Brooklyn, New York, with his family in 1921. He earned his bachelor's and master's degrees in electrical engineering from City College of New York and went to work as a mechanical engineer for the National Bureau of Standards in 1938. Rabinow eventually became the Chief of the Electro-Mechanical Ordnance Division before he left in 1954 to start his own firm. During World War II he worked with **Harry Diamond** and began his inventing career by designing fuses, including safety features, and guidance systems for bombs and missiles. Rabinow's wartime work on defense systems garnered him the Certificate of Commendation from the National Defense Research Council and the Naval Ordnance Development Award in 1945 as well as the President's Certificate of Merit in 1948.

Among Rabinow's inventions were a camera to view flight paths of airplanes, the optical scanner and mail handling equipment, headlight dimmers, the first magnetic disk memory, automatic clocks and watches, an automobile clutch, a pick-proof lock, and the straight-line phonograph.

Rabinow left the position of vice president of Control Data Systems to return to the National Bureau of Standards (now the National Institute of Standards and Technology) in 1972 as chief research engineer, retiring in 1975 to consultancy status for the Institute's Office of Energy-Related Inventions until 1989. He died on September 11, 1999.

Benjamin F. Shearer

RAMO, SIMON (1913–)

Simon Ramo's company, Ramo Woolridge Corporation, successfully managed the intercontinental ballistic missile (ICBM) program of the 1960s and closed the "missile gap" with the Soviet Union.

The son of Lithuanian immigrants, Ramo was born on May 7, 1913, in Salt Lake City. He moved quickly through his education, completing a B.S. in electrical engineering at the University of Utah and a Ph.D. in electrical engineering and physics at the California Institute of Technology by age twenty-three. Ramo was immediately hired by General Electric, where he was central to the company's development of microwave technology and its electron microscope. By 1945, he held twenty-five patents and had published *Introduction to Microwaves*.

The following year, Ramo moved to Hughes Aircraft, where he masterminded the company's rise to prominence as a contractor for the U.S. Department of Defense. Hughes' contracts typically involved performing research and development for guided missiles. By 1953, the Department of Defense was becoming nervous about giving a single company too much responsibility for major defense programs. At the same time, Ramo and colleague Dean

Woolridge were becoming frustrated with management problems at Hughes. In mid-September 1953, Ramo and Woolridge resigned, then formed Ramo Woolridge Corporation.

In *The Business of Science*, Ramo reminisces that he was surprised to receive a call from the secretary of the air force within three days of forming Ramo Woolridge. The assignment was to participate in analysis that would shape the future of the United States' missile program, which Secretary of Defense Charles Wilson thought included too many expensive ways to bomb the Soviet Union. Only after starting the project was he told that ICBMs had already been established as a high priority.

ICBMs became vital in late 1953 because intelligence analysts pieced together clues that the Soviet Union was successfully developing its own ICBM system. It was estimated that, using these bombs, the Soviet Union could destroy the United States in less than thirty minutes. While intermediate range ballistic missiles (IRBMs) placed in friendly countries could protect the United States in the short term, it was essential that the nation develop its own ICBMs.

An ICBM is essentially a rocket with a nuclear bomb in the nose. Like space rockets, the missile requires multistaged fuel tanks, a guidance system, and a landing segment that is shielded against the heat of reentry. Ramo notes that there were a number of technical problems with developing a usable ICBM. Existing guidance systems could not target accurately enough. Hydrogen bombs were heavy, and the shielding needed for re-entry would make them heavier. Lifting the weight required huge rockets, which meant more vibration, which meant less accurate navigation. New developments provided hope: a lighter-weight, more powerful h-bomb was in the works, and **Charles Stark Draper** of MIT developed an inertial guidance system for more accurate targeting. However, a workable ICBM would still need to increase rocket power by a factor of ten without sacrificing accuracy. These were the problems that Ramo Woolridge, given responsibility for developing ICBMs as fast as possible, would have to overcome.

Ramo's plan was for his engineers to agree on a rough design for the missile, then each team would develop its own segment concurrently. This process was a change from the traditional research and development (R&D) method of solving the first problem, then solving the second one, and so on.

It did. The Atlas missile passed its short-range test flight in late 1957 and was successful in long-range tests in 1959. By then, the United States and the Soviet Union were at about the same stage in developing launchable ICBMs, but the Atlas was more accurate than Soviet missiles. In 1961, the new secretary of defense, Robert McNamara, declared that there was no longer any "missile gap" with the Soviets. Ramo was pleased that the ICBM project stayed on schedule and had few cost overruns.

Ramo also provided technical leadership on the earlier Thor (IRBM) and later Titan (ICBM) projects. Ramo Woolridge became TRW, which later merged with Fujitsu. Ramo went on to write several popular books on business and science, including *What's Wrong with Our Technological Society and How to*

Fix It. He was awarded the National Science Medal in 1979 and served on numerous government committees during the Reagan administration. As of mid-2005, Ramo was retired in southern California.

Since 1982, the Institute of Electrical and Electronics Engineers (IEEE) has awarded the Simon Ramo Medal for achievements similar to Ramo's management of the ICBM project.

Wende Vyborney Feller

RAMSEY, NORMAN FOSTER JR. (1915–)

Norman F. Ramsey headed the MIT Radiation Laboratory's Fundamental Development Group during World War II, and developed X-based, 3cm wavelength radar systems, which later led into research that won him the Nobel Prize. Ramsey was born on August 27, 1915, in Washington, DC, into a military family. He was extremely bright and used the frequent moves as a child to advance grades according to his growing talent. He entered Columbia University at the age of sixteen and graduated with a math degree at while not yet twenty. He studied physics at the Cavendish Laboratory of Cambridge University and got a second bachelor's degree in 1937. Upon his return to New York City, he joined **Isidor Isaac Rabi**'s physics research group at Columbia University, working in the newly discovered magnetic resonance field and sharing in the exciting breakthroughs in the lab at the time, which earned Rabi the Nobel Prize.

Ramsey obtained his doctorate from Columbia in 1940 and took a position at the University of Illinois, but immediately became immersed in war-related research. From 1940 to 1943, he worked on experiments with radar at MIT's Radiation Laboratory. He was in charge of the magnetron group, working on the 3 cm wavelength variant of radar. Ramsey and his group also focused on using waveguides instead of beaded lines for determining radar signals. The 10 cm wavelength radar that ended up in later use took a great deal of the insights determined by the 3 cm group. He also took a demonstration of his work to England during 1941, allowing the scientists on both continents to share data, and in Ramsey's case, equipment, as the British gave him some crystals to use in their lab.

Near the end of 1942, Ramsey began to serve as a consultant on radar to the secretary of war in Washington, DC, as a result of his work at the Radiation Lab. The navy was particularly interested in receiving working radar systems as soon as possible, both 3 cm and 10 cm wavelengths, and Ramsey advised the Army Air Corps (AAC), which had not got on board quite as quickly, on the possibilities presented by the project. He heavily influenced part of the AAC war budget, quietly advising a young officer who was responsible for writing the preliminary report on radar requirements on the new aircraft that were being built.

In 1943, **Julius Robert Oppenheimer** recruited Ramsey, and he remained at Los Alamos until 1945. There was an initial problem with the transfer, as the secretary of war was reluctant to turn the young scientist over to the new project. In a negotiated compromise, Ramsey was officially designated the secretary of war's expert consultant on the project, and though he was a normal group member and few knew about the distinction, he was not a regular employee of the project. Later, when the Los Alamos team was honored by the War Department, Ramsey would not technically be included in that group, which he found amusing.

At Los Alamos, Ramsey worked on improving the bomb shape and aerodynamics, as part of the Delivery Group. He also served as a liaison with the air force in arranging the tests of the early models. His group observed that on high altitude drops, accuracy was difficult because of warping of the bomb's fins. The report that Ramsey created to inform the military of this problem in other applications, he later discovered, had been suppressed for security concerns about the Manhattan Project. After the bomb specifications had been determined, he supervised the physical assembly of the bombs. He also led the briefings of the pilots and bombardiers who were assigned the drops onto Hiroshima and Nagasaki.

After the war ended, Ramsey returned to Columbia briefly before accepting a professorship at Harvard University that lasted over forty years. At Harvard, Ramsey began research into molecular beam magnetic resonance, and frustrated with problems achieving accuracy, created a new method for measuring particle resonance called the separated-oscillatory-field method. In 1960, he developed the atomic hydrogen maser, which is used for hyper-accurate measurements of atomic resonance and led to the development of the cesium atomic clock. These two developments won him the 1989 Nobel Prize, which he shared with Wolfgang Pauli and Hans Dehmelt. Ramsey retired from Harvard in 1995, becoming the Higgins Professor of Physics emeritus. He is currently active in the Union of Concerned Scientists, which recently wrote a letter condemning the distortion of science promoted by the administration of President George W. Bush.

Ellen Baier

RAMSEY, PAUL (1913–1988)

During World War II, Paul Ramsey was a pacifist and a conscientious objector. His central moral concern was: how can one love one's neighbor and yet kill him? Eventually he developed an answer that led him to abandon pacifism for the just war doctrine.

Ramsey concluded that war to save the life of another person was a moral act that justified the use of violence. He discussed this issue in his book, *Basic Christian Ethics* (1950). He concluded that the love commandments could not only justify war, but also specify limits so that the conduct of war could be moral.

Ramsey argued for the idea that noncombatants should be immune from attack. This idea was developed in *War and the Christian Conscience* (1961) and *The Just War* (1968). He also used the Roman Catholic moral principle of a double effect to say that while civilians may not be attacked, injury as "collateral damage," if an unintended consequence, is morally acceptable.

Ramsey defended American actions during the Vietnam War as both moral and politically justified. He rejected claims that the war was immoral.

Ramsey was born in Mendenhall, Mississippi on December 10, 1913, the son of a Methodist minister. He graduated from Millsaps College and Yale Divinity School, earning a B.D. in 1940 and a Ph.D. in 1943. In 1944 he moved to Princeton University's new Department of Religion, remaining there until 1982. Ramsey died on February 20, 1988, in Princeton, New Jersey.

Andrew J. Waskey

RANDOLPH, ASA PHILIP (1889–1979)

A. Philip Randolph was a journalist, the organizer of the Brotherhood of Sleeping Car Porters, a socialist, and an activist for civil rights for African Americans. He was born in Crescent City, Florida, on April 15, 1889. His father was a minister in the African Methodist Episcopal Church and his mother was also quite religious. Despite early inclinations to the ministry, Randolph became an atheist. Education was important for his family, and Randolph attended the Cookman Institute (later Bethune-Cookman College) in Jacksonville in 1903.

A. Philip Randolph. Courtesy of the Library of Congress.

In 1911, Randolph moved to New York, which became home for the rest of his life. He had a variety of jobs to support himself, including one as an elevator operator. To fight against bad working conditions, he founded the Elevator and Switchboard Users Union. Randolph was also exposed to socialism and unionism, which would become influential to his style of leadership. Additionally, he began lessons on Shakespeare in Oxford-style English, which impacted his speech and his accent. In 1913, he married Lucille Campbell Greene, who introduced him to Chandler Owen. Randolph and Owen developed a theory that blacks could only be free if they were not deprived economically, and since most blacks were workers, they should be socialists because the Socialist Party supported workers.

In 1917, Randolph and Owen founded *The Messenger* to espouse their beliefs. In 1918, both were jailed because they did not support World War I owing to the treatment of African-American soldiers. In 1920, Randolph and Owen founded the Friends of Negro Freedom as an organization to bring about equality, but the organization ultimately shattered because of dissension in the ranks. By the 1930s, the radicalism of

The Messenger and its owner had become muted because of the association of socialism with communism.

Despite his dismissal of forthright radicalism, Randolph still believed that organizing black labor was a method to gain equality. In 1925, he helped organize the Brotherhood of Sleeping Car Porters to protest working conditions. However, he had a hard time gaining support for his organization because of his socialism, atheism, and accent, but Randolph appealed to the porters in biblical terms that proved effective. Yet Pullman refused to negotiate with the union until twelve years later because of the National Industry Recovery Act, which guaranteed workers the right to organize and be recognized as a union. In 1937, Pullman signed a contract with the first black union. Due to his success with black labor, the National Negro Congress chose Randolph to lead their organization. However, by 1940 he left the NCC because of its ties to Communism, and he shifted his focus to civil rights more broadly. The American economy was beginning to turn around as well because of defense contracts, but African Americans were not allowed to work at defense industries and many were still reliant upon federal relief monies.

To protest the segregation of the defense industries, Randolph proposed a march in Washington, DC, of 10,000 blacks. He promoted the march in his paper, the *Black Worker*. President Franklin Roosevelt and the administration worried that the march might cause race riots in the nation's capital. When Randolph noted that the march might include 100,000 blacks, Roosevelt called him and **Walter Francis White** to the White House for negotiations. Randolph proposed that both the military and the defense industries be desegregated. In 1941, Roosevelt created the Fair Employment Practice Committee with Executive Order 8802, which was supposed to place minorities in jobs in the defense industries, and in return, Randolph called off the march.

Randolph succeeded in using pressure tactics to achieve equal employment rights for African Americans in World War II. Also, in the 1940s, Randolph formed two campaigns against the segregated military, one that focused on legal action and the other that encouraged young African Americans not to join a "Jim Crow" army because of its segregation. In March 1948, President Harry Truman introduced his Universal Military Training (UMT) initiative, which basically amounted to a draft. During Senate testimony on the UMT, Randolph warned that he would encourage blacks to participate in mass civil disobedience rather than join a racially discriminatory military. Truman issued Executive Order 9981, which desegregated the military. In the 1950s and 1960s, Randolph joined forces with the National Association for the Advancement of Colored People (NAACP) in the battle for civil rights as well as work on poverty programs for President Lyndon Johnson. He died on May 16, 1979.

Further Reading: Leeman, Richard. *African-American Orators: A Bio-Critical Sourcebook.* Westport, CT: Praeger, 1996; Pfeffer, Paula. A. *Philip Randolph, Pioneer of the Civil Rights Movement.* Baton Rouge: Louisiana University Press, 2000.

Kelly J. Baker

RAPER, KENNETH BRYAN (1908–1987)

Kenneth Raper was a member of the "Penicillin Team" formed in 1941 at the United States Department of Agriculture's (USDA) Northern Regional Research Laboratory in Peoria. That team, including **Andrew J. Moyer**, successfully developed penicillin strains and production methods that made mass-production of penicillin possible, thereby saving countless lives of soldiers during World War II.

Raper was a North Carolina native, born in Welcome on July 11, 1908, and completing his undergraduate education at the University of North Carolina in 1929. He went on to George Washington University to earn a master's degree in 1931 and then to Harvard for both a master's degree and a doctorate in 1935 and 1936. Raper worked at the USDA's Bureau of Plant Industry as a mycologist from 1936 to 1940 and then joined the research lab in Peoria as a microbiologist, where he remained until 1953. He left there for a faculty position at the University of Wisconsin, where he had a distinguished academic career in bacteriology and botany.

Raper's work at the research lab earned him membership in the National Academy of Science and the American Academy of Arts and Sciences in 1949, the year in which he co-authored the classic A Manual of the Penicillia. Although the penicillin produced during the war through the effort of the team in Peoria had priority for military use, penicillin was also in demand by the civilian civilization. It was the first wonder drug, and it ushered in the age of antibiotics.

Benjamin F. Shearer

RAUSCHENBUSCH, WALTER (1861–1918)

Walter Rauschenbusch was born on October 4, 1861, in Rochester, New York. His father and mother had come to the United States from Germany after the revolutions of 1848. His father arrived as a Lutheran missionary to German immigrants, but after arriving, become an American Baptist minister.

After graduating from the Rochester Free Academy, Rauschenbusch went to Westphalia, Germany, where he studied for the next four years. He returned to Rochester in 1883 and he soon graduated from the University of Rochester (B.A., 1884). Seminary training began shortly afterward at the Rochester Theological Seminary from which he graduated in1886.

Rauschenbusch was ordained on June 1, 1886, as minister of the Second German Baptist Church in New York City. The church was located in an immigrant area beside the area known as "Hell's Kitchen." His experiences with the social problems of poverty, unemployment, deprivation, hunger, disease and crime inspired him to become involved in applying the Gospel to social problems.

The challenge for Rauschenbusch was to develop a socioeconomic theology that would enable him to give a theological rational for his advocacy of reforms to aid the poor. In doing so he was also opposing current ideologies of social Darwinism and individualism. He read many works by radicals and reformers popular at the time and also became involved in the mayoralty campaign of Henry George, as he called for radical changes.

Rauschenbusch was influenced by two young Baptist preachers, Leighton Williams and Nathaniel Schmidt. With Rauschenbusch they formed a Society of Jesus, later expanded into the Brotherhood of the Kingdom. In November 1889 they began publishing a pro-labor monthly periodical called *For the Right*. The goal of the publication was to mobilize the working people for their Christian socialist program. *For the Right* ran until March 1891, when it ceased publication. At this time Rauschenbusch left America for a year of study in Germany.

On his journey to Germany Rauschenbusch visited England. While there he became acquainted with Fabian Socialism, the Salvation Army, and other reformers and ministers to the poor. In Germany he was attracted to the teachings of Albert Ritschl (1822–1889) and his followers on Jesus' preaching of the Kingdom of God.

Rauschenbusch was called to teach New Testament at Rochester Theological Seminary in 1897. In 1902 he became professor of church history. In 1907 he published *Christianity and the Social Crisis* (1907). The book spotlighted him as a major advocate of the Social Gospel in the United States. Considered both dynamic and compassionate, Rauschenbusch always regarded himself as an evangelist seeking to win people to a "new birth" in Christ. At the same time, he believed that the Kingdom of god required social as well as individual salvation and he demanded a "new order that would rest on the Christian principles of equal rights and democratic distribution of economic power."

Among Rauschenbusch's writings were *Prayers of the Social Awakening* (1910), *Christianizing the Social Order* (1912), and *A Theology for the Social Gospel* (1917). In *Theology for the Social Gospel*, he sought to offer a systematic Christian theology with a social perspective. He made the Kingdom of God central to Christian theology so that the Church would shift its focus from being a mission society to being a social service organization. He did not see this as reducing the Gospel to a mere political ideology. To him the Kingdom of God was a divine creation that was present, and progressing toward fulfillment. What was needed for the world's social problems was a return to the simple perspective of Jesus.

Rauschenbusch was very unhappy over the outbreak of World War I in 1914, especially for its anti-German fervor. He published *Dare We Be Christians* in opposition to war and "Be Fair to Germany" in 1914. The latter was an article that tried to present a neutral view of Germany and England, but was viewed as supporting German aggression. As a pacifist he opposed the entry of the United States into the war. He suffered emotionally as relatives fought on both sides of the war. He believed the war demonstrated the presence of sin in the world.

In 1915 Rauschenbusch helped to circulate "Private Profit and the Nation's Honor, a Protest and a Plea," a statement against the export of munitions from the United States. His stance on the war damaged his reputation. He died in Rochester on July 25, 1918.

Further Reading: Minus, Paul M. *Walter Rauschenbusch: American Reformer*. New York: Macmillan, 1988.

Andrew J. Waskey

RAYMOND, HENRY JARVIS (1820–1869)

During the Civil War, Henry Jarvis Raymond used his position as the editor and founder of the *New York Times* to promote his pro-Union views. Born on January 24, 1820, near Lima, New York, Raymond attended the University of Vermont, but moved to New York to become a journalist. He worked first with the *New York Tribune* under **Horace Greeley**. However, after a personal dispute with Greeley, Raymond left the *Tribune* and in 1851, founded the *New York Times*, with George Jones. It was intended to be a decent and respectable paper, though the famous tagline, "All the News That's Fit to Print," was added by a later editor.

Henry Jarvis Raymond. Courtesy of the Library of Congress.

Raymond's level-headed approach to reporting garnered approval from the readers tired of luridly sensationalized news, particularly during the Civil War, in which he personally served as a war correspondent. Adding to his renown as a practical and devoted publisher was his defense of the paper during the New York draft riots in 1863. Blacks and anti-slavery Republicans were the main targets of the mobs, and Raymond and others in the *Times* building used Gatling guns from an upper window to repel the rioters bent on destruction.

After the war, Raymond delved more deeply into politics, serving as the chairman of the Republican National Committee and as a congressman, but after political infighting denied him a second nomination to the House, he returned to the paper. He died on June 18, 1869, in New York City, a newsman to the end.

Ellen Baier

REA, GEORGE BRONSON (1868–1936)

During the Spanish-American War, George Bronson Rea worked as a correspondent for the *Herald*, and though he stayed with the Cuban forces, his reports showed his pro-Spain slant. Born in Brooklyn, New York, in 1868, George Bronson Rea was educated as an engineer, though he embraced the career of a reporter during the height of so-called "yellow journalism." In 1896, Rea worked as a war correspondent for the *Herald*, and though he stayed as an embedded reporter with the Cuban revolutionary forces of General Maximo Gomez, he did not profess any particular sympathy with the rebels, especially after Gomez objected to some of the reports Rea filed that criticized the new Cuban government by threatening the reporter with execution. The book that Rea later published, *Facts and Fakes about Cuba*, made his sympathy with the Spanish side of the conflict clear.

During his time in Cuba, Rea shared travels and adventures over the Cuban countryside with **(Henry) Sylvester Scovel**, a reporter for the *World*, both with Gomez's troops and with General Antonio Maceo. Rea was particularly talented at sneaking his reports out of the country, frequently a problem for journalists covering the Cuban rebellion. He returned to the United States in August 1896, but was back in Cuba in time to be present for the destruction of the U.S.S. *Maine* in February 1898. After the Spanish-American War, he became known for his reporting on the politics of the Far East. He died in 1936.

Ellen Baier

READ, JOHN BRAHAM (?–?)

Surgeon John Read of Tuscaloosa, Alabama, invented the Read projectile shell, which, when improved by **Robert Parker Parrott**, was one of the most common rifle projectiles used by both sides during the Civil War. A projectile shell, in contrast to a bullet with solid metal, contains an explosive or other filling. The shell was fitted with a hollow forged-iron plug, filled with slow-burning powder. Read patented a method for constructing cannon projectiles, or shells. His invention consisted of the attachment to the butt of elongated cannon shells of a cupped cylinder of wrought-iron fastened to the body by having the perforated bottom embedded in the metal of which the shot is composed.

The Confederates manufactured the Read projectile by placing the wrought iron sabot in the bottom of the mold formed by the pattern for the shell and pouring the necessary amount of cast metal into the mold. Read's patent also covered almost every possible way to attach a sabot to the bottom of a rifled projectile. In 1856, Read sold his invention to Parrott, superintendent of the West Point Foundry, for the sole right to manufacture it for the U.S. government. In spite of Parrott's giving credit to Read when Parrott made improvements to it, Read nevertheless claimed patent infringement, but it was Parrott's improved design that was used during the Civil War.

Further Reading: Dickey, Thomas S., and Peter C. George. *Field Artillery Projectiles of the American Civil War.* Atlanta, GA: Arsenal Press, 1980.

Michael L. McGregor

REED, JOHN SILAS (1887–1920)

A protestor as well as journalist, John Reed reported on World War I for the radical newspaper *The Masses* and was arrested many times for expressing views the United States government felt were seditious. Born into a wealthy family on October 22, 1887, in Portland, Oregon, Reed grew up privileged, attending Harvard College. In 1913, his social conscience was stirred, and he embarked on his short but fraught career. He began writing for *The Masses* that year, working with noted socialist **Max Forrester Eastman**. His accounts of striking workers led him to travel to Mexico, where he reported for four months on the Mexican Revolution for the *Metropolitan Magazine*.

John Reed. Courtesy of the Library of Congress.

This stint as a war correspondent led to his assignment in Europe—Germany, Serbia, Bulgaria, and Russia—at the first sign of conflict in 1914, with illustrator **Boardman Robinson**. Reed wrote of his wartime visit in 1916's *The War in Eastern Europe*, illustrated by Robinson. The two men contributed reports back to Eastman's radical paper *The Masses*, and were among those named when the newspaper was charged with violating the Espionage Act in 1917. Though none of the contributors was convicted, the newspaper folded.

After the war, Reed briefly visited Russia to witness the revolution in Petrograd. He soon returned to the United States, where he underwent trial after trial for his "incendiary speech[es]" and headed the Communist Labor Party until he was finally convicted of sedition and fled the country. He died of typhus on October 19, 1920.

Ellen Baier

REES, DAVID (1973–)

In September 2001 Chapel Hill, North Carolina, native and Oberlin College graduate David Rees self-published a pair of comic books called *My New Fighting Technique Is Unstoppable* and *My New Filing Technique Is Unstoppable*. His cartoons were composed using clip art downloaded from the Internet. In addition to self-publishing them in book format, he also put them on the Internet, where they gained a small but loyal following.

After the September 11, 2001, attack, and the subsequent American invasion of Afghanistan, Rees, then living in Brooklyn, began writing a cartoon called *Get Your War On*. He continued to use Internet clip art. The cartoon tells the story of a group of office workers discussing current events, particularly the Afghanistan and, later, the Iraq wars. The comments of these characters, often profane and always ironic, seem to indicate that they are in support of the war efforts. However, the tone of the comic makes it plainly clear that Rees is opposed to the war.

The popularity of the comic within the Internet community was huge, and under pressure from his fans, Rees was convinced to publish a collection of the comics as a book. Unwilling to profit from the endeavor, he donated the book profits from the first printing, and a second printing, to a group called Adopt-a-Minefield, which was devoted to clearing minefields in northern Afghanistan. He has continued to support this organization with subsequent printings of his second book.

Mike Timonin

REID, WHITELAW (1837–1912)

Whitelaw Reid, a Civil War correspondent, began as the editor of the *New York Tribune* in 1869. After the Tribune's founder, **Horace Greeley**, died in 1872, Reid gained ownership of the newspaper and continued its tradition as a leading voice of political and social issues in the United States.

Born on October 27, 1837, near Xenia, Ohio, Reid graduated from Miami University in 1856. By 1859, he was editor of Xenia's newspaper and began writing for other Ohio-based publications. In 1861, he became the city editor of the *Cincinnati Gazette*, reporting about the Civil War for that newspaper. The following year, he began a one-year term as clerk of the military committee for Congress and, from 1863 to 1866 he was also the librarian for the House of Representatives.

Reid's writing and editorial tenure at the *New York Tribune* lasted from 1868 (when he was named lead editorial writer) until 1905, when he retired from active participation but still managed the publication's finances.

Although he refused diplomatic appointments to Germany in 1877 and 1881, Reid did accept an offer to serve as minister to

Whitelaw Reid. Courtesy of the Library of Congress.

France in 1889; three years later, he unsuccessfully ran as vice president of the United States under Benjamin Harrison.

Throughout the end of the nineteenth century and beginning of the twentieth, Reid served the United States in foreign ambassador positions. He also published many political books ranging from *After the War* (1867), which shared his impressions of the southern states in 1866, to *How America Faced Its Education Problem*, which was published in 1906. Reid died in London, England, on December 15, 1912.

Further Reading: Cortissoz, Royal. *The Life of Whitelaw Reid.* London: Thornton Butterworth, 1921.

Kelly Boyer Sagert

REMINGTON, FREDERIC (1861–1909)

Frederic Remington's drawings of Cuba were used to incite anti-Spanish sentiments and bolster support for the Cuban revolution during the Spanish-American War. Born to Seth Pierre and Clara (Sackrider) Remington on October 4, 1861, in Canton, New York, Remington studied at the Yale School of Fine Arts and at the Art Students League in New York. He spent some time in the American West, drawing Geronimo's Apache tribe; it was these sketches—his first successful pieces—that created his reputation as an artist of the West. Remington was a critic of American policies toward Native Americans, writing articles and essays in an attempt to enlighten Easterners on reservation conditions, as well as providing drawings of the West on commission for *Harper's Weekly*.

Remington worked as a war correspondent for *Harper's* during the Spanish-American War, sending back reports and drawings of the Cuban struggle. Quickly disillusioned by the horrors that he witnessed, he was present at the charge on San Juan Hill, led by Theodore Roosevelt, and he presented readers back in America with a view of war not as heroic, but as deeply disturbing. His distress at the atrocities of war came through in his pictures and articles, and he could not remain in Cuba long.

After the war, Remington devoted himself primarily to his fiction, writing novels about the dying wildness of the West. He was considered slightly less sentimental than many contemporary authors, especially after his experiences in Cuba. He died of appendicitis on December 26, 1909.

Ellen Baier

REUTHER, WALTER (1907–1970)

A prominent World War II–era labor leader, Walter Reuther headed the United Auto Workers, creating a base of solid anti-communist, though liberal, union support through the Cold War and into Vietnam. Born on September 1, 1907, in Wheeling, West Virginia, to Valentine and Anna (Stocker)

Reuther, Reuther grew up in a strongly liberal and hard-working family. He began work at the age of sixteen, though he managed to complete high school and several years of college at Detroit City College (now Wayne State University). He began to show his socialist leanings when he worked for the Ford Motor Company, which fired him in 1932, reportedly for supporting **Norman Mattoon Thomas** in the 1932 presidential election and joining the Auto Workers Union. Following this firing, unable to find work in America, Reuther and one of his brothers traveled to Eastern Europe and Japan. He worked briefly in an auto factory in Russia, but felt stifled by the lack of scope for his political activities. He returned to the States in 1935, and it was then that he became truly active in the growth of industrial unionization.

During the turbulent labor relations of the pre–World War II era, Reuther earned his reputation of working for the rights of the common man. He also split decisively with Communism at this time, though when he was elected United Auto Workers (UAW) president in 1946, he was still more liberal than many of his colleagues. As the war approached, Reuther was involved in plans to move from civilian to war production, advising owners on the likely labor relations that would arise with changing production goals and employee needs that the war would create. His earliest plans for creating over five hundred planes per day in converted automobile factories through a reconstructed and empowered labor force, though scorned by owners, soon proved to be both efficient and farsighted. Even the production goal, which seemed laughably high in 1940, was met and exceeded at the height of wartime production. The war provided an opportunity for Reuther to further his political goals for the advancement of labor's power, and it was an opportunity that he embraced. He not only worked toward a greater presence of labor in decision-making and bargaining, but also worked to eliminate racism within the union and exploit the potential for a full-employment wartime economy.

Reuther's primary method of organization was to single out a company, or even a shop, that promised to provide militant strikers, then build upon the success there to reach out to the rest of the challenged company and industry. In negotiations, he often requested unemployment benefits, pensions, and company-paid insurance in exchange for tractable employees, and the companies generally, though not always, willingly cooperated. During the final days of the war in 1945, when factories were changing back to a civilian economy, Reuther attempted an even bolder than usual stance towards the management of General Motors, demanding that the company "open the books" for inspection by the unions; in effect, he led his workers in fighting for more transparent accounting of the relationship between prices and wages. However, his attempt was not backed by the rest of the striking unions—not even other UAW local branches—and his bold move failed.

After the war, Reuther's involvement with politics and union leadership only increased, causing him to be the target of an assassination attempt in 1948, which permanently injured his right arm. Elected president of the UAW after a bitter struggle, he worked to entrench himself, purging the rolls of his opponents.

He also worked to eliminate the communist influence, successfully avoiding reprisals for his own pre-war socialism. His objection to the communists was based less on ideological bases than on practical ones; communists were less committed to the union objectives than to their own political goals, he felt, and therefore were more likely to present resistance to union solidarity.

Reuther became president of the Congress of Industrial Organizations (CIO) in 1952, though when the CIO rejoined the American Federation of Labor (AFL), he was too far left of center to support the merger, and stepped down from his leadership position. Reuther disagreed with conservative **George Meany**, the AFL president, on union support for the war in Vietnam, civil rights issues, and environmental protection, among other things. Following a dispute in labor policy, Reuther withdrew the UAW in 1968 to pursue a new organization, the Alliance for Labor Action (ALA), but it was largely unsuccessful, limited by Reuther's untimely death from a plane crash in Michigan on May 9, 1970.

Ellen Baier

REVERE, PAUL (1735–1818)

Paul Revere was born on January 1, 1735, in Boston and raised there, attending North Grammar School. During the French and Indian War, he saw

brief service. After the war, he married and joined his father's silversmith business. He learned copper engraving and produced several anti-British caricatures widely published before the Revolution. Revere was an early supporter of American liberty, having become close friends with Samuel Adams, James Otis, and John Hancock. When British troops fired on Boston citizens on March 5, 1770, Revere produced an engraving widely distributed of the Boston Massacre. It served to further enflame the anti-British, pro-liberty feelings of Boston.

A member of the "Sons of Liberty," Revere participated in the Boston Tea Party. When England occupied Boston, Revere became one of thirty North End mechanics patrolling the streets and monitoring troop movements. In December 1774, he urged New Hampshire patriots to seize Fort William and Mary and the military stores there. On April 18, 1775, Revere and William Dawes were sent to warn Samuel Adams and John Hancock that British troops were marching. Revere reached Lexington around midnight then left for Concord an hour later. Captured by British sentries, he was

Paul Revere. Courtesy of the Library of Congress.

released on foot to return to Lexington where he joined Hancock in fleeing into safety. He later commanded a garrison at Castle Williams, Boston, before leaving service in disrepute. He died on May 10, 1818.

Further Reading: Langguth, A. J. *Patriots: The Men Who Started the American Revolution.* New York: Simon and Schuster, 1988.

Jerry L. Parker

RICHARDS, ALFRED NEWTON (1876–1966)

Alfred Newton Richards served as the Chairman of the Committee on Medical Research of the Office of Scientific Research and Development (OSRD) for the U.S. government from 1941 to 1946. In this capacity, he oversaw the first successful penicillin mass-production effort as well as the largest and most expensive but effective effort to discover antimalarial drugs. Before assuming this administrative position, Richards had been a respected scientist, renowned for organizing the Department of Pharmacology at the University of Pennsylvania in 1910 and for his research on kidney function, which formed the basis of modern nephrology.

Born in Stamford, New York, on March 22, 1876, Richards was admitted to the Yale College in 1893. He took an elective in physiological chemistry under R. H. Chittenden during his time at Yale, and additional laboratory courses in chemistry allowed him to graduate in June 1897 with honors in chemistry. Subsequent graduate work with Chittenden resulted in a joint publication in the first volume of the *American Journal of Physiology*; thus, Richards is considered a pioneer in American physiology. Chittenden next invited Richards to join his permanent staff when he moved to the Department of Medical Chemistry in the College of Physicians and Surgeons at Columbia. Richards stayed at Columbia from 1898 through 1908, earning his Ph.D. in physiological chemistry in 1901. The Rockefeller Institute awarded him its very first scholarship, which he used for a year of study with Columbia professor Christian A. Herter on epinephrine's glycosuric effects on the dog pancreas.

Richards assisted George B. Wallace of Cushny's Department of Pharmacology in his already established course at Bellevue for further preparation in his new role at Columbia, organizing an elective in experimental pharmacology at Columbia at Wallace's suggestion. He next served as associate editor of the *Journal of Biological Chemistry*; in 1910, he became managing editor. Richards established a pharmacology department for the medical school at Northwestern and later joined the pharmacology faculty of the University of Pennsylvania. As professor of pharmacology, his most recognized accomplishment was his laboratory's finding of the filtration-reabsorption concept of kidney function using frogs as the experimental model. He worked during World War I with Henry H. Dale through the British Medical Research Committee on the cause of wound shock and also as a major in the U.S. Sanitary Corps. In 1939, the University of Pennsylvania appointed him

701

vice-president in charge of medical affairs. Subsequently, President Franklin Roosevelt appointed him chairman of the Committee on Medical Research for the newly created OSRD.

The purpose of the Committee on Medical Research was to "advise and assist" the Director of OSRD by planning and coordinating medical research in universities, hospitals, scientific institutions, and industries and by recommending and overseeing research contracts. The committee recommended more than five hundred research proposals, which resulted in 135 contracts and a total of $25 million in expenditures. Richards' committee also set priorities for research on the major problems in military medicine at the time, namely infection prevention and treatment of wounds and malaria prevention.

When a team of Oxford scientists had achieved success in producing penicillin, Richards suggested the drug might be produced on a large scale if there were collaboration among chemical manufacturers. The Committee on Medical Research supported Richards' proposal by passing a resolution on October 2, 1941, which authorized the chairman to pursue the possibility of research on penicillin on a pooling of information basis. Pharmaceutical manufacturers joined the program, and successful treatments led to increased production. By war's end, enough penicillin was produced to treat all infections in the Allied military. Shortly thereafter, production also grew sufficient to treat the civilian population. Richards had also administered a successful cooperative program between the United States and England for the development of antimalarial drugs through which more than 14,000 compounds were developed and tested.

Richards later headed a group to study how the research collaboration with academia, government, and industry begun during the war could continue postwar. Their recommendations for a national research foundation were published in *Science—The Endless Frontier*. Richards served as president of the National Academy of Sciences from 1947 to 1950. At age eighty-one, he addressed a faculty research group at the medical school of the University of Pennsylvania about the advantages and dangers of government grants-in-aid for medical research. He died on March 24, 1966, two days after his ninetieth birthday.

Further Reading: Schmidt, Carl F., Ed. "Alfred Newton Richards: Scientist and Man." *Annals of Internal Medicine* 71, Supplement 8 [Memorial Issue] (1969): 1–89.

Ximena Chrisagis

RICHARDSON, ALBERT DEANE (1833–1869)

Albert Richardson was a newspaper correspondent in the Civil War for the New York *Tribune*. Born in Franklin, Massachusetts on October 6, 1833, and educated at Holliston Academy, he worked for several newspapers in Pittsburgh and Cincinnati before joining the *Boston Journal* to cover the sectional conflict in Kansas.

During the Civil War Richardson became the *Tribune*'s chief correspondent in the West. Adventurous and self-assured, he risked being hanged as a spy to travel through the South as a secret correspondent for the *Tribune* in 1861. Richardson accompanied Hooker's forces at the Battle of Antietam. At the Battle of Vicksburg he attempted to run the Confederate batteries aboard a hay barge with fellow *Tribune* correspondent Junius Henri Browne. The barge was hit by gunfire, killing the captain and three crewmembers. Richardson and Browne survived, but were captured and imprisoned in a military prison at Salisbury, North Carolina. The following year the intrepid correspondents escaped. After a daring four-hundred-mile, four-week journey through the Blue Ridge Mountains, they reached Knoxville, Tennessee.

Richardson wrote several books about his Civil War exploits. He met a tragic end shortly after his engagement to the recently divorced Abby Sage McFarland on November 25, 1869, when her ex-husband fatally shot him at his desk in the *Tribune* office. Richardson and McFarland were wed in a death-bed ceremony a week before his death.

Further Reading: Andrews, J. Cutler. *The North Reports the Civil War*. Pittsburgh: University of Pittsburgh Press 1955.

Michael L. McGregor

RICKARD, CLINTON (1882–1971)

A veteran from a long line of Tuscarora Indian veterans, Chief Clinton Rickard enlisted during the Spanish-American War and the Filipino Insurrection. For the remainder of his long life, Rickard was simultaneously a proud U.S. Army veteran and the most prominent Iroquois leader opposing the draft. This seeming contradiction cannot be understood without looking at Native American treaty rights. Rickard was born on May 19, 1882, on the Tuscaroras' Cattaraugus reservation in western New York state. The Rickard family's history of military service went all the way back to his great-great-grandfather, who fought in the Revolutionary War. For the Tuscarora and the other members of the Haudenosaunee Confederacy (also known as Six Nations of the Iroquois) military service is seen as part of reciprocal treaty obligations. The Six Nations often point in particular to the Jay Treaty of 1794 and the 1814 Treaty of Ghent since they both recognize Haudenosaunee sovereignty and set conditions and obligations for all parties: the Six Nations, the United States, and Great Britain (which later passed these obligations on to Canada.)

Rickard fought in the Philippines from 1901 to 1904. Just prior to that he was part of the guard detail for, ironically, then Vice President Theodore Roosevelt, a man noted for his intense hatred of Indians. Rickard saw veterans' organizations as similar in purpose to now-defunct Iroquois warrior societies. After the war he joined the Army and Navy Union, the United Spanish War Veterans, and a Masonic Lodge. Rickard also played the lead role in organizing Post 8242 of the Veterans of Foreign Wars on the Tuscarora reservation.

In 1917, when the United States entered World War I, the Iroquois had already issued their own declaration of war against the Central Powers in reaction to the abusive treatment their citizens endured in Germany. At war's end, the U.S. government "awarded" citizenship, first to Native American veterans in 1919, then to all Native Americans in 1923. Most Iroquois were strongly opposed to both acts, which they saw as forcible assimilation, an attempt to strip away their treaty rights and sovereignty, and the imposition of mainstream culture and taxes upon their lands. The final act many Iroquois found intolerable was the Immigration Act of 1924, which restricted the movements of Iroquois between Canada and the U.S.

Rickard played a leading role in opposition to these acts, founding the Indian Defense League of America (IDLA) in 1926. The catalyst for him was when Deskaheh or Levi General, a Cayuga sachem (counselor), became ill after traveling to the League of Nations in Geneva to make an appeal for aid in the loss of indigenous rights. Unable to be treated by medicine men from his reserve in Canada because of immigration laws, Deskaheh died in Rickard's home. Rickard vowed to dedicate his life to fighting treaty violations such as border restrictions and the draft. He organized an annual celebration/march to assert border-crossing rights as contained in the Jay Treaty.

In 1928, when Native Americans could vote for the first time, most Iroquois refused to, seeing voting as accepting the loss of sovereignty. Those Iroquois who did vote were stripped of the privilege of ever becoming a chief or clan mother in their nations. Their opposition to forcible citizenship continued into World War II. A faction of Iroquois issued its own declaration of war against the Axis powers. The Six Nations Council refused to cooperate with the Selective Service Act and took its case to court claiming that the Citizenship Act of 1924 was unconstitutional. Rickard presented the Confederacy's position. The Iroquois lost their case, but their young men volunteered as foreign nationals to avoid being drafted as citizens.

Rickard continued to lead the IDLA in struggles against the loss of Iroquois land, termination, and against conscription of Iroquois in the Korean and Vietnam Wars. In 1928, the IDLA had won unrestricted rights for Indians to trade and travel across the U.S./Canadian border. In 1968 the Canadian government tried to collect tolls at border crossings. Mohawks at the reserve of Akwesasne, supported by Rickard and the IDLA, blockaded the bridge in protest. In February 1969 the Canadian government backed down. The bridge blockade led to the founding of the newspaper *Akwesasne Notes*, which played a huge role in the Red Power movement and Native American veterans' confrontations with the U.S. government during the Vietnam era. Rickard died on June 14, 1971.

Further Reading: Carroll, Al. *Medicine Bags and Dog Tags*. Lincoln: University of Nebraska Press, 2005; Graymont, Barbara, Ed. *Fighting Tuscarora*. Syracuse, NY:

Syracuse University Press, 1973; "Indian Defense League of America." Accessed January 7, 2005, at http://idloa.org.

Al Carroll

RICKENBACKER, EDWARD VERNON (1890–1973)

Born on October 8, 1890, to Swiss parents, Eddie Rickenbacker grew up poor in Columbus, Ohio, where he began working full-time in 1904 after his father's death. He worked in a variety of jobs until he finally took an International Correspondence School course in mechanical engineering and landed a job with the Frayer-Miller automobile company. He went on work for Firestone-Columbus, raced in the first Indianapolis 500 in 1911, and then moved to Duesenberg in 1912, where he formed his own racing team.

Rickenbacker went into the U.S. Army in 1917 as a driver for John Pershing. He then joined the air corps and became an ace with twenty-six kills. After the war he headed the Rickenbacker Automobile Company until it went bankrupt. In 1927 he bought the Indianapolis Speedway. He kept the track until 1947, but he was more interested in running Eastern Airlines.

Eastern came into being after passage of the 1925 Air Mail Act as Florida Airways. A 1926 hurricane destroyed the airline, and in 1929 Rickenbacker moved to General Motors' Fokker Aircraft Company, then to American Airways, then back to General Motors (GM). By 1938 Rickenbacker re-established Eastern under GM ownership. He was forced out as chief executive officer (CEO) in 1957, but remained chairman of the board until 1963.

Rickenbacker was strongly opposed to Franklin Roosevelt and the New Deal, and he was a member of the "America First" committee that opposed U.S. entry into World War II. He supported the effort after Pearl Harbor, touring bases in the United States, Europe, and the Pacific in 1942 and 1943. He died on July 23, 1973.

John H. Barnhill

RIDENOUR, LOUIS NICOT JR. (1911–1959)

When Louis Ridenour died at only forty-seven on May 21, 1959, he left a legacy of significant contributions to American war efforts. Born on November 1, 1911, Ridenour obtained his undergraduate physics degree at the University of Chicago in 1932 and his doctorate at the California Institute of Technology in 1936. He received an appointment to Princeton's Institute for Advanced Study in 1935 and left there for the University of Pennsylvania in 1938. In January of 1941, Ridenour was among the first physicists to join MIT's Radiation Laboratory (Rad Lab) in the search for effective radar systems.

Ridenour, who became the first Chief Scientist of the Air Force in 1950, led a group that began the design of what became the successful SCR-584 gun-laying radar. **Ivan A. Getting** became responsible for the final design of this system because Ridenour left the Rad Lab for North Africa as an expert consultant for the secretary of war, where he convinced commanders of the effectiveness of the SCR-584. Returning to the lab from abroad, Ridenour took over the Airborne Radar Division and was made the lab's assistant director. In that position he furthered the development of **George Edward Valley Jr.**'s H2X radar bombsight, an airborne targeting radar system first employed in combat in 1943. With a group of scientists in Europe in 1944, Ridenour invented the use of the SCR-584 to control bombers in bad weather and he strategically engaged radar-controlled anti-aircraft resources to knock out 90 percent of incoming German buzz bombs over Britain.

Benjamin F. Shearer

RIGDON, CHARLES (?–1866)

Charles Rigdon and **Thomas H. Leech** made pistols and swords for the Confederate Army. Before the Civil War, Rigdon had made scales in St. Louis, Missouri. Sympathetic to the South's cause, he moved to Memphis in 1861, where he joined up with Leech to make pistols and swords sometime in late 1861 or early 1862. During 1862 they secured a contract with the Confederate government to produce pistols based on the Colt Model 1851 Navy pistol. In May 1862, the company was forced to move to Columbus, Mississippi, as Union troops moved on Tennessee. The company moved again in December 1862 to Greensboro, Georgia. Leech and Rigdon stopped making swords in April 1863 to concentrate on making pistols.

On December 13, 1863, Leech sold his interest in the company to Rigdon. The sale was not official until January 1, 1864. After Leech left, Rigdon took on James A. Ansley as a partner and the company was renamed Rigdon, Ansley and Company. Rigdon continued to make pistols under the contract he and Leech had obtained from the Confederate government. Also after Leech left, the pistol design was modified to hold twelve shots. The plant was moved to Augusta, Georgia, early in 1864 where the company continued to produce pistols until January 1865.

Rigdon died on October 9, 1866, in Memphis, Tennessee.

Further Reading: Albaugh, William A., III, and Richard D. Steuart. *The Original Confederate Colt: The Story of the Leech & Rigdon and Rigdon-Ansley Revolvers.* New York: Greenberg, 1953.

Dallace W. Unger Jr.

RINEHART, MARY ROBERTS (1876–1958)

Mary Roberts Rinehart worked as a war correspondent during World War I. She was born on August 12, 1876, in Pittsburgh, was married in 1896, and had three sons and one daughter. Rinehart trained as a nurse at the Pittsburgh Homeopathic Hospital, but began to write after her husband's investments failed in 1903. Though she wrote in multiple genres, Rinehart was especially known for her mysteries and romances. She was influential in the development of the mystery genre and twentieth-century detective fiction.

At the start of World War I, Rinehart served as a war correspondent in Europe for the *Saturday Evening Post*, publishing eleven articles in spring and summer 1915. Back on the home front, she wrote articles for the military for the purposes of public information. In an effort to return to the war zone, she became an official Red Cross nurse, but since she had a son serving on the front, she was not allowed to go. Rinehart finally received a war assignment as an official representative of the War Department. Though she arrived just two days prior to the armistice, she remained in Europe to tour Red Cross facilities on the front. If poor health had not prevented her, she would have contributed to the war effort during World War II as well.

Mary Roberts Rinehart. Courtesy of the Library of Congress.

Rinehart died in New York, on September 22, 1958.

Further Reading: Conn, Jan. *Improbable Fiction: The Life of Mary Roberts Rinehart.* Pittsburgh: University of Pittsburgh Press, 1980.

Stacy Dorgan

RINES, ROBERT H. (1922–)

Born in Boston on August 20, 1922, Robert Rines was accepted to MIT when he was only fifteen years old, where he pursued an undergraduate degree in physics and had the opportunity on work on radar at the Radiation Laboratory. After leaving the Signal Corps, Rines got his law degree at Georgetown in 1946, specializing, like his father, in patents. Rines went on to lead an incredible life as a patent lawyer, musician, inventor, and Loch Ness monster chaser. He founded both the Academy of Applied Science and the Franklin Pierce Law Center, a law school for intellectual property law. The Inventor's Hall of Fame, to which Rines was elected in 1994, noted that his high-definition image-scanning radar patents are the basis for weapons fire-control, early warning, and missile detection radars that have been used in all

American wars since World War II. Rines used his own sonar system to look for Nessie the Loch Ness monster, and it was also employed to find the *Titanic*. In his spare time, Rines has written music for ten plays.

Rines' invention of a modulations technique for the Microwave Early Warning System (MEW, also known as the AN/CPS-1) during World War II helped to make the more than 60-ton MEW an effective system. The two MEWs installed in Britain in 1944 were effective in defending against German V-1 buzz-bombs. The MEW was also installed on the beachhead at Normandy to protect invasion forces and monitor air traffic.

Benjamin F. Shearer

RITER, BENJAMIN FRANKLIN JR. (1886–1966)

Franklin Riter spearheaded the American Legion's post–World War II campaign to reform the military justice system. Born on September 27, 1886, in Logan, Utah, Riter graduated from Utah State Agricultural College in 1907. He earned a law degree from Columbia in 1910 and joined a local law firm. In 1911, he married Lesley Woodruff, daughter of a prominent Salt Lake City doctor.

Though Riter attended Infantry Officers' Training School during World War I, the war ended before his training did. In 1923, he received a reserve commission as a captain in the Judge Advocate General's department (JAG). During the 1930s, he rose to lieutenant colonel. He also chaired the Utah branch of Fighting Funds for Finland.

In 1941, Riter was called into service, promoted to colonel and became chair of the first JAG Board of Review (a military appeals court) in the European theater. After the invasion of Europe, he coordinated five boards of review. Riter presided over the case of Private Eddie Slovik, the first deserter executed since the Civil War. He was promoted to Brigadier General and received the Legion of Merit for his service.

Scandals in 1947 resulted in public interest in reforming military justice. In hearings that resulted in the Uniform Code of Military Justice (UCMJ), Riter testified for the American Legion on the importance of recognizing the needs of draftees who serve for short terms. He also testified that an interim measure, the Elston Act, lacked penalties for violating procedures. The UCMJ became law in 1950.

Wende Vyborney Feller

RIVERA, GERALDO (1943–)

Geraldo Rivera has been a familiar face on American television since 1970, when he got his first job at WABC in New York City as a reporter. A native of Brooklyn, by the time he got into television he had served two years with the Merchant Marine Corps, completed his B.S. degree at the University of

Arizona and his law degree at Brooklyn as well as graduate work at the University of Pennsylvania and the Columbia School of Journalism. When his legal career primarily in poverty law left him with few means, he turned to television journalism, in which he was remarkably successful. Rivera appeared on ABC's *Good Morning America*, hosted its *Good Night America* show, and spent eight years on *20/20*. From 1987 until 1998 *The Geraldo Rivera Show* represented what many called a foray into tabloid journalism. Yet Rivera continued to produce serious, well-received documentaries for NBC thereafter and hosted *Rivera Live* on CNBC.

In 2001 Rivera took the opportunity to become a war correspondent for Fox News Network. He reported first from Afghanistan. In 2002, he joined fellow correspondents **Peter Arnett**, **David Bloom**, and **Walter C. Rodgers** to report Gulf War II from Iraq. Rivera's reportage was characterized by incendiary and vindictive rhetoric. Indeed, he caused quite a stir when he announced, on the air, the mission of the airborne division with which he was traveling.

Since July 2002 Rivera has been an investigative reporter for Fox.

Benjamin F. Shearer

RIVINGTON, JAMES (1724–1802)

A loyalist publisher during the American Revolution, James Rivington also operated as a double agent who passed British military secrets to General George Washington. Rivington was born in London, where he and his brother took over their father's printing business in the 1740s. Having declared bankruptcy in England, Rivington immigrated to America in 1760. After pursuing several different moneymaking schemes, he established a successful printing firm in New York.

On March 18, 1773, Rivington published the first issue of his newspaper, *Rivington's New-York Gazetteer*. Within two years, the *Gazetteer* had a circulation of 3,600, making it one of the largest newspapers of the Colonial era. Rivington maintained a balanced view of politics at first, but by the end of 1774 he was printing stridently loyalist articles and earning the wrath of patriots. In November 1775, an angry mob destroyed Rivington's printing press. According to legend, the type was melted down to make bullets for the militia.

Rivington fled to England in January 1776, but returned to British-occupied New York the following year to serve as the royal printer. He resumed publication of his newspaper under the new title *Rivington's New York Loyal Gazette*, which was later changed to the *Royal Gazette*. During this same period, Rivington, unbeknown to his contemporaries, was furnishing General George Washington with secret military information. At the end of the war, Washington not only allowed Rivington to remain in New York, but also sent troops to safeguard him from vengeful patriots. Rivington died in poverty in 1802.

Kathleen Ruppert

ROBERTSON, JAMES (1742–1814)

James Robertson, the "Father of Tennessee" and founder of Nashville, was born in Brunswick County, Virginia, on June 28, 1742, to John and Mary Gower Robertson. After moving to North Carolina, he married Charlotte Reeves, daughter of a Presbyterian minister, in 1768 and the two had thirteen children together. The year after he married, Robertson and several of his North Carolina neighbors traveled west into what is today eastern Tennessee, arriving at the Holston Valley near the Watauga River. Once there, they established the Watauga Association and chose Robertson as one of the five magistrates. They also nominated him commander of the Watauga Fort. The Watauga Association later founded a settlement along the Cumberland River, which they called Fort Nashborough in honor of General Francis Nash.

During the American Revolution, several Indian wars broke out on the frontier of eastern Tennessee. Robertson was among the American soldiers who helped defend the white settlements from the Cherokees.

President George Washington appointed Robertson Brigadier General of the U.S. Army in 1791. Three years later, Robertson petitioned the North Carolina legislature to incorporate Nashville as a town. He later sought to establish a school there called Davidson Academy. In 1804, Robertson was elected as Indian Agent for the Chickasaw and Choctaw tribes. He died on September 1, 1814.

Further Reading: Matthews, Thomas E. *General James Robertson*. Nashville: Parthenon Press, 1934; Putnam, A.W. *History of Middle Tennessee; or, Life and Times of Gen. James Robertson*. Knoxville: University of Tennessee Press, 1971.

Nicole Mitchell

ROBERTSON, PAT (1930–)

A controversial televangelist and 1988 presidential candidate, Pat Robertson is one of the few Christian leaders to support the post-9/11 war in Iraq. Born on March 22, 1930, into a prominent family of Virginia Democrats, Robertson attended military prep schools before enrolling in Washington and Lee University. He joined the Marines in 1948, graduated from college in 1950, and began service in Korea. Though Robertson claimed during his presidential campaign to have seen combat, veterans testified that he had been "liquor officer." In 1959, Robertson earned a divinity degree from the New York Theological Seminary. A Southern Baptist, he launched a successful career in televangelism, including hosting *The 700 Club*, and founded the Christian Coalition.

The 1990 Gulf War is credited with silencing Robertson's efforts to divide the Republican Party on social and taxation issues. In his best-selling book, *The New World Order*, Robertson argued that an international conspiracy was eroding Christian values throughout the world, and that the United States should therefore withdraw from the United Nations.

Following the 9/11 attacks, Robertson approved **Jerry Falwell**'s remarks blaming the attacks on pagans, abortionists, feminists, gays, lesbians, the ACLU and the People for the American Way. Though many Christian leaders oppose the Iraq war, Robertson vocally supports the war, arguing also for judicial activism to silence excess liberalism at home. He is less supportive of the government: in October 2004, Robertson announced that God had told him to expect massive casualties in Iraq, but that his efforts to warn President George W. Bush had gone unheeded.

Wende Vyborney Feller

ROBINSON, BOARDMAN (1876–1952)

During World War I, Robinson worked as a political cartoonist, and his anti-war drawings were published in radical newspapers, where they drew criticism from government officials anxious to quash such seemingly unpatriotic dissent. Robinson was born on September 6, 1876, in Nova Scotia, Canada, to John Henry and Lydia Jane (Parker) Robinson. He grew up in Wales, but returned to North America to attend the Massachusetts Normal Art School in Boston, then studied in Paris, Italy, and San Francisco. He moved to New York to pursue a career in commercial illustration in 1904, and soon found that his bold political cartoons sold well to magazines and newspapers, including the *New York Times*, *New York Tribune*, and *Morning Telegraph*.

Robinson went to Russia with journalist **John Silas Reed** in 1914, studying the conditions under socialism and reporting back to the *Metropolitan Magazine*. In 1916, Robinson illustrated Reed's book, *The War in Eastern Europe*, which also grew out of that visit. Many of his cartoons appeared in *The Masses*, a radical journal, and in 1917, the government accused the journal and its contributors of undermining the war effort, and in the ensuing legal battle, the newspaper folded.

After the war, Robinson contributed to **Max Forrester Eastman**'s newspaper, *The Liberator*, until 1922. He also illustrated books, painted murals and frescoes, and taught at the Art Students League of New York. He also served as the first director of the Colorado Springs Fine Art Center. He died on September 5, 1952.

Ellen Baier

ROCKWELL, NORMAN PERCEVEL (1894–1978)

Norman Rockwell was born in New York City on February 3, 1894, and as he grew up, he shared illustrated magazines with his father. Rockwell dropped out of high school to take classes at the National Academy of Design, and he also studied at the Art Students League of New York. He began his career illustrating for children's magazines. In 1916, Rockwell sold his first cover to the *Saturday Evening Post*, and his work continued to grace the front of the

Norman Rockwell. Courtesy of the Library of Congress.

magazine for over forty years. With over three hundred cover prints, his work had a larger audience than most artists.

Rockwell also illustrated advertisements, calendars, and books. During World War II, he painted "Four Freedom" posters, which symbolized President Franklin Roosevelt's war goals. The most famous of these, *Freedom of Speech*, is now located at the Metropolitan Museum of Art. The *Post* published these prints beginning in February 1943. Also in 1943, Rockwell painted his famous *Rosie the Riveter* for a *Saturday Evening Post* cover. Rockwell's Rosie represented the influx of women in the workforce as a patriotic act. Rosie was dressed in blue jeans with her riveting gun nearby. Rockwell's painting of this woman patriot was embraced by the women's movement of the 1970s as an example of what women could accomplish. Throughout his career, Rockwell painted the humorous as well as the painful in American life. He died on November 8, 1978.

Further Reading: Claridge, Laura. *Norman Rockwell: A Life*. New York: Random House, 2001.

Kelly J. Baker

RODGERS, WALTER C. (1940–)

Walter Rodgers completed his B.A. in 1962 and his M.A in 1964, both in history, at Southern Illinois University—Carbondale. He came to prominence as a correspondent for Cable News Network (CNN) who was "embedded" with the U.S. Army during the war with Iraq. Journalists were first embedded with military units during Operation Iraqi Freedom in a distinct about-face from U.S. government policy during previous modern military actions. During the U.S. invasion of Grenada in 1983, for example, journalists were distanced from the action. During the Gulf War, pool journalists were given limited access to selected military maneuvers and operations.

The U.S. military had been preoccupied with press coverage of war ever since Vietnam, when military leaders blamed extensive television coverage of nasty guerilla war for the American public's abandonment of its support for the action. Prior to the Iraqi war, however, the military came to terms with the media to allow news organizations to embed their reporters in the battlefield units. Walter Rodgers was one of the most prominent of these embedded journalists as a CNN correspondent whose reports were broadcast around the world.

Rodgers served with the U.S. Army's Third Squadron, Seventh Cavalry during the charge toward Bagdad in 2003. Armed with the most modern technology (including a videophone and a mobile antenna system) and encased in a sandbag-lined Humvee, Rodgers chronicled the trek through the Iraqi desert and into Bagdad itself.

Rodgers joined CNN in 1993 and served as a correspondent for Berlin and Jerusalem. Prior to that, Rodgers wrote for the Associated Press, the *Washington Post*, and the *Christian Science Monitor* and joined ABC News in London in 1981. He served as Moscow bureau chief for that network from 1984 to 1989 and retired from CNN in September 2005.

Agnes Hooper Gottlieb

RODMAN, THOMAS JACKSON (1815–1871)

Thomas Jackson Rodman developed an improved method of casting cannon barrels and a prismatic powder that improved the performance of artillery guns. Born on July 30, 1815, in Salem, Indiana, he attended West Point and graduated from there on July 1, 1841. He spent his entire life in the army.

Serving as an ordnance officer in various locations, Rodman developed a method of hallow-casting gun barrels that increased their strength significantly. The army was unwilling to accept the new process, so Rodman obtained permission to patent and develop it himself in 1845. Finally, in 1859 the army contacted Rodman about using the process to build a gun. The gun was the Model 1861 Columbiad, a fifteen-inch coastal gun, which also became known as the Rodman Gun.

From March 1855 to June 1856, Rodman commanded the arsenal at Baton Rouge, where he started to work on prismatic powder. The powder charge then in use actually produced less pressure as the shell left the barrel of the gun because it burned from the outside in. What Rodman did was to create a new charge that burned not just from the outside in, but also from the inside out. This caused the pressure to remain the same as the shell moved down the barrel of the gun. This principle is still used today in the design of artillery ammunition.

Rodman worked at various arsenals throughout and after the war until his death on June 7, 1871.

Dallace W. Unger Jr.

ROEBLING, WASHINGTON AUGUSTUS (1837–1926)

Washington A. Roebling improved the ability of armies to build suspension bridges while campaigning. The son of an engineer, Roebling was born on May 26, 1837, in Saxonburg, Pennsylvania. His family moved to Trenton, New Jersey, where he was educated at the prestigious Trenton Academy. After graduating from Rensselaer Polytechnic Institute in 1857, Roebling immediately assumed responsible engineering positions.

The outbreak of the Civil War prompted Roebling to enlist in the army as a private. Quickly becoming a staff officer, he participated in several battles and campaigns of the Army of the Potomac and supervised the construction of temporary suspension bridges over the Rappahannock and Shenandoah rivers. He distilled his knowledge into a short manual with illustrative plates, *Instructions for Transport and Erection of Military Wire Suspension-Bridge Equipage* (1862). As an engineer, Roebling also sited defensive lines, designed fortifications, and observed enemy movements from a tethered balloon.

Roebling earned fame after resigning from the army. He assisted his father in building a suspension bridge over the Ohio River at Cincinnati and then became chief engineer for the Brooklyn Bridge after his father's death. Carefully monitoring underwater work on the towers, Roebling was permanently disabled from prolonged breathing of compressed air. Overcoming hazards and hardships, he completed the majestic project in 1883.

Roebling devoted his long retirement to reading, research, and family business interests. He died in Trenton on July 21, 1926.

Further Reading: Schuyler, Hamilton. *The Roeblings: A Century of Engineers, Bridge-builders and Industrialists.* Princeton, NJ: Princeton University Press, 1931.

William M. Ferraro

RONFELDT, DAVID (1942–)

With collaborator **John Arquilla** of the Navy Postgraduate School, David Ronfeldt has explored the concept of "netwar" as the next step in warfare. Ronfeldt earned a bachelor's degree in international relations from Pomona College in 1962, followed by a master's degree in Latin American studies from Stanford in 1964 and a doctorate in political science from Stanford in 1971. He has been a member of the RAND Corporation think tank for more than thirty years.

Netwar is a theory that attempts to explain the use of networked organizational structures as tools of conflict. The concept first appeared in a 1993 article in *Comparative Strategy*, titled "Cyberwar Is Coming!" It was expanded in Arquilla and Ronfeldt's 1996 book, *The Advent of Netwar*, and revisited in their 2001 follow-up book, *Networks and Netwars*.

While traditional military organizations are hierarchical, with commands following downward from a high-level authority, networked organizations consist of roughly equal individuals who are connected in one of several ways. A *chain* network moves information or substances from person to person, with each member knowing only the prior and next people in line. A *hub* network consists of multiple centers, each of which distributes information to a number of contacts. An *all-channel* network is made of people who all communicate with one another freely.

Network organizations are found in criminal cartels, guerilla forces, terrorist organizations, anti-war activist groups, and social reform movements. Specific groups named as engaging in netwar range from the Zapatistas to drug-smuggling organizations to Greenpeace. In general, netwarfare appeals to organizations that are opposing a hierarchical authority that could easily overpower them in a direct confrontation. The advantages of netwar stem not from use of the Internet—though that can be a tool for netwar—but from how information and action are distributed. A common feature of networked organizations is that many individuals know some or all of the organizations' plans and are thus capable of acting autonomously. Where hierarchical organizations would mount an offensive, networked organizations "swarm": numerous small units independently converge on a target. The convergence need not be military; it can be an information campaign or an attempt to disrupt civilian activities.

The September 11, 2001, attacks illustrate netwar in action. A covert network conveys information through nodes, so that removing a node does not prevent the network from functioning. Individuals work separately to take coordinated action: in this case, to hijack four airplanes. The goal is not to capture a military target, but to achieve psychological disruption. Personal loyalty and ideological fervor link the warriors to their cause.

In "Networks, Netwars, and the Fight for the Future," which appeared in the October 2001 issue of *First Monday*, Ronfeldt and Arquilla defined the five characteristics of a successful network organization. First, a network always consists of dispersed, relatively leaderless, nodes. Where leadership exists, it is more likely to stem from shaping the organization's story than from traditional rank or administrative functions. Second, a network organization requires a compelling story about its goals and methods. This narrative feeds a shared organizational culture: instead of waiting for top-down commands from a leader, members of the organization act autonomously to "do the right thing." Third, aspects of networking are often explicit elements of the organization's doctrine. For example, "leaderless resistance" is the rallying cry of right-wing activist Louis Beam, who promotes the concept as a means of obtaining flexibility and robustness. Incorporating networking concepts as doctrine makes the organization more resistant to pressures to reshape itself into a hierarchy as it grows. Fourth, although Internet-based technologies are not essential, they are especially appropriate to network organizations. E-mail, cell phone, and peer-to-peer computing technologies support the organization's efforts to distribute information broadly. Finally, successful network organizations usually start from a core of kinship groups, friendships, or other social networks. Trust and loyalty are essential to the network's functioning.

Ronfeldt and Arquilla argue that hierarchical organizations face enormous difficulties in fighting networks. To win against a networked enemy, it is necessary to adopt some of the characteristics of a network organization. Thus, some of the most effective maneuvers of the Iraq war involved U.S. troops organized into smaller, networked units that swarmed around objectives, coordinated through the flow of information.

Netwar builds on an earlier concept explored by Ronfeldt and Arquilla, "cyberwar." Cyberwar, discussed in the 1997 book *In Athena's Camp*, focuses more specifically on exploiting and disrupting computer technology, from using the web for propaganda to launching hacker-style attacks on enemies' web sites. The focus here is primarily on the importance of information security.

Wende Vyborney Feller

ROOT, ELISHA (1808–1865)

Elisha Root invented the Colt-Root repeating rifle, a revolving firearm, in 1855 and after the death of **Samuel Colt** on January 10, 1862, became president of Colt Firearms. Root was born on May 10, 1808, in Ludlow, Massachusetts. Beginning work at the age of ten, he engaged in a number of jobs until 1849, when he went to work for the Colt Firearms Company. He remained at Colt until his death on August 31, 1865.

Root invented and patented a number of items including several involving firearms during his career. In 1849, he developed a revolving cylinder for firearms. He also invented a machine that could bore chambers in revolving cylinders in 1854. In 1855 he developed a machine that could rifle four gun barrels at a time, and later that year he developed a rifle that used a revolving cylinder, thus allowing it to fire multiple times before it had to be reloaded. The rifle was named the Colt-Root Model 1855. He also worked with cartridges, and in 1859 developed a machine for packing a cartridge and a cap together. He also developed a machine that shaped stocks and barrels for pistols for the Colt Firearms Company. When Colt died, Root took over as president and helped build the company.

Root was married twice. His first marriage was to Charlotte Bridgeman on October 15, 1832. They had one son. Root remarried on October 7, 1845, to Matilda Colt. The couple had three children.

Dallace W. Unger Jr.

ROOT, GEORGE FREDERICK (1820–1895)

George Frederick Root, also known as G. Friedrich Wurzel, was born in Sheffield, Massachusetts on August 30, 1820. His musical talents were noticeable at an early age. By age thirteen, he could play thirteen different instruments. He moved to Boston in 1838 to study music under George Webb. Moving to New York City in 1845, he played the organ for the Church of the Strangers and taught music at the Abbott Institute for Young Women. In 1850, he went to Paris to study before joining Lowell Mason at Boston's Academy of Music. It was there he began to compose. Stephen Foster greatly influenced his work. Under the pseudonym G. Friedrich Wurzel, he produced lighthearted songs such as "Hazel Dazel" and "Rosalie, the Prairie Flower." As Root, he preferred sacred and patriotic music such as "The Shining Shore."

His brother, E. T. Root, founded a music store in Chicago in 1858, and a year later Root bought into Root & Cady and moved to Chicago to work. The outbreak of the Civil War fueled his patriotic talents. He produced twenty-eight songs, including "Tramp, Tramp, Tramp, the Boys Are Marching," "The Vacant Chair," and "Just Before the Battle, Mother." His biggest hit was inspired by President Lincoln's proclamation for troops. "The Battle Cry of Freedom" sold 12,000 copies between August and November 1862. By 1867, Root & Cady claimed sales of 350,000 copies. It was also popular with Southern troops. Root died on August 6, 1895.

Jerry L. Parker

ROREM, NED (1923–)

Ned Rorem's musical composition *War Scenes* was written in 1969 during the height of American involvement in the Vietnam War. In this piece, Rorem utilized texts from Walt Whitman's Civil War diaries. These texts describe the brutality and horror of war in intimate detail. Rorem used these texts, which describe a battle between North and South, and applied them contextually to the "North" and "South" war raging during his time. It was a piece that neither advocated nor protested, but rather informed the listeners about the realities of war. Rorem dedicated it to those who died on both sides in Vietnam during the time that he composed it (June 20–30, 1969).

Ned Rorem was born in Richmond, Indiana, in 1923, but his childhood was spent in Chicago. His composition teachers/mentors included Leo Sowerby, Virgil Thomson, Aaron Copland, and Arthur Honegger. From 1949 until 1958, Rorem lived in France. During his time in France, he was awarded both a Fulbright (1951) and a Guggenheim (1957) fellowship. Upon his return to the United States he taught at the University of Buffalo (1959–1960), the University of Utah (1965–1967), and the Curtis Institute (1980 to present).

Rorem is best known for composing more than four hundred songs. In fact, *Time* magazine has proclaimed him the greatest composer of songs in the world. He also has composed in many other genres, however, and is author of fourteen books.

Further Reading: McDonald, Arlys L. *Ned Rorem, a Bio-Bibliography.* Westport, CT: Greenwood Press, 1989.

David Diehl

ROSENWALD, JULIUS (1862–1932)

Armed with an education in the public schools of Springfield, Illinois, where he was born on August 12, 1862, Julius Rosenwald parlayed his business sense as a clothing manufacturer into a half-interest in Sears, Roebuck & Company as the twentieth century dawned. His original investment of $37,500 for a quarter-interest in the company in 1895 made him a multimillionaire long before

Julius Rosenwald. Courtesy of the Library of Congress.

America entered World War I. President of Sears from 1910 until he became board chair in 1925, Rosenwald was admired as a prolific philanthropist.

Rosenwald philosophically opposed war, but he believed in service to his nation at time of war. With the argument that the best preparation for peace is to be prepared for war, President Wilson appointed the Advisory Commission of the Council for National Defense late in 1916 with Rosenwald as a member. Commission members organized around committees. Rosenwald chaired the committee on supplies, which included food and clothing. Certainly his stature in the business and philanthropic communities assisted him in bringing business leaders into the war effort, but members of the Advisory Commission were continually frustrated by the lack of centralized authority in trying to mobilize the nation's industry and even by competing committees.

Rosenwald, however, had one certain success during his time as a volunteer in Washington. As the military began to let construction contracts for cantonments across the country, it was Rosenwald who suggested that the profit on any one contract could not exceed $250,000, thus negating the effect of war-inflated construction costs. Rosenwald died in Chicago on January 6, 1932.

Benjamin F. Shearer

ROSS, JOHN (1790–1866)

John Ross led the Cherokee Nation in its fight against forced removal, enduring the infamous Trail of Tears and guiding his people through their own civil war during the U.S. Civil War. Ross served as a Lieutenant in the Creek War, fighting alongside Sam Houston and serving under Andrew Jackson. His lifelong role was to be a liaison between whites and Cherokees, first serving as a translator for missionaries, Indian agents, and diplomats. He was president of the Cherokee Constitutional Convention in 1827 and elected principal chief in 1828. When Andrew Jackson became President, he seized Cherokee land, refusing to abide by the Supreme Court's decision upholding Cherokee treaties. A separate faction led by Major Ridge and Stand Watie signed away Cherokee lands in 1834. The Cherokee Nation was forcibly removed on the Trail of Tears. Once in Oklahoma Territory, Watie's followers allied with pro-slavery forces while Ross' followers were pro-Union. With the advent of the Civil War, the Cherokee Nation was isolated on three sides by Confederates. Ross first urged the Cherokees to remain neutral, then temporarily allied with the Confederacy. After the first Confederate defeat, Ross led the Cherokee Nation back to the Union and isolated the Treaty Party from the rest of the tribe. Watie's Confederate bands led devastating guerilla raids, killing almost one quarter of the Cherokee. Yet Ross recognized the need to heal internal wounds within the tribe, and welcomed back Watie's followers after the war. He died in 1866 during treaty negotiations with the United States.

Further Reading: Hauptman, Laurence. *Between Two Fires: American Indians in the Civil War.* New York: Free Press, 1995.

Al Carroll

John Ross, a Cherokee chief. Courtesy of the Library of Congress.

ROSS, MARY G. (1908–)

Mary Ross was born in the former Indian Territory of Oklahoma on August 9, 1908. Her great-great-grandfather, **John Ross**, principal chief of the Cherokee Nation from 1828 until his death in 1866, had led his people on the Trail of Tears from Tennessee to Tahlequa, Oklahoma. Mary, who had always loved mathematics, earned her undergraduate math degree in 1928 at Northeastern State College in Tahlequa, which her famous ancestor founded. For the next nine years Ross taught high school math and science, then took a position as a statistical clerk for the Bureau of Indian Affairs, and attained her master's degree in math in 1938 at Colorado State Teachers College.

With the United States fully engaged in war in 1942, Ross went to work for Lockheed as a mathematical research assistant. She first worked on the compressibility of the P-28 fighter as it approached the speed of sound. With Lockheed's encouragement and assistance Ross received further education and her certification as a mechanical engineer in 1949. Already moving up the ranks, Ross became one of the forty engineers who formed the Lockheed Missiles and Space Company.

By the time Ross retired as senior advanced systems staff engineer at Lockheed in 1973, she had made important contributions to the development of the Polaris ballistic missile that was launched from submarines, the Agena rocket, and various ballistic missile and satellite systems, including the

Poseidon and Trident missiles. She also developed specifications for interplanetary space exploration. The recipient of numerous awards, Ross is America's most celebrated Native American female aeronautical engineer.

Benjamin F. Shearer

RUBIN, JERRY C. (1938–1994)

Jerry Rubin and Abbie Hoffman co-founded the Yippies, a group of social radicals during the 1960s and 1970s. While *Yippie* officially stood for Youth International Party (YIP), the name Yippie may have came first. The Yippie Festival of Life drew a large number of young people to Chicago, resulted in considerable violence and the infamous Chicago Seven trial.

That trial was not Rubin's first time in court. Likewise, the protests in Chicago were not his first acts of social activism. Born in Cincinnati on July 14, 1938, Rubin graduated with a degree in sociology from the University of Cincinnati, and then spent some time in Tel Aviv with his younger brother. Upon returning to the United States in 1964, Rubin enrolled at the University of California at Berkley, where he became involved in protests against a local grocer who refused to hire African Americans. In 1965, Rubin organized rallies against the Vietnam War, becoming the founder of the Vietnam Day Committee (VDC). His involvement with the VDC resulted in his appearance before the House Un-American Activities Committee (HUAC).

During the HUAC hearings, Rubin displayed a flair for the theatrical. Dressed as an American Revolutionary soldier and handing out copies of the Declaration of Independence, Rubin turned the room into a circus. He and his case were eventually thrown out.

Rubin remained active in the 1960s counterculture, associating with the Diggers, a guerilla theater group in the Haight-Ashbury district of San Francisco. In 1967 he went to New York to help organize an East Coast protest of the war. He met Abbie Hoffman there, and joined in the first of a series of publicity stunts. With some friends, Rubin and Hoffman entered the New York Stock Exchange and, from the visitor's balcony, gave a speech to the traders on the floor about the war and the economy. This speech was greeted with applause from the traders, but chaos ensued as Hoffman's group threw dollar bills onto the trading floor.

Later in 1967, during a three-day protest of the Vietnam War in Washington, DC, Rubin and Hoffman led fifty thousand hippies on a march to the Pentagon where they initiated a "siege" of the building, tried to convince guards to give up their military careers, performed an exorcism on the building, and then attempted to levitate it using positive energy. Rubin and Hoffman understood this as staged media events meant to focus American public attention on military actions.

Following the 1967 war protests in Washington, a larger event was planned for Chicago during the 1968 Democratic Party Convention. The stated goal of the Chicago protest was to disrupt the convention and to once again focus public attention on the political process. Rubin and Hoffman proposed a Festival of Life as an alternative to the Festival of Death represented by the convention. The Yippies were organized as an element of the Festival of Life, and plans were made to nominate "Pigasus the Immortal" as president on the YIP ticket.

The Yippies were organized primarily as a media stunt. To highlight the absurdities they saw in the political process, the Yippies gave out copies of their party platform—blank sheets of paper—to reporters. The Chicago stunt went badly wrong. Instead of being peaceful, it became a violent riot as police attempted to shut down the students and they responded by attacking the police. The end result was a trial of the Chicago Eight (seven after Seales was dismissed) by Judge Julius Hoffman. After Seales was removed, Rubin, Hoffman and the others took over the courtroom in protest. They appeared in costumes and wearing judicial robes. They accused Judge Hoffman of being a Nazi, giving him the Nazi salute as they entered the courtroom. They handed out jellybeans, kissed witnesses, and generally threw the whole process into a shambles. They were cited for contempt of court two hundred times over the course of the trial. In the end, Judge Hoffman convicted them. Their convictions were overturned by the U.S. Supreme Court.

Following the end of the Vietnam War, Rubin became a successful entrepreneur, working with the health food industry. Accused by many of selling out, Rubin tried hard to remove himself from the image of the 1960s radical. He died on November 28, 1994, after being hit by a car.

Further Reading: Gitlin, Todd. *The Sixties: Years of Hope, Days of Rage.* New York: Bantam Books, 1987.

Mike Timonin

RUML, BEARDSLEY (1894–1960)

When a new tax code enacted in 1942 made it likely that thousands of Americans would be delinquent in payments, Beardsley Ruml proposed income tax withholding as a solution.

Born in Cedar Rapids, Iowa, on November 5, 1894, Ruml earned a B.S. from Dartmouth in 1915, followed by a doctorate from the University of Chicago. His research on intelligence testing led to his participating in the Army's trade testing programs.

After working in public administration, Ruml became dean of the University of Chicago in 1930. He left four years later to join R. H. Macy Company. There, he developed the idea of installment payments on purchases. In 1937, he became a director of the Federal Reserve Bank of New York, which he chaired from 1941 to 1947.

Ruml's withholding tax plan resulted from taxation changes in 1942. To support the war effort, taxes were increased and the income tax extended to millions of Americans who had not previously paid federal taxes. When a poll showed that only 15 percent of taxpayers were saving to meet their annual obligation in March 1943, the government wondered what to do about delinquents. Ruml proposed a 75 percent amnesty on 1942 and 1943 income taxes, along with a new system for withholding taxes from paychecks so that taxpayers would "pay as you go." This plan was incorporated in the Revenue Act of 1942.

Ruml was also part of the 1944 conference that established the International Monetary Fund. He became chair of Macy's in 1945 and retired in 1949. Ruml died on April 18, 1960.

Wende Vyborney Feller

RUSH, BENJAMIN (1746–1813)

Dr. Benjamin Rush, often cited for his friendships with Thomas Jefferson and John Adams and for signing the Declaration of Independence, was a widely published writer on both medical and non-medical topics. He became a manufacturer of saltpeter (potassium nitrate), a key ingredient in gunpowder, and published the results of his experiments in November 1774. Subsequently, he published *An Account of the Manufactory of Salt-Peter*, using pseudonyms for both pieces. In April 1777, the Continental Congress appointed Rush as surgeon general for the middle department of the Continental Army.

Rush was born on January 4, 1746, graduated from Princeton in September 1760, and obtained an apprenticeship with renowned Philadelphia physician John Redman. He then studied medicine in Edinburgh, defending his thesis in 1768. During his time in Europe, he initiated an acquaintance with fellow Philadelphian Benjamin Franklin, who was in London at the time. Franklin became his benefactor, lending him money and introducing him to important contacts such as Sir Alexander Dick, the president of the Royal Society of Physicians.

Rush returned to Philadelphia in 1769 to establish his own practice. He also volunteered his services to the Society for Inoculating the Poor. On August 1, 1769, the College of Philadelphia's Board of Trustee's appointed him professor of chemistry at age twenty-three; he was the youngest member of the medical faculty. Rush used his post to indoctrinate his students in his medical philosophies, although his colleagues among the medical faculty often disagreed with his views.

Rush continually sought publication of his medical papers in hopes of being elected to the Royal College of Physicians. He also published political essays, including an anti-slavery essay (*An Address to the Inhabitants of the British Settlements in America, Upon Slave-Keeping, By a Pennsylvanian*), despite the fact that he held slaves himself. After the passage of the Regulating Act (also known as the Tea Act), Rush published *On Patriotism* as well as another essay in which he described tea as toxic to the body, thus mixing politics and medicine.

In 1774, Rush published his experiments on the manufacture of potassium nitrate and the United Company for Promoting American Manufacturers elected him president, as he was a staunch proponent of producing the goods that had previously been imported from Britain. In 1775, Congress published Rush's essays on potassium nitrate in a pamphlet with an introduction by Benjamin Franklin and the Pennsylvania Committee of Safety chose him to help direct the building of a "saltpeter manufactory." The committee also chose Rush to be physician-surgeon to their fleet of gunboats. After meeting Thomas Paine in 1775, Rush encouraged him to publish his views on independence, even suggesting the title *Common Sense* and connecting him with the printer.

On July 20, 1776, Pennsylvania's Constitutional Convention chose Rush as one of its delegates to Congress. On August 2, 1776, he signed the incorporated legal copy of the Declaration of Independence, although he continued to see patients throughout his tenure in Congress. On April 11, 1777, Congress chose Rush as the surgeon general for the middle department of the army, having selected **William Shippen Jr.** as Director General. The *Pennsylvania Packet* published Rush's essay, "To the Officers in the Army of the United States: Directions for Preserving the Health of Soldiers," on April 22. Rush later criticized Director Shippen for what he considered negligent medical care of the soldiers; in fact, he insisted that the entire medical department was substandard, and that changes were necessary. Congressional hearings ensued in which Shippen denied the charges, and Rush resigned from the medical department on January 30, 1778.

Rush began teaching at the University of the State of Pennsylvania in 1780, and he founded the first free dispensary in the United States. He also served as a member of the Pennsylvania Convention that ratified the U.S. Constitution in 1787. Rush's commitment to the poor remained steadfast as he treated Philadelphians stricken by the Yellow Fever epidemics of 1793 and 1797. A proponent of heroic medicine, which espoused bloodletting and purging, he adhered to his views even after the field began to move away from these extreme measures. Rush later held the offices of the presidency of the Pennsylvania Society for the Abolition of Slavery (1803) and treasurer of the United States Mint (1797–1813), a post to which President John Adams appointed him. Rush and his wife Julia (Stockton), who was fourteen years his junior, had thirteen children. He died on April 19, 1813.

Further Reading: Hawke, David Freeman. *Benjamin Rush: Revolutionary Gadfly*. Indianapolis: Bobbs-Merrill, 1971.

Ximena Chrisagis

RUSK, HOWARD A. (1901–1989)

Howard A. Rusk, MD, is widely regarded as the modern father of the medical specialty of Physical Medicine and Rehabilitation (also referred to as physiatry). Rusk was a tireless proponent of the view that the care of injured and disabled persons required not only attention to the physical and vocational aspects of their injuries, but also to their social and psychological well-being as well.

Born in Brookfield, Missouri, on April 9, 1901, Rusk attended the University of Missouri and went on to complete his medical studies at the University of Pennsylvania in 1925. Upon completing a yearlong internship at St. Luke's Hospital in St. Louis, Rusk married and established a private practice specializing in internal medicine. In 1942 Rusk left his practice to support the war effort as a medical officer in the U.S. Army Air Corps. As chief medical officer of the Jefferson Barracks in St. Louis, Rusk took a negative view of the passive convalescence that he witnessed and he set about discharging from hospital anyone who appeared to be well enough to return to active duty. Much to his chagrin, Rusk discovered that a majority of those he discharged ended up being rehospitalized because they were indeed unfit for the rigors of military duty.

Based on his experiences Rusk came to believe that service personnel recovering from illness or injury should be involved in more active forms of convalescence including physical re-conditioning, vocational training, and psychological support to deal with the emotional sequela of injury. Rusk's ideas were slow to take hold among those in charge of the Medical Corps. However, he was permitted to put his approach to a test by comparing outcomes of patients assigned to a medical barracks employing this active approach to convalescence with the outcomes of service men assigned to a traditional care setting. The results of this field experiment vindicated Rusk's approach and he was subsequently reassigned to Washington, DC, with the mandate to oversee the establishment of similar rehabilitation units throughout the Army Air Corps. Rusk would later be awarded the Distinguished Service Medal for his contributions to the improved care of injured and disabled service personnel.

Following his wartime service, Rusk joined the faculty and medical staff of New York University (NYU) School of Medicine where he set about transferring his ideas about rehabilitation medicine to the civilian sector. In 1950 the Institute of Physical Medicine and rehabilitation was opened at NYU under his direction. During this period, Rusk also successfully lobbied with the American Board of Physical Medicine to add rehabilitation to its designation. Today, this professional organization and accreditation body is known as the American Board of Physical Medicine and Rehabilitation.

Rusk was a tireless advocate for mobilizing resources for the care and rehabilitation of disabled persons throughout the United States and the world. He was active in many national and international organizations including the Health for Peace movement in the 1950s, the International Society for Rehabilitation of the Disabled, and the National Council on the Handicapped, which he chaired from 1979 to 1982. A prolific writer, Rusk wrote for both professional and lay audiences on a variety of topics related to the well being of disabled persons and the rehabilitation of patients suffering from a variety of medical conditions ranging from stroke to cancer. In 1972, Rusk published an autobiography aptly titled A World to Care For.

Rusk was the recipient of many honors. In addition to recognition for his military service, he was the recipient of three Albert Lasker Awards and the

French Legion of Honor. In 1984, NYU re-named its rehabilitation institute in his honor as the Howard A. Rusk Institute of Rehabilitation Medicine. Rusk died in 1989 at the age of eighty-eight.

Further Reading: Rusk, Howard A. *A World to Care For: The Autobiography of Howard A. Rusk, MD.* New York: Random House, 1972.

David J. Steele

RUSSELL, JANE (1921–)

Ernestine Jane Geraldine Russell was born on June 21, 1921, in Bemidji, Minnesota. By the time she was nine years old, her family had moved to Burbank, California. Her mother, a former actress, encouraged Russell to study music and drama. Russell attended Max Reinhardt's Theatrical Workshop and studied with the noted Maria Ouspenskaya. After some failed auditions, **Howard Robard Hughes Jr.** hired her in 1940 with a seven-year contract. Russell debuted in the 1941 film *The Outlaw*, for which Hughes eventually took over direction.

The film was considered risqué at the time and opened to only a limited release in 1943. Its full release occurred after the war ended, but this film made Jane Russell famous in spite of, or perhaps because of, its censorship problems. A still shot of Russell from the film displaying her full figure and sultry look against a stack of hay became one of the most popular pinups during World War II, along with the shot of **Ruth Elizabeth "Betty" Grable** looking over her shoulder. It was said that these pinups reminded soldiers why they were fighting.

Russell's quick rise to fame based on her physical attributes was in some ways inauspicious. Known as "the sweater girl," many did not take her seriously as an actor. She was to prove them wrong. With a long list of films to her credit as well as success on Broadway and television, Russell became one of America's most popular personalities. In addition, she founded the World Adoption International Fund in 1955.

Benjamin F. Shearer

RUSSELL, ROBERT PRICE (1898–1965)

Robert Russell's research on incendiary bombs led to the M69 bombs used against Japan in World War II. Born in 1898 in Massachusetts, Russell worked his way through Clark University. After graduating in 1917, he served in the marines, and earned a doctorate from the Massachusetts Institute of Technology in 1922. In 1927, he became director of research for Standard Oil Company. He shifted to Standard Oil Development Company in 1933 and became president in 1944.

Russell's war work included membership on the National Defense Research Committee (NDRC) and chair of the Oil, Chemical, Rubber, and Explosives division of the U.S. Strategic Bombing Survey. In 1946, he won the gold medal of the American Institute of Chemists for his war work, specifically processes for increasing production of 100-octane aviation gasoline, for producing a necessary component of synthetic rubber from petroleum, and for synthesizing toluene for production of TNT.

Russell's research also included development of a jellied-oil explosive suitable for use in incendiary bombs. This explosive—later known as napalm—was packed in cheesecloth bags. The bags were packed in the middle of a bomb, with a fuse in the head and a stabilizer in the tail. When the bomb reached its target, the lit napalm sprayed from the tail. This M69 bomb was tested against fake towns at the Dugway Proving Grounds, and then used against Japanese cities. Variants were also used in the Korean War.

Russell's awards included the Medal of Merit and the French Legion of Honor.

Wende Vyborney Feller

RUSSO, ANTHONY "TONY" JOSEPH (1937–)

Tony Russo was the co-defendant with **Daniel Ellsberg** in the Pentagon Papers case, which exposed government secrecy about the origins of the Vietnam War. In 1963, Russo volunteered to travel to Vietnam as part of the Rand Corporation's Viet Cong Motivation and Morale Project contracted by the Pentagon. He worked on the project for four years, spending two years in Vietnam interviewing prisoners captured by the United States as well as refugees fleeing military action. This experience convinced him that American policy in Southeast Asia was immoral.

He urged his Rand colleague, Daniel Ellsberg, to release the classified intelligence report that would become known as the Pentagon Papers. Ellsberg was indicted for taking the papers, which the *New York Times* began publishing on June 13, 1971. The Supreme Court rejected the Richard Nixon administration's efforts to halt publication.

Russo was subpoenaed to testify against Ellsberg before a federal grand jury. Russo refused and was imprisoned for his civil disobedience. The trials of Russo and Ellsberg ended in victory for the defendants because the administration's burglaries and wiretaps directed against Ellsberg had been illegal. Russo had hoped to use the trial as a forum to denounce Nixon's Vietnam policies.

Following the trial, Russo worked in a Los Angeles alcoholism treatment program and taught time series analysis at California State University, Dominguez Hills. In 1991, he was elected chair of the education committee of the Los Angeles Anti-Gulf War Coalition, and he continues to lecture on the lessons of the Vietnam War.

Ron Briley

RYAN, JOHN DENNIS (1864–1933)

As president of the giant Anaconda Copper Mining Company starting in 1909, John D. Ryan was an important figure in American business. The burgeoning electrification of the nation had made copper a vital commodity. **Bernard Mannes Baruch** among others sought Ryan's expertise on the Advisory Commission of the Council of National Defense when America entered World War I. In fact Ryan's name was on the original list of men recommended for the Advisory Commission, but since he was Republican he was vetoed by the Democratic Wilson administration and replaced with **Hollis Godfrey**.

Ryan was born on October 10, 1864, in Hancock, Michigan. Although his father was a mining authority, young Ryan took no immediate interest in his father's profession, forsaking a college education to be a clerk and salesman. When he finally got into the copper business at the turn of the century, his rise was meteoric. Yet he resigned as president of Anaconda in 1917 to serve on the American Red Cross War Council. Soon he was serving in government, first as director of the Bureau of Aircraft production in May 1918 and then in August as an assistant secretary of war and chair of the Aircraft Board. He resigned in November when the armistice was declared. While there was some discord over his role at the Aircraft Board, his agreement with the War Industries Board to produce copper for 23.5 cents a pound was crucial to the war effort. Ryan died on February 11, 1933, in New York City.

John D. Ryan. Courtesy of the Library of Congress.

Benjamin F. Shearer

RYERSON, DONALD M. (1885–1932)

Donald Ryerson had joined the family steel manufacturing business in Chicago soon after his graduation from Yale in 1907. An enthusiastic patriot, he burst one afternoon into **George Creel**'s Washington office of the Committee on Public Information (CPI). The committee was composed of the heads of the army, navy, and several others. Ryerson had developed an idea for putting speakers in Chicago's motion-picture theaters. He left Creel's office with instructions to form a national organization called the Four Minute Men.

Ryerson, as head of the Speakers Division of the CPI, was able to train 150,000 speakers to deliver the government's message across the country by the end of 1917. They gave four-minute long speeches promoting the draft, the purchasing of Liberty Bonds, saving food, and other war related topics. They began speaking in movie theaters where it normally took about four minutes to change reels in a feature movie. Speakers eventually were sent to colleges, churches, camps, lodge meetings, and other places.

American entry into World War I in 1917 was quite controversial. To counter adverse public opinion and promote the war effort, George Creel used an enormous number of channels of communication to further Woodrow Wilson's war aims. By the war's end Ryerson's Four Minute Men (and some women) had given millions of speeches persuading the nation to support the war.

Ryerson became chairman of the board of Joseph T. Ryerson & Son, Inc., in 1928. In ill health, he killed himself on May 8, 1932.

Andrew J. Waskey

S

SACHS, ALEXANDER (1893–1973)

Although Alexander Sachs made his career as an economist, his most important role may have been convincing Franklin D. Roosevelt to fund research into atomic bombs. Born in Lithuania on August 1, 1893, Sachs came to the United States with his family as Jewish refugees in 1904. He graduated from Columbia University in 1912 and subsequently did postgraduate work in philosophy at Harvard, although he did not earn a doctorate. He became an economist with Lehman Brothers, known for his scorn of stock market hype in the 1920s and his disdain for Hoover administration recovery efforts.

Sachs was an acquaintance of **Albert Einstein** and had served President Roosevelt on a number of New Deal projects. He therefore struck Einstein, **Enrico Fermi**, and **Leo Szilard** as the appropriate go-between to explain their atomic theories—and the dangers of other countries developing an atomic bomb—to the president. Sachs' October 11, 1939, visit to the White House led to Roosevelt's forming a series of committees that ultimately approved the Manhattan Project. Sachs also served the war effort as an economic consultant for several government agencies.

His enthusiasm for the atomic bomb paled after the bombing of Hiroshima and Nagasaki. Sachs had expected its first uses to be test detonations that would convince Germany and Japan to surrender. Feeling that the United States had made a moral error in using the bomb on civilians, he became an advocate of nuclear arms control. Sachs died on June 23, 1973, in New York.

Wende Vyborney Feller

SAFFORD, MARY JANE (1831–1891)

Born on December 31, 1831, in Vermont, Mary Jane Safford moved to northern Illinois as a child and later to southern Illinois. She was teaching in Cairo, Illinois, at the beginning of the Civil War when sick and wounded Union soldiers arrived there for medical treatment. She left teaching and helped organize and establish temporary hospitals. According to Mary A. Livermore of the Northwest Sanitary Commission, Safford was the first woman in the West to go into Civil War military camps and hospitals.

The morning after the battle of Belmont, Safford went onto the battlefield to look for wounded soldiers. Similarly, she took supplies to the field of Shiloh where she worked for three weeks and returned to Cairo by steamboat with wounded soldiers for the hospitals in Cairo; Paducah, Kentucky; and St. Louis. While working in Cairo, she worked with **Mary Ann Ball Bickerdyke**, who was known for her crude manners and explosive tirades. In contrast, Safford, called "the Angel of Cairo," was petite, dignified, well educated and diplomatic. They were said to have complemented each other well.

After eighteen months of Civil War nursing, her health suffered and her brother sent her to Europe to recover. Later Safford graduated from the New York Medical College for Women, took graduate training in Austria and Germany, and practiced medicine in Chicago. She died on December 8, 1891.

Further Reading: Wheeler, Adade Mitchell and Wortman, Marlene Stein. *The Roads They Made: Women in Illinois History.* Chicago: Charles H. Kerr Publishing, 1977.

Marjorie A. Baier

SALISBURY, HARRISON EVANS (1908–1993)

A prolific journalist, non-fiction writer, and novelist, Harrison Salisbury is known best for his work on the Soviet Union, China, and the Vietnam War. Born in Minneapolis on November 14, 1908, Salisbury served as editor of the University of Minnesota's campus newspaper as an undergraduate. He then was hired by the United Press and worked all over the country. In 1943, he was sent to London to cover World War II.

After much effort, he joined the *New York Times* in 1949 as a correspondent in Russia, where he spent six years. Although his work on the Soviet Union drew censure from Senator Joseph McCarthy and others, it was generally hailed as groundbreaking. In 1955, Salisbury won the Pulitzer Prize in international reporting for his series entitled "Russia Re-Viewed." Further, his account of the Nazi blockade of Leningrad, *The 900 Days: The Siege of Leningrad* is regarded as the definitive text on the subject.

Salisbury remained influential and controversial for the rest of his career. The *Times* sent him to the American South in 1960 to cover the civil rights movement; his unflinching coverage sparked an unsuccessful libel suit against the paper. From 1966 to 1967, Salisbury covered the Vietnam War, also traveling extensively in North Vietnam. This reporting was expected to have earned him another Pulitzer, but after political dispute, it was awarded to another journalist.

Salisbury stayed with the *Times* until 1973, when he retired to focus on his writing. He died on July 5, 1993.

Rebecca A. Adelman

SALMON, THOMAS W. (1876–1927)

Thomas Salmon was a pioneer psychiatrist during World War I. Born on January 6, 1876, in Lansinburgh, New York, he was the son of Thomas Henry, a surgeon, and Annie Frost. At the age of nineteen, Salmon entered Albany Medical College where he met his future wife, Helen Ashley. In April 1899, he graduated from medical school with honors and tried, unsuccessfully, to run a family practice. In 1903, Salmon worked on Ellis Island performing psychiatric evaluations on immigrants. This position led to his appointment as the first Medical Director of the National Committee for Mental Hygiene in 1912.

Three years after war erupted in Europe, Salmon traveled to England to examine shell shock, where he concluded that psychological factors, not mental disorders, were the primary causes of war neurosis. By December 1917, Salmon became the director of psychiatry for the Allied Expeditionary Force (AEF) and his investigations led to the creation of the Division of Neurology and Psychiatry, headed by Dr. **Pearce Bailey**. The division implemented many of Salmon's suggestions for treating shell-shocked victims, such as moving treatment hospitals closer to the front lines, increasing resources to treat victims, and reorganizing the military's medical departments. For his contributions, Salmon received the Distinguished Service Medal.

Following the war, Salmon became a professor of psychiatry at Columbia University and from 1923 to 1924 served as president of the American Psychiatric Association. He died on August 13, 1927.

Further Reading: Bond, Earl D. *Thomas W. Salmon: Psychiatrist.* New York: W. W. Norton, 1950.

Donald C. Force

SANFORD, E. S. (1817–1882)

E. S. Sanford was president of the American Telegraph Company, and military supervisor of telegrams. As president of what then was a major communications company, Sanford recognized that the telegram would be important to military communications, especially between civilian and military leaders in conducting the war. Sanford also recognized that the government did not possess its own telegraph system and did not possess the funds to build its own system.

Sanford authorized the American Telegraph Company to extend its wires to certain government installations, as well as to purchase telegraph equipment and hire telegraph operators. As a result, the president and the secretary of war could send telegrams to the battlefront without going to the American Telegraph office to send and receive information about battles at the War Department, only a short walk from the White House.

In addition to the government's using the telegraph to send war news, correspondents employed by newspapers used the telegraph to send accounts of battles to their editors for publication in the newspaper. Increasingly Secretary of War Edwin M. Stanton became concerned that newspaper correspondents communicated information about military movements that could be used by the Confederacy. To prevent this, on February 25, 1862, Stanton appointed Sanford to the position of military supervisor of telegrams to censor correspondent and reporter telegrams.

Further Reading: Bates, David Homer. *Lincoln in the Telegraph Office: Recollections of the United States Military Telegraph Corps during the Civil War*. Lincoln: University of Nebraska Press, 1995.

Michael L. McGregor

SARANDON, SUSAN (1946–)

Susan Sarandon. Courtesy of Photofest.

As a young child in New Jersey, born on October 4, 1946, actress and political activist Susan Sarandon always asked difficult questions. She has continued this probing, often using her celebrity to call attention to social injustices. After filming the movie *A Dry White Season*, Sarandon immediately got involved in the opposition to the Gulf War. She and partner Tim Robbins were among a handful of other Hollywood actors who gathered to protest America's involvement in the war. Sarandon had been a longtime supporter of the anti-war organization Military Families Support Network. From her association with this group, Sarandon drew many parallels between the Persian Gulf War and the conflict in Vietnam. With the upcoming 1992 presidential election, she was still incensed that America's presence in the Persian Gulf was continuing to escalate.

Sarandon's anti-war stance conflicted with Hollywood's pro-war position. Sarandon, however, joined a number of other speakers in Washington, DC, in 1991 to inform politicians that not every nation was involved in the Persian Gulf. In an interview for the *Washington Post*, Sarandon berated the reporter for not being more aggressive with stories about the Gulf War. She was outraged at the media's kid-glove treatment of the military when it came to the Persian Gulf. Sarandon has continued to take a role in social causes, opposing America's detainment of HIV-positive Haitians in Guantanamo Bay. The *Thelma and Louise* star has been named a UNICEF goodwill ambassador.

Further Reading: Shapiro, Marc. *Susan Sarandon: Actress-Activist.* Amherst, NY: Prometheus Books, 2001.

Nicole Mitchell

SARNOFF, DAVID (1891–1971)

David Sarnoff was the long-time head of the Radio Corporation of America (RCA). An immigrant success story, he was born on February 27, 1891, in Uzlian, a *shtetl*, or Jewish village, in the Pale of Settlement, the region of western Russia where the czar obligated his Jewish subjects to live. When Sarnoff was five, his father immigrated to the United States to earn the rest of the family's passage west. Five years later David set out with his mother and younger brothers. While in Minsk, he witnessed an attack by Cossack horsemen upon a Jewish crowd, an incident that left an indelible impression upon him.

In America Sarnoff soon shouldered much of the responsibility for the family's income as his father's failing health made employment impossible. Although he was making good money selling newspapers, young Sarnoff's drive to better himself led him to a job as a radiotelegraph operator with American Marconi. By 1912 he held a responsible position. However, the story of his being the sole radio link to the sinking *Titanic* is part of his self-promotional legend, and cannot be documented in contemporary reports.

By the time of the U.S. entry into World War I, Sarnoff was already the commercial manager of the entire American Marconi Company. In spite of his success in business, Sarnoff still had a burning desire to serve his adopted country and prove himself a true American. He applied for a commission in the navy, but received no answer. Suspecting that he was facing anti-Semitic prejudice, he then tried to be drafted as a private in the army, but the War Department ordered an exemption on the basis that he was too valuable to the war effort in his civilian job.

Between the two World Wars, Sarnoff applied himself to building RCA, which had been created to ensure that foreigners could not control America's radio technology. During this period he became a reserve officer in the Army Signal Corps, positioning himself to be able to serve in the next armed conflict. All the time he had an uneasy eye upon events in Germany, where the Nazis were rising to power and implementing their racial policies against his coreligionists. After the Kristallnacht attacks on Jewish synagogues and businesses, Sarnoff grew certain that armed conflict was only a matter of time.

When the Japanese bombed Pearl Harbor on December 7, 1941, Sarnoff immediately informed President Franklin D. Roosevelt that all of RCA's resources were at his command. Sarnoff knew that radio would be critical to the conduct of the war and had been putting military contracts ahead of civilian television manufacturing for months beforehand. He had also overseen the development of an "alert receiver" that would turn on a radio and summon listeners to warn of an attack. (This technology was an ancestor of the weather alert radio.) However, Sarnoff resisted the government's pressure to license RCA's patents to the government for war production without the payment of royalties.

Critical as his role at RCA might be to the war effort, Sarnoff still wanted to go on active duty. After some lobbying, his reserve colonelcy was activated and he served on various advisory committees in Washington, DC. He soon established a reputation as a skillful troubleshooter and as a result he was assigned to set up the communication systems for the D-Day invasion of Normandy. Although his organizational skills and straightforward style offended some people, communications for the invasion went smoothly. Sarnoff remained on active duty until he was promoted to brigadier general and proudly displayed his star in his corporate office. He considered it a symbol of the partnership between big business and the military and was known as "the General" at RCA.

Sarnoff continued to play an important part in the Cold War, providing military communication systems. In 1953 he was present at the dedication of a giant wireless telegraph station that would power a global network for the navy. He also was involved in the creation of the Voice of America. He even wanted to do mass airdrops of cheap radios into the Soviet Union so that everyone behind the Iron Curtain could hear about freedom. At times the stridency of his anti-communism was off-putting to those factions within the Soviet Union who were trying to liberalize.

Sarnoff remained in control of RCA until the last years of his life, when failing health made it impossible for him to continue working. He died of a heart attack on December 12, 1971.

Leigh Husband Kimmel

SAYRE, JOHN NEVIN (1884–1977)

During World War I, John Nevin Sayre was an outspoken pacifist. He joined the Fellowship of Reconciliation (FOR) and worked with the National Civil Liberties Bureau, the predecessor of the American Civil Liberties Union. He defended imprisoned conscientious objectors against abuse, gaining access to President Woodrow Wilson because his brother had married Wilson's daughter. He was instrumental in restoring to *World Tomorrow* and *The Nation* access to the mails after they had been banned as subversive by appealing to President Wilson.

In the 1920s Sayre edited the *World Tomorrow*, the publication of FOR. He organized the Committee on Militarism in Education in order to end compulsory Reserved Officer Training Corps in civilian colleges.

In 1927 Sayre traveled to Nicaragua to oppose American intervention. He later helped to organize church and labor leaders in Europe into Embassies of Reconciliation to prevent World War II. In 1939 Sayre organized the Episcopal Pacifist Fellowship and soon afterward fellowships and other pacifist groups.

During World War II Sayre aided pacifists, Jews, pastors and people persecuted by the Nazis. He also began a War Victims Fund. He visited Japanese Americans in internment camps. After World War II, Sayre participated in the peace movements advocating pacifism during the Korean and Vietnam Wars.

Sayre was born on February 4, 1884, near Bethlehem, Pennsylvania. He graduated from Princeton University (1907) and Union Theological Seminary in New York City (1910). He was ordained an Episcopal priest in 1911. He died on September 13, 1977.

Andrew J. Waskey

SCHAEFER, VINCENT JOSEPH (1906–1993)

Though Vincent Joseph Schaefer worked on government projects during World War II dealing with weather research, including cloud physics and aircraft icing, his most notable achievement, the development of cloud seeding, occurred just after the war, in 1946 while working with Nobel prize-winning chemist **Irving Langmuir** at General Electric's Research Laboratory on Mount Washington in New Hampshire. Using a deep freeze box, he formed clouds by his own breath, adding dry ice to create a miniature snowstorm. (Earlier experiments to modify weather apparently began in Massachusetts in 1924 and 1938 by Emory Chaffee at Harvard and Henry Houghton at MIT and by W. Veraart in Holland in 1930). In November of 1946, Schaefer flew over Mount Greylock in Massachusetts, depositing pellets of dry ice into a cloud that resulted in a snowfall.

Schaefer was born in Schenectady, New York, on July 4, 1906, leaving high school in 1922 to become an apprentice machinist at General Electric (GE). After a detour into landscape gardening, he rejoined GE, eventually becoming Langmuir's research associate. From 1954 to 1958, Schaefer was director of research at the Munitalp Foundation's meteorological research program; then, from 1959 to 1961, he joined the American Meteorological Society and the Natural Science Foundation and worked to develop summer programs for high school students. In 1960, he founded and directed the Atmospheric Sciences Research Center at the State University of New York at Albany, where he remained until his retirement in 1976. Schaefer died in Schenectady on July 25, 1993.

Patricia Marton

SCHAIRER, GEORGE SWIFT (1913–2004)

Even before victory had been declared in Europe, George Schairer was sent to Germany in April 1945 with, among others, **Theodore von Kármán** and **Hugh Latimer Dryden** to sift through technical papers left behind by retreating German scientists. Schairer came across wind tunnel data that indicated a swept-wing aircraft could perform better than a straight-wing aircraft. In May he wrote to his colleagues at Boeing instructing them to confirm the data in Boeing's wind tunnel. As a result, the B-47 Stratojet bomber was born in 1951, the first swept-wing, multiengine bomber, followed by the B-52 Stratofortress, which was redesigned with jet engines by Schairer and **Edward C. Wells** in a Dayton, Ohio, hotel room. It was first flown in 1952 and saw extensive use in the Vietnam and Persian Gulf Wars.

Born in Wilkinsburg, Pennsylvania, on May 19, 1913, Schairer earned his undergraduate engineering degree at Swarthmore in 1934 and his master's at MIT in 1935. He joined Boeing's aerodynamics department in 1939 after two years each at Bendix and Consolidated Vultee. In 1959 he became Boeing's vice president for research and development and in 1973, vice president for research. Schairer remained a consultant for Boeing ten years after his retirement in 1978. He died on October 28, 2004.

Schairer was a pioneer in aerodynamics. He received the Spirit of St. Louis Medal in 1958 from the American Society of Mechanical Engineers and the Daniel Guggenheim Medal in 1967. He was elected to the National Academy of Sciences in 1968.

Benjamin F. Shearer

SCHAWLOW, ARTHUR L. (1921–1999)

Arthur Schawlow shared the 1981 Nobel Prize of physics with Nicolaas Bloembergen for their development of the laser and their work in laser spectroscopy. Schawlow was born in Mount Vernon, New York, on May 5, 1921. His family moved to Toronto, Canada, where he studied physics at the University of Toronto. After completion of his undergraduate degree in 1941, Schawlow initiated graduate studies, which were interrupted during World War II. For several years he worked at Research Enterprises building radar equipment. He received a Ph.D. in physics at the University of Toronto in 1949, and became a research associate and fellow at Columbia University, where he started working with **Charles Hard Townes**.

From 1951 to 1961, Schawlow was a physicist at Bell Telephone Laboratories, where he did research in superconductivity and nuclear quadrupole resonance. He worked with Townes in 1953 on the construction of the first working maser. The invention of the laser is attributed to them too. In 1958, Schawlow and Townes, a consultant to Bell Labs, published the paper, "Infrared and Optical Masers," in *Physical Review*. This paper was the beginning of a new scientific field and a new multibillion-dollar industry.

Schawlow joined the faculty of the physics department at Stanford University in 1961 and was chairman from 1966 to 1970. He continued at Stanford until his retirement in 1991. He died on April 28, 1999.

Further Reading: Chu, Steven, and Charles H. Townes. "Arthur Schawlow, May 5, 1921–April 28, 1999." *Biographical Memoirs of the National Academy of Sciences* 83 (2003): 197–215.

Nestor L. Osorio

SCHENCK, CHARLES T. (?–?)

Charles T. Schenck was the general secretary of the Socialist Party (USA). He was convicted of violating the Espionage Act of 1917 in Federal District Court and sentenced to six months in jail. His conviction was upheld by the U.S. Supreme Court in *Schenck v. United States*, 249 U.S. 47 (1919).

Schenck had been indicted for conspiracy to violate the Espionage Act, for causing and attempting to cause insubordination in the armed forces, and for obstructing the recruiting and enlistment into the armed services of the United States in a time of war. Schenck's socialist ideology taught pacifism. He had printed materials urging potential draftees to reject participation in the war, and he had mailed fifteen thousand pieces of material urging refusal to participate in the draft. Schenck argued that the draft was involuntary servitude prohibited by the Thirteenth Amendment. Furthermore, his leaflet passionately argued that the draft promoted despotism in the interests of Wall Street barons.

At his trial Schenck had argued that the Espionage Act of 1917 violated the First Amendment guarantee of Freedom of Speech, claiming that the protection was absolute. Justice Oliver Wendell Holmes Jr. delivered the opinion of the court upholding Schenck's conviction. Holmes' opinion argued that there are limits to freedom of speech. He argued that if speech is close to action, and if there is a clear and present danger that may be likely to produce a "substantive evil," then the speech may be stopped, prohibited or punished.

Andrew J. Waskey

SCHNEIDERMAN, WILLIAM (1905–1985)

William Schneiderman was born in Russia in 1905. His family immigrated to America, first living in the slums of Chicago and later in a poor neighborhood in Los Angeles. He joined the U.S. Communist Party at the age of sixteen and became a party organizer as a young adult. Eventually, he became the chairman of the California delegation of the U.S. Communist Party.

In 1939, the government took Schneiderman to court in an attempt to revoke his American citizenship. The government maintained that at the time of his naturalization in 1927 he was a member of the U.S. Communist

Party and, therefore, did not support the principles of the Constitution. He was also charged with supporting the overthrow of the American government by force, given his participation in the U.S. Communist Party. A federal court initially supported the government's position, revoked his citizenship, and threatened him with deportation.

Wendell Willkie, the 1940 Republican candidate for president, appealed Schneiderman's conviction before the U.S. Supreme Court in 1943. His conviction was overturned, thus benefiting over seven million naturalized citizens. In 1952, Schneiderman was a key defendant in the Los Angeles Smith Act trial. Various members of the U.S. Communist and Socialist parties were charged with violating the Alien Registration Act of 1940, known as the Smith Act. The act made participation in any organization defined as "un-American" a crime, punishable by a twenty-year prison sentence. Later in the 1950s, the U.S. Supreme ruled the Smith Act unconstitutional. Schneiderman died in 1985.

Gene C. Gerard

George S. Schuyler. Courtesy of the Library of Congress.

SCHUYLER, GEORGE SAMUEL (1895–1977)

George S. Schuyler's work as a journalist commented on important issues of World War II, from his concern for Italian-occupied Ethiopia in 1936 to his opposition of Japanese internment camps in America. He was born on February 25, 1895, in Providence, Rhode Island, educated in Syracuse public schools, married in 1928, and had one daughter, Philippa. From 1912 to 1919, Schuyler served in the army and achieved the rank of lieutenant. Thereafter he worked as a journalist, international correspondent, and satirist. His work was often controversial, especially when it criticized leaders such as **Martin Luther King Jr.** and Malcolm X.

Schuyler opposed America's entrance into World War II. Believing that fascism in the form of American racism must first be fought in America, he joined the America First Committee in 1940. During World War II, Schuyler continued his muckraking journalism, citing the ideological similarities between the Nazis and the American South and speaking out against Japanese internment camps. He believed nonetheless that African Americans should continue faithfully to serve America's cause. Indeed, he suggested that a long war would benefit African Americans, who would thereby prove a valuable American resource.

Schuyler was an ardent anti-communist by 1939 and worked with organizations such as the Congress for Cultural Freedom and the John Birch Society in the postwar years. He died in New York City on August 31, 1977.

Further Reading: Peplow, Michael W. *George S. Schuyler*. Boston: Twayne, 1980.

Stacy Dorgan

SCOVEL, (HENRY) SYLVESTER (1869–1905)

During the Spanish-American War, Sylvester Scovel served as a correspondent for the New York *World* and traveled with revolutionary forces in Cuba. Scovel was born on July 29, 1869, in Denny Station, Pennsylvania. He attended both the University of Wooster and the University of Michigan, working as an engineer when he was not in classes. Though he was not a trained journalist, his aggressiveness won him, in 1895, a position as a war correspondent to Cuba for the *Pittsburgh Dispatch* and the *New York Herald*. He was arrested by Spanish military police in 1896, and when he escaped to return to the United States, the New York *World* engaged his journalistic and histrionic talents to infiltrate the camp of the Cuban revolutionary leader Maximo Gomez. Scovel sent back reports of Spanish oppression designed to heighten American sentiments in sympathy with the Cuban rebels. He remained there for eleven months, until Spanish officials again arrested him on February 7, 1897. Released after a prolonged diplomatic struggle on the part of the United States, Scovel took only a short break from the conflict before returning to Cuba, and he remained there with American forces until 1899. His lack of respect for authority led to trouble with American troops as well, however, and he was threatened with court martial for disobeying regulations in order to pursue his stories.

After the war's end, Scovel worked in various engineering posts around Cuba. He died in Havana on February 11, 1905.

Ellen Baier

SEABORG, GLENN THEODORE (1912–1999)

Glenn Seaborg was a world-renowned chemist who shared the 1951 Nobel Prize in chemistry with Edwin McMillan for work with transuranium elements (those listed after uranium on the periodic table). He won the National Medal of Science, the highest science award in the United States, in 1991.

Seaborg was born in Ishpeming, Michigan, on April 12, 1912, to a Swedish immigrant mother and a father whose parents had also emigrated from Sweden. Seaborg attended the University of California, Los Angeles, where he worked as a fruit packer, ship stevedore and lab assistant to earn money for school. He received his Ph.D. in chemistry from the University of California—Berkeley in 1937. Seaborg worked at the Lawrence Berkeley National Laboratory as a graduate student, and was hired to teach at the school in 1939.

His most significant World War II–related discovery came in the middle of the night on February 23–24, 1941, when a group of scientists produced the first element beyond neptunium. (Neptunium had been produced in 1940 by Edwin McMillan and **Philip Hauge Abelson**.) Seaborg, McMillan, fellow teacher Joseph Kennedy, and graduate student Arthur Wahl used **Ernest Orlando Lawrence**'s cyclotron to bombard uranium to create plutonium. The element was not officially confirmed and named until later that year. The researchers, along with scientist Emilio Segré, were also able to continue the research to discover Plutonium-239, a significant advance because this was a fissionable isotope. This discovery, which showed that fission was more possible with "slow neutrons," led to the development of nuclear energy.

Seaborg developed the "actinide concept" along with noted physical chemist Gilbert Newton Lewis in the late 1930s. Their work developed a new theory of primary and secondary acids and bases. When Seaborg placed transuranium elements on the periodic table, it was perhaps the most significant changes the table had undergone since its inception. He used this concept to discover a series of elements including americium, californium, einsteinium, seaborgium and others. Seaborgium was the first element named for a living person.

With the entrance of the United States into World War II, and as a result of his plutonium research, Seaborg was appointed to the Manhattan Project as a development researcher to create a method for mass production of large quantities of plutonium in what was called a "chain reactor." Scientist **Enrico Fermi** and his group demonstrated the process in 1942, and Seaborg was charged with separating the plutonium from the remainder of the fission products left in the uranium. His official role was to develop a multi-stage process for the separation, concentration and isolation of plutonium. A pilot plant, the Clinton Engineer Works, was constructed in Oak Ridge, Tennessee, and a production plant in Hanford, Washington. The results of this experimentation with separating uranium led to the uranium-235 product that was used to create the bomb dropped on Hiroshima. Seaborg's method yielded enough plutonium to create a test bomb for the site at Alamogordo, New Mexico, on July 16, 1942. When the test proved successful, additional plutonium was produced to make the Hiroshima bomb that was used on August 9, 1945.

Seaborg, along with a group of scientists, lobbied for the test demonstration of the atomic bomb in the hope that if the president and military leaders saw its power and force, it would never be used in warfare. A report was made on the July 1942 test, but it is not known if President Harry Truman ever reviewed the details. Truman ordered the atomic bombs to be dropped on Japan.

After World War II, Seaborg continued to join with other scientists in exploring nuclear reactions, including using a new cyclotron at Lawrence Berkeley Laboratory in classifying types of nuclear reactions and isotopes.

Truman appointed Seaborg to serve on the first General Advisory Committee to the Atomic Energy Committee, where he served from 1947 until 1950. President John F. Kennedy appointed Seaborg as head of the Atomic Energy Commission in 1961, where he remained until 1971.

Seaborg's work in radioisotopes was instrumental in advances in nuclear medicine, including the use of Iodine-131 and Cobalt-60. Seaborg served as a teacher and chancellor at the University of California and worked for nuclear arms control. He was an advocate of international cooperation in scientific endeavors. By the end of his life, he held fifty honorary degrees and over forty patents. He died on February 25, 1999.

Further Reading: Seaborg, Glenn T. *A Chemist in the White House: From the Manhattan Project to the End of the Cold War.* New York: Oxford University Press, 1997.

Pamela Lee Gray

SEALE, ROBERT "BOBBY" GEORGE (1936–)

Bobby Seale founded the Black Panther Party for Self-Defense with **Huey P. Newton** in 1966. He was also a defendant in the notorious Chicago Seven (actually eight for a while), joining **Jerry C. Rubin**, Abbie Hoffman, and other white anti-war protesters who demonstrated during the 1968 Democratic National Convention.

Seale was born in Dallas, Texas, on October 22, 1936, but his family eventually moved to Oakland, California, where he attended high school, but failed to graduate. He joined the Air Force, and after a three-year stint was dishonorably discharged. At home again, he worked, got his high school diploma, and began attending Merritt Community College. There he met Huey Newton, in whom he found a kindred spirit as an activist for the rights of black and oppressed people. The Black Panthers, angry over the victimization of blacks in virtually every phase of American life—housing, education, law enforcement, health care, employment—issued a Ten Point Plan that included their desire for peace, but they were to be militant in seeking peace.

Seale's anti–Vietnam War activism preceded the founding of the Panthers. He believed, correctly, that black soldiers were dying at astoundingly higher rates—at least double their percentage of total population— than white soldiers in Vietnam. More importantly, however, Seale could not see why any black soldier should risk his life for a country that refused to recognize his civil rights.

Seale earned jail time for his contemptuous behavior during the Chicago Eight Trial, but in 1972 his sentence was suspended. He ran a failed campaign for mayor of Oakland, California, in 1973, formally left the Panthers in 1974, and devoted his life to community organization and development, writing, and speaking.

Benjamin F. Shearer

SEEGER, PETE (1919–)

Songwriter, musician, and social activist Pete Seeger composed a number of songs during World War II, at first opposing American involvement in the conflict and later supporting the Allied war effort. He was drafted into the army in 1942 and served for three years in the Pacific theater. In later years, Seeger was at the forefront of the peace movement opposing American involvement in Vietnam.

Seeger was born on May 3, 1919, in Patterson, New York. His parents, musicologist Charles Seeger and concert violinist Constance Edison Seeger, were both faculty members at Julliard. Seeger was educated at private schools in New York and Connecticut before entering Harvard as a sociology student in 1936. He left Harvard in the middle of his sophomore year in order travel throughout the U.S. collecting folk songs and attempting to master the five-string banjo.

In 1939–1940 Seeger worked as assistant archivist at the Library of Congress' Archive of Folk Song. He met folksinger **Woodrow "Woody" Wilson Guthrie** at a March 1940 benefit for California migrant workers. Seeger and Guthrie traveled together throughout the United States performing at union rallies and migrant camps. In the same year Seeger founded the Almanac

Pete Seeger entertains at the opening of the Washington labor canteen, 1944. Courtesy of the Library of Congress.

Singers, a loosely knit group of folksingers that performed mainly at union rallies, strikes, and protest meetings.

As communist sympathizers—Seeger would later join the Party in 1942—the Almanac Singers opposed American involvement in the European war, at least during the short-lived alliance between the Soviet Union and Nazi Germany. In March 1941 the group recorded *Songs for John Doe*, a collection of anti-war songs that included Seeger's "'C' for Conscription," "Plow Under," and "Washington Breakdown." When Hitler invaded the Soviet Union in June 1941, Seeger and the other Almanac Singers insisted that all copies of *Songs for John Doe* be recalled and destroyed. Rather than continue to protest the war, the group directed its efforts toward writing and performing anti-Hitler songs.

In January 1942, the Almanac Singers were featured on *We the People*, a radio show intended to boost morale during the war. "Round and Round Hitler's Grave"—a song that Seeger co-wrote with Woody Guthrie—became very popular as an antifascist anthem and was featured on a CBS series entitled *This Is War*. The Almanac Singers quickly fell from grace, however, when the press got wind of the group's earlier anti-war album, *Songs for John Doe*. Thereafter, the Almanac Singers found themselves increasingly unable to secure bookings, despite the release of a new pro-Roosevelt album in May 1942 entitled *Dear Mr. President*.

Seeger was drafted in 1942; he spent the next three years serving in the army, primarily in the Pacific arena, where he entertained the troops and compiled a collection of soldier songs. He was discharged as a corporal in 1945. Following his return to civilian life, Seeger formed a new musical group, the Weavers. The group sold four million records within three years, but was blacklisted during the Joseph McCarthy era. Seeger and the Weavers were banned from national television and many radio stations stopped playing their songs.

In 1955 Seeger was called to testify before the House Committee on Un-American Activities. When he invoked the First Amendment (rather than the Fifth Amendment) to justify his refusal to answer the committee's questions, Seeger found himself facing criminal charges of contempt of Congress. He was convicted five years later and sentenced to a year in jail, but he served only four days of his sentence. A federal judge finally dismissed the charges against him in 1962.

During the 1960s, Seeger became a regular feature at civil rights rallies and anti-war protests. His songs "Where Have All the Flowers Gone?" and "Turn, Turn, Turn" became closely identified with the peace movement. Other Seeger compositions, such as "The Ballad of the Fort Hood Three," were more overtly concerned with the Vietnam conflict. "Waist Deep in the Big Muddy," while it never mentioned President Lyndon Johnson or the Vietnam War explicitly, was a scathing indictment of the Johnson administration's policies in Vietnam: "Every time I read the paper, those old feelings come on/We are waist deep in the Big Muddy, and the big fool says to push on."

Now in his eighties, Seeger remains active in promoting social and environmental issues and opposing a war that he considers unjust. In 2003 Seeger led thousands in song as part of the Global March for Peace. He recently updated one of his anti-Vietnam songs, "Bring Them Home," to apply to the invasion of Iraq.

Kathleen Ruppert

SENN, NICHOLAS (1844–1908)

Considered a "Master of Abdominal Surgery," Nicholas Senn was born in Switzerland, but immigrated to America in 1852 settling in Ashford, Wisconsin. Senn attended Chicago Medical College and graduated in 1868 with top honors. After his internship he organized a general practice specializing in surgery. Senn became an attending physician at Milwaukee Hospital in 1874. Then in 1877, he traveled to the University of Munich in Germany, where he received a second M.D. just a year later.

Senn became a professor of surgery in the College of Physicians and Surgeons in Chicago in 1884, where he emphasized three main elements of surgery: clinical microscopy, animal experimentation, and use of antiseptics in surgery. He held a number of other professorships, including professor of principles and practice of surgery at the College of Physicians and Surgeons and professor of surgery and surgical pathology and professor of military surgery at Rush Medical College. In 1888, Senn developed a test using hydrogen for diagnosing gastrointestinal canal injuries by experimenting on himself. He also served as surgeon general of the Wisconsin National Guard and founded the Association of Military Surgeons.

During the Spanish-American War, Senn served in Cuba where he became known for his surgical techniques on gunshot wounds. In 1908, he suffered from an attack of myocarditis while mountain climbing in South America; he died shortly after returning to Chicago.

Further Reading: Hamilton, Shari. "The Great Master of Abdominal Surgery: Nicholas Senn, MD, 1844–1908." *Wisconsin Medical Journal* 91 (May 1992): 245, 247–249.

Lisa A. Ennis

SERBER, ROBERT (1909–1997)

Robert Serber, a theoretical physicist, was **Julius Robert Oppenheimer**'s assistant in the Manhattan Project. Born in Philadelphia in 1909, he obtained a B.S. degree from Lehigh University (1930), and a Ph.D. in physics from the University of Wisconsin (1934). After attending a lecture given by Oppenheimer at the University of Michigan, he decided to join the faculty of the University of California at Berkeley, where Oppenheimer became his mentor.

From 1936 to 1945 Serber was a member of the physics faculty at the University of Illinois, but in 1941 Oppenheimer recruited him to work for the Manhattan Project. In April of 1943, Serber gave a series of five lectures summarizing all that was known about building an atomic bomb. These lectures were known as the *Los Alamos Primer*. Serber's job was to provide the diverse team of scientists and engineers assembled at Los Alamos with a description of each one's role in the project, and to give them what was known about nuclear fission as well as what was needed to produce a bomb. Because he was very interested in how experimental research physics was done, Serber was an ideal bridge between the experimental and the theoretical part of the project. He was also the first one to develop a good theory of bomb disassembly hydrodynamics.

After the war, Serber became a professor at Columbia University. He was chair of the physics department in 1975 until his retirement in 1978. He was also an expert on proton-proton interactions and in particles detecting instrumentation.

Nestor L. Osorio

SHAHN, BEN (1898–1969)

During World War II, Ben Shahn worked for the Office of War Information making posters, pamphlets, and other graphic art. Shahn was born to a Jewish family on September 12, 1898, in Kovno, Lithuania, then a province of Russia, from which his father sought escape from persecution for his socialist activities. The family immigrated to Brooklyn, New York, in 1906 where Ben apprenticed as a teenager in his uncle's lithography shop. In 1918 Shahn became a naturalized American citizen. After taking art courses at New York University, City College of New York, and the National Academy of Design, he traveled to Europe for further study. In the 1920s, Shahn became a social realist and his work was often inspired by news reports. He held strong socialist views and was an ardent supporter of Roosevelt's New Deal policies.

Working for the Farm Security Administration from 1935 to 1938, Shahn made thousands of photographs that depicted the hardship of the Great Depression. In 1942–1943 he worked for the Office of War Information designing pamphlets and executing a number of anti-fascist offset lithographic posters. Many of his fear-inspiring posters depicted Nazi acts of atrocity like the destruction of Lidice, a Czech mining village that was obliterated by the Nazis in retaliation for the 1942 shooting of a Nazi official by two Czechs. All men of the village were executed; the women and children were sent to concentration camps. Lidice became a symbol for the brutality of Nazi occupation during the war. Shahn died on March 14, 1969.

Further Reading: Greenfeld, Howard. *Ben Shahn: An Artist's Life*. New York: Random House, 1998.

David M. Carletta

SHAKESPEARE, EDWARD ORAM (1846–1900)

Physician, bacteriologist, and public health advocate Edward O. Shakespeare is best known for his work with Walter Reed and **Victor Clarence Vaughan** on conditions in the army camps of the Spanish-American War. Born in New Castle County, Delaware, on May 19, 1846, Shakespeare attended medical school at the University of Pennsylvania. After graduating in 1896, he established an ophthalmology practice where he investigated using cocaine as an eye anesthetic and invented a new ophthalmoscope. His success led to appointments in both eye surgery and refraction. He also served as county coroner and curator of the Philadelphia General Hospital. Interest in science and social reform led Shakespeare to serve as a government consultant. In 1885 the mayor of Philadelphia asked him to investigate a typhoid fever outbreak in the city, which he traced to the town's water supply. That same year, Shakespeare was asked by President Cleveland to study cholera in Spain and Italy, resulting in a thousand-page report. A year later Shakespeare was one of ten physicians invited to become charter members of the Association of American Physicians. Then, in 1892, he was called on to serve as port physician in Philadelphia during a cholera scare.

Shakespeare's final appointment was with Reed and Vaughan. Charged with investigating health in army camps, the group reported that almost all malaria cases were really typhoid fever and called for safety measures, especially hygiene. This disease had proved as deadly as bullets. Shakespeare died unexpectedly of a heart attack in 1900.

Lisa A. Ennis

SHANNON, CLAUDE ELWOOD (1916–2001)

Claude Shannon is generally recognized as the father of information science. His 1948 article, "A Mathematical Theory of Communications," revolutionized communications theory. During World War II, however, Shannon not only applied his genius to practical issues, but he also helped to make cryptography a scientific pursuit.

Shannon was born on April 30, 1916, in Gaylord, Michigan. He finished his B.S. degree at the University of Michigan in 1936. His master's thesis, "A Symbolic Analysis of Relay and Switching Circuits," got him a graduate degree in electrical engineering at MIT and immortality for laying the foundation of digital computing and integrated circuits. In his Ph.D. dissertation, also done at MIT, he tried to apply mathematics to genetics. Degrees in hand, Shannon went to work for Bell Laboratories in 1941.

Bell Labs was deeply interested in war work. Shannon worked on secrecy systems and anti-aircraft gun directors. His encryption work developed into the secrecy system used for Allied conferences. His anti-aircraft directors, which accurately detected flying objects and aimed counter-missiles at them, helped England survive the German Blitz.

Shannon left Bell Labs to teach at MIT in 1956. From 1958 until his retirement in 1978, he was Donner Professor of Science. In 1966, Shannon received the National Medal of Science. A victim of Alzheimer's disease, he died on February 24, 2001.

Further Reading: Shannon, Claude Elwood. *Claude Elwood Shannon: Collected Papers.* Edited by N. J. A. Sloane and Aaron D. Wyner. New York: IEEE Press, 1993.

Benjamin F. Shearer

SHARPS, CHRISTIAN (1811–1874)

Christian Sharps developed and patented a breech-loading system in 1848. Born in New Jersey in 1811, Sharps became a machinist and worked on a number of inventions during his life, receiving patents on more the fifty of them. Of these fifty patents Sharps obtained, more than twenty were for guns, parts of guns, and cartridges and machinery used in producing guns. He married Sarah Chadwick.

Sharps received his first patent on September 12, 1848, for a self-capping sliding breech-loading pin. His patent for a breech-loading firearm was issued on July 9, 1861. The breech-load system allowed the gun to be loaded from the top instead of from the end of the barrel. A paper cartridge was used (he did not switch to metal ones until after the Civil War) and closing of the breech would cut open the cartridge. In 1854, Sharps moved to Hartford, Connecticut, and worked as superintendent at the factory that manufactured his guns.

Initially the U.S. Army was resistant to using the breech-loading weapons during the Civil War, but by the end of the war the army had placed orders for more than nine thousand rifles and eighty thousand carbines of Sharps' design. While the army had purchased most of Sharps' weapons, the navy also purchased some of them.

Sharps died on March 13, 1874, in Vernon, Connecticut.

Further Reading: Rywell, Martin. *The Gun That Shaped American Destiny.* Harriman, TN: Pioneer Press, 1957.

Dallace W. Unger Jr.

SHARPTON, ALFRED CHARLES JR. (1954–)

As a preacher, activist, and erstwhile Democratic presidential candidate, the Reverend Al Sharpton has been an outspoken critic of American involvement in the Second Gulf War. Alfred Charles Sharpton Jr. was born in Brooklyn, New York, on October 3, 1954, and ordained a Pentecostal minister ten years later. In 1971 Sharpton founded the National Youth Movement to combat drug use and poverty and to mobilize young urban voters. He attended Brooklyn College for two years before dropping out in 1975. Sharpton achieved national recognition as a controversial civil rights activist, leading demonstrations on a number of high-profile racially charged court cases. In 1991 he founded the National Action Network (NAN), a civil rights organization aimed at empowering the disenfranchised. After two unsuccessful bids for the U.S. Senate and one for the mayoralty of New York, Sharpton ran unsuccessfully for president of the United States in 2004.

In the months preceding the outbreak of the Second Gulf War, Sharpton stridently opposed an American invasion of Iraq. Addressing anti-war demonstrators at a huge rally in Washington, DC, on January 18, 2003, Sharpton objected to the use of low-income Americans in particular as targets in a war for oil. Since the outbreak of hostilities, Sharpton has remained critical of the Bush administration's policies in Iraq. Joining **Cindy Sheehan** and other protesters in Crawford, Texas, in August 2005, Sharpton compared the anti-war movement to the civil rights struggle and called Sheehan the conscience of the nation.

Kathleen Ruppert

SHAW, BERNARD (1940–)

Bernard Shaw was an original anchor for CNN. He was born on May 22, 1940, in Chicago, Illinois. Owing to his father's sustained interest in current affairs, Shaw developed a taste for news reporting and a high respect for journalists. **Edward Roscoe Murrow**, the distinguished World War II reporter, was his idol in youth.

With a natural eloquence and sharp conversational skills, Shaw pursued his dream with perseverance. As he told Peter Benjaminson in an interview for *Contemporary Authors* (1987), "I worked very hard; I slept very little: a typical instance of a young novice getting an opportunity and going berserk in the process of doing the job." His efforts bore fruit as in 1965 he earned a job as news writer for the Chicago station WFLD. He moved to CBS News, got promoted from reporter to correspondent, shifted to ABC network for better prospects, and joined CNN in 1980 as a news anchor. CNN, an emerging TV network, was a challenge for the journalist and his unfaltering ethics.

The outstanding experience in Shaw's entire journalistic journey was his commendably courageous reportage during the 1991 Gulf War. His round-the-clock live coverage, dramatic and riveting, brought him worldwide visibility and instant recognition. This coverage by mainstream prime-time media also generated sympathy and consent for the war policies of the U.S. administration. For this, Shaw received the George Foster Peabody Broadcasting Award and the Award for Cable Excellence for best newscaster for 1991. Shaw retired from CNN in 2001.

Jitendra Uttam

SHAW, IRWIN (1913–1984)

Irwin Shaw was born in Brooklyn on February 27, 1913, and graduated from Brooklyn College in 1934. He began a career in theater and literature. In 1936 his anti-war one act play, *Bury the Dead*, appeared and gave him his first taste of fame. He was also involved in the writing of screenplays for directors like George Stevens. Perhaps his major accomplishment was the writing of a series of short stories that have become American classics.

Shaw enlisted in the army in 1942 and served in Europe. Toward the end of the war he joined the photographic unit led by George Stevens and remained with it through the liberation of France and the defeat of Germany. He witnessed the freeing of Paris and the horror of the liberated concentration camps.

Following the war, Shaw published the acclaimed novel *The Young Lions* in 1949, which became, with **Norman Kingsley Mailer**'s *The Naked and the Dead*, one of the great books to come out of the war. Shaw told the compelling story of three soldiers—a Nazi, an American Jew and another American who had been pursuing a theater career—from before the war, through the war from North Africa to Europe, until their paths cross. Shaw wove these fictional figures with real events to attain a vivid picture of combat and the affect of war on individuals and societies.

Following the publication of *The Young Lions*, Shaw pursued a successful career writing popular novels as well as screenplays. He died on May 16, 1984.

Marc L. Schwarz

SHEEHAN, CINDY (1957–)

On April 4, 2004, Army Specialist Casey A. Sheehan, a Humvee mechanic from Vacaville, California, was killed in action in Sadr City, Iraq. His mother, Cindy Sheehan, was devastated. Realizing she could not bring her son back, the former Roman Catholic youth minister set out to give meaning to his death by trying to end the war in Iraq and bring the soldiers home before other mothers felt her heartbreak. Sheehan's activism was motivated by her son's death and what she saw as betrayal. When weapons of mass destruction—cited by President George W. Bush as the reason for the war—turned out never to have existed, Sheehan set out to make the record straight. She blamed Bush directly for Casey's death. Sheehan told an interviewer that she believed her son had died for naught.

Early in 2005 Sheehan and a small like-minded group founded the Gold Star Mothers for Peace. Its dual purpose is to end the occupation of Iraq and to act as a support group to Gold Star families by supporting and empowering those victimized by the war in Iraq, raising awareness about the human costs of the war, and reaching out to families who lost loved ones in the war. While membership is open to anyone who lost a relative because of war, the organization is primarily concerned with those who lost relatives in the war in Iraq. Sheehan has spoken and protested around the country and appeared before Congress with her message.

Benjamin F. Shearer

SHEEHAN, JOHN CLARK (1915–1992)

World War II brought American science, government and industry together in a number of successful projects to advance the war effort. The development of radar and the atomic bomb were notable successes of this collaboration. The discovery of a method to mass-produce penicillin from a fermentation process was another outstanding accomplishment that succeeded in saving countless lives. The task of synthesizing penicillin, however, was a dismal failure. When that research was halted at the end of the war, $20 million had been wasted, in the opinion of most scientists, supporting about one thousand British and American scientists in this futile task. Twelve years later, chemist John Sheehan did what had eluded one of America's and Great Britain's most extensive and intensive scientific research efforts. His synthesis of penicillin led to the development of many "wonder drugs" now in common use.

Even before the United States officially entered the war, the nation was on a war footing. President Roosevelt created the Office of Scientific Research and Development (OSRD) by Executive Order on June 28, 1941. **Vannevar Bush**, OSRD director, soon created the Committee on Medical Research (CMR), with **Alfred Newton Richards** as chair. Early in October 1941 the CMR decided to pursue a coordinated research program on penicillin. By February, however, only a small grant had been given to at the Northern Regional Research Laboratory in Peoria to study the fermentation process. Although the "Penicillin Team" in Peoria, which included **Kenneth Bryan Raper** and **Andrew J. Moyer**, was ultimately able to ferment the right mold and **Jasper H. Kane** at Pfizer found the right deep fermentation process to mass-produce it, their success was not assured. In October of 1943, the OSRD and CMR agreed to attack the synthesis of penicillin in a secret and coordinated effort. By the end of 1943, however, the fermentation process was producing millions of doses and the synthesis project languished only to be cancelled in 1945.

Although Merck was involved in the synthetic penicillin project, Sheehan was working on streptomycin and B vitamins, which by this time were produced synthetically, while employed there from 1941 to 1946. Born in Battle Creek, Michigan, on September 23, 1915, he finished his undergraduate work at Battle Creek College in 1937, and obtained his M.S. (1938) and Ph.D. (1941) in organic chemistry from the University of Michigan. Sheehan contributed to the war effort while still at Michigan by co-developing a mass process to manufacture the explosive RDX. In 1946 Sheehan accepted a position in the chemistry department at MIT, where he remained throughout his academic career, accepting emeritus status in 1977. He served as a science advisor to presidents Kennedy and Johnson from 1961 to 1965.

Sheehan and his MIT group took on the penicillin synthesis problem in 1948 with financial support from Bristol Laboratories. Neither pharmaceutical companies nor research chemists wanted to pursue synthesis after the war. Pfizer, for example, counted penicillin made from natural molds as its biggest selling drug up until 1953. Most research chemists could not find funding to discover a drug that already existed in plenty and furthermore, the penicillin molecule was believed to be too difficult to get any positive results. Sheehan, on the other hand, relished the opportunity to do pure research and saw in synthetic penicillin the opportunity to conquer the molecule and modify it to create new and better drugs. He predicted in the early 1950s that synthetic penicillin would lead the way to an enhanced, stronger, more stable, less degradable drug with a broader spectrum, that caused less allergic reaction. In 1951 Sheehan received the American Chemical Society Award in Pure Chemistry for synthesizing a penicillin (5-phenylpenicillin). This penicillin, however, lacked any antibiotic properties, but it was a significant step forward.

By 1956 Sheehan had synthesized the penicillin molecule's chemical nucleus. His final work was completed during 1957 and reported in 1958. Thirty years after Alexander Fleming's discovery of penicillin, it could now be made in a laboratory. On March 1, 1957, Sheehan applied for a patent. He made a new patent application on May 1, 1959. A long legal battle ensued after Beecham, Inc., made numerous claims for having first synthesized penicillin. In 1979, the U.S. Board of Patent Interferences finally found that Sheehan should prevail. Sheehan's predictions about synthetic penicillin all came to fruition. He himself discovered ampicillin. In 1959 the American Chemical Society again honored him with its Award for Creative Work in Pure Chemistry. Sheehan died on March 21, 1992.

Further Reading: Sheehan, John C. *The Enchanted Ring; The Untold Story of Penicillin.* Cambridge, MA: MIT Press, 1982.

Benjamin F. Shearer

SHEEN, MARTIN (1940–)

Born Ramón Estevez in Dayton, Ohio, on August 3, 1940, actor and political activist Martin Sheen debuted on television in 1961 and in film in 1967. He starred in the 1979 film *Apocalypse Now*, set during the Vietnam War, and has long been a protestor of American military actions. Arrested more than fifty times for his protest activities, Sheen is a member of the organization Consistent Life, which opposes abortion, euthanasia, and the death penalty in addition to war.

In August 2005, Sheen attended a protest rally held by **Cindy Sheehan** to oppose the second war in Iraq. The actor has been highly vocal in his belief that America should not be involved in the war in Iraq. In December 2004, Sheen joined a number of other celebrities in signing an open letter to President George W. Bush urging him not to engage in war in Iraq. He also led an anti-war march in Los Angeles the following January. Sheen has also been featured in television advertisements, launched by the organization Win without War, requesting that Americans inundate the White House and U.S. Congress with anti-war letters, phone calls, faxes, and e-mails. Sheen believed that this "virtual" march on Washington, DC, would alert Congress that American citizens are vehemently opposed to America's military actions in Iraq. He has often taken advantage of his celebrity status to gain media attention, resulting in a flood of hate mail sent to the actor because of his opposition to any American military action in Iraq.

Nicole Mitchell

SHEERAN, JAMES B. (1819–1881)

Born in Ireland, young James Sheeran migrated to Canada at age twelve with his parents and then moved on to Monroe, Michigan, where he received his education by the Redemptorist priests. He married in 1842, but after the death of his wife in 1849, he joined the Redemptorist order and was ordained a priest in 1858. In his first parish, a congregation in New Orleans, he adopted the politics and values of his flock. On September 2, 1861, he received assignment as Catholic chaplain in the Fourteenth Louisiana Infantry in the Army of Northern Virginia. His partisanship was legendary, referring to the invading Union army as "Lincoln's bandits." In 1864, while imprisoned by Union forces, he tried harder to convert the Yankees to the Confederate cause than Catholicism.

Sheeran's two-volume diary spanned the period between August 1862 and his return to New Orleans in 1865, and within its pages he wrote of his dealings with Stonewall Jackson, Robert E. Lee, Confederate stragglers, ministry to the troops, and relationships with his Union captors. He returned to New Orleans after the war, and in 1867 began a short ministry in Newark, New Jersey. In 1871, he received appointment as pastor of the Church of the Assumption in Morristown, New Jersey. Sheeran died of apoplexy on April 3, 1881.

Further Reading: Durkin, Joseph T., Ed. *Confederate Chaplain: A War Journal of Rev. James B. Sheeran, c.ss.r, 14th Louisiana, C.S.A.* With a preface by Bruce Catton. Milwaukee: Bruce Publishing, 1960.

James S. Baugess

SHERROD, ROBERT LEE (1909–1994)

Robert Sherrod contributed to American public information during World War II through his articles on the war in the South Pacific. He was born in Thomas County, Georgia, on February 8, 1909, earned his degree from the University of Georgia in 1929, was married three times (widowed twice), and had two sons. Sherrod worked in journalism as a reporter, a correspondent, and an editor for publications such as the *New York Herald Tribune, Time, Life,* and the *Saturday Evening Post.*

As a correspondent during World War II, Sherrod wrote articles on the military and foreign affairs and personal accounts of his experiences in the war zones of the South Pacific from 1942 to 1945. Several of these articles are compiled in Samuel Hynes' two-part *Reporting World War II* (New York: Library of America, 1995). Sherrod's book *Tarawa: The Story of a Battle*, published in 1944, is his account of the marine battle there in 1943. *On to Westward: The Battles of Saipan and Iwo Jima* (1945) and *History of Marine Corps Aviation in World War II* (1952) are Sherrod's valuable histories of American battles against Japan. His awards included a commendation from the U.S. Navy in 1943 for his coverage of the Battles of Attu and Tarawa.

In the postwar years, Sherrod became managing editor and then editor-in-chief of the *Saturday Evening Post*, worked as an editor and co-author of texts, and became the president of the Curtis Publishing Company in 1965. He died in Washington, DC, on February 13, 1994.

Stacy Dorgan

SHERWOOD, ROBERT EMMET (1896–1955)

Robert E. Sherwood made major literary, political, and strategic contributions to America's fight against fascism. He was born on April 4, 1896, in New Rochelle, New York, graduated from Harvard in 1918, married twice, and had one daughter. Sherwood served in the Canadian Black Watch Regiment during World War I and was wounded in action. Thereafter, he worked as a drama and movie critic, an editor, a playwright, an advisor and speechwriter to President Franklin Roosevelt, a special assistant to the secretary of war (1939–1942), the secretary of the navy (1945), and the director of the Overseas Branch of the Office of War Information (OWI) (1942–1944). He is also known as one of the founders of the Algonquin Hotel Round Table (1920) and the Playwrights' Producing Company (1938).

Sherwood's many awards include the Pulitzer Prize for Drama for *Idiot's Delight* in 1936, *Abe Lincoln in Illinois* in 1939, and *There Shall Be No Night* in 1940 and the Pulitzer Prize for Nonfiction for *Roosevelt and Hopkins* in 1948.

Sherwood was strongly opposed in the 1930s to America's involvement in the war; however, his attitude changed by the end of the decade, when he became an ardent antifascist. His dramatic work at this time expresses these sentiments and his belief in American democracy. He helped organize the Committee to Defend America by Aiding the Allies and to sell the war at home through his work on Roosevelt's "Four Freedoms" and other speeches and as a leader of the OWI.

He died in New York City on November 14, 1955.

Stacy Dorgan

SHIPPEN, WILLIAM JR. (1736–1808)

William Shippen Jr. was one of the pioneers of medical education and military medicine in the United States. He was born in Philadelphia in 1736 the son of a prominent medical doctor. Following in his father's footsteps, he graduated from Princeton University in 1754 and did four years as an apprentice to his father. He then traveled to Britain where, in 1761, he was awarded a medical degree from the University of Edinburgh.

Following his return, Shippen lectured about anatomy and worked to expand medical education in the colonies. When the Revolutionary War broke out, he entered the medical service of the Continental Army and dedicated himself to military medicine. In 1776, he gained the position of medical director of the Flying Camp, a force of ten thousand troops operating in New Jersey. The following year, after Shippen submitted a plan for the reorganization of army medical service that was accepted nearly in its entirety, the Continental Congress named him director general of all the military hospitals for the Armies of the United States—making him, in effect, the surgeon general of the United States.

In this post, Shippen established uniform surgical procedures for all military hospitals, and promoted programs for the training of medical personnel and for the care of soldiers' families. Unfortunately, the circumstances in which he replaced his predecessor as director general, **John Morgan**, led to accusations from Morgan and his allies that Shippen had gained his appointment through political intrigue. Morgan's supporters circulated reports that Shippen had misappropriated funds, and falsified morbidity and mortality statistics. These accusations led General George Washington to order a court-martial for Shippen in summer 1780. On August 18, that court-martial cleared Shippen of any wrong doing and ordered him returned to duty. Nevertheless, an exhausted Shippen resigned from the military in January 1781.

Further Reading: Conner, B. C. *William Shippen, Jr.* Philadelphia: American Philosophical Society, 1951.

Walter F. Bell

SHOCKLEY, WILLIAM BRADFORD (1910–1989)

Physicist William Shockley was one of the three inventors of the transistor. He was born in London, England, on February 13, 1910, to William Hillman Shockley, an American mining engineer, and May (Bradford) Shockley, a mineral surveyor. In 1913 his family returned to the United States and he grew up in California. He was home-schooled until the age of eight, but subsequently followed a more typical pattern of schooling. He received a B.S. in physics from the California Institute of Technology (CalTech) in Pasadena in 1932, and in 1936 he received his Ph.D. from the Massachusetts Institute of Technology in Cambridge, for work exploring quantum mechanics and the movement of electrons through crystalline substances.

With his doctoral work completed, Shockley went to Bell Telephone Laboratories to work on an alternative to vacuum tubes, which had several major drawbacks—size, fragility, and heat generation among them. During

World War II he set that work aside to apply himself to more immediately practical work on military radars. In 1942 he became research director for the Anti-Submarine Warfare Operations Research Group at Columbia University. From 1944 to 1945 he was a consultant to the secretary of war, advising him on military applications of technology.

After the war, Shockley returned to Bell Labs and his research on vacuum tube alternatives. However, **John Bardeen** soon determined that Shockley's initial design for a solid-state equivalent to the vacuum tube could not work and developed an alternate design with the aid of **Walter Houser Brattain**. Using a slab of germanium, a wedge of plastic and a piece of gold foil, they were able to amplify a signal a hundredfold. As a result, Shockley's name was not included on the original patent for the transistor, a fact that he would come to resent greatly. Driven by this turn of events, he invented two other forms of transistor in the next two months, alienating Bardeen and Brattain. In 1956 Shockley was included with them as a co-laureate for the Nobel Prize in Physics as a result of his contributions to the invention of the transistor.

After the breakup of their team, Shockley went to California's Santa Clara Valley to found Shockley Semiconductor, a company to build transistors and design other semiconductor devices. His decision was at least in part responsible for the development of Silicon Valley, the enormous concentration of electronics and computer industry activity in the Santa Clara Valley.

Transistors had enormous implications for the military, at least as critical as the invention of the Audion tube by **Lee De Forest**. Transistors solved the problems of size, fragility and heat production that had always kept military radios large and temperamental. With solid-state components, radios in the field could become small enough to be held in the hand and rugged enough to survive the bumps and shocks of the battlefield. Furthermore, transistors allowed the military to build smaller and more powerful computers than had been possible with vacuum tubes. While even the most sophisticated vacuum tube computer might take hours to complete a relatively simple calculation and had to be tended by squads of technicians constantly ready to replace burnt-out tubes, a transistor-based computer could be built far more compactly, perform its calculations far more rapidly, and produce less heat, thus running far more reliably.

Transistors also made militarily useful satellites possible. A simple satellite like the Soviet Union's original *Sputnik* could send down a radio signal, but not much else of use. With rugged miniature and micro-miniature solid-state electronics, satellites could facilitate communications, take extremely accurate pictures of enemy installations from orbit, and perform many other activities useful to the military.

After surviving a near fatal head-on automobile collision in 1961, Shockley emerged a changed man, although not all would consider the changes to be for the better. Shockley became increasingly interested in human betterment through genetics and particularly through its application in eugenics, a science brought into disrepute by the Nazis during World War II by their pseudoscience of "racial hygiene." Shockley became involved in very controversial studies linking intelligence to genetics, particularly when he claimed that African Americans were inherently inferior to European-Americans and that the admixture of African and European stocks in America was causing a deterioration of the overall intelligence of the American public.

Shockley became estranged from his children, partly because of his naturally abrasive personality and partly because of his espousal of such racist views. In response to their outrage at his statements, he condemned them as a "degeneration." Shockley died in San Francisco, California, on August 11, 1989.

Leigh Husband Kimmel

SIKORSKY, IGOR IVANOVICH (1889–1972)

Igor Sikorsky was a Russian immigrant whose brilliance was revealed in his engineering of the first modern, practical helicopter. Born in Kiev, Ukraine, on May 25, 1889, Sikorsky studied at the Naval War College in St. Petersburg before moving to Paris to study aeronautics. By 1910, back in Kiev, he was piloting his own aircraft and two short years later was hired as the designer and chief engineer of a Russian aircraft plant. Sikorsky designed and built two- and four-engine planes used by the Russians during World War I.

Unsympathetic to Marxist philosophy, Sikorsky immigrated to the United States in 1919 after the Bolshevik Revolution. Without much to his name, Sikorsky settled in New York and cultivated a group of investors from among other Russian immigrants, including the famous composer, Sergei Rachmaninoff. Sikorsky Aero Engineering Corporation opened its doors for business in 1923.

The 1920s was a time in American aviation of barnstormers and not of serious pursuits such as passenger air travel. That changed after **Charles Augustus Lindbergh**'s historic 1927 transatlantic flight, and the possibilities for commercial aviation quickly expanded. Lindbergh touted commercial aviation as safe and reliable and partnered with both Trans World Airlines and Pan Am. Needing passenger planes, Sikorsky responded with a ten-seat amphibian, the S-38, receiving orders from the navy and Pan Am Airlines. In 1931, Sikorsky introduced the largest passenger plane built in the United States, the S-40 flying boat (later succeeded by the S-42). Pan Am used these flying boats on its Latin American and transatlantic routes and, at the time, were the ultimate in luxury flying. Sikorsky correctly believed that only these big planes could compete against passenger rail travel, providing comparable seating, lavatories, and service with that of the Pullman cars.

After moving its operation to Stratford, Connecticut, the company was bought by United Aircraft and Transport Corporation in 1929. United was a huge conglomerate that had also absorbed Boeing Airplane Company, Boeing Air Transport, Inc., Pratt & Whitney, Stearman, and Chance Vought, to name but a few. It gave Sikorsky some stability and he began work again on developing a practical helicopter. In 1939 he flew his VS-300, which set the standard for helicopter design, using a large rotor blade on top for lift and propulsion and a smaller tail rotor to counteract torque. Although its use was limited, his helicopter, the R-4, did see some action in World War II as a rescue craft in the South Pacific.

After World War II, there were many optimistic predictions of a helicopter in every garage, as a *Popular Mechanics* magazine cover depicted in February 1951. Sikorsky himself certainly believed that the potential for helicopters as urban commuters was not far-fetched. The machine would contribute to the depopulation of the city, as workers could live in the country and conveniently fly to work. Ultimately, logistics such as traffic restrictions in urban areas and high operating costs impeded the success of that vision. However, small utility helicopters in the civilian sector have proven to be very significant. Sikorsky envisioned a necessity for a small, mobile flying machine that could get to remote and urban areas alike in order to save lives and help with search and rescue. He was right. Helicopters are used to travel to oil rigs in the ocean, can land in mountains and difficult terrain, are heavily used by the coast guard in search and rescue, help put out forest fires, and are used by most hospitals to medivac patients and organs.

In addition to civilian uses, Sikorsky also advocated that the army could use the helicopter as flying cavalry to place troops behind enemy lines, thus seizing the advantage. The U.S. Army was interested in the machine so that it would not have to rely on the air force for close air support. Its value was proven during the Vietnam conflict, as the infantry commuted back and forth to war via the "Huey." The air force also utilized the helicopter in a variety of ways. One of particular note was the Sikorsky HH-3E "Jolly Green Giant," used by the U.S. Air Force in their Rescue and Recovery Service during the Vietnam conflict. The pilots of this helicopter risked their own lives daily to save the lives of soldiers wounded in the field.

Sikorsky retired from Sikorsky Aircraft in 1957, but kept a close relationship with the company up until his death on October 26, 1972.

Further Reading: Sikorsky, Igor. *The Story of the Winged-S.* New York: Dodd, Mead, 1944.

Valerie L. Adams

SILKO, LESLIE MARMON (1948–)

A mix of Laguna Pueblo, Keresan Pueblo, Mexican, and Anglo ancestry, Leslie Silko was born in Albuquerque on March 5, 1948, and grew up at Laguna Pueblo in northern New Mexico. She received her B.A. degree at the University of New Mexico in 1969.

Best known for her landmark work, *Ceremony*, Silko together with **Navarre Scott Momaday**, author of *House Made of Dawn*, virtually created Native American literature, mixing traditional Native American oral storytelling with Western literature's use of the novel and using it to promote renewed cultural pride while critiquing mainstream society. Both also produced highly acclaimed novels about the alienation of World War II Native American veterans that many saw as allegories about both the Vietnam War and the Indian Wars.

Other works by Silko include her collection of poetry, *Laguna Woman; The Man to Send Rain Clouds*, with seven of her short stories; and *Almanac of the Dead*, with its depiction of Western culture as failing and indigenous cultures returning to ascendancy in the Americas, juxtaposing a doomed Western city and Laguna Pueblo before the arrival of missionaries.

Silko also founded the Laguna Film Project, filming and producing *Arrowboy and the Witches*. She was named a Living Cultural Treasure by the New Mexico Humanities Council and also received the Native Writers' Circle of the Americas Lifetime Achievement Award.

Further Reading: "Laguna Woman." Accessed January 8, 2005, at www.richmond. edu/~rnelson/woman.html; "Leslie Marmon Silko." Accessed January 8, 2005, at http://www.utm.edu/stafflinks/lalexand/ceremony.htm; "Voices from the Gap: Leslie Marmon Silko." Accessed January 8, 2005, at http://voices.cla.umn.edu/newsite/authors/silkolesliemarmon.htm.

Al Carroll

SIMMONS, HEZZLETON ERASTUS (1885–1954)

Rubber was both a scarce and vital commodity during World Wars I and II. Hezzleton Simmons was one of the nation's foremost authorities on the chemistry of rubber and as such, made important contributions to America's war efforts on the home front.

Simmons was born in Lafayette, Ohio, on January 3, 1885. He finished his undergraduate degree in chemistry in 1908 at Buchtel College (later the University of Akron). After completing his master's degree in chemistry at the University of Pennsylvania in 1910, Simmons returned to Akron as an assistant professor. Two years later he became a full professor. By the time America entered World War I, Simmons' lectures on rubber chemistry were themselves valuable commodities in the training of those involved in rubber production. The lectures were published as *Rubber Manufacture: The Cultivation, Chemistry, Testing and Manufacture of Rubber* in 1921. The book included sections on recycling rubber and manufacturing rubber substitutes.

Simmons remained at the University of Akron throughout his career, which culminated in his assuming the presidency of the university in 1933. Although somewhat removed from primary rubber research when the United States entered World War II, he nevertheless served the war effort by joining the War Production Board's Rubber Branch as associate chief. Serving in that capacity from 1942 until 1944, Simmons helped to form the government-sponsored rubber research program.

Simmons retired from the University of Akron in 1951. He died on December 30, 1954.

Benjamin F. Shearer

SIMMONS, RUSSELL (1957–)

Entrepreneur Russell Simmons was born to a middle-class family on October 4, 1957, in Queens, New York. He attended the Harlem branch of City College of New York in the mid-1970s, but dropped out to begin promoting local rap groups such as Run DMC, which included his older brother, Joseph. In 1984, he joined with Rick Rubin to form Def Jam Records, a pioneering hip-hop label. Defending his rap artists against critics, Simmons argued that rappers "keep it real" and generally provide positive role models for black youth. Def Jam Records also found a large audience in the white suburbs.

Def Jam was only one part of the Simmons empire. Rush Communications included a clothing company called Phat Farm, television shows such as *Def Comedy Jam*, and a movie production company. In 1999, Simmons sold DefJam for $100 million, and in 2004, he sold Phat Farm for $140 million.

Simmons used his fortune to fund the Hip-Hop Summit Action Network (HSAN), employing hip-hop music to encourage education and address social concerns for at-risk youth. HSAN worked to increase youth participation and registration for the 2004 election. Simmons is also an outspoken vegan, who participated in campaigns against the slaughterhouse policies of Kentucky Fried Chicken. In 2004, he joined with Musicians United to Win without War, an industrywide peace alliance, to oppose U.S. military action in Iraq.

Further Reading: Simmons, Russell, and Nelson George. *Life and Def: Sex, Drugs, Money and God.* Pittsburgh: Three Rivers Press, 2002.

Ron Briley

SIMMS, WILLIAM GILMORE (1806–1870)

William Gilmore Simms was a prolific writer whose depictions of Southern society influenced the region's cultural identity. Born on April 17, 1806, in Charleston, South Carolina, Simms was raised by his maternal grandmother after his mother died and his father relocated to frontier Mississippi. Indifferently schooled, Simms developed his deep attachment to the South through extensive travel and reading.

Simms began his career editing literary journals. He achieved general recognition during 1834 and 1835 for historical novels. Over the next decades, Simms wrote in several genres and actively promoted southern literature. He acquired a wide circle of literary and political friends. While Simms frequently visited northern publishers, he resided contently on a South Carolina plantation after marrying a planter's daughter.

Staunchly proslavery, Simms experienced the increasing sectional polarization in 1856 when a lecture he gave in the North on southern sensibilities provoked newspaper censure. Over the next decade, Simms endured the deaths of his wife and several children as well as the burning of his home. Despite wartime travails, Simms unwaveringly supported the Confederacy. His unconquerable spirit animates *Sack and Destruction of the City of Columbia, S. C.* (1865), written immediately after the city's notorious burning following Union occupation.

Stigmatized by northerners, Simms struggled after the war to generate income through his writing. He died on June 11, 1870.

Further Reading: Simms, William G. *The Letters of William Gilmore Simms.* Edited by Mary C. Simms Oliphant et al. 6 vols. Columbia: University of South Carolina Press, 1952–1982.

William M. Ferraro

SIMON, BOB (1941–)

As a correspondent for CBS news, Bob Simon covered crises, war, and unrest from sixty-seven countries. He chronicled the withdrawal of American troops from Vietnam, the Yom Kippur War in 1973, and the student unrest in Tiananmen Square before being captured by Iraqi troops during the Persian Gulf War in 1991.

Simon and four of his TV crew were captured when they crossed from Saudi Arabia into Iraqi-occupied Kuwait on the fifth day of the air campaign in Iraq and spent forty days in an Iraqi prison. For most of his imprisonment, he was held in solitary confinement and suspected of spying. Simon said subsequently that it was a careless mistake that he and the film crew crossed the border.

By the time the Persian Gulf War began, he was the chief Middle East correspondent for CBS, a position he had held for four years. Born in the Fort Apache section of the Bronx on May 29, 1941, he graduated with a history degree from Brandeis University and joined CBS in 1967. He transferred to the London bureau in 1969, then to the Saigon bureau. In the early 1980s, he was a State Department correspondent in Washington, DC, and in 1982 he became a national correspondent based in New York. He was named chief Middle Eastern correspondent in 1987.

After his release from Iraqi prison in 1991, he wrote a book, *Forty Days*, about the experience. He became a correspondent for CBS' *60 Minutes* in 1996 and, in 1999, for *60 Minutes II*.

Agnes Hooper Gottlieb

SINATRA, FRANCIS ALBERT (1915–1998)

Frank Sinatra was a memorable performer as well as a mercurial personality. Born on December 12, 1915, in Hoboken, New Jersey, Sinatra's first brushes with music happened when his uncle gifted him with a ukulele. On a fateful day in 1936, when Sinatra went to a Bing Crosby performance, he decided intuitively to become a singer.

Pursuing his dream with strong dedication, he grabbed any and every opportunity to sing, from amateur nights to local radio stations and traveling bands. Admiration and fame followed as he developed a distinctively spontaneous and emotive crooning style. E. J. Kahn, writing in the *New Yorker* (November 2, 1946), attributed Sinatra's popularity to World War II, observing that young women "turned to him as compensation for the absence of their young men."

In 1943, the crooner debuted in films with *Higher and Higher* (RKO). In 1945, he played himself in *The House I Live In* (RKO), a short musical drama about religious and racial tolerance. Sinatra hoped that the social unity America achieved in wartime would continue after the war. The film won a special Academy Award.

Sinatra was a quietly generous man who never tolerated any kind of racial prejudice. He received the Jean Hersholt Humanitarian Award (1971) for his various contributions to charity over the years. With numerous awards to his credit and countless admirers, he died

Frank Sinatra in *From Here to Eternity*. Courtesy of Photofest.

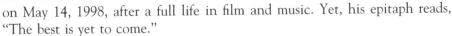

on May 14, 1998, after a full life in film and music. Yet, his epitaph reads, "The best is yet to come."

Jitendra Uttam

SINCLAIR, UPTON BEALL (1878–1968)

Upton Sinclair is best known today for his novel *The Jungle*, which exposed abuses in the meat packing industry and was instrumental in passing of the federal Pure Food and Drug Act of 1906. He was born in Baltimore on September 20, 1878, and was writing pulp fiction even before he graduated from the City College of New York. *The Jungle* established him as a writer and a muckraking socialist in 1905. Sinclair broke with his fellow socialists, however, over World War I. His 1919 book *Jimmie Higgins* was a somewhat veiled fictionalization of his personal disillusionment with socialism. Sinclair favored the war because of German aggression.

Breaking with socialism did not mean ceasing social action. When over six hundred striking union longshoremen and dockworkers in southern California were arrested in April 1923 for peacefully protesting on the private property they named "Liberty Hill," an outraged Sinclair applied for a speaking permit,

Upton Sinclair. Courtesy of the Library of Congress.

which was denied, and continued the protest on May 15 by reading the Bill of Rights. He was promptly arrested, before he could finish the First Amendment. The charges against Sinclair and the three other men were dropped, and all but twenty-eight of the six hundred strikers were released from jail as a result of Sinclair's public protest. Sinclair later ran for California governor 1934, and lost by a narrow margin.

Sinclair's Lanny Budd novels of World War II were pro-war. He eventually abandoned socialism completely and became anticommunist. Sinclair died on November 25, 1968.

Pamela Lee Gray

SKILLIN, EDWARD JR. (1904–2000)

Edward Skillin Jr. was editor and publisher of *Commonweal*, a lay Catholic magazine independent of the Catholic Church and founded in 1924. He was born in New York City on January 23, 1904, but was raised in Glen Ridge, New Jersey. After receiving a bachelor's degree from Williams College, Skillin earned a master's degree in political science from Columbia University in 1933, the same year he joined the staff of *Commonweal*. He served as editor from 1938 to 1967 and publisher from 1967 until he retired in 1998.

Skillin, an undaunted liberal, helped shift the magazine to a more socially attuned and renewal-minded vision of an open and pluralistic Catholic Church. In the first issue under Skillin's editorship, Skillin and his co-editor declared their recognition of the importance of movements among industrial workers, farm laborers, and the underprivileged. At the same time, they asserted opposition to both fascism and Marxist communism. Over the next several decades, Skillin kept discourse civil while leading *Commonweal* through a series of political controversies. *Commonweal* refused to join in the U.S. Catholic admiration for Francisco Franco during the Spanish Civil War. As a member of the National Peace Conference and the Catholic Association for International Peace, Skillin backed isolationism. Once the U.S. government entered World War II, *Commonweal* condemned area bombing and the use of atomic weapons. Under Skillin's editorship *Commonweal* opposed McCarthyism and supported resistance to U.S. involvement in Vietnam. Skillin died on August 14, 2000.

Further Reading: Bredeck, Martin J. *Imperfect Apostles: The Commonweal and the American Catholic Laity, 1924–1976*. New York: Garland Publishing, 1988.

David M. Carletta

SKINNER, CLARENCE RUSSELL (1881–1949)

Clarence Skinner, widely regarded as one of the most influential Universalists of his time, was born in Brooklyn on March 23, 1881, into a family of Universalists. He studied for the ministry at St. Lawrence College and was ordained in 1906, serving as secretary on the Commission for Social Services.

After ordination, Skinner led the Universalist Church of Mt. Vernon, New York, until 1911, and then moved to Grace Universalist Church in Lowell, Massachusetts. In 1914, Skinner accepted a position as Professor of Applied Christianity at the Crane Theological School of Tufts College. While there, Skinner published *The Social Implications of Universalism*, in which he more broadly and radically interpreted the Social Gospel, an ecumenical movement for social and economic justice, than did the traditional Protestant denominations, in fact verging on socialism.

After the United States entered World War I in 1917, Skinner was criticized for his publicly held views on pacifism. While defended by the dean of the Theological School, Skinner's socialistic views eventually resulted in termination of a ministry at a nearby Universalist Church, and an investigation by the District Attorney of Massachusetts. During World War I and the early interwar period, pacifism and socialism were clearly linked in the public mind as dangerous and subversive ideas. Skinner's views did not change, but by the time the United States entered into World War II, his pacifism prompted no public attacks. Skinner died on August 27, 1949.

Further Reading: Dictionary of Unitarian and Universalist Biography. "Clarence Russell Skinner." Accessed May 2005 at http://www.uua.org/uuhs/duub/articles/clarencerussellskinner.html.

Mike Timonin

SMALL, LYNDON FREDERICK (1897–1957)

As editor-in-chief of the *Journal of Organic Chemistry* since 1938, Lyndon F. Small was already an admired chemist when World War II took him away from his primary research in morphine chemistry to develop substitutes for quinine. Born in Allston, Massachusetts, on August 16, 1897, Small graduated from Dartmouth in 1920, received his master's degree from Harvard in 1922, and his Ph.D. from the Massachusetts Institute of Technology in 1926. After studying further abroad, he became a researcher in the University of Virginia's chemistry department.

James Bryant Conant, with whom Small had studied at MIT, recommended him to direct the Drug Addiction Laboratory, which was established at the

University of Virginia by the National Research Council's Division of Medical Sciences in 1929. For ten years, Small led a research group who tried to separate the beneficial pain-killing qualities of opiates from their addictive qualities. They found success in an opiate derivative called Metopon. Small was known to keep the hundreds of opiates he prepared for further evaluation in cigar boxes.

Preparing for war, the National Institutes of Health requested Small and his group to move to Bethesda, Maryland, and change their research focus to the development of antimalarials. Here again, the research group found success, developing numerous effective substitutes for quinine and other drugs. Malaria left untreated would decimate troops in the field, notably in the Pacific theater.

Small returned to his original research interests after the war. He died on June 15, 1957.

Benjamin F. Shearer

SMITH, GERALD LYMAN KENNETH (1898–1976)

Gerald L. K. Smith was a Disciples of Christ minister and a follower of both Father **Charles Edward Coughlin** and Huey Long. Born in Pardeeville, Wisconsin, on February 27, 1898, Smith was ordained in 1916. He moved to Louisiana in 1928 and began broadcasting over the radio. Smith had a reputation as an outstanding orator, and he ran the "Share Our Wealth" program for a time after Huey Long's 1935 assassination. Smith, Coughlin, and Francis Townsend formed the Union Party for the 1936 presidential election. Getting only 2 percent of the vote, the party disbanded.

Smith lost his job with Share Our Wealth because of his white supremacy and links to the isolationist America First Committee. He became leader of the America First Party and candidate for the U.S. Senate from Michigan. He ran for president in 1944 and again in 1956. His periodical, *The Cross and the Flag*, was among the first to express Christian Identity ideas.

Smith belonged to William Dudley Pelly's fascist Christian American Patriots, the Silver Shirts. In 1942 the federal government brought indictments against native fascist individuals and groups, including the America First Committee. The government's conspiracy charge was impossible to prove, the judge died, and a mistrial was declared after eight months. The case was dismissed in 1946.

Smith was a Holocaust denier and increasingly rabid anti-Semite after World War II. He started building a religious theme park in Hot Springs, Arkansas, in 1964 and died of pneumonia on April 15, 1976.

Further Reading: Jeansonne, Glen. *Gerald L. K. Smith: Minister of Hate.* New Haven: Yale University Press, 1988.

John H. Barnhill

SMITH, HORACE (1808–1893)

Horace Smith, along with **Daniel Wesson**, developed a pistol and metal cartridge for it that they manufactured together. Smith was born on October 28, 1808, in Cheshire, Massachusetts. His family moved to Springfield, Massachusetts, in 1812 where his father worked in the United States armory. As he was growing up, Smith would assist his father at the armory and at age sixteen became an apprentice at the armory and remained working there for eighteen years. After that Smith worked for a number of different arms manufacturers and from 1846 to 1849 produced his own gun. In 1853, he met Daniel Wesson and they began to work together.

Smith and Wesson first developed a repeating rifle, but never pursued production it. Over the next several years they developed, patented and then sold the rights to several improvements to the rifle they had developed. In 1856, they began producing a pistol that used a metal cartridge, which they had designed. They were then issued a patent in 1860 for a metal cartridge that they had invented for their pistol. Over the following years they made a number of other improvements to the pistol they had patented. Their pistol was extremely popular. After twenty years of working together, Smith sold his part of the business to Wesson in July 1873.

Smith was married three times, the last time to Mary Lucretia Hebbard on February 5, 1873. He died on January 15, 1893 in Springfield, Massachusetts.

Dallace W. Unger Jr.

SMITH, J. ANDRE (1880–1959)

The leader of eight official war artists during World War I, J. Andre Smith was the most prolific of the battlefront recorders. Born in Hong Kong in 1880, Smith moved to New York for his education after his father died in 1887. He received a master's degree in architecture from Cornell University in 1904 and practiced in that field for several years before deciding to pursue art professionally. He was known for his painting and for his etching as well as for his lightning-fast technique and ability to finish a work in a single sitting. As World War I began, he entered the army as a first lieutenant with the Engineer Reserve Corps; when he was selected for the art assignment with the American Expeditionary Force, he was promoted to captain. As the only one of the eight to have any military training, he was chosen to lead the group. He was the first in France, arriving on March 15, 1918.

At the front, when the artists were criticized for lack of productivity or battlefront action, Smith defended them to his superiors in Washington, claiming that the mostly sedate artwork they were supplying was the truest representation of life at the front.

After the war, Smith published a book called *In France with the A.E.F.*, showcasing over a hundred pieces of his own work. He hoped that the book would help launch his postwar freelance career, which indeed it did. He died in 1959.

Ellen Baier

SMITH, ROY LEMON (1887–1963)

Roy L. Smith, editor of the *Christian Advocate* and a prominent minister, opposed what he saw as American hysteria about war. Smith was born in Nickerson, Kansas, on January 28, 1887. He graduated from Southwestern College in nearby Winfield in 1908 and earned a Bachelor of Divinity degree from Garrett Bible Institute in 1915. He became a Methodist minister, working at congregations in Kansas, Chicago, and Minneapolis, as well as writing columns for the *Chicago Tribune* and the *Minneapolis Star*. In 1935, he was voted one of the seven most representative Methodist ministers in America.

From 1940 to 1948, Smith edited the *Christian Advocate*, a weekly that boasted the largest circulation of any Protestant denominational newspaper. Smith argued in a series of 1941 editorials that American clergy had been victims of pro-war propaganda in World War I, and that "the hope of peace lies, not in damning Hitler and the Nazis, but in setting our own house in order before God." He advocated Christianity as an antidote to growing nationalism, both at home and abroad. This revulsion with war accompanied concern for social issues at home. In 1948, in the early stages of the Cold War, Smith admonished the General Conference of the Methodist Church that, if Christianity was to defeat communism, it must offer more hope of a better life, including practical benefits such as sanitary housing.

Smith's numerous books were popular in their day. He died in San Bernardino, California, in April of 1963.

Wende Vyborney Feller

SMITH (SAID), STEPHAN (1971?–)

Stephan Smith's song "The Bell" gave voice to anti-war sentiments as the United States was considering going to war with Iraq. Both lyrically and melodically, he followed in the vein of **Pete Seeger** (who joined Smith on the recording), **Woodrow "Woody" Wilson Guthrie**, and Phil Ochs, who on occasion used deceptively simple imagery and rhythm to underscore points of political and social opinion. Smith was born in Cleveland, Ohio. His mother is an Austrian Jew and his father is Iraqi; Smith credits his family background for his calling to write songs of confrontation and social justice.

Smith grew up in West Virginia playing in fiddle contests, absorbing the music of the American south along with music from his parents' international families. At the same time, he was involved in punk music, quitting high school to tour with a punk band. Later he spent time as a migrant worker across the United States and traveled as a hobo around Europe before relocating to New York. There he began to listen to the music of Guthrie and **Bob Dylan**, and met beat poet **Allen Ginsberg** and folk protest legend Seeger. Pulling his varied musical and sonic stories together, Smith released the albums *Now's the Time* (Rounder) in 1997, *New World Wonder* (Universal Hobo), which includes "The Bell," in 1999, and *Slash and Burn* (Artemis) in 2004. "The Bell" has also been released as an extended play disc (EP) with video.

Kerry Dexter

SOUSA, JOHN PHILIP (1854–1932)

Composer John Philip Sousa, known as the "March King," was born in Washington, DC, on November 6, 1854, to John Antonio and Maria Elisabeth Trinkhaus Sousa. His father played trombone in the U.S. Marine Band. By the time he was six years old, Sousa had started learning to play musical instruments including the violin, piano, flute, and trombone. When he was just thirteen years old, his father sent him to the marines as an apprentice. Sousa briefly left the marines though he returned in 1880 to become leader of the marine band. He remained in this role until 1892 when he left to form his own concert band.

While returning to America from a trip to Europe, Sousa was inspired to compose the song, "The Stars and Stripes Forever," on December 25, 1896. The song quickly became the official march of the United States. Another 1896 Sousa composition, the "El Capitan March," was played to send off the ships going to fight in the Philippines.

Sousa's band made several European tours in the years before World War I. In 1917, Sousa joined the U.S. Naval Reserve at the age of sixty-two. Inventor of the sousaphone

John Philip Sousa. Courtesy of the Library of Congress.

and one of America's most famous composers and conductors, Sousa died on March 6, 1932, in Reading, Pennsylvania, after conducting a final band rehearsal. The last piece Sousa conducted was "The Stars and Stripes Forever."

Further Reading: Delaplaine, Edward S. *John Philip Sousa and the National Anthem.* Frederick, MD: Great Southern Press, 1983.

Nicole Mitchell

SPARKS, WILLIAM JOSEPH (1905–1976)

With the closing of shipping lines from the start of World War II, natural rubber was in short supply. While the U.S. government intervened to assure synthetic rubber production in government plants, scientists all over the country scurried to find the formulae for effective man-made products. William Sparks and his colleague, Robert Thomas, at Esso Research and Engineering developed butyl rubber and found a way to mass-produce it by 1943.

Sparks was born in Wilkinson, Indiana, on February 26, 1905. He got his chemistry degree in 1926 and a Master of Arts degree in 1929 from Indiana University. When he finished his doctorate in chemistry at the University of Illinois in 1936, he joined the Standard Oil Development Company, which became Esso and then Exxon. Sparks left Esso in 1939 to work at the Department of Agriculture's Northern Regional Research Lab, but he went back to Esso a year later to work on synthetic rubber and remained there in positions of increasing importance until he retired in 1967. Sparks died on October 23, 1976.

Standard Oil had been making a product called Vistanex, which was an additive to grease and oil, since 1933. It was known to have some qualities of rubber, but it lacked elasticity and strength. One day in 1937, Sparks and Thomas added butadiene to a mixture of Vistanex and butyl rubber was suddenly created. Butyl rubber is the flexible, airtight rubber found in inner tubes.

Benjamin F. Shearer

SPEDDING, FRANK HAROLD (1902–1984)

Elected to the National Academy of Sciences in 1952, Frank Spedding was a major figure in the Manhattan Project, America's World War II effort to produce an atomic bomb. Born in Hamilton, Ontario, on October 22, 1902, Spedding held a bachelor's degree in chemical engineering and a master's in analytical chemistry from the University of Michigan. He earned his doctorate in physical chemistry at the University of California at Berkeley in 1929. After fellowships and two years as an instructor at Berkeley and another two years at Cornell, Spedding went to Iowa State University, where he remained until his death on December 15, 1984, having taken emeritus status in 1973.

When **Arthur Holly Compton**, who headed the Chicago Manhattan Project at the University of Chicago, determined that chemists were needed, he invited Spedding, an expert on rare earth elements, to head the Chemistry Division in 1942. Spedding divided his time between Ames, Iowa, and Chicago, but owing to space limitations in Chicago, he formed a team at Iowa. There Spedding's team undertook the problem of processing uranium to the purity needed for the critical reaction. By November 1942, the team had perfected the process and delivered two tons of uranium for the reactor at Chicago. A month later the desired reaction was attained with Spedding's processed uranium. Within a few months, the scientists at Ames produced over 2 million tons of the purified product. In 1947 the Atomic Energy Commission opened the Ames Laboratory with Spedding as its director to continue his groundbreaking work.

Benjamin F. Shearer

SPENCE, DAVID (1881–1957)

David Spence was one of the pioneers of rubber chemistry. Born in Udny, Scotland, on September 26, 1881, he earned his Ph.D. at the University of Jena in 1906. In 1909 he left the university of Liverpool to join the Diamond Rubber Company in Akron, Ohio, as director of its research laboratories. B.F. Goodrich Company bought out Diamond in 1912, but Spence stayed on until 1914, when he and a partner started the Norwalk Tire & Rubber Company. Spence was vice president and general manager of Norwalk until 1925. He left Norwalk to become vice president for research and development at International Rubber Company in New York. Walker retired to California in 1931 to do rubber research independently, but returned to New York in 1952.

A few years before World War I broke out in Europe, natural rubber prices had spiked up owing to heavy demand. This began the search in America for a synthetic rubber. Spence, while still at Diamond Rubber, successfully synthesized isoprene to be used in synthetic rubber that he produced on a small scale. Over his career, Spence had found processes to vulcanize and devulcanize rubber, dye it, extract it from guayule, and change its qualities. He was the first recipient of the American Chemical Society's Charles Goodyear Medal in 1941.

Spence headed the National Research Council's Rubber Division during World War I and was a consultant to the War Production Board during World War II. He died on September 24, 1957.

Benjamin F. Shearer

SPENCER, CHRISTOPHER M. (1833–1922)

Christopher M. Spencer invented a repeating rifle in 1860 that was used by the Union during the Civil War. Born on June 20, 1833, in Manchester, Connecticut, Spencer developed a love for working on mechanical devices. He worked in a number of different fields until 1854 when he went to work for the Colt armory and became interested in the idea of a repeating rifle. After working for Colt, he invented an automatic silk-spooling machine.

Spencer finally built a wooden version of his repeating rifle. With encouragement, he built a working model and patented it on March 6, 1860. The rifle, an improvement over the muzzle-loading rifles that most of the troops used at that time, was tested and ordered by the Union Army. The Spencer could hold seven bullets, reloaded in half the time of a muzzle-loader, was accurate to two thousand yards, and was very reliable.

In May 1861, Spencer sold his rights to the design, but continued to work at the plant and received a royalty. He also turned his attention to other inventions, developing a horseless carriage (1862), a repeating shotgun (1866), an automatic turret lathe (1873), and pump action guns (1882).

Spencer married Frances Theodora Peck in June 1860, but she died in 1881. On July 3, 1883, he married Georgette T. Rogers and had four children with her. Spencer remained active until his death on January 14, 1922.

Further Reading: Gies, Joseph, and Frances Gies. *The Ingenious Yankees.* New York: Thomas Y. Cromwell, 1976.

Dallace W. Unger Jr.

SPERRY, ELMER AMBROSE (1860–1930)

Elmer Sperry's active gyroscope became a central technology for submarine warfare, aerial warfare, and accurate gunnery. He also sold arc lights to the U.S. Navy during World War I.

Born October 12, 1860, on a farm in Cortland County, New York, Sperry spent his youth exploring how equipment worked. His first invention was reputedly a superior horseradish grater, developed for his aunt at age six. At twenty, he completed his studies at the local State Normal School. The same year, he developed an arc light system that would be the first of numerous inventions. His first venture, Sperry Electric Illuminating and Power Company, enjoyed initial success in Chicago. However, the company failed within its first five years, despite well-publicized successes at the World's Fair of 1892. Sperry sold his patents to General Electric. While in Chicago, he also married Zula Goodman, daughter of a local Baptist deacon, in 1887.

For the next two decades after the arc light venture, Sperry moved from one invention and start-up company to the next, dabbling successfully in electric rail cars, electric automobiles, automobile batteries, chemical manufacturing, lead purification, and chrome detinning. Around 1907, his interest shifted to gyroscopes, a technology that had caught his interest when he needed a way to stabilize his electric automobiles.

French physicist Leon Foucault originally invented the gyroscope in 1852. It is simply a heavy, spinning wheel mounted so that its axis can reorient itself freely. If the wheel's mounting is moved or turned, the spinning wheel will remain in the same orientation to the earth. (This principle is why it is possible to stay balanced on a unicycle.)

Gyroscopes were wanted by the U.S. Navy to stabilize ships. Sperry's gyroscope was the first to predict the ship's roll actively and prevent the undesirable motion before it started. By 1908, Sperry was working on modifying his gyroscope into a gyrocompass, in which a device mounted to the axis of the gyroscope is given a high degree of friction. When the friction limits the gyroscope's movement, it orients its axis toward true north. A gyrocompass thus provides more accurate navigation than a magnetic compass, which orients to magnetic north. As ships became constructed of iron rather than wood, the iron in the hulls also interfered with magnetic compasses.

Sperry's gyrocompass was tried in the Brooklyn Navy Yard on the U.S.S. *Delaware* in 1910, and then tested at sea in 1911. During World War I, the device was used by all of the Allies' navies, and it was later sold to more than sixty steamship lines. It ultimately became part of the standard automatic pilot system for U.S. Navy ships. The device was nicknamed "Metal Mike."

Among Sperry's navy contracts was also one for development of a gyroscopic stabilizer and autopilot for airplanes. This technology was not fully developed until 1930, although it won an award from the French government as early as 1913. The airplane stabilizer was first installed in commercial planes in 1933 and was widely used by the U.S. military in World War II. Gyroscopes also make it possible to aim artillery accurately from moving platforms such as ships and planes.

Arc lights returned to prominence in Sperry's work for the navy during World War I. Starting in 1914, he developed a high-intensity arc light with one billion candlepower, the strength needed to match the range of naval turret guns. These lights were also used in London and Paris as search lights to scan for incoming enemy planes. In peacetime they were used for flood lighting and beacons at airports.

Sperry's work in the 1920s also encompassed an automatic car transmission, signaling and sighting devices for the military, a device to detect flaws in rail tracks, and improvements to the diesel engine. He held more than four-hundred patents by his death in Brooklyn on June 16, 1930. He had also received numerous awards, including two medals each from the czar of Russia and the emperor of Japan. Sperry also was one of the founders of the American Electrochemical Society and the American Institute of Electrical Engineers.

Sperry Gyroscope, founded in 1910, became Sperry Corporation in 1933, Sperry Rand in 1955, and Unisys in 1986. Sperry's gyroscope technology remains fundamental to guiding missiles.

Further Reading: Hughes, Thomas Parke. *Elmer Sperry: Inventor and Engineer.* Baltimore: Johns Hopkins University Press, 1971.

Wende Vyborney Feller

SPILHAUS, ATHELSTAN FREDERICK (1911–1998)

Athelstan Spilhaus received the Legion of Merit award in 1946 for his research during World War II. In 1937, he had invented the bathythermograph (BT), a device for measuring water temperature and pressure as it passed through ocean depths, in the hope of learning more about ocean currents and deep-water life. **Columbus O'Donnell Iselin** developed the BT into a sonar device for the U.S. Navy that would allow submarines to hide from as well as to find enemy ships. The BT was used extensively during the war. Spilhaus, however, went on during the war to develop meteorological instruments for aircraft and do research on radar and radio.

Spilhaus was born near Capetown, South Africa, on November 25, 1911. He got his undergraduate engineering degree at the University of Capetown in 1931, his master's at MIT in 1933, and his doctorate from Capetown in 1948. Spilhaus' long relationship with the Woods Hole Oceanographic Institute began in 1936, when he left MIT. He organized New York University's department of meteorology beginning in 1942, where he continued to make contributions to the war effort. He became a U.S. citizen in 1946.

Spilhaus' many positions included president of the American Association for the Advancement of Science (1970), president of the Franklin Institute (1967–1969), U.S. representative to UNESCO (1954–1958), and scientific director of weapons effects for atomic tests in Nevada (1951). The air force awarded him its Exceptional Civilian Service Award in 1952. Spilhaus died on March 30, 1998.

Benjamin F. Shearer

SPILLER, EDWARD N. (1825–1871)

Edward Spiller and **David Judson Burr** started firearms company Spiller & Burr that made pistols for the Confederate States during the Civil War. Spiller was born in 1825 near the town of Washington, Virginia. He married a woman from Harrisonburg, Virginia. Before the war he was a teacher until he moved to Baltimore, Maryland, and got involved in the dry goods business. When the war began he moved his business to Richmond, Virginia.

The Confederate government was sorely in need of its own arms-manufacturing capability. When Spiller and Burr, both wealthy businessmen, were asked by the government to create a business to make arms for the Confederacy, they jumped at the opportunity for easy profit. Since Spiller did not know much about making firearms, he relied on small arms expert and partner James Burton. When Burton was transferred to Atlanta, Georgia, Spiller and Burr moved their company to there also. What would become the Spiller and Burr pistol was based on Burton's selection of one of **Eli Whitney Jr.**'s .36 caliber single-action revolvers as a model. While Spiller and Burr were to produce 15,000 pistols over two years by their contract, only about 1,500 were actually produced owing to labor and materials shortages.

The Confederate government purchased the company before Sherman arrived in Atlanta and moved production to Macon. After the war Spiller lived in Atlanta for a while, and finally moved back to Baltimore and started a second dry goods business. He died in 1871.

Dallace W. Unger Jr.

SPOCK, BENJAMIN MCLANE (1903–1998)

Well known for his liberal and assuring advice on child rearing, Dr. Benjamin Spock was an active Vietnam War protestor, arrested and convicted for helping young men circumvent the draft. Born on May 2, 1903, Spock grew up in New Haven, Connecticut, the eldest of six children, helping to parent his siblings, half-protecting them from an overly authoritative mother. He attended Phillips Academy at Andover and then Yale University, like his lawyer father before him. While in college, he won a place on the crew team, earning a gold medal at the 1924 Paris Olympics. He graduated at the top of his class from Columbia University's College of Physicians and Surgeons in 1929.

Dr. Benjamin Spock speaks at the Count Each Day war protest. Courtesy of Photofest.

A pediatric specialist and father of two sons, Spock wrote the wildly successful *The Common Sense Book of Baby and Child Care* in 1946 (originally for sale for only 25 cents), which rocketed him to public fame. The book, written in a warm and friendly tone, appealed to post-war parents cowed by the prevailing authoritarian methods of raising children. He recommended that parents trust in their own judgment, even above his own advice, and though critics scorned this liberal attitude, many young parents eagerly embraced it. During the 1950s and early 1960s, he taught child development courses at the University of Pittsburgh, the University of Minnesota, and Case Western Reserve University, and wrote several other books on childcare. He even hosted a television program that focused on advice to parents.

As both the Cold War and the Vietnam War escalated, Spock became more politically active. He served as a lieutenant commander in the naval reserve during World War II, and he had previously been rather approving of the American military agenda, in a lukewarm manner, but the nuclear arms race frightened him into action. He was against the development of nuclear weapons and opposed the American encroachment into the Vietnamese civil war, which he saw as unnecessary and imperialistic. The slogan "war is bad for children and other living things," may well have been coined to describe Spock's sentiments; he viewed his involvement in the peace movement as protecting the baby boom children his book had helped to raise. Though at first reluctant to alarm the parents he advised, he overcame his objections when President John F. Kennedy announced his intention to carry out more nuclear development and testing in response to Russia's tests of 1961. Ironically, Spock had supported and campaigned for Kennedy two years previously. In 1962, he became a member of the board of the National Committee for a

Sane Nuclear Policy (SANE), after publicly issuing warnings of the dangers that nuclear testing posed for children, pregnant women, and nursing mothers. He wrote letters of protest to the White House at first, but then began to join demonstrations with increasing enthusiasm.

Over six feet tall and in his late fifties at the start of his career as an agitator, Spock stood out in more than one way among the throngs of angry young people who were his fellow protestors. He connected with them, however, and in 1967, he was part of a group that collected over three hundred draft cards and returned the cards defiantly to the Department of Justice along with a petition entitled "A Call to Resist Illegitimate Authority," signed by over two thousand protestors, many of them prominent academics and clerics. Because of this act of protest, Spock and three of the four other loosely connected leaders were indicted, convicted, and sentenced to two years in prison for conspiring to aid and abet draft resisters, as violators of the United States Universal Military Training and Service Act. Rev. **William Sloane Coffin** Michael Ferber, Mitchell Goodman, and Marcus Raskin were the other four accused, and Raskin was the only one to avoid a conviction. The case was based on a total of eleven overt acts that the Department of Justice found compelling, of which the petition was the first. The prosecution also mentioned anti-war speeches made by each of the defendants around the time of the protest, a press conference held by all but Ferber, as well as the collection of draft cards from young men and the return of a briefcase full of those cards to the Department of Justice. In 1968, the case was reversed on appeal and all charges were dismissed.

Spock and the others were perfectly willing to go to prison for the cause, ready to test the legality of the draft—not to mention the war. In the petition he and the others wrote, the "Call to Resist," they called upon the "higher law" mentioned at the Nuremberg trials immediately after World War II, claiming that the American actions in Vietnam constituted war crimes, which were codified and condemned at the Geneva Conventions and ratified by the United States. The young men who declined to obey the draft were, therefore, not in the wrong: they were defying laws that they considered unjust, immoral, and unconstitutional. After the news of the indictment was released, Spock stated to a *New York Times* reporter that he hoped hundreds of thousands of young people would refuse to be party to the draft, and that patriotic Americans should throw President Lyndon Johnson out of office.

Detractors of the protest movement, particularly the virulently antagonistic Vice President Spiro Agnew, blamed Spock not only for his own anti-war actions, but also for corrupting children by creating the "spirit of permissiveness" that brought about the youngest generation of hippies. Spock, who of course approved of his fellow protestors' rebellion, retorted that at least he could not be blamed for Agnew's upbringing. Many, appalled by the lack of respect shown by the young and radical (to say nothing of the old and radical), echoed Agnew's view during the Vietnam War, but Spock believed that he had empowered the young to believe that their own opinions mattered, and that they had the right to act on their own beliefs. He could only take pride in fostering such a rebellious spirit.

In 1972, Spock ran for president, nominated by the People's Party. He earned over 75,000 votes on an ultra-liberal platform. He supported universal health care, a high minimum wage, the legalization of abortion and marijuana, and the immediate cessation of hostilities in Vietnam. During the 1980s and into the 1990s, Spock's involvement in anti-nuclear and pro-social welfare protests included many acts of trespassing, civil disobedience, and deliberate vandalism. He was arrested more than a dozen times between his sixtieth birthday and his ninety-fourth. During this time, he also found time to revise and update his original childcare book, which underwent seven editions, in the process becoming retitled *Dr. Spock's Baby and Child Care*. Over the years, most of the original sexism had been removed, and changing family structures and mores had been recognized, including an acceptance of divorce, blended families, and single, lesbian, and gay parents. Above all else, the book continually emphasized the importance of mutual respect between parent and child. Dr. Spock's book has, in the last sixty years, sold over 50 million copies and been translated into over forty-two languages. He died on March 16, 1998, having been active in demonstrations to the end of his life.

Further Reading: Bloom, Lynn Z. *Doctor Spock: Biography of a Conservative Radical.* Indianapolis: Bobbs-Merrill, 1972; Maier, Thomas. *Dr. Spock: An American Life.* New York: Harcourt Brace, 1998; Spock, Benjamin and Mary Morgan. *Spock on Spock.* New York: Pantheon, 1989.

Ellen Baier

STAFFORD, PATRICK P. (1954–)

Patrick Stafford is a poet and writer working to bring poetry to a deprived world. Born in Los Angeles on March 13, 1954, he went into the United States Marine Corps in 1971, attended the Armed Forces Institute, and served in Vietnam. Stafford attended the University of California—Irvine from 1980 to 1981 and set out on a career in which he could survive on his writing skills, settling down finally in Grants Pass, Oregon, where he lives with his wife, child, and novelist father. In 2002 Stafford gained notoriety with his publication of "Homage to a Princess," a poem dedicated to the memory of Britain's Princess Diana. He has written a number of poems, plays, and articles for various magazines and he has garnered several awards for his poetry.

Throughout his career Stafford has been writing poetry based on his experiences in Vietnam. In 2005, one hundred of these poems were published as an e-mail book under the title *Asian Darkness*. Taken as a whole, Stafford's poems in *Asian Darkness* juxtapose the contradictions of the Vietnam War that made it ineffable to many Americans and certainly to American soldiers fighting an unpopular war. In "Vietnam Thesis (1 Narrative)," for example, Stafford cleverly links warriors and cowards in Vietnam by choice or decree into a kindred group feeling guilt and shame rather than pride and honor, only to realize that they had two enemies, the North Vietnamese and the people on the home front who greeted them with scorn and showered them with apathy.

Benjamin F. Shearer

STANLEY, WENDELL MEREDITH (1904–1971)

Wendell Meredith Stanley performed valuable work for the government on the development of a virus vaccine during World War II, winning the Nobel Prize for chemistry in 1946. Born in Ridgeville, Indiana, on August 16, 1904, he received a B.S. (1926) in chemistry from Earlham College in Indiana, and then obtained an M.S. (1927) and Ph.D. (1929) from the University of Illinois, Champaign. After graduation, he was a National Research Fellow in Chemistry in Munich, Germany (1930–1931), returning in 1931 to the Rockefeller Institute for Medical Research in New York City, moving with the Institute to Princeton, New Jersey, the following year.

In 1942, Stanley worked on the Committee on Medical Research at the Office of Scientific Research and Development, created in 1941 to provide research in science and medicine for problems of national defense. There was no means of protection available against influenza and the government wanted to avoid the results of an outbreak similar to that in 1918 that led to the death of millions. The vaccine was successfully developed and adapted first for army use in 1945 and then for civilian use. In 1948, Stanley established a virus institute at the University of California—Berkeley, remaining there until 1969, when he returned to the Rockefeller Institute in Princeton until his death on June 16, 1971. His wife, Marian Stanley, was also a scientist. They had four children: a son, who followed in the same field, and three daughters. He held many other positions, including consultant to the secretary of war from 1945 to 1946.

Patricia Marton

STARR, EBENEZER "EBAN" TOWNSEND (1816–1899)

Ebenezer "Eban" Townsend Starr founded the Starr Arms Company of New York that produced pistols for the Union Army during the Civil War. He was born on August 18, 1816, in Middletown Connecticut. Starr joined the United States Navy at the age of seventeen and served until 1837. He married Almira Babcock on August 17, 1842, and they had two children.

Starr invented a breech-loading carbine that was produced by his company. Over 20,000 Starr 21 inch, .54 caliber barrel carbines, known to be completely reliable, were sold and delivered to the Union Army under contract for $25 each. Starr Arms was perhaps best known for its pistols. The first revolver was the double-action Starr D.A. model 1858 Navy .36-caliber for military use. The second, which led to a contract for 20,000, was the double-action, six-shot Starr D.A. model 1858 Army .44 caliber revolver, which weighed three pounds. In the midst of the war, however, competition forced Starr to make a cheaper and more efficient single-action revolver, the Starr S.A. model 1863 Army .44 caliber. By the end of 1864, Starr received another contract for 25,000 of these guns.

Starr Arms Company was so dependent on the sale of arms to the government that after the end of the war with no contracts, the company was out of business by the end of 1867 after eleven years of existence. Starr died on October 27, 1899, in Brooklyn, New York.

Dallace W. Unger Jr.

STEDMAN, EDMUND CLARENCE (1833–1908)

Born in Hartford, Connecticut, on October 8, 1833, Edmund Stedman attended Yale, where he published his first poem. He went on to edit newspapers, and by 1856 he was writing for popular magazines like *Harper's*. In 1860 he published a book of poetry and joined the editorial staff of the New York *World*, acting as its war correspondent from 1861 to 1863.

Stedman was also a Union Soldier. He sometimes took an active part in fighting the battles he covered. The high point of his Civil War campaigning was the first battle of Bull Run. In the spring of 1862, McClellan and his staff fed Stedman "news leaks" and in turn Stedman brought the *World* to support McClellan. After the failure of McClellan's peninsula campaign, Stedman lost confidence in him and called for new military leadership. His doubts about the *World*'s financial health and disapproval of its Copperhead (northern anti-war Democrats) leanings prompted him to accept a government clerkship in Washington, DC, in 1862.

Although Stedman continued to cover important battles for the *World*, his new Washington job marked the first step in his withdrawal from the conflict he had welcomed so enthusiastically. Stedman recognized that the war had changed everyone, including himself. In March 1863, Stedman wrote his brother of his discouragement at not being rich, or having high political or military office. In 1864, he opened his own successful brokerage business and continued his literary career as poet and critic.

Further Reading: Scholnick, Robert J. *Edmund Clarence Stedman*. Boston: Twayne Publishers, 1977.

Michael L. McGregor

STEINBECK, JOHN (1902–1968)

John Steinbeck, probably most famous for his novels *The Grapes of Wrath* and *Of Mice and Men*, also wrote scripts for war propaganda movies—*The Lifeboat, The Moon Is Down, A Medal for Benny*—during World War II. Steinbeck was born on February 27, 1902, in Salinas, California. In 1920, he entered Stanford University and remained there until 1925, but never graduated.

From Stanford Steinbeck moved to New York City. He worked as a manual laborer there, part of the time on the construction of Madison Square Garden. He attempted to publish his freelance writing, but was unsuccessful. Returning to California in 1926, Steinbeck was then able to publish three novels, starting in 1929. None of these, however, was either a critical or popular success. He married his first wife, Carol Henning, in 1930. Finally, in 1935, Steinbeck had his first success, *Tortilla Flat*, followed the next year by *Of Mice and Men*.

Steinbeck published his most famous novel, *The Grapes of Wrath*, in 1938. He received the Pulitzer Prize for this novel in 1940. This was also the year that the highly successful and critically acclaimed movie version of the book was released. 1941 signaled an important shift in subject matter for Steinbeck. It was the year that America entered World War II, after the bombing of Pearl Harbor in December. Steinbeck's creative output now focused on presenting wartime values, often of a propagandistic nature. Primarily, he would do this through the cinema.

Steinbeck's first war-related movie was based upon a book published in 1942 (his first book since *The Grapes of Wrath*) titled, *The Moon Is Down*. It appeared in stage form on Broadway for a short period, and then came out as a movie in 1943. In this movie, the setting is a village somewhere in the European theater of action. The Nazis have invaded the village and the plot revolves around the abuses of the Nazis and the courage of the villagers to resist. It is a clear-cut presentation of good verses evil. In the movie, resistance continues despite continued executions. One of the villagers reminds the audience: "The little people won't go under."

Also in 1943, Steinbeck went to work for the New York *Herald Tribune* as a war correspondent. For several months, he reported from England, North Africa and then went with the Allied forces as they invaded Italy. During the invasion, his eardrum burst from the shelling and he returned home. He would later publish these war dispatches in a book titled *Once There Was a War* (1958).

In 1944, another movie, *Lifeboat*, written by Steinbeck and directed by Alfred Hitchcock, was released. The movie was made at the behest of the Coast Guard that wanted the country to know how important the convoys in the North Atlantic were. The story was about the attack and sinking of a freighter by a German submarine, which was also destroyed. The survivors, including the Nazi submarine captain, are afloat together on a lifeboat. Unfortunately, Hitchcock changed Steinbeck's script in ways that angered Steinbeck and he disowned the movie. Nevertheless, the movie showed the evil nature of the Nazis and was popular.

Steinbeck's final wartime movie was *A Medal for Benny* (1945). The script was originally a collaborative effort between Steinbeck and Jack Wagner, but was reworked by others. Despite some bad reviews, the movie was popular, perhaps because it contained comedy, unlike the other movies, along with a strong dose of sentimental patriotism.

In addition to these movies, Steinbeck also wrote a nonfiction work in 1942 for the military. Entitled *Bombs Away!* it documented the training process of a bomber crew from boot camp to just before their first mission, and was very well received. Steinbeck gave the profits from the book to the Air Force Aid Society.

Steinbeck continued to write until his death on December 20, 1968, in New York City. His books would include popular titles like *East of Eden* (1952), *The Winter of Our Discontent* (1961) and *Travels with Charley* (1962). He also wrote the script for *Viva Zapata!* (1952). He was a recipient of many awards, including the New York Drama Critics' Circle Award for *Of Mice and Men* in 1938, and the United States Medal of Freedom in 1964 as well as the Press Medal of Freedom in the same year. Steinbeck was also a trustee of the John F. Kennedy Memorial Library and a member of the National Arts Council. In 1962, he received the Nobel Prize for Literature.

William P. Toth

STETTINIUS, EDWARD REILLY JR. (1900–1949)

An influential industrialist, Edward Stettinius headed the War Resources Board and was a civilian member of the National Defense Advisory Committee during World War II, as well as serving as secretary of state for President Franklin Roosevelt. Stettinius was born on October 22, 1900, in Chicago, Illinois. He attended the University of Virginia, though he did not receive a degree, and in 1924, he took a job as a stock clerk with the General Motors Company. Within seven years, he was a vice president in charge of public and industrial relations, and in another seven years, he was the chairman of the board. As Stettinius was a politically active, liberal businessman involved in unemployment relief during the Depression, Roosevelt asked him to serve on the Industrial Advisory Board of the National Recovery Administration in 1933. Unfortunately, his service was curtailed by his business commitments, namely his move to the board of U.S. Steel, but he retained close ties with Roosevelt.

These ties led directly to the chairmanship of the War Resources Board in 1939, meant to provide counsel on economic policies to the Munitions Board, prioritizing scarce resources in the event that the United States join the war. The War Resources Board soon dissolved, however, amid public protests that no labor or farm representatives had been appointed. The board was also considered to be the first step to taking the United States into war, which few believed would be necessary at that point. Roosevelt was unwilling to pursue the matter, as the board's proposals would have placed the already precarious economy directly into the hands of the military, a step Roosevelt did not think Congress was likely to approve.

Instead, Roosevelt created the National Defense Advisory Commission, with the industrial leaders, Stettinius among them, reporting directly to Roosevelt. The loose organization of the commission was not efficient enough to command wide-ranging wartime mobilization, however, nor were its members given enough information on what exactly the government wished to have produced, to be as effective as possible, and Roosevelt soon created the Office of Production Management (OPM). The OPM was a more straightforward organization, and was given more official status and authority for increasing production.

In 1941, Stettinius was appointed as the director of priorities in the OPM. This experience soon encouraged Roosevelt to appoint Stettinius as administrator of the Lend-Lease Program. The motivation behind Lend-Lease was that even though the United States was neutral at the time that the program was begun, private industry would offer credit to U.S. allies, especially Britain. The private sector would then be responsible for selling, renting, or lending arms and munitions to countries at war, helping America's allies while greatly benefiting the war industries as well. The companies involved converted their factories entirely to war-related production, and Roosevelt called them the "arsenal of democracy." Accusations have been leveled at the foreign subsidiaries of many of the companies involved in the Lend-Lease program, claiming that they took advantage of Lend-Lease to make a profit arming Germany and Italy at the same time they were arming the Allies, but those accusations were not aimed directly at Stettinius.

The diplomacy skills acquired in the Lend-Lease program served Stettinius well. In September 1943, Stettinius became the secretary of state for President Roosevelt, replacing Cordell Hull, and promptly began to reorganize the department for increased efficiency and improved relations with the public. He also assisted in the creation of the United Nations at the Dumbarton Oaks Conference. At the Yalta Conference in 1945, Stettinius was present at the meeting with Roosevelt, Josef Stalin, and Winston Churchill, and was responsible for many of the concessions that the Union of Soviet Socialist Republics (USSR) received in the Far East, for which he was widely regarded as foolish. At the time, he believed that the Russians could be invaluable allies against Japan, but of course, the decision was bitterly regretted by his critics as the Cold War began to advance.

After Roosevelt died, President Harry S. Truman replaced Stettinius with James Byrnes. Truman appointed Stettinius the U.S. representative to the United Nations, which pleased him, as he was a staunch supporter. Thus Stettinius led the American delegation at the UN conference in San Francisco. He resigned the post a year later in frustration that Truman refused to use the resources of the UN to broker peace with the USSR. He served as the rector of the University of Virginia for a time, and he died on October 31, 1949, from a heart attack.

Ellen Baier

STEVENS, JOHN (1749–1848)

Better known as the father of American railroads, John Stevens also built the first ironclad ship, almost four decades before the famous *Monitor* and *Merrimac*.

The son of a shipmaster, merchant, and landowner in New Jersey, Stevens was born in 1749 and completed his law studies at King's College, now Columbia University, in 1771. During the Revolutionary War, he served as treasurer of New Jersey. After the war, he married, then built an estate near Hoboken, New Jersey.

Starting around 1788, Stevens became fascinated with improving on the steamboat designs of John Fitch and James Rumsey. Frustrated in his efforts to obtain sole steamboat-building rights in New York, Stevens used his personal influence toward the development of the first U.S. patent law, passed in 1790. In 1809, his *Phoenix* became the first seagoing steamboat.

In 1812, Stevens incorporated his patented engine design in a steam vessel with an iron-plated hull to repel shot. The ship was to be anchored to a swivel, using a screw-propellor to rotate as it discharged guns. This design was intended for a battery defending New York, but the project was never built.

After 1810, John Stevens shifted his attention to promoting railroads. He died on March 6, 1838. His son, Robert Livington Stevens, began a prototype for an ironclad battleship in 1842, but the project was still unfinished when its inventor died in 1856. With the start of the Civil War, the Union backed the newer design of **John Ericsson**, which became the *Monitor*.

Wende Vyborney Feller

STEVENS, O. NELSON (1883–1966)

O. N. Stevens helped the Southern Alkali Company achieve national recognition for producing alkalis such as chlorine and caustic soda during World War II. Born on February 27, 1883, in Avon, Illinois, Stevens studied engineering at the University of Kansas, School of Mechanical Engineering. His work with alkali production included positions at Kansas Chemical and Alkali Company and the Solvay Process Company in Detroit. He was a natural candidate to manage the Southern Alkali Company.

Under Stevens' supervision, Southern Alkali produced high levels of soda ash and caustic soda. The plant supplied weapon manufactories around the country with alkali products like chlorine, which was needed because it "neutralized" the effects of mustard gas. Weapon manufactories demanded caustic soda because it produced glycerin, a major ingredient for making TNT. The army and navy issued the Army-Navy Production Award for Excellency in War Production to the Southern Alkali Company, managed by Stevens, on November 20, 1943. In a letter, the Under Secretary of War, Robert P. Patterson, praised the Southern Alkali Company for producing alkalis at the highest production rate possible.

These accolades resulted from both Stevens' managerial style and the employees' willingness to increase their productivity level. He allowed the Southern Alkali Corporation to serve Corpus Christi as well as the national home front during World War II. Stevens, who became vice president of

Southern Alkali, remained the company's most respected operations manager, even after his death on May 9, 1966, in Corpus Christi, Texas.

Madalyn Ard

STEVENSON, EARL PLACE (1893–1978)

Born in Logansport, Indiana, on October 2, 1893, Earl Stevenson received his B.S. degree from Wesleyan University in 1916. He then went to the Massachusetts Institute of Technology to teach chemistry and work on his master's degree. Although he completed his master's in 1919, Stevenson, like many other scientists, was called into the service during World War I. (In World War I scientists were often conscripted rather than contracted with through universities. The vision of **Vannevar Bush** for government/university cooperation would change the model for World War II.) As a lieutenant in the Chemical Warfare Service, Stevenson helped to develop gas mask filters.

Stevenson became the director of research at Arthur D. Little Company in 1919, and in 1922, vice president. The company had specialized in testing and analytical service up until Stevenson succeeded Arthur D. Little as president in 1935. It was left to Stevenson to take the company into new technical and managerial directions, which he did successfully. He became known as a leading industrial chemical engineer. Before and during World War II he was again called into service on the home front. Stevenson was the chief of the Chemical Engineering Division of the National Defense Research Committee and then chaired the Eleventh Division of the Office of Scientific Research and Development.

Stevenson retired as chair of Arthur D. Little in 1961, continued his service to several government committees as well as to his community, and died on June 28, 1978.

Benjamin F. Shearer

STEWART, JAMES MAITLAND (1908–1997)

Having already acquired his pilot's license, famed actor James Stewart, born on May 20, 1908, enlisted in the Army Air Corps in March 1941 before the Japanese bombed Pearl Harbor on December 7 of that year. He was first sent to Moffett Field, California, where he hosted a radio broadcast called *We Hold These Truths*, a tribute to the Bill of Rights 150th anniversary. He hosted other radio shows as well to encourage people to enlist in the military. During the summer of 1942, Stewart narrated documentaries for the Office of War Information in addition to hosting the *Your Air Force—This Is War* documentary. He also made appearances on *Letter at Midnight*, a program that portrayed American soldiers writing letters to their families that described their reasons for fighting.

Many celebrities who enlisted in the military were essentially used for publicity purposes and to encourage morale among troops. Stewart, however, requested that he be treated as any other soldier and be assigned to combat duty. By the end of World War II, he had flown twenty different missions to Europe. Stewart remained in the Air Force Reserves when the war ended. By 1959, he had reached the rank of Brigadier General. In addition to serving in World War II, Stewart also flew a bombing mission over North Vietnam during the Vietnam War. He retired from the Air Force in May 1968 and died on July 2, 1997.

Further Reading: Dewey, Donald. *James Stewart: A Biography.* Atlanta: Turner Publishing, 1996.

Nicole Mitchell

James Stewart (circa 1950s). Courtesy of Photofest.

STICKNEY, JOSEPH L. (1848–1907)

Joseph Stickney was a prominent war correspondent in the Philippines during the Spanish-American War. He was born in Marion, Kentucky, on July 12, 1848, and served as a lieutenant in the U.S. Navy during the Civil War. In 1867, he graduated from the Naval Academy and took up journalism. Stickney worked for several newspapers before joining the *New York Herald*, where he was employed as a foreign editor and editorial writer from 1887 to 1898. He wired Asiatic Squadron leader Commodore George W. Dewey in April 1898 promising to only submit for publication news approved by Dewey.

Stickney joined the squadron while it was in Hong Kong preparing for battle. He asked Dewey if he could observe the attack on the Spanish fleet from the flagship *Olympia*'s bridge. As the fleet was short of officers, Dewey appointed Stickney to be his aide, thus freeing up an officer for gunnery duty during the victorious Battle of Manila Bay on May 1. Stickney accompanied Dewey's chief of staff Commander Benjamin P. Lamberton when he went ashore the following day to take possession of the principal Spanish naval station in the Philippines at Cavite. Thanks to reporters like Stickney, Americans went "Dewey Mad" over their new hero, who was quickly promoted to admiral. After the war, Stickney wrote "With Dewey at Manila" for the February 1899 edition of *Harper's Magazine*. That same year he published his congratulatory biography *Life and Glorious Deeds of Admiral George Dewey*.

David M. Carletta

STIEGLITZ, JULIUS OSCAR (1867–1937)

During World War I, Julius Stieglitz developed gases, dyes, and chemicals for use in war, and advised the government how to obtain chemicals that had previously come from Germany. Born in Hoboken, New Jersey, on May 26, 1867, to Edward and Hedwig (Werner) Stieglitz, he and his identical twin, Leopold, attended the Realgymnasium in Karlsruhe, Germany, for their primary education. Stieglitz attended the University of Berlin for his doctorate in organic chemistry, while his twin attended medical school. He worked in the chemistry industry briefly before taking a teaching position at the University of Chicago, and he became a full professor in 1905. His students knew him as a particularly thoughtful and organized teacher.

Stieglitz was vital during World War I in reverse engineering and recreating the synthetic dyes and chemicals, not to mention medications, which had previously been imported from Europe. He chaired the committee on synthetic drugs of the National Research Council, and vice-chaired the council on pharmacy and chemistry of the American Medical Association. In addition to his work with medicines, he also was instrumental in the development of gases and chemicals for offensive use by the American troops in response to Germany's use of chlorine and nerve gases. Though the chemical weapons were potent, they were also unpredictable and volatile for use in the field, and Stieglitz preferred his work on medicines. After the war, he returned quietly to his teaching duties. He died of pneumonia in Chicago on January 10, 1937.

Ellen Baier

STILLÉ, CHARLES JANEWAY (1819–1899)

A member of the U.S. Sanitary Commission during the Civil War, Charles J. Stillé also authored the influential pamphlet, *How a Free People Conduct a Long War*. The brother of groundbreaking pathologist Alfred Stillé, Charles Stillé was born in Pennsylvania on September 23, 1819, and graduated from Yale in 1839. Though he became a lawyer, his primary interests were in literature and history.

The Sanitary Commission was organized in 1861 as a grassroots relief effort to provide medical and hygiene assistance along with comforts such as quilts and cider to Union soldiers. In his *History of the United States Sanitary Commission*, published in 1866, Stillé credited the commission's work with mobilizing Union morale before the capture of Vicksburg as well as minimizing the number of deaths from complications. Stillé was also one of the organizers of the Great Central Fair held in Philadelphia in 1864. This fair raised $1 million for the war effort.

In 1862, Stillé published *How a Free People Conduct a Long War*. This pamphlet sold 500,000 copies and was also reprinted in the March 7, 1863, issue of *Harper's Magazine*. Stillé compared the Civil War to Britain's struggles against Napoleon, arguing that periods of discouragement were inevitable, but that fortitude and patriotism would carry the day.

After the war, Stillé became a professor of literature at the University of Pennsylvania. He served as provost there from 1868 to 1880, and authored several books on the Revolutionary War, including a biography of John Dickinson. He died on August 11, 1899.

Wende Vyborney Feller

STONE, ISIDOR FEINSTEIN (1907–1989)

Isidor Feinstein was born in Philadelphia, Pennsylvania, on December 24, 1907. He grew up in Haddonfield, New Jersey, where he published and distributed his own newspaper at the age of fourteen. Feinstein began working for a Camden newspaper while still in high school and he left the University of Pennsylvania without a degree, worked at various papers, and in 1931 joined the *Philadelphia Record*. In 1933 he became an editorial writer at the *New York Post*. He left the *Post* in 1938, the year after he legally changed his last name to Stone, and became capital correspondent of the *Nation* the next year. Stone was fired from the *Nation* in 1946, wrote for failed leftist papers, and jobless, founded the *I.F. Stone Weekly* in 1953, which lasted as a biweekly until 1971.

Stone was not a republican or a democrat, but an independent social democrat. He had hoped that the end of World War II would usher in a period of world peace, but cooperation between the Soviet Union and the United States that had attained victory, soon gave way to virulent anti-communism in the United States, which Stone saw as irrational and unbalanced. He became a consistent critic of the Cold War, of President Harry Truman in particular, and regularly uncovered government lies. During the Korean War, Stone persistently questioned policy makers and suggested negotiating tactics to end the war. He was also one of the first critics of American involvement in Vietnam. Stone died on June 18, 1989.

Benjamin F. Shearer

STONE, ROBERT ANTHONY (1937–)

One of the most important novelists of his generation, Robert Stone was born in Brooklyn, New York, on August 21, 1937, and raised by his mentally ill mother. He went into the navy in 1955, left in 1958, and enrolled for a year in New York University. He was a fellow at Stanford in 1962. Stone has synthesized elements of two very different novelistic traditions. The romantic-naturalistic tradition, represented by **Ernest Hemingway**, emphasized a controlled narrative style, the treatment of "masculine" subjects, and a hardboiled worldview. The counterculturalist or protest tradition, represented by John Dos Passos and Henry Miller, emphasized a spontaneous narrative style, the treatment of illicit subjects, and a progressive worldview.

In each of Stone's novels, the male protagonist has enough experience of the world to have assumed a hardened view toward life's possibilities, but not quite enough experience of the world beyond his own relatively safe American life to appreciate the full dangers of entering other realms without recognizing the naivete inherent in even the wandering itself. Often these protagonists have wandered into "war zones" under the misguided sense that the experience will somehow give meaning to their seemingly increasingly purposeless lives and cleanse their troubled psyches.

In his first novel, A *Hall of Mirrors* (1967), Stone explored the deeply rooted tensions between reactionary and radical extremes simmering just under the surface of American political life in the years immediately preceding the convulsive protests against the Vietnam War. Drawing on his own experiences in New Orleans, where he and his wife scraped by for several years in the early 1960s, Stone focused on a spiritually empty radio "personality" who has accepted a position at a right-wing station that exists to promote the expediently populist agenda of its wealthy and politically ambitious owner.

After freelancing in Vietnam as a reporter for several British newspapers, Stone produced one of his most highly acclaimed novels, *Dog Soldiers* (1974). The protagonist is a journalist who thinks that the horrors to which he has been exposed have made him sufficiently hard and have provided a sort of moral justification to smuggle heroin from Vietnam to the United States. When he returns to the United States, the journalist, along with his wife and a confederate, discovers that far from being an "easy score," the heroin smuggling has made him a target of both the truly vicious criminals who control heroin distribution and the equally ruthless police who have become corrupted by the great sums to be made from the drug trade. The novel serves as a sort of parable about the confused ironies in both the competing interests that sustained the American involvement in the Vietnam War and the counterculture's rejection of that involvement.

In the later chapters, the setting of *Dog Soldiers* shifts to northern Mexico, a region associated in the American consciousness with the near-anarchic lawlessness of Geronimo's Apache raiders and Pancho Villa's bandit revolutionaries. In his third novel, A *Flag for Sunrise* (1981), and his seventh novel, *Bay of Souls* (2003), Stone focused on similar American views of Central America and the Caribbean. Historically, these settings have been regarded as both decidedly "foreign" and yet within the American sphere. They have attracted both "freebooters" and "do-gooders." Stone's American protagonists aren't sure what they are doing in these places and further mistake dark schemes and passions for exotic adventures. The civil disorder, violent politics, and rapacious corruption of these places reflect the protagonists' confusion and make it seem ridiculously self-involved and ultimately inconsequential.

In his fifth novel, *Outerbridge Reach* (1989), Stone focused on a Vietnam vet who grossly underestimates the physical and spiritual challenges in participating in a solo sailing race around the globe. In *Damascus Gate* (1998), his sixth and most acclaimed novel since *Dog Soldiers*, another American journalist travels to Jerusalem in order to research religious delusions, a subject of increasingly personal as well as professional interest to him. Of course, because it represents most all of the deep religious differences fueling the bitter political conflicts in the region, Jerusalem is both the perfect and worst possible setting for exploring such a subject—and an extremely dangerous place to try to work out one's spiritual uncertainties.

Further Reading: Shelton, Frank W. "Robert Stone's *Dog Soldiers*: Vietnam Comes Home to America." *Critique: Studies in Contemporary Fiction* 24 (Winter 1983): 74–81; Solartoff, Robert. *Robert Stone*. New York: Twayne, 1994; Stephenson, Gregory. *Understanding Robert Stone*. Columbia: University of South Carolina Press, 2002.

Martin Kich

STONER, EUGENE MORRISON (1922–1997)

Eugene Stoner was born in Gasport, Indiana, in 1922. He began working for the Vega Aircraft Company after graduated from high school in Long Beach, California. At the outbreak of World War II, Stoner enlisted in the U.S. Marine Corps to do his part in supporting the war effort. His main job in the marine corps was to work in Aviation Ordinance. With his tour of duty completed, Stoner was working in the machine shop for Whittaker, an aircraft equipment company, at the end of 1945. He rose to the management level position of design engineer.

The Armalite Division of the Fairchild Engine and Aircraft Corporation hired Stoner as its chief of engineering in the 1950s. There Stoner developed and created the prototypes of the military assault weapon known as the M16 Rifle. It is lightweight and eventually became a dual-action weapon convertible from semi-automatic to fully automatic rapid-fire action.

Today, the M16 rifle is widely used in all the U.S. armed services as well as in law enforcement. The M16 has seen action during the Vietnam War, the Cold War, Gulf Wars I and II, the War on Terror, and in Afghanistan.

Stoner eventually held more than one hundred patents in the ordinance field for four different companies. He co-founded ARES, Inc., in 1971, and retired from ARES in 1989. Stoner then acted as a consultant with the company until he passed away on April 24, 1997, at his home in Palm City, Florida.

Erskine L. Levi Jr.

STOUFFER, SAMUEL ANDREW (1900–1960)

Samuel Stouffer was the director of the professional staff of the War Department's new Research Branch in the Special Services Division from 1941 until 1946. He headed an effort to research the attitudes of men enlisted in the army. While the purpose of this research was to provide the army with quick information about soldiers that would lead to policy formation, what finally resulted from Stouffer's research was the classic sociopsychological study, *The American Soldier*, condensed to four volumes from surveys of 500,000 soldiers and published in 1949.

Stouffer was born in Sac City, Iowa, on June 6, 1900. He obtained his B.A. from Morningside College in 1921, his M.A. in English from Harvard in 1923, and his Ph.D. in sociology from the University of Chicago in 1930. He remained a year at Chicago to teach statistics before going to the University of London to do postdoctoral work in statistics. From 1932 to 1935 Stouffer taught social statistics at the University of Wisconsin and then moved to the sociology department at Chicago, where he remained until 1946. He was professor of sociology and director of the Laboratory of Social Relations at Harvard from 1946 until he died on August 24, 1960.

Stouffer's pioneering work in military sociology set standards for survey research and opened new issues for understanding soldiers before, during, and after military service. Those issues included race, educational background, age, the effects of combat, religious sentiment, social cohesiveness, and the influence of mass media.

Benjamin F. Shearer

STOUT, REX TODHUNTER (1886–1975)

Rex Stout worked as a propagandist during World War II and played an important role in public information. He was born in Noblesville, Indiana, on December 1, 1886, was married twice, and had two daughters. From 1906 to 1908, he served in the U.S. Navy. Stout worked many jobs throughout his life, but is renowned for his political activism and fiction writing, especially his series of detective novels featuring characters Nero Wolfe and Archie.

On the eve of World War II, Stout worked to promote America's war preparedness and aid to the Allies. He was a member of the Fight for Freedom Committee as well as Freedom House, an organization dedicated to promoting democracy, and was active in Friends of Democracy, which campaigned for the Allied cause. He also conducted the radio programs, *Speaking of Liberty* in 1941, *Voice of Freedom* in 1942, and *Our Secret Weapon* in 1942–1943. During the war years, he served the Writers' War Board, helping to create media in support of the war effort on the home front, and as president of the Society for Prevention of World War Three. Finally, in 1945, he went as a correspondent on a tour of the war zone.

Stout continued to work for a peaceful world order in the postwar years. From 1949 to 1975, he was involved in the Writers' Board for World Government, an organization whose mission was to lobby for world government. As an ardent anti-communist (though accused otherwise by the government), he staunchly supported America's war in Vietnam.

Stout died in Danbury, Connecticut, on October 27, 1975.

Stacy Dorgan

STOUT, SAMUEL HOLLINGSWORTH (1822–1903)

Samuel Stout was a Confederate surgeon during the Civil War. After graduating from the University of Nashville, Stout taught school and apprenticed in medicine before graduating from the University of Pennsylvania's medical school in 1848. After a brief residence in Nashville, he and his wife moved to Giles County, near Pulaski, where he owned land and slaves, and practiced medicine.

Stout was surgeon of the Third Tennessee Infantry from May to November 1861, then he was placed in charge of the Gordon Hospital in Nashville until February 1862. After the fall of Nashville, Stout was sent to Chattanooga, where he was soon in charge of all Army of Tennessee hospitals behind the lines. In this capacity, he supervised doctors and other personnel, selected hospital sites, and coordinated the needs of the medical department with military and civilian suppliers. During summer 1864, Stout supervised more than sixty constantly relocating hospitals in Georgia, Alabama, and Mississippi.

After the war, Stout lost his farm to bankruptcy and moved to Atlanta, where he practiced medicine and helped establish the public school system. In 1882 he moved to Cisco, Texas, and eventually to Dallas, where he continued his medical and educational activities, though he never again achieved financial stability. At his death, he left a collection of 1,500 pounds of Army of Tennessee hospital records.

Further Reading: Schroeder-Lein, Glenna R. *Confederate Hospitals on the Move: Samuel H. Stout and the Army of the Tennessee.* Columbia: University of South Carolina Press, 1994.

Michael L. McGregor

STRONG, GEORGE TEMPLETON (1820–1875)

Attorney, amateur musician, and civic leader George Templeton Strong was treasurer of the U.S. Sanitary Commission. He was born on January 26, 1820, in New York, the son of George Washington Strong, a prominent attorney. While at Columbia College (1835), he began to compile a diary. By 1838 he graduated, and served as a law clerk in his father's practice, with admission to the bar in 1841. Three years later he became a partner in the firm. Strong married Ellen Caroline Ruggles (1825–1891) in 1848.

In June 1861, Strong was appointed treasurer of the U.S. Sanitary Commission. As a commissioner, Strong severely criticized what he saw as bureaucratic incompetence in the War Department's Medical Bureau. He visited army camps and battlefields, and personally met with President Abraham Lincoln, Secretary of War Edwin M. Stanton, and Generals Ulysses S. Grant and George McClellan.

In 1862, the Union issued a call for nurses and doctors. Against her husband's misgivings, Ellen Strong served on hospital ships during the Civil War, displaying administrative abilities. She later acted in a play, *The Follies of a Night*, for the commission's Metropolitan Fair (1864).

With landscape architect **Frederick Law Olmsted**, George Strong cofounded the Union League Club of New York to promote respect for the Union. Both men later established *The Nation* magazine in 1865. Strong died on July 21, 1875, in New York.

Further Reading: Strong, George Templeton. *The Diary of George Templeton Strong*. Edited by Allan Nevins and Milton Halsey Thomas. New York: Macmillan, 1952.

Ralph Hartsock

STRYKER, ROY EMERSON (1893–1975)

Roy Emerson Stryker was responsible for overseeing much of the photographic documentation of the home-front mobilization in World War II. He was born on November 5, 1893, and grew up in Montrose, Colorado. During World War I he served in the army. After the war he returned to Colorado and met Alice Frasier, whom he married.

In 1920 they moved to New York City. Stryker enrolled in Columbia University, from which he received both his bachelor's and master's degrees in economics. He and his wife moved to Washington, DC, in 1935 and Stryker was hired to be the chief of the Historical Section of the Farm Security Administration, responsible for coordinating photographers to document the administration's work helping farmers affected by the Great Depression.

During Word War II, Stryker was transferred to the Office of War Information. He was in charge of the office's photographic unit where he directed photographers in documenting America's mobilization for the war. He documented automobile factories as they converted over to the production of aircraft for the air force. He also heavily documented the entrance of women into the workforce and extensively photographed the growth of the armament industries.

After the war, Stryker was hired by the Standard Oil Company to coordinate the photographic documentation of the company and its workers. He later directed various documentary projects for the city of Pittsburgh. Stryker eventually returned to Colorado and died in Grand Junction in 1975.

Gene C. Gerard

SUMMERS, CLYDE WILSON (1918–)

Clyde Summers, professor emeritus at the University of Pennsylvania, has taught labor law for over sixty years and authored over 150 publications focusing upon the individual rights of workers with employers and within their unions. He was a conscientious objector during World War II.

Summers was born on November 21, 1918, in Grass Range, Montana. In 1935, he left the family farm to study accounting at the University of Illinois, but he found law more interesting, and in 1942, earned his law degree. A Christian pacifist, he had considered a career in the ministry before settling on the law, and because of his anti-war beliefs, the state of Illinois refused to admit him to the bar. Although Summers lost his Supreme Court challenge, Justice Hugo Black, in a dissenting opinion, found Summers to be an "honest, moral, and intelligent" young man who "would strive to make the legal system a more effective instrument of justice" (325 U.S. 561).

While he was admitted to the New York State bar in 1951, Summers eschewed practicing law in favor of teaching, carving out a career that earned him the title of "Mr. Labor Law." Before moving to the University of Pennsylvania in 1975, Summers taught at the University of Toledo, University of Buffalo, and Yale University. He also was an arbitrator in over a thousand cases involving unions. Summers played a key role in drafting the 1959 Landrum Griffin Act to promote greater democracy within the union movement.

Ron Briley

SWOPE, HERBERT BAYARD (1882–1958)

On August 19, 1918, President Woodrow Wilson named Herbert Swope to the War Industries Board, headed then by **Bernard Mannes Baruch**, who became his lifelong friend. Swope was already a well-known journalist, having won the first Pulitzer Prize in 1917 for his reporting on German U-boats' sinking of British ships and German troops marching into Belgium. Baruch referred to Swope as one of his executive assistants, but officially Swope was designated as an associate member of the Board.

Born in St. Louis on January 5, 1882, Swope's youth did not augur a successful newspaper career. He was kicked out of high school once, never went to college, and was fired from most of the newspaper jobs he got. In 1909, however, Swope began writing for **Joseph Pulitzer**'s *New York World*, and he excelled there, becoming its executive editor from November 1920 until the end of 1928. For the next thirty years, until his death on June 20, 1958, Swope was a publicist, a diplomat, served on boards, and consulted for the army public relations department during World War II.

Swope had started working informally for Baruch and the War Industries Board before his appointment. He wrote letters and speeches for Baruch, but more importantly, he pumped up both Baruch's and the board's public image. Swope was interested in government and counted himself a Wilsonian Democrat, but he also harbored the hope that his contact with Baruch would lead to further opportunities. Indeed, it was rumored that Swope, who never outgrew his youthful profligacy, was on Baruch's payroll.

Benjamin F. Shearer

SZILARD, LEO (1898–1964)

A brilliant theoretical physicist, Leo Szilard worked on the building of the atomic bomb and then dedicated his life to seeing that the weapon was never again used against humanity. Born in Budapest, Austro-Hungary, on February 11, 1898, Szilard was a student of **Albert Einstein** in Berlin. Earning a Ph.D. in physics from the University of Berlin in 1922, he stayed there as a professor for ten years. Szilard eventually fled Germany in 1933 when Hitler assumed power. In 1938 he left Britain for the United States because he was largely disgusted at Britain's policy of appeasement toward Hitler at Munich. Columbia University welcomed Szilard in 1939.

In 1939 Szilard and fellow scientist **Walter Henry Zinn** completed an experiment in which they proved that when atoms of uranium were split, neutrons were emitted. This discovery implied that the massive energy of an atom could be unleashed. Szilard remembered going home the night of that experiment and thinking that it could only lead to sorrow. His fellow Columbia colleague, **Enrico Fermi**, made the same discovery almost simultaneously. Alarmed that the Nazi regime might develop an atomic weapon, Szilard and Fermi encouraged Szilard's old mentor, Einstein, to convince President Franklin Roosevelt to begin an atomic weapons program.

The famous Einstein Letter of 1939 was in fact written by Szilard, but signed by Einstein as his was the much greater reputation and influence. In the letter, Einstein explained the findings of Szilard and Fermi and their implications. After Roosevelt approved the establishment of the Manhattan Project, which was the code name of the atomic bomb project, Szilard worked primarily at the Chicago Metallurgical Lab. It was here that Szilard and Fermi witnessed the first controlled nuclear chain reaction on December 2, 1942. Afterward, Fermi went to Los Alamos while Szilard stayed in Chicago, working on a process to extract plutonium from uranium.

While at Chicago, Szilard had trouble with the implications of this new weapon of mass destruction and sought to influence President Roosevelt's use of the bomb. He sent a letter to the first lady, Eleanor Roosevelt, and scheduled a meeting with her for May 8, 1945, to discuss the dangers of the bomb. His hope was that she might in turn influence her husband and encourage him not to use the weapon, but Franklin Roosevelt died on April 12, 1945, and Harry Truman assumed the presidency. Szilard then tried to convince Truman not to use the bomb directly on Japan. He was one of seven scientists from Chicago who wrote "The Report of the Committee on Political and Social Problems, Manhattan Project 'Metallurgical Laboratory,'" or the Franck Report. **Glenn Theodore Seaborg** was also among the committee members. Written in June 1945, the scientists asked President Truman to give Japan advance warning of the bomb through a demonstration "before the eyes of representatives of all United Nations, on the desert or a barren island." They also argued "nations could still be diverted from a path which must lead to total mutual destruction, by a specific international agreement barring a nuclear armaments race." In July, Szilard went even further, drafting a strongly worded petition to Truman identifying the moral issues of the bomb. Signed by over sixty other scientists, Szilard asked Truman not to use the bomb at all, calling atomic bombs "a means for the ruthless annihilation of cities." Ultimately Szilard was unsuccessful in halting the atomic bombings against Japan in August.

Although Szilard played a significant role in the development of the bomb, afterward he devoted his time to ensuring that the military did not have complete control over the development of atomic weapons. He led a fight against the May-Johnson Bill, a bill that would have placed complete control of atomic power in the hands of the military. Along with Einstein, he helped establish the Emergency Committee of Atomic Scientists in order to help shape public opinion about the dangers of atomic power. In 1957 he helped organize the first Pugwash Conference in Nova Scotia, a conference set up for scientists from around the world to discuss peace and world security. In 1962 he organized the Council for Abolishing War. Szilard eventually left nuclear physics for biophysics and did astounding work in the field of molecular biology. He died on May 30, 1964, in La Jolla, California.

Further Reading: William Lanouette. *Genius in the Shadows: A Biography of Leo Szilard*. Chicago: University of Chicago Press, 1994; Leo Szilard. *The Voice of Dolphins*. New York: Simon and Schuster, 1961.

Valerie L. Adams

T

TALBOT, FRANCIS XAVIER (1889–1953)

During the Spanish Civil War, Francis Xavier Talbot supported General Francisco Franco's nationalist position because of its heavy support for Roman Catholicism and its opposition to modernism and communism. He took similar positions in other struggles because of his support for Catholicism. During both world wars, he strongly supported the United States in its war effort.

Talbot was an intellectual with a career mainly in the literary field. He was editor of the Jesuit weekly *America* for over two decades. He also edited the *Catholic Mind* and *Thought*, also Jesuit periodicals, and played a major role in the foundation of *Theological Studies*, the theological journal of the Jesuits.

Talbot served for twelve years as chaplain to the National Motion Picture Bureau of the International Federation of Catholic Alumnae. This group previewed movies for the Legion of Decency. Talbot also served three years as the president of Loyola College in Baltimore, Maryland. He died on December 3, 1953, in Washington, DC, where he was doing archival work at Georgetown University as well as parish work.

Talbot was born in Philadelphia, Pennsylvania, on January 25, 1889. He joined the Society of Jesus in 1906 and was ordained a priest on June 29, 1921. He was trained at St. Andrew-on-the-Hudson in Poughkeepsie, New York. He studied philosophy (1910–1913) and theology (1918–1921) at Woodstock College in Woodstock, Maryland. Talbot then taught English at the Loyola School in New York City from 1913 to 1916. From 1917 to 1918 he taught religion and English at Boston College.

Andrew J. Waskey

TALLANT, ALICE WELD (1875–1958)

Obstetrician and gynecologist Alice Weld Tallant graduated from Smith College in 1897 and Harvard Medical School in 1902. She was professor of obstetrics at the Women's Medical College of Pennsylvania and physician-in-chief of the College Hospital from 1905 to 1923.

During World War I, Tallant volunteered to serve for six months (July 1917–February 1918) in the Smith College Relief Unit in France, first serving as assistant director and then director. Later, she served as a physician for the American Committee for Devastated France (May 1918–1919). Next, she became aide-major, first class (honorary) with the Sixth French Army, serving as a physician in the Military Evacuation Hospital (H.O.E., B-52) at Coulommiers and Château-Thierry (June–August 1918), after the American Army rejected her request to serve as a physician. Following her hospital service, Tallant cared for French civilians who had been "bombed-out" and were infected with influenza. For those services to the army and the civilian population, the French government awarded her its highest honor, the Croix de Guerre.

Tallant's career as an obstetrics professor and practitioner continued to flourish after her return to the United States. She published medical articles as well as the 1922 monograph, A Text-Book of Obstetrical Nursing, and she was reported to have delivered more than three thousand babies during her years in Philadelphia.

Further Reading: Day, Blanche. "Woman Physician Reminisces about World War I Exploits." *Germantown* (Pennsylvania) *Courier* 21, no. 31 (July 4, 1957): feature page. Provided by Smith College Archives.

Ximena Chrisagis

TAYLOR, ALBERT HOYT (1879–1961)

Late September 1922 Albert Taylor and **Leo Clifford Young**, his engineering colleague at the U.S. Naval Aircraft Radio Laboratory, made an amazing discovery while testing high-frequency radio waves near a river. The ships passing by broke up their radio signals. They soon realized that radio detection and ranging (radar) could make a tremendous contribution to the navy in detecting enemy ships.

Born on New Year's Day of 1879, Taylor was already investigating the possibilities of radio when he graduated from Northwestern University in 1902. He earned his doctorate from the University of Göttingen in 1909 and taught at the University of North Dakota until accepting a commission in the Naval Reserve in 1917, which eventually brought him to the Aircraft Radio Laboratory as its head in 1919. When the Naval Research Laboratory (NRL) was created in 1923, Taylor became superintendent of the Radio Division and remained in that position until 1945. He retired in 1948 and died on December 11, 1961.

Under Taylor's guidance along with his active involvement in high-frequency radio and transmitter control investigations, the navy employed a ship-worthy radar system in 1937 only a few years before the United States entered World War II. Working with him at the NRL, Leo Young and **Robert Morris Page** perfected and built a pulse radar system that could detect planes as well as ships. The Institute of Radio Engineers recognized Taylor's outstanding achievements as a researcher and executive by awarding him its Medal of Honor in 1942.

Benjamin F. Shearer

TAYLOR, SUSIE BAKER KING (1848–1912)

Susie King Taylor served as a laundress and nurse with the Union regiment of the First South Carolina Volunteers from 1862 to the end of the Civil War. She used this opportunity to teach the soldiers of the regiment and many other African American children and adults to read.

Born on August 5, 1848, to a woman who was a slave on the Isle of Wight, Taylor was brought up by her grandmother in Savannah, Georgia. A friend of her grandmother surreptitiously taught Taylor to read. She caught the attention of a Union commander who enrolled her as a laundress in his African American regiment. She eagerly used the opportunity to teach the soldiers to read, and she learned how to clean and fire a musket, provide nursing care, and cook, all without pay. While visiting soldiers in the hospital at Beaufort, she met **Clarissa Harlowe Barton**.

Taylor married a sergeant in the regiment, Edward King, who was killed in an accident in 1866. Their son was born after King died. Taylor returned to teaching and married Russell Taylor in 1879. Susie King Taylor helped organize a chapter of the Woman's Relief Corps in Boston and held several offices. Unfortunately, Taylor never qualified for a Civil War pension because she had not signed a contract as a nurse. She died on October 6, 1912.

Further Reading: Susie King Taylor. *Reminiscences of My Life in Camp with the 33d United States Colored Troops Late 1st S. C. Volunteers.* Boston: Author, 1902. Accessed May 10, 2005, at http://digilib.nypl.org/dynaweb/digs/wwm97267/Susie_King_Taylor.

Marjorie A. Baier

TELLER, EDWARD (1908–2003)

A noted figure in nuclear physics, Edward Teller's calculations on atomic implosion determined it would be contained to a certain area rather than continuing indefinitely. He is considered the "father of the H-bomb" for his groundbreaking work on nuclear fusion.

Teller was born on January 15, 1908, in Budapest, and educated in Germany, receiving his doctorate in 1930 from the University of Leipzig. He spent two years teaching at the University of Göttingen, and fled Germany in 1934 with the help of the Jewish Rescue Committee. He then worked with Niels Bohr in Copenhagen for a year, researching the quantum mechanics of the hydrogen ion. In 1935, he moved to Washington, DC, where he became a professor of physics at George Washington University. He was primarily a theoretical physicist until just before the United States entered World War II, when he gained interest in the practical applications of the nuclear fission and fusion discoveries that were coming thick and fast in the physics field.

In 1942, **Julius Robert Oppenheimer** asked Teller to be part of the original planning sessions of the Manhattan Project. Teller was particularly interested, but he was intrigued by the idea that the atomic bomb, which relied on a chain reaction of nuclear fission to set off a massive explosion, could then trigger an even larger explosion using nuclear fusion. This idea was later to become the theoretical basis for the hydrogen bomb. For the meantime, however, Teller agreed to move to Los Alamos, New Mexico, and work in the Theoretical Physics division under **Hans Bethe**, though he was irked that he was not chosen to head the division. His idea for the hydrogen bomb was considered a low priority until the atomic bomb was first created. This prioritization angered Teller, and he was frequently difficult to work with on the fission project. He was easily distracted by the impractical yet interesting, and overly willing to work off of incomplete calculations, some of his colleagues alleged in retrospect. He did contribute, figuring out a key component of the implosion mechanism and the shock-wave propagation with Bethe, but many scientists breathed easier when Teller returned to the University of Chicago in 1946.

Teller's project was approved, however, in 1949, when the Soviet Union exploded its first atomic bomb. President Harry S. Truman announced that the hydrogen bomb would be put into development as soon as possible, and Teller returned to Los Alamos. He was not any easier to work with, demanding more staff, especially theorists. Stanislaw Ulam came up with a workable theory for a megaton hydrogen bomb utilizing greater quantities of trinium than Teller had thought necessary, though Teller later took full credit for the discovery. The key was in the separation of the fission and fusion reactions, using the blast from the primary fission to fuel the secondary fusion. Despite the discovery, Teller was not chosen to lead the development project, and he joined the Livermore Laboratory at the University of California Radiation Laboratory. After the "Super" tested successfully on an atoll in the Pacific Ocean on November 1, 1952, Teller became known as the "father of the hydrogen bomb," despite his limited involvement. He was adamantly pro-nuclear, and refused to acknowledge his role in advancing the Cold War, though in 1973, **Isidor Isaac Rabi** stated bluntly that a world without Teller would have been better.

He drew more ire from fellow scientists by testifying to the Atomic Energy Commission that Oppenheimer may have been a security risk at the trial to determine Oppenheimer's loyalty to the government. He and Oppenheimer clashed, and had done so for many years, because of Teller's support of the government's nuclear program and Oppenheimer's opposition to it. Though Teller had initially lobbied for a demonstration of the atomic bomb before it was dropped on a civilian city in Japan, he quickly came to earn his hawkish reputation during the Cold War, and Oppenheimer became his self-defined rival in the scientific community.

As a research fellow at the Hoover Institute for the Study of War, Revolution, and Peace at Stanford University, Teller later provided support for President Ronald Reagan's Strategic Defense Initiative, an elaborate system based on lasers and atomic bomb mid-air interception popularly known as "Star Wars," as well as the second Bush administration's revival of the missile defense program in the early 2000s, earning a Presidential Medal of Freedom from President George W. Bush. He died on September 9, 2003 in Stanford, California.

Ellen Baier

TERMAN, FREDERICK EMMONS (1900–1982)

Frederick Terman, who published the first edition of *Radio Engineering* in 1932, was one of America's most celebrated electrical engineers. He was elected to the National Academy of Sciences in 1946 and received the National Medal of Science in 1976. The Presidential Medal of Merit was also among his many honors, awarded to him in 1948 for his vital work during World War II.

Terman was born on June 7, 1900, in English, Indiana, the son of psychologist **Lewis Madison Terman**. Raised in California, he received his undergraduate degree in chemistry in 1920 and his engineer's degree in 1922 from Stanford. Working under **Vannevar Bush** at MIT, Terman earned his doctorate in electrical engineering in 1924. He returned to Stanford as an instructor in 1925 and remained there in increasingly responsible positions until his retirement in 1965. Terman's determination to form business and government relationships around a highly respected research institution— Stanford—earned him the epithet "Father of Silicon Valley."

From 1942 to 1946 Terman went on leave from Stanford to contribute his expertise to the American war effort. In December 1941, Vannevar Bush asked his former student to head the newly formed Radio Research Laboratory, originally an office of MIT's Radiation Laboratory that soon became independent and moved to Harvard. Terman led the successful effort of more than 800 Lab employees to produce offensive and defensive countermeasures to radar.

Terman was very active in professional organizations as well as in government service throughout his life. He died on December 19, 1982.

Benjamin F. Shearer

TERMAN, LEWIS MADISON (1877–1956)

Lewis Madison Terman was born on January 15, 1877, in Johnson County, Indiana, to parents Jim Terman and Martha Cutsinger Terman. Terman was the twelfth of fourteen children and was educated in a one-room schoolhouse until the age of thirteen. The only available option for Terman to further his education was Central Normal College, whose mission was to prepare students to become teachers. Terman did not enroll at Central Normal College until two years after eighth grade graduation for financial reasons. He took courses at Central Normal and gained teaching experience at local grade schools from age fifteen to twenty-one. He then served as principal of a high school in Smith Valley, Indiana, for three years. By this time, Terman had a wife, Anna, whom he had met and married in 1899 while at Central Normal. Loans from his family and a fellowship enabled Terman to realize both a master degree from Indiana University and a Ph.D. from Clark University in 1905. Terman was now equipped to teach psychology or pedagogy at the college level.

Terman worked in several positions at various universities after obtaining his doctorate degree. His battle with tuberculosis would be a deciding factor in where the Terman family would establish themselves. Terman was offered a position within the Department of Education at Stanford. He would later move to the psychology department and would remain at Stanford for thirty-three years, serving as chairman of the Psychology Department for twenty years. With the beginning of World War I, psychologists were seeking a way to assist in national defense. **Robert Mearns Yerkes**, president of the American Psychological Association, formed a committee to develop a psychological test that would determine the fitness of army recruits. From 1917 to 1919 Terman and his associate, Arthur Otis, were heavily involved in the development of these tests and the final report of the results. Despite questions from the military, the military testing project brought the use of psychological testing to the forefront of public consciousness and established Terman as a reputable psychologist.

Terman's support of eugenics was a critical factor in his work. The eugenics movement determined that characteristics that brought success in life were genetic in nature. Therefore, society could be improved by eliminating those with weaker traits. One such example would be the forced sterilization of patients in mental institutions, which Terman supported. The concept of eugenics was a driving force behind Terman's works in intelligence testing. Though fervent in his support of eugenics early in his career, Terman would back away from eugenics later in his career when faced with the harsh reality of eugenics put into action in the atrocities of Nazi extermination camps. Terman never, however, publicly recanted his views on eugenics.

Terman's work at Stanford began with a revision of the intelligence test established by French psychologist Alfred Binet. As a result, a single index of intelligence known as "intelligence quotient" (IQ) was developed. Terman was also heavily involved in the development of group testing for school children, which has become common practice in nearly all modern educational systems. In the mid-1900s Terman launched his famous longitudinal study of gifted children. The focus of the study was to determine the effect intelligence has on one's success as an adult. In this study over one thousand young people were surveyed over their lifetimes to determine the relationship of giftedness and success in life. This remains an ongoing study.

Terman was a pioneer in the development of psychological tests such as the Stanford-Binet and the concept of IQ. His longitudinal study provided scientists with a wealth of information such as the effect of military combat on men after World War II. In contrast, Terman's Darwinian-like approach concerning the use of intelligence testing brought about disagreement from colleagues. If not carefully constructed and administered there are many limitations to group testing such as cultural bias that can lead to invalid results. The limitations of psychological testing and the proper use of those tests are topics that Terman introduced and will continue to be discussed for many years to come. Terman died on December 21, 1956.

Further Reading: Minton, Henry L. *Lewis M. Terman, Pioneer in Psychological Testing.* New York: New York University Press, 1988; Seagoe, May V. *Terman and the Gifted.* Los Altos, CA: W. P. Kaufmann, 1975; Terman, Lewis M. *Genius and Stupidity.* New York: Arno Press, 1975.

Diane Foster

THAYER, ABBOTT HANDERSON (1849–1921)

Artist Abbott Thayer's observations and theories on animal coloration led to the efforts during World War I to camouflage military installations and ordnance. Thayer was born to privilege on August 12, 1849, in Boston. From 1863 to 1869 he attended the Chauncy Hall School and thereafter studied art in Boston and New York. Thayer opened a studio in Brooklyn in 1869 and after marrying in 1875, studied further in Europe, returning to New York in 1879. He found success in painting portraits, but in 1887 the first of his idealized winged women appeared in "Angel," his daughter the model. With the death of his wife in 1890, Thayer turned to psychological paintings, and in 1901 he forsook New York for a rustic life in Dublin, New Hampshire.

Thayer, a staunch Darwinist, believed natural laws determined animal coloration. In an 1896 article he sought to explain the law of protective coloration. Thayer's law was essentially that animals seem to disappear because of optical illusions based on their color, which is lighter where least illumined and darker where most illumined (obliterative counter shading). A 1903 article followed in which he explained how animal markings function for protection. Thayer's son Gerald elucidated his work in *Concealing-coloration in the Animal Kingdom; An Exposition of the Laws of Disguise through Color and Pattern: Being a Summary of Abbott H. Thayer's Discoveries* (1909). Thayer's 1907 painting *Peacock in the Woods* illustrated his theories. He died on May 29, 1921.

Benjamin F. Shearer

THOMAS, CHARLES ALLEN (1900–1982)

The holder of numerous awards and patents, Charles Thomas was the director of central research at Monsanto when he was called into government service for

801

the Manhattan Project. He worked on solid rocket fuels and coordinated the successful research effort to purify plutonium for the atomic bomb. He was present at the first test of the bomb and the recipient of the Medal of Merit from President Harry Truman in 1946 for his contributions to the Manhattan Project.

Born in Kentucky on February 15, 1900, Thomas grew up across the street from Transylvania College in Lexington, Kentucky. A budding chemist prone to blow up his home, he was allowed to use Transylvania's labs when just a teenager and he graduated from there in 1920. After completing his master's in chemistry at MIT, Thomas went to work for General Motors Research Corporation in Dayton, Ohio, the creation of **Charles Francis Kettering**. He and another young chemist, Carroll Hochwalt, were members of the team that developed ethyl gasoline. In 1926 the two formed Thomas and Hochwalt Laboratories with seed money from General Motors to study synthetic rubber. Ten years later their company was purchased by Monsanto to be its research arm. Thomas became a vice president of Monsanto in 1945. He then held the positions of president from 1951 to 1960 and chairman of the board until his mandatory retirement in 1965. Thomas was active in civic affairs and a founding member of the National Academy of Engineering.

Benjamin F. Shearer

THOMAS, ISAIAH (1750–1831)

Isaiah Thomas' *Massachusetts Spy*, founded in 1770, was important to the Patriot cause in the years leading up to and during the Revolutionary War. Thomas was born in Boston in January 1750, impoverished following his father's death, and sent at the age of six to work for a printer, Zechariah Fowle. At seven he was indentured to the printer for fourteen years. He broke his indenture after ten years, intending to sail for London, where he hoped to learn the art of printing, but he never made it there. En route to London, he stopped in Halifax, where he was hired to assist in printing a newspaper, the *Halifax Gazette*. He often chose to include news about opposition to the Stamp Act in the colonies, a strategy that eventually got him fired from his position. After short stays in Portsmouth, New Hampshire, Boston, and Wilmington, North Carolina, Thomas settled briefly in Charleston, South Carolina, where he worked for printer Robert Wells and married Mary Dill (they divorced in May 1777). He and Mary had a daughter, Mary Ann, and a son, Isaiah.

Thomas returned to Boston in 1770 to form a partnership with Fowle, began publishing the *Massachusetts Spy*, and soon bought out Fowle and increased the size and frequency of the paper. Though his credo was to be "Open to all Parties, but influenced by None," Thomas' paper supported the Patriot cause. This reflected the political stance of those who provided him financial and editorial support: John Hancock and revolutionary contributors Joseph Greenleaf and Thomas Young. The paper became the voice of independence and a primary source for information on the work of Patriot organizations such as the Sons of Liberty and the Committees of Correspondence as well as the issues they supported. The network that delivered the paper is believed to have been a means through which the radicals' Committees of Correspondence communicated—and thus also, considering the paper's wide distribution, supported a broader network of revolutionaries. It is also likely that Thomas contributed to the revolutionary cause by printing Patriot handbills and allowing his shop to be used as a meeting place.

After the start of the Revolutionary War in 1775, the *Spy* moved to Worcester, Massachusetts, which was to become Thomas' permanent home. But before following the paper to Worcester, Thomas further contributed to the war cause by joining **Paul Revere** on his ride to warn of the imminent British attack. He then joined the militia at Lexington, an experience about which he subsequently published a scathing, inciting account of British atrocities, describing them as inhumane murderers.

At the start of the hostilities, the *Spy* was a lucrative publication, with a readership throughout the colonies. However, the war challenged Thomas' success. Debts, short supplies of ink and paper, and the British occupation of Boston resulted in severe financial difficulties. He overcame them by diversifying his publications and expanding his business. Thomas was also appointed postmaster at Worcester in May 1775, a post he held until 1802. His good fortune extended to his personal life as well when he married Mary Thomas Fowle (no relation to Thomas' early master) in May 1779.

Thomas' publishing empire grew in the post-war years to span the former colonies. In addition to his newspapers and almanac, he published, together with his partners, more than 900 books, including Richardson's *Pamela* (1794), Goldsmith's *The Vicar of Wakefield* (1795), and Rousseau's *Letters of an Italian Nun* (1796). He was also an important printer of textbooks, children's books, magazines, music, and medical books. In addition, he was an author. His 1810 history of American printing remains an important source for scholars today.

Among the societies Thomas organized was the American Antiquarian Society, for which he also served as president from 1812 until his death. He endowed the society and donated a large portion of his imprints, including newspapers he had begun to collect in the early 1790s. It is but one of his efforts on behalf of historic preservation—especially of the United States. Thomas grew conservative in later years. His wife, Mary, died in November 1818 and his son died in 1819. He married Rebecca Armstrong that same year, but the couple separated in May 1822. His life and business activities slowed down in the years to follow. Thomas died in Worcester on April 4, 1831.

Further Reading: Batchelder, Frank Roe. "Isaiah Thomas, the Patriot Printer." *New England Magazine*, New Series 25 (November 1901): 284–305.

Stacy Dorgan

THOMAS, NORMAN MATTOON (1884–1968)

Born on November 20, 1884, to a Presbyterian minister in Marion, Ohio, Thomas graduated in 1905 from Princeton, where he studied under Woodrow

Wilson. He was a volunteer social worker in New York before studying at Union Theological Seminary. He read about Christian Socialism and became a socialist by the time he was ordained in 1911 and became pastor of East Harlem Presbyterian Church.

The pacifist Thomas opposed World War I and was among the founders of the Fellowship of Reconciliation, National Civil Liberties Bureau, and the American Civil Liberties Union. He also edited *World Tomorrow* and *The Nation*.

Thomas was the Socialist candidate for governor of New York in 1924 and ran unsuccessfully for various other offices. He ran for president in 1928, 1932, and 1936. In 1940 Thomas became a founder of the isolationist America First Committee, which at the end of a year was 800,000 strong, but dissolved on December 11, 1941. Thomas supported the war effort although he objected to internment of Japanese Americans and the influence of big business over war production.

Again in 1940, 1944, and 1948 Thomas was the Socialist presidential candidate. He opposed communism, poverty, racism, Cold War rearmament, and the Vietnam War. He was involved in labor and civil rights groups such as the League for Industrial Democracy, National Association for the Advancement of Colored People (NAACP), Congress of Racial Equality (CORE), and the Committee for a Sane Nuclear Policy (SANE). The author of numerous works, Thomas died on December 19, 1968.

John H. Barnhill

THOMPSON, JOHN TALIAFERRO (1860–1940)

John T. Thompson was born on December 31, 1860 in Newport, Kentucky. He grew up at army posts from California to Ohio. At 16 he decided to follow his father into the military. Thompson entered West Point in 1878 and graduated in 1882. He was commissioned a second lieutenant in artillery. Thompson was recognized for his skills in logistics, and restored order to an army supply system that had become hopelessly broken down. He was transferred to the Army Ordnance Department in 1880.

During the Spanish-American War, Thompson was appointed chief ordnance officer. He became a small arms specialist, and took charge of the army's ordnance supplies and logistics in Cuba. He was recognized for delivering over eighteen thousand tons of munitions without a single accident. Thompson was one of the first to recognize the merits of automatic pistols and rifles. He also developed the .45 caliber bullet for handguns.

Thompson retired a general in 1914 because of the difficulties in convincing the military to adopt automatic weapons. He went to work for the Remington Arms Corporation, managing the world's largest rifle factory at Eddystone, Pennsylvania. Remington Arms was producing British Army and Russian Army rifles for use during World War I. Yet Thompson still wanted to make a lightweight personal machine gun and began working, in his spare time, at home on this project. In 1915 he began his research and eventually created the "Tommy Gun," the world's first hand-held submachine gun. Thompson died on June 21, 1940.

Erskine L. Levi Jr.

THOREAU, HENRY DAVID (1817–1862)

Walden; or, Life in the Woods (1854) established Henry David Thoreau's reputation as a naturalist. "On the Relation of the Individual To the State," an 1848 lecture to the Concord Lyceum, established his reputation as a conscientious objector. The speech was published in 1849 as "Resistance to Civil Government," but it is known better today by the title given to it when republished after his death, "Civil Disobedience."

Thoreau was born on July 12, 1817, in Concord, Massachusetts. He graduated from Harvard in 1837. Thoreau and his brother operated a school until 1841. When the school closed Thoreau went to live in Ralph Waldo Emerson's home for two years, tutored in Emerson's brother's home in New York for a year, and returned to Concord, having published a few articles. On Independence Day 1845, he began his stay at Walden Pond, remaining until September 6, 1847.

During the middle of his stay at Walden, Thoreau was arrested for failure to pay his poll tax, which he had not paid in several years as a protest against slavery. He spent a late July night in jail. A relative paid the tax for him. Whether or not Thoreau chose that moment in 1846 to protest the newly declared Mexican-American War as well as slavery is debatable. In

Henry David Thoreau. Courtesy of the Library of Congress.

his now famous 1848 lecture, however, Thoreau declared that government can be abused and perverted: "Witness the present Mexican war, the work of comparatively a few individuals using the standing government as their tool."

Benjamin F. Shearer

TILLMAN, FLOYD (1914–2003)

Floyd Tillman was born in Ryan, Oklahoma, on December 8, 1914. He grew to become a pioneer of the "honky-tonk" and "Straight Ahead" country music era as an American country singer and songwriter. Tillman could also play the guitar, mandolin and banjo. His wife's name was Frances Inez and his children were Larry, Floyd, Donald and Frank. Tillman began his musical career by playing backup for fiddlers at local dances in Texas in his early childhood years. In 1933, at the age of nineteen, he became a member of Adolph and Emil Hofner's band playing at Gus' Palm Garden in San Antonio, Texas. At age twenty-one, in 1935, Tillman led his own band, called the Blue Ridge Playboys.

Eventually, Tillman played on other bands and orchestras, before enlisting in the U.S. Army during World War II as a radio operator, serving his tour in Texas. While in Texas, and not being in a direct combat zone, he was able to keep recording songs with Decca Records. In 1944 Tillman released one of the Top 5 country hits of the year, called "G.I. Blues." After the war, he made appearances at the Grand Old Opry and all together created over one thousand songs during his long life. Tillman was a charter inductee into the Nashville Songwriters International Hall of Fame in 1970, and he was inducted into the Country Music Hall of Fame in 1984. Tillman died in Texas on August 22, 2003, at the age of eighty-eight.

Erskine L. Levi Jr.

TILTON, JAMES (1745–1822)

Born on June 1, 1745, in Duck Creek Hundred, Delaware, James Tilton attended Rev. Samuel Finley's school with **William Shippen Jr.**, **Benjamin Rush**, and **John Morgan** before attending the College of Philadelphia, where he graduated as a physician in 1771. At the outbreak of the Revolution, Tilton joined a Delaware light infantry regiment as a lieutenant, going into battle at White Plains, Long Island, and Trenton before becoming the regiment's surgeon.

Tilton's own illness and time spent in the Morristown, New Jersey, military hospital appalled him, as he saw wounded and contagious patients crowded together and the hospitals badly organized and supplied. Transferring to the hospital service, Tilton insisted on cleanliness, the separation of wounded and sick men, examining boards for physicians and proper clothing and food for recovering patients. At Basking Ridge, New Jersey, Tilton erected experimental "Tilton Huts," well-ventilated, easy-to-clean wards for small numbers of men.

After the war, Tilton served in the Continental Congress and the Delaware House, was a founding member of the Medical Society of Delaware, and was a promoter of the Constitution. In 1813, as one of the last surviving Revolutionary War medical personnel, he was appointed physician and surgeon general of the army. Despite poor health and the amputation of a leg, Tilton inspected hospitals and pushed for the implementation of his earlier reforms, as published in *Economical Observations on Military Hospitals* (1813). Tilton died on May 14, 1822.

Further Reading: Saffron, Morris. "The Tilton Affair." *Journal of the American Medical Association* 236 (1976): 67–72.

Margaret D. Sankey

TINKER, CHARLES ALMERIN (1838–1890)

Charles Tinker was a Union military telegraph cipher operator during the Civil War. In March 1857, Tinker was employed as a telegraph operator in the Tazewell House in Pekin, Illinois. This was the headquarters of the circuit court judge. After watching Tinker manipulate the Morse key, and seeing him write down an incoming message, President Abraham Lincoln asked him to explain the operation. Tinker explained how the battery creates an electric current, which passes through the coils of the magnet. The electric current attracts an iron arm connected to a spring, which pulls the arm back from the magnet whenever the electric current is broken. By this method, the dashes and dots of the telegraph are created. Lincoln was very interested in this new method of communication.

With **David Homer Bates** and **Albert Brown Chandler** in the War Department's military telegraph office, Tinker and his comrades were the center of wartime communications. President Lincoln was a frequent visitor at the communications hub. On January 1, 1863, the day Lincoln's Emancipation Proclamation became effective, after a long reception at the White House at which the president was obliged to stand for hours shaking hands with all sorts of people, he came over to the telegraph office, settled himself in his accustomed place, and placing his feet on a nearby table, relaxed from the strain and fatigue of the day.

Further Reading: Bates, David Homer. *Lincoln in the Telegraph Office*. Lincoln: University of Nebraska Press, 1995.

Michael L. McGregor

TITTLE, ERNEST FREMONT (1885–1949)

During World War I, Ernest Fremont Tittle served in France with the Young Men's Christian Association (YMCA). Working with American troops, he was present at the St. Mihiel Offensive. His war experiences so radicalized him that he became an absolute pacifist.

Viewing any support for war as militarism, Tittle served with committees and organizations opposed to war. These included the Methodist Church World Peace Commission, the Commission to Study the Basis of a Just and Durable Peace and the Commission on the War in the Light of Christian Faith.

Tittle was appointed pastor of the First Methodist Church, Evanston, Illinois, shortly after he returned from France in 1918. His preaching on social justice issues of economic inequality, racism, nationalism, and war were often controversial. Prior to America's entry into World War II, Tittle urged negotiations to end the conflict. Even the attack on Pearl Harbor did not modify his absolute pacifism.

Tittle was born October 21, 1885, in Springfield, Ohio. He began his undergraduate education at Wittenberg College, but finished at Ohio Wesleyan in 1906. He graduated from Drew Theological Seminary with a B.D. in 1908, and was ordained a Methodist minister in 1910. From 1908 to 1918, Tittle served as pastor at Ohio churches in Christiansburg, Dayton, Delaware, and Columbus (1916–1918). During these pastorates, he was recognized as a liberal preacher who advocated the progressive beliefs of the Social Gospel. At his death on August 3, 1949, he was a major leader of liberal and pacifist Methodists.

Andrew J. Waskey

TOCH, MAXIMILIAN (1864–1946)

Maximilian Toch was born in New York City on July 17, 1864. When he was only eighteen years old he earned both his bachelor's degree in chemistry and his law degree from New York University. He then transformed the family's paint and pigment import business into Toch Brothers Paint Company, started another company, Standard Varnish Works, and worked as a patent attorney. Toch was also a heavily published expert on the chemistry of paints, pigments, and drying oils. His fame brought him a visiting professorship at the University of Beijing and even more fame came his way when he questioned the authenticity of several Rembrandt paintings based on his own scientific evidence.

On October 1, 1917, the U.S. Treasury Department's Bureau of War Risk Insurance declared that merchant ships had to be camouflaged to protect them from German submarines or pay a war risk penalty in addition to insurance premiums. The Bureau approved five competing camouflage systems, one of them being the Toch system. This system employed S-shaped diagonal streaks of battleship gray (a color Toch is credited with inventing), dark blue-gray, dark green, and light purple-pink to help ships fade out and blend into distant backgrounds. The Toch system was used on a large number of transports. By the middle of 1918, however, a more effective British dazzle camouflage replaced all five of the original systems. Toch was also in charge camouflaging fortifications on the East Coast. He died on May 28, 1946.

Benjamin F. Shearer

TOLMAN, RICHARD CHACE (1881–1948)

Chemist and physicist Richard Tolman interrupted his academic career to make contributions to American war efforts in both World War I and World War II. Born on March 4, 1881, in West Newton, Massachusetts, Tolman graduated from MIT in 1903 with a chemical engineering degree. He returned to MIT in 1907 and earned his doctorate in chemistry in 1910. Tolman taught chemistry successively at the University of Michigan, the University of California at Berkeley, and the University of Illinois until 1918, when he took a commission as a major in the army to become chief of the

Dispersoid Section of the Chemical Warfare Service. There he worked on smoke screens and tested ammunition. Tolman remained in Washington after the war ended as assistant director and then director of the Agriculture Department's Fixed Nitrogen Research Laboratory.

Tolman left Washington to become professor of physical chemistry and mathematical physics at the California Institute of Technology in 1922. He was elected to the National Academy of Sciences in 1923. He was also active in the Committee of Scientific Aids to Learning of the National Research Council. This group, which included **Vannevar Bush**, **Karl Taylor Compton**, **Frank Baldwin Jewett**, and **James Bryant Conant**, were convinced that America would enter the war and that successful warfare would depend on scientific research. In June 1940, President Franklin Roosevelt approved the formation of the National Defense Research Committee. Bush became its chair and Tolman, already in Washington, became its vice chair, in charge of armor and ordnance. Tolman returned to Caltech in 1947 and died on September 5, 1948.

Benjamin F. Shearer

TOMPKINS, SALLY LOUISE (1833–1916)

Born in Virginia, the daughter of a wealthy planter and politician, Sally Louise Tompkins was the only woman commissioned in the Confederate Army. Tompkins grew up on a Virginia plantation and moved to Richmond with her mother after her father's death shortly before the Civil War.

After the first Battle of Manassas/Bull Run, the necessity for hospitals and nurses became clear. Wounded soldiers needed care, and Judge John Robertson offered Tompkins the use of his house for a hospital. Tompkins opened Robertson Hospital on August 1, 1861. Because of deteriorating conditions in other small hospitals that had sprung up across the South, the Confederacy enacted a law that hospitals treating soldiers were required to be under the control of the Confederacy and managed by a commissioned officer. Tompkins appealed to Jefferson Davis, president of the Confederacy, who commissioned her a captain in the Confederate Army and made her head of the hospital. She asked to work without pay and continued to support the hospital financially above and beyond the food, medicine, and supplies for the sick and wounded that were provided by the government. The Robertson Hospital provided care for 1,333 patients over the four years of the Civil War with only seventy-three deaths, a statistic reflecting the excellent nursing care Tompkins and her nurses provided.

When the war ended, Tompkins' personal resources were depleted and she could not support herself on her salary as a nurse, so she entered the Home for Confederate Women in Richmond.

Marjorie A. Baier

TOWNES, CHARLES HARD (1915–)

In 1964, Charles H. Townes won the Nobel Prize for Physics, based on his co-invention of the maser, a quiet and reliable means of amplifying the radar used in many military applications. This invention formed the basis for the more popularly known laser.

Townes was born in Greenville, North Carolina, on July 28, 1915. He earned degrees from Furman University, Duke, and finally the California Institute of Technology, from which he received a doctorate in physics in 1939. After graduating, he was recruited by Bell Telephone Laboratories, where he remained until 1947. During World War II, his work there concentrated on radar bombing technology.

Radar inspired Townes' subsequent research, after he left Bell Labs to become a professor of physics at Columbia University. In the early 1950s, he focused on amplifying radar, building on principles established by **Albert Einstein** about thirty years earlier. The essential idea behind this work was that passing a beam of energy through a chamber that contained excited molecules will amplify the energy. For radar, amplification means more accurate signals for navigation, communication, and locating enemy vessels.

The first device for microwave amplification by stimulated emission of radiation—a name promptly reduced to its acronym, *maser*—used ammonia as the medium. A beam of ammonia particles was sent through a series of four magnets, which sorted the excited from the unexcited particles. The excited particles were then focused through a small hole into a resonator, where the energy of the vibrating particles generated a microwave signal of 24 billion cycles per second.

In January 30, 1955, *New York Times* article, Townes' maser was touted as providing the basis of a highly accurate "atomic clock": that is, an accurate means of measuring time precisely enough to calculate tiny shifts in the earth's rotation. The maser could be used this way because the oscillation of the ammonia molecules was highly regular. It was reported that such an atomic clock would lose no more than a single second in three hundred years.

Townes, however, was more interested in touting the maser as a potential "noiseless amplifier," noting that, if a microwave beam was passed through the resonant cavity, the excited ammonia particles amplified it without the noise typical of vacuum tubes. He envisioned using the maser to increase the sensitivity of microwave beams and to provide more accurate radar navigation.

One flaw in Townes' ammonia-based maser was that it could not provide continuous output. Soviet scientists Nikolai Basov and Aleksander Prokhorov, whose maser used more than two energy levels, solved this problem. In 1964, Basov, Prokhorov, and Townes shared the Nobel Prize for Physics and were lauded for "fundamental work in the field of quantum electronics."

A second flaw was that the ammonia-based maser could not be tuned to specific frequencies. It was therefore made obsolete by masers with other gain mediums—either other gasses or solids such as synthetic rubies.

From 1956 onward, Townes had been working with his brother-in-law and former Bell Labs colleague, **Arthur L. Schawlow**, now a professor at Stanford, to develop an "optical maser." This device was to pass light through a "gain medium," which performed the same function as the excited ammonia particles. In 1958, they established the workability of an optical maser and subsequently shared patents for optical and infrared masers, now more commonly known as lasers (for light amplification by stimulated emission of radiation). The term *laser* was actually coined by **Richard Gordon Gould**, who, after years of court battles, was recognized as its inventor.

Townes was also Vice President and Director of Research of the Institute for Defense Analyses from 1959 to 1961. He left Columbia in 1961 for the Massachusetts Institute of Technology, where he stayed until moving to the University of California at Berkeley in 1967, where he led research into radio and infrared astronomy. Townes was designated an emeritus professor in 1986. In March 2005, his many awards were increased by the Templeton prize for his work on the relationship between science and religion.

Masers are still used in microwave amplification and radio telemetry. Lasers, called in 1960, a solution looking for a problem have found potential military uses in targeting and range finding. Research is also in progress for laser-based energy weapons, use of lasers to destroy incoming intercontinental ballistic missiles (ICBMs), orbital nuclear defenses, and airborne missile shields against enemy spacecraft. However, the handheld laser gun of science fiction fame is likely to prove impractical for the foreseeable future.

Wende Vyborney Feller

TOWNSEND, HARRY EVERETT (1879–1941)

Harry Everett Townsend was a popular artist and painter born on March 10, 1879 in Wyoming, Illinois. After finishing high school, he entered the Chicago Art Institute and in 1900, studied abroad in Paris and London, returning to Chicago in 1903. In 1904 he married Cory Schiedewend, an aspiring artist.

During the next ten years, Townsend worked in his studio in Leonia, New Jersey, where he developed his etching, lithography, and sculpting skills. He became known for his scenic drawings of rural landscapes and many of his sketches appeared in popular magazines such as *Harper's*, *Century*, *Scribner's*, and *McClure's*.

When the United States entered World War I, Townsend joined the Division of Pictorial Publicity to assist in documenting the war. Townsend drew over two hundred sketches of soldiers in the trenches and of the war's new technologies, such as airplanes and tanks. Following the war, he was able to

Harry Everett Townsend. Courtesy of the Library of Congress.

attend the Paris Peace Conference, but did not create any major sketches of the event.

When Townsend returned from Europe in 1920, he moved his family to Connecticut where he continued to paint scenic landscapes. In the 1930s, he created numerous murals and taught at his studio in Norwalk. Townsend died on July 25, 1941.

Further Reading: Cornebise, Alfred E. *Art from the Trenches: America's Uniformed Artists in World War I.* College Station: Texas A&M University Press, 1991; Townsend, Harry Everett. *War Diary of a Combat Artist.* Edited by Alfred E. Cornebise, Niwot, CO: University Press of Colorado, 1991.

Donald C. Force

TRUDEAU, GARRETSON BEEKMAN (1948–)

Garry Trudeau is the creator of the *Doonesbury* cartoon strip that runs in over one thousand newspapers around the world. While his characters explore the themes of everyday life, Trudeau also focuses squarely on the political issues from the front pages of the newspapers.

Trudeau was born in July 1948 to well-to-do conservative parents in the Saranac Lake region of upstate New York. He attended the private St. Paul's Academy and then entered Yale University. His father was a doctor, and Trudeau's family includes the Beekmans of New York's Beekman Place. He began his cartooning career with a strip he drew in 1968 for the Yale *Daily News*. That strip, *Bull Tales*, focused on college life and humor. After graduation, Trudeau was invited to join the newly formed Universal Press Syndicate. *Bull Tales* morphed into another strip, *Doonesbury*, created by combining the then-popular slang word "doone," which meant a good-natured fool, and the last part of the name Pillsbury, the last name of Trudeau's college roommate. Michael Doonesbury is the main character of the strip. Trudeau was influenced by Walt Kelly and Al Capp, and while both cartoonists covered World War II and the issues of the war, Trudeau was the first American cartoonist to parody real-life political figures in a daily strip.

The *Doonesbury* comic strip first ran on October 26, 1970, and introduced the main characters of D.B., Michael, and Zonker, commune-dwelling students at the fictional Walden College. The content topics of the strip ranged from life in the commune to the war in Vietnam. The strips focusing on the war parodied U.S. President Richard Nixon and other government officials.

When the Watergate scandal broke, the Trudeau-drawn White House became a symbol of remoteness from the American people. As the war continued and the Watergate investigation expanded, the White House was drawn in darkness, sometimes with a cloud surrounding the entire structure, and then Trudeau added drapes to cover the official residence—the cartoonist's symbolic interpretation of the attempts of Nixon and his associates to hide from controversy. Many critics were puzzled as to the success of the cartoon, since some of the daily strips consisted of a basic drawing of the White House in four frames with balloon captioned dialogue offering the only distinction from frame to frame.

The biting critiques of politicians and the timeliness of the content separated *Doonesbury* from other editorial pieces. Trudeau developed each character with a unique history that readers followed with interest. *Doonesbury* created a day-to-day satire for each of the complicated congressional and presidential inquiries and focused on the important details and issues. Many *Doonesbury* strips were controversial, leaving editors to decide to run the strip and receive angry letters, or to remove specific offending strips. Some papers canceled syndication subscriptions. Many editors chose not to print the cartoons for certain days, creating a public debate on the role of free speech in American newspapers. Some compromised by moving the strip to the editorial pages, where it runs today in most newspapers.

Trudeau won the Pulitzer Prize for Editorial Cartooning in 1975, the first time a comic strip won the highest honor for cartooning. He was nominated again for the Pulitzer in 1989, and while he was a finalist, Trudeau did not win a second award. The cartoonist also won an Oscar for Best Animated Feature for the *Doonesbury* Special aired in 1977. Trudeau was made a member of the American Academy of Arts and Sciences in 1993. American cartoonist Matt Groening, creator of *The Simpsons*, cites Trudeau as his major influence.

Today *Doonesbury* is syndicated around the world. Trudeau also contributes written and cartoon work to the *Washington Post, Time, Harper's*, and the *New Yorker*. With the exception of one brief hiatus, *Doonesbury* continued and its characters moved into middle age. They confronted home and family issues until the American war in Iraq, when Trudeau began a pointed commentary on the new war. B.D., one of the original characters who first joined the military during the Vietnam War and who has worn his combat helmet in all but one strip, has lost his leg in service in the current war in Iraq. As American support for the war has waned and President George W. Bush's popularity has fallen, the *Doonesbury* strip has increased its focus on the Iraq war.

Further Reading: Rall, Ted. *Attitude 2: The New Subversive Alternative Cartoonists.* New York: Nantier Beall/Minoustchine Publishing, 2004; Trudeau, Garry. *Flashbacks: Twenty-Five Years of Doonesbury; Got War?; Peace Out, Dawg.* Kansas City, MO: Andrews McMeel Publishing.

Pamela Lee Gray

TRUMBULL, JOHN (1756–1843)

John Trumbull, born on June 6, 1756, in Lebanon, Connecticut, the son of Governor Jonathan Trumbull, entered Harvard in 1772, where he taught himself drawing and painting by studying the university's collection. When the Revolution began, he joined the First Connecticut Regiment, but his family's prominence brought him to Washington's attention and he was soon assigned to make sketches of British fortification and work with Polish military engineers on Fort Ticonderoga's defenses.

In 1779, however, Trumbull left the army to handle family business interests in New England and Paris, possibly also participating in secret missions there for Congress. In 1780, he went to London to study under Benjamin West, but was arrested on the vindictive testimony of Loyalist refugees in England, his conviction for treason halted only by the intervention of Edmund Burke. Trumbull's works were portraiture and monumental, epic works of North American history.

Although Trumbull's engravings and portraits, including those of George Washington were popular, he took a position in 1794 as John Jay's Secretary at the London embassy, where he helped to reveal France's bribery attempts in the XYZ Affair. Trumbull returned to America after the War of 1812 and lobbied Congress to allow him to paint historical canvases for the restored Capitol, which he installed in 1826, the *Declaration of Independence*, being his most famous. Trumbull died on November 10, 1843.

Further Reading: Jaffe, Irma. *John Trumbull, Patriot-Artist of the American Revolution.* Boston: New York Graphic Society, 1975.

Margaret D. Sankey

TRUMBULL, JOSEPH (1737–1778)

Congress appointed Joseph Trumbull, at George Washington's suggestion, the first Commissary General of the Continental Army on July 19, 1775. With few funds, he set out to feed the growing American Army.

Trumbull was born in Lebanon, Connecticut, on March 11, 1737. After graduating from Harvard in 1756, he joined his father's trade business, which was done directly with English merchants. By the end of the 1760s the business had failed. Trumbull, like his father, who was elected governor of Connecticut in 1769 and retired as governor in 1784, had political ambitions. He served in Connecticut's militia and its General Assembly in the 1760s. In the early 1770s, Trumbull served on committees of correspondence. In April 1775 he accepted the assembly's appointment as commissary general for the Connecticut military. Having served ably, a few months later he was commissary general of the Continental Army.

In November 1775 Congress established a day's army ration as 1 pound of beef; 18 ounces of flour; 1 pint of milk; 1 quart of spruce beer; 6.8 ounces of peas; 1.4 ounces of rice; 0.183 ounces of soap; and 0.0686 ounces of candle. By the next month a Court of Enquiry criticized the prices Trumbull was paying for food. His idea for a state-based provisioning system that would overcome logistical problems failed completely. Yet the army was fed, mostly by employing local sutlers, and Trumbull remained commissary general until 1777, when Congress appointed him to the Board of War. He died on July 23, 1778.

Benjamin F. Shearer

TRUMP, JOHN GEORGE (1907–1985)

John G. Trump was responsible for bringing effective radiation therapy to victims of cancer. A little more than a year after this new treatment was put into place, Trump put aside his medical research and joined the government's effort to develop radar systems.

Trump was born in New York City on August 21, 1907. He completed his undergraduate degree in electrical engineering at the Brooklyn Polytechnic Institute in 1929, his master's degree in physics at Columbia University in 1931, and his doctorate in electrical engineering at MIT in 1933. Remaining at MIT, Trump developed the Van de Graaf accelerator, working with its inventor, into a mechanism that could generate high-energy x-ray beams, which could target tumors. By 1940 Trump had created smaller and more powerful machines that were put into therapeutic use.

Radar and the atomic bomb were the two World War II research and development priorities of the U.S. government. Trump served as the chair of the National Defense Research Committee's Radar Division. MIT's Radiation Laboratory (the Rad Lab) was the focus of radar research. In 1944, Trump headed the Rad Lab's British branch, as the United States and Britain had shared information on radar from the start. Indeed, the Rad Lab's many successes during the war saved many lives from German blitzes in Great Britain.

When the war was over, Trump headed MIT's High Voltage Research Laboratory, remaining there until 1980. He died on February 21, 1985, and was awarded the National Medal of Science the next year.

Benjamin F. Shearer

TSUI, DANIEL CHEE (1939–)

An experimental solid-state physicist, Daniel Tsui shared the Nobel Prize in Physics in 1998 with Horst L. Störmer and Robert Laughlin for their contribution to the discovery of the fractional quantum Hall effect (FQHE), a phenomenon in which the effects of low temperature and powerful magnetic field force electrons to come together to form a new type of incompressible quantum liquid.

Tsui was born in the Henan Province, China, on February 28, 1939. His family allowed him to move as a teenager to Hong Kong where he completed high school and pre-college training. In 1958 he was admitted to Augustana College, completing his B.A. degree in 1961. He earned his Ph.D. in physics at the University of Chicago in 1967. Tsui joined the staff of Bell Laboratory in 1968, where he worked with Störmer and others in the study of two-dimensional electron gas in semiconductor interfaces, which eventually led them to the discovery in 1982 of the fractional quantum Hall effect.

Tsui became a professor in the department of electrical engineering at Princeton University in 1982. With the support of the Air Force Office of Scientific Research, he continued his work on conduction in ultra-small structures and quantum physics of electronic materials, which is now used in the design of high performance wave components for military surveillance and communication systems.

Elected to the National Academy of Sciences in 1987, and recipient of the Physics Medal of the Benjamin Franklin Institute in 1998, Tsui has over 240 scientific publications.

Nestor L. Osorio

TUOHY, WILLIAM KLAUS (1926–)

William Tuohy received the Pulitzer Prize for his international reporting on the Vietnam War in 1969. Tuohy was born on October 1, 1926, in Chicago, Illinois. In 1951, he earned a B.S. degree from Northwestern University, and began his journalism career with the *San Francisco Chronicle*, working his way up from copy boy to night city editor between 1952 and 1959. In 1959, he joined *Newsweek* as an editor and worked as a foreign correspondent for the magazine in 1966. Later that year, Tuohy transferred to the *Los Angeles Times* and covered the Vietnam War from 1966 to 1968. He also served as the paper's Middle Eastern correspondent from 1969 to 1971 and then as the *Los Angeles Times* bureau chief in Rome and London. In addition to his Pulitzer Prize for coverage of the Vietnam War, Tuohy received an award in 1970 from the Overseas Press Club of America for his Middle Eastern coverage. Tuohy described the American desertion of Vietnamese allies as one of the sorriest episodes in contemporary American history.

He concluded in his memoirs that citizens in a democracy need the information that reporters may provide. Nevertheless, his experiences left him increasingly skeptical of human motivation and the arrogance of those in power. Tuohy has often expressed his frustration that American policymakers continue to repeat the same foreign policy mistakes, at considerable cost in human life.

Further Reading: Tuohy, William. *Dangerous Company: Inside the World's Hottest Trouble Spots with a Pulitzer Prize–Winning War Correspondent.* New York: Morrow, 1987.

Ron Briley

TURRENTINE, JOHN WILLIAM (1880–1966)

When the supply of potash in the United States was endangered in 1910 as negotiations with the German potash producing monopoly faltered, the government allocated funds to support development of domestic resources. The next year John Turrentine went to work for the U.S. Department of Agriculture's Bureau of Soils in the search for sources of potassium other than potash.

Turrentine was born in Burlington, North Carolina, on July 5, 1880. He earned his bachelor's and master's degrees at the University of North Carolina, taught chemistry at Lafayette College for three years, and then did his doctoral work at Cornell, graduating in 1908. Turrentine taught at Wesleyan University until he joined the U.S. Bureau of Soils.

By the time America entered World War I, there was a serious shortage of potash, a source of soluble potassium. Potassium, with nitrogen and phosphorous, are the three primary nutrients of plants. Not only did a lack of potash as fertilizer endanger American agriculture, especially the growing of potatoes, wheat, and cotton, but potash also had wartime applications in the manufacture of black explosive powders, optical glass, and gas masks.

Turrentine was sent to Summerland, California, to take charge of an experimental plant that was to make potash out of kelp. There he succeeded in inventing a new process that indeed produced the potash and iodine as well from kelp. The plant remained in operation until 1922. Turrentine left government service in 1935 to found the American Potash Institute. He died on June 11, 1966.

Benjamin F. Shearer

TUVE, MERLE ANTONY (1901–1982)

World War II changed physicist Merle Tuve's research priorities. Tuve had worked with **Gregory Breit** to prove the existence of the ionosphere in the mid-1920s, thus intimating the possibility of radar. He then turned to nuclear physics and made more important discoveries. Shortly after war broke out in Europe, however, Tuve enthusiastically began research on proximity fuses, which when placed in anti-aircraft shells, promised to defend soldiers and civilians more effectively from enemy attacks.

Tuve was born in Canton, South Dakota on June 27, 1901. He earned his B.S. in physics in 1922 and his M.S. a year later at the University of Minnesota. He received his doctorate from Johns Hopkins University in 1926 based on his work with short-pulse radio waves in the course of his pioneering ionospheric studies. Tuve then joined the Department of Terrestrial Magnetism at the Carnegie Institution where he pursued his research in nuclear physics until 1940, when he began developing the proximity fuse. By August of 1942 the fuses were ready for production and Tuve was transferred to the

Applied Physics Laboratory at Johns Hopkins as director. He remained there throughout the war, managing the production of millions of proximity fuses for various uses. The fuses were used extensively in the Pacific, in Great Britain, and at the Battle of the Bulge.

Tuve received the Presidential Medal of Merit for this work in 1946. He became director of the Department of Terrestrial Magnetism also in 1946 and remained there until 1966. He died on May 20, 1982.

Benjamin F. Shearer

TYLER, ROYALL (WILLIAM) (1757–1826)

Royall Tyler was a soldier in the Revolutionary War, a judge on the Vermont Supreme Court, and a law professor at the University of Vermont. He was also the author of America's first successful stage comedy, *The Contrast* (1790). Tyler was born in Boston on July 18, 1757. After graduating from Harvard in 1776, he began to study law, but suspended his studies to fight in the Revolution as a member of the Boston Independent Company. When the war ended, Tyler earned his law degree and began practice in Massachusetts. He re-entered the service in 1787 to help suppress Shays' Rebellion.

It was on official business connected to Shays' Rebellion that Tyler first visited New York City. Entranced by the theater scene, he remained in the city. Within a month Tyler had staged his first play, *The Contrast* (1790). The play contrasted the manners and mores of its hero, Revolutionary War veteran Colonel Henry Manley, with those of the oversophisticated, "Europeanized" New Yorkers Manley encountered when he came to the city petitioning the government on behalf of wounded veterans. While his cause was represented as just, Manley himself was gently satirized for his windy rhetoric of independence. A great success in New York, the play was subsequently staged in Baltimore and Philadelphia.

Tyler wrote one more play before returning to New England, where he became a judge and a professor. He continued to write, producing occasional pieces for newspapers, such as his patriotic "Ode Composed for the 4th of July" (1797), as well as a novel, *The Algerine Captive* (1797), and a book contrasting English and American culture, *A Yankey in London* (1809). Tyler's career, health, and finances flagged toward the end of his life, and he died in poverty on August 26, 1826.

Matthew J. Bolton

U

UREY, HAROLD CLAYTON (1893–1981)

Harold Urey won the Nobel Prize in Chemistry in 1934 for the discovery of heavy water. His expertise in separating isotopes brought him into the nation's service during World War II through the Manhattan Project just as his sense of duty took him to a Philadelphia chemical plant to assist America's efforts in World War I in spite of his pacifism.

Urey was born in Walkerton, Indiana, on April 29, 1893. After graduating with a zoology degree from the University of Montana in 1917 he went on to Berkeley, where he received his doctorate in chemistry, and then for a year of study in Copenhagen with Neils Bohr. He began his distinguished academic career at Johns Hopkins University in 1924, moving to Columbia in 1929, the University of Chicago in 1945, and finally to the University of California—San Diego in 1958.

In May 1940 Urey and his colleagues at Columbia were working on separating uranium isotopes under a government contract. Urey was appointed head of an advisory committee to the Committee for Uranium. When the Office of Scientific Research and Development was created in 1941 under **Vannevar Bush**, Urey was a member of the Uranium Section's executive committee, which made recommendations in 1942 for a program to make atomic weapons. As director of War Research at Columbia, Urey had hundreds of people working for him to separate uranium isotopes by three different methods. Although Urey's research eventually proved successful, it did not produce uranium for use in the war.

Benjamin F. Shearer

V

VALLEY, GEORGE EDWARD JR. (1913–1999)

George Valley made two notable contributions to American war efforts. During World War II he developed the H2X radar bombsight, which was used extensively as it made bombing through overcast possible. During the Cold War as a member of the U.S. Air Force Scientific Advisory Board from 1946 to 1964, Valley conceptualized the Semi-Automatic Ground Environment (SAGE), which combined twenty-four operational centers and three combat centers with radar and computers to detect and respond to enemy attacks on the country.

Valley was born in New York City on September 5, 1913. He graduated from MIT in 1935 and finished his doctorate in nuclear physics at the University of Rochester in 1939. He then went to Harvard as a research assistant for a year and then as a National Research Council fellow, leaving Harvard for MIT's Radiation Lab in 1941. After the war Valley continued his academic career at MIT and founded the government-funded Lincoln Laboratory there in 1949. Valley died on October 16, 1999.

Late in 1942 Valley became convinced that bombing Germany would be more effective than trying to shoot down its planes. He set aside his gun-laying radar project to develop a targeting radar. While **Luis Walter Alvarez** was working on such a radar system, Valley believed he could more quickly adapt the existing English H2S system into radar accurate enough for successful use by using the X-band rather than the S-band. Valley's H2X was first employed in combat in November 1943.

Benjamin F. Shearer

VAN HYNING, LYRL CLARK (?–?)

Lyrl Clark Van Hyning became active in the ultra-conservative isolationist movement that sprang up in the late 1930s. She believed that America's involvement in World War II was a mistake, and that it was part of a large Jewish conspiracy. As with many women active in the isolationist movement, she was stridently anti-Semitic. She accused Jews of inspiring the Civil War, the assassination of President Abraham Lincoln, and World War I, and also accused President Woodrow Wilson of being Jewish. She argued that the election of President Franklin D. Roosevelt and World War II were part of an international Jewish conspiracy.

Van Hyning lived in Chicago and published a weekly newspaper, *Women's Voice*, which reached a circulation of twenty-five thousand by 1945. She also founded the group We the Mothers Mobilize for America with **Elizabeth Dilling** in February 1941. In only three months this organization, which Dilling soon left, claimed to have 1,000 members in Chicago and 150,000 across the country. The organization, comprised mostly of middle-class mothers, held protests against World War II.

Van Hyning received financial backing from some very prominent businessmen. Automobile tycoon **Henry Ford**, publisher **William Randolph Hearst**, and aviator **Charles Augustus Lindbergh** all supported Van Hyning's newspaper and organization. She was active in the so-called Mother's Movement, a coalition of conservative women who protested against American actions in World War II, and brought a portion of her organization to an antiwar demonstration in Washington, DC, in 1943. The following year, she sponsored a national women's peace conference.

Gene C. Gerard

VARGAS Y CHÁVEZ, JOAQUÍN ALBERTO (1896–1982)

Artist and illustrator Alberto Vargas was born in Arequipa, Peru, on February 9, 1896. After studying photography in Geneva and London, he went to New York in 1916, where he survived by painting and retouching photographs. His big break came in 1919 when Florenz Ziegfeld hired him to do posters for his Follies. In 1934 Vargas headed for Hollywood to paint the stars and do other film-related artistic work. Back in New York in 1940, he was hired by *Esquire* magazine to replace the famous illustrator George Petty, whose depictions of women had set the male standard of feminine beauty in the 1930s.

Working out of *Esquire*'s Chicago headquarters, Vargas was an instant success even before America was involved in World War II. His Varga girls (a romantic variation on Vargas) appeared not only in the magazine, but also on calendars and playing cards. During the war, Varga girls made their way throughout the world in *Esquire*'s military editions and other products. Among the troops, Vargas' idealized women became pinups as famous as the posters of **Jane Russell** and **Ruth Elizabeth "Betty" Grable**.

A protracted contract dispute eventually left *Esquire* with ownership of the brand "Varga" in 1950. Vargas managed to make a living until Hugh Hefner hired him in 1960 to paint nude foldouts for *Playboy*. These Vargas girls created an entirely new audience for his work. He retired from *Playboy* in 1976 and died on December 30, 1982.

Benjamin F. Shearer

VAUCLAIN, SAMUEL MATTHEWS (1856–1940)

Samuel Vauclain headed the Advisory Committee on Plants and Munitions of the War Industries Board during World War I. This committee, originally the production committee of the Council of National Defense's Munitions Standards Board, came about after the March 1918 reorganization of the War Industries Board.

Vauclain, born in what is now part of Philadelphia on May 18, 1856, was raised in Altoona where his father was a railroad mechanic. He left school at sixteen to work on the railroad, and in 1883 he went to work for the Baldwin Locomotive Works back in Philadelphia. There he developed into a leading expert on locomotive design with a number of inventions to his credit. By 1911, he became the company's vice president and in 1919, its president. Although known to be autocratic and irascible, Vauclain was also a superb salesman who had opened European markets for Baldwin's products when war broke out and even began making munitions for the British.

Vauclain credited the ordinary Americans like himself who gathered in Washington to manage the war with the eventual victory. His Committee's support of standardizing the British Enfield rifles and redesigning them to use Springfield rifle ammunition increased production and quality dramatically. Most significantly, however, Vauclain's personal appeals to cease business as usual and start making needed munitions were critical in swaying

Samuel Matthews Vauclain. Courtesy of the Library of Congress.

wary manufacturers who had always been suspicious of government work to the war effort.

Having become chair of the board at Baldwin in 1929, Vauclain died at home on February 5, 1940.

Benjamin F. Shearer

VAUGHAN, VICTOR CLARENCE (1851–1929)

A division surgeon in the U.S. Army during the Spanish-American War, Victor Vaughan led groundbreaking research into the spread of typhoid in the training camps. Born in 1851, he attended Central College in Fayette, Missouri, then taught at and was dean of the University of Michigan Medical School, where he fought for the inclusion of women, until his retirement in 1920. He promoted the germ theory of contagion, and worked extensively with the army, whom he served as a surgeon for many years.

Many of the army training camps had a problem with typhoid outbreaks throughout much of the Spanish-American War. The War Department, on the advice of the Surgeon General, appointed Major Vaughan, along with Majors Walter Reed and **Edward Oram Shakespeare**, to the Typhoid Board from 1898 to 1900. Their task was to discover the cause of the typhoid problem in the army encampments and make recommendations for the correction of any unsanitary conditions. The board investigated the medical histories of over ninety regiments. They discovered that the source of the infection was primarily contact with human carriers, not contaminated water, as had previously been believed. They also discovered that carriers were infectious during their own incubation period, and may spread the disease unknowingly before they were even diagnosed and after they were pronounced recovered. The board's suggestions for prevention were largely unheeded, however, as the Army Medical Department's resources were overstretched by that point.

Vaughan died in 1929, having trained four generations of noted physicians.

Ellen Baier

VEAZEY, WILLIAM REED (1883–1958)

Magnesium is an abundant element in the earth's crust, but it is found only in combination with other minerals. World War I was the first war in which magnesium was required in large amounts. It was used in tracer bullets, artillery shells, gas masks, flashlights, alloys for castings, and as an alternative for aluminum. The need for magnesium grew higher as the war churned on. England alone had asked the United States for 250,000 pounds a year, and other allies placed a constant demand on U.S. production. Thanks to **Herbert Henry Dow** and William Veazey, the United States had three plants turning out 30,000 pounds of magnesium a month by fall 1918. Another plant in Canada produced 15,000 pounds a month.

Veazey was already well established teaching chemistry and chemical engineering at the Case School of Applied Sciences when Dow asked him to consult on magnesium production in 1916. Veazey had been born in Chase City, Virginia, on December 29, 1883, and did his undergraduate work at Westminster College. After completing his doctorate in chemistry at Johns Hopkins in 1907, he began teaching at Case. Veazey, a frequent consultant for Dow over the years, was finally persuaded to leave Case in 1936 to work for Dow. He remained with Dow until retiring in 1953. He died on September 20, 1958.

In that summer 1916, Veazey led a small group at Dow who produced the first pound of magnesium metal in the United States using the process he developed.

Benjamin F. Shearer

VIGUERIE, RICHARD A. (1933–)

Richard Viguerie, born on September 23, 1933, in Golden Acres, Texas, is a conservative and anticommunist whose fund-raising skills helped establish the new political right during the 1970s. He got his political start in 1961 as the executive secretary of the conservative Young Americans for Freedom. In 1963, he joined the Committee for the Monroe Doctrine to oppose accommodation with Cuba. After Goldwater's loss in 1964, Viguerie, using a public list of 12,000 contributors to the Goldwater campaign, began direct-mailing solicitations for such conservative causes as anti-communism and opposition to abortion.

Viguerie's vision was both politically successful and financially lucrative, earning him over $100,000 his first year in the business. Among his most controversial clients was the Korean Cultural Freedom Foundation, an anticommunist front organization for Reverend Sun Myung Moon's Unification Church. In 1974, Viguerie established the *Conservative Digest*, and by 1980 he was earning between $35 and $40 million annually for his clients.

With the election of President Ronald Reagan in 1980, Viguerie was one of the most influential political consultants in the nation. He was, however, willing to criticize the Reagan administration for its budget deficits. In 1987, he was on the board of the American Freedom Coalition, formed to bring conservatives together with the Christian right in support, among other things, of "freedom fighters" against communists and America's duty to spread freedom everywhere.

Viguerie continues to raise funds for conservative causes and assert that the dominant culture discriminates against Christians.

Ron Briley

VILLARD, HELEN FRANCES "FANNY" GARRISON (1844–1928)

Fanny Garrison Villard was a World War I protestor, an ardent and absolute pacifist, and an advocate for women's rights. The daughter of William Lloyd

Garrison, a well-known abolitionist, and Helen Eliza Benson, she was born Helen Frances Garrison in Boston, Massachusetts, on December 16, 1844. Despite her family's poverty, she attended the Winthrop School in Boston. She taught piano to help support her family until she married **Henry Villard**, a German journalist, in 1866. Deeply influenced by her father's progressive politics, and empowered by her husband's successful business enterprises, she was an active philanthropist. She worked first with the Diet Kitchen Association, which provided food for the sick and poor, and contributed money and time to several such charitable organizations. She also helped found Barnard College and the Harvard Annex (later Radcliffe College).

After her husband died in 1900, however, Villard became much more active in especially controversial circles: women's rights and peace. She was a lovely woman, even in later years, and commanded the complete attention of audiences whenever she spoke. Though she was active in suffrage circles in New York, her main contributions emerged with the beginning of World War I. At the age of seventy, she organized the Women's Peace March down Fifth Avenue on August 29, 1914, hoping to bring together pacifists demonstrating their commitment to the cause of peace and their outrage at the war crimes being committed. Several thousand women, and a bare handful of men (including Villard's son), dressed all in black paraded silently down the street, accompanied only by the beating of a bass drum. In November of that year, the Women's Peace Party (WPP) was founded, and Villard was active in the New York chapter, making sure that her time and efforts were going toward absolute nonresistance, with no compromise. When the party vowed to support the war if the United States were overtly threatened, however, she was outraged. Because of her refusal to acknowledge that any aggression on the part of Germany would warrant a response from the United States, Villard left the Women's Peace Party in 1916. Her son described her as uncompromising, but without guile.

Villard's son, **Oswald Garrison Villard Jr.**, was also a noted peace activist, as well as the editor of *The Nation* and the *New York Evening Post*, and the two of them often collaborated in working on the paper or in working for peace. Her uncompromising stance and strength of character strongly influenced her son, who became even better well known than she; in particular, he helped to found the National Association for the Advancement of Colored People, to which she also donated time and money.

In 1919, Villard and several other firm pacifists formed the Women's Peace Society, an organization that vowed to support no war efforts, however slight. This organization was considerably smaller than the WPP, and spent its time and resources lobbying politicians rather than demonstrating or agitating. Several members of Villard's Women's Peace Society who were more inclined to action, in turn, left to form the Women's Peace Union, but the Peace Society remained active until 1932, and Villard headed it until her death on July 5, 1928, in Dobbs Ferry, New York.

Further Reading: Villard, Oswald Garrison. *Fighting Years; Memoirs of a Liberal Editor*. New York: Harcourt, Brace, 1939; *William Lloyd Garrison on Non-resistance,*

Together with a Personal Sketch by His Daughter, Fanny Garrison Villard, and a Tribute by Leo Tolstoi. Edited by Fanny Garrison Villard, New York: Nation Press Printing, 1924.

Ellen Baier

VILLARD, HENRY (1835–1900)

Henry Villard became well known for his coverage of several major Civil War battles for the *New York Herald* and the *New York Tribune*. Born in Bavaria on April 10, 1835, as Ferdinand Heinrich Gustav Hilgard, he immigrated to the United States in 1853, "Americanized" his name and began his writing career.

Unable to speak English, Villard worked a series of menial jobs while learning the language. By 1858, he worked for a German newspaper, covering the Abraham Lincoln-Stephen Douglas presidential debates. Villard reported battles such as First Manassas in July 1861, Fredericksburg in December 1862, and the Wilderness in May 1864 for several different newspapers, earning a reputation as an outstanding war correspondent.

Villard married Helen Frances Garrison, daughter of the radical abolitionist and editor of *The Liberator*, William Lloyd Garrison, on January 3, 1866. Shortly thereafter, Villard traveled to Europe to cover the Franco-Prussian War for the *New York Tribune*. By 1881, he owned a significant portion of the *New York Evening Post* and *The Nation*.

Post-war, Villard also became a railroad entrepreneur, financing railways in the United States. Befriending **Thomas Alva Edison**, he invested in the Edison Electric Light Company. In 1888, Villard was named chairman of the board for Edison's company, now called the Edison General Electric Company. Retiring in 1893, he and his family toured Europe and Villard wrote his memoirs, focusing significantly on the Civil War years. He died on November 12, 1900, leaving his business concerns to his son, Harvard graduate **Oswald Garrison Villard Jr.**

Further Reading: de Borchgrave, Alexandra, and John Cullen. *Villard: The Life and Times of an American Titan.* New York: Doubleday, 2001.

Kelly Boyer Sagert

VILLARD, OSWALD GARRISON JR. (1916–2004)

Mike Villard, as he was called, did not follow the paths of his grandfather, **Henry Villard**, or his father into journalism at the family's enterprises, the *New York Evening Post* and *The Nation*. Neither did he follow the path of his father and grandmother, **Helen Frances "Fanny" Garrison Villard**, into pacifist activism. Born on September 17, 1916, in Dobbs Ferry, New York, and also claiming abolitionist William Lloyd Garrison as his great-grandfather, Villard had an early fascination with radio, becoming a licensed operator at the age of 16. While he got his undergraduate degree in English at Yale in

1938, he turned to his personal interest in electrical engineering for graduate work. Villard went to Stanford as a research associate in 1939 to work under **Frederick Emmons Terman**.

When Terman took over the Radio Research Laboratory at Harvard, he employed Villard to work on radar jamming devices there. Villard got his engineering degree in 1943 with Terman's assistance, but his Ph.D. was delayed until 1949, three years after his return to Stanford as a member of the faculty. Thus began a distinguished career at Stanford and the Stanford Research Institute, which ended with his official retirement in 1987 and his death on January 7, 2004.

A member of the National Academy of Sciences, Villard received the Air Force's Meritorious Civilian Service Award and the Secretary of Defense's Medal for Outstanding Service for proving the efficacy of stealth technologies and designing an over-the-horizon radar system to detect missiles and aircraft.

Benjamin F. Shearer

VINCENT, JESSE G. (1880–1962)

Jesse Vincent took a leave of absence from the Packard Motor Car Company during World War I to work in the war effort, thus earning the title of colonel. He was among other things, commander of McCook Field in Dayton, Ohio, from February to September 1918. Yet his greatest contribution to the war was made over a few days in rooms at Washington's Willard Hotel when he helped to design the Liberty engine.

Vincent was born in rural Arkansas in 1880. With no formal training in mechanical engineering beyond a correspondence course, he honed his natural skills at the American Arithmometer Company from 1903 until he went to Hudson Motors in 1910 as chief engineer. He left Hudson for the same position at Packard in 1912 and became a vice president in charge of engineering in 1915. Vincent retired from Packard in 1949, but remained a consultant until 1954. He died on April 20, 1962.

Edward Andrew Deeds of the Aircraft Production Board asked Vincent and **Elbert John Hall** of Scott-Hall Motors to work together on the design of a standardized aircraft engine for military use. They met on May 29, 1917, at the Willard and in two days had preliminary drawings, in four days, finished drawings, and a prototype in six weeks. By December 1917 engines were in production, and by the end of the war, nearly 16,000 Liberty engines had been produced and 6,000 had been installed in aircraft. Liberty engines played an important part in the Allied victory.

Benjamin F. Shearer

VON KÁRMÁN, THEODORE (1881–1963)

Best known for his work in aeronautics, Theodore von Kármán began life on May 11, 1881, in Budapest, Hungary, and quickly became a mathematical prodigy. After leaving gymnasium, von Kármán won the Eotvos Prize as the top student in mathematics and science in Hungary. Instead of allowing him to pursue mathematics, von Kármán's father insisted that he study mechanical engineering at the Palatine Joseph Polytechnic in Budapest. It soon became clear, however, that von Kármán's interests and talents lay in the realm of theoretical mathematics. After serving a compulsory stint in the Austro-Hungarian army, von Kármán won a two-year fellowship from the Hungarian Academy of Sciences, which allowed him to pursue his studies at Göttingen University in Germany. Although von Kármán would earn his Ph.D. for creating mathematical models explaining buckling in large structures, it was during this period that his interests shifted from engineering to aeronautics.

At Göttingen, von Kármán could develop his new interest at the large wind tunnel built for the Zeppelin airships. In 1911, his research in the wind tunnel led to the creation of a mathematical model that explained why alternating double rows of vortices form behind flat bodies in a fluid flow. This observation and explanatory model came to be known as Kármán's Vortex Street. (In time von Kármán's name would be attached to a dozen different mathematical formulations). In 1913, von Kármán accepted the post of director of the Aeronautical Institute in Aachen, Germany, where he conducted theoretical work on aircraft design. With the outbreak of World War I, von Kármán was called into military service, designing and testing aircraft. During his time in the army, von Kármán helped to develop a helicopter that needed to remain tied to the ground, but could replace the unreliable and troublesome observation balloons then in use. After the war, von Kármán continued his work in Aachen and in an attempt to reunite scientists whose relationships had been frayed during the long war, he established the International Applied Mechanics Congress Committee, which, after World War II, became the International Union of Theoretical and Applied Mechanics.

In 1930 von Kármán became the director of the new Aeronautical Laboratory at the California Institute of Technology where his intellectual curiosity and open-mindedness quickly drew top graduate students to the university. While others thought rocket propulsion was strictly a science fiction fantasy, von Kármán encouraged his students in the field. Their work was so promising that by 1938 the U.S. Army Air Corps was sponsoring the Jet Assisted Take-off Rockets (JATO) program at Cal Tech. The JATO program would be the first of many collaborative efforts between von Kármán and the U.S. military. The first planes using JATO technology were tested in August 1941, and by April 1942 the Douglas A-20 became the first airplane to use permanently mounted JATOs.

Despite this early success, jet propulsion research remained a relatively small endeavor with no coordinated planning or centralized facilities. That situation changed after 1943 when the Allies learned of the German V-2 rocket, which could deliver a 743-kilogram payload to a target 240 kilometers away. In August 1943 von Kármán was asked to write a report on the possibilities for the United States developing similar long-range rockets, which could be fired from beyond the horizon and travel faster than intercepting aircraft. In October 1943 the National Defense Research Committee appointed General Hap Arnold of the Army Air Corps to create a coordinated guided missile research and development program. Thus the Jet Propulsion Laboratory (JPL) was born, with von Kármán as its first director. Created too late to make any practical contributions to the war effort, the JPL would become a center of research and development during the Cold War. The JPL would be instrumental in both weapons development and the space program.

Von Kármán retired in 1949, but remained politically and scientifically active, helping to create AGARD, the scientific research program of the North Atlantic Treaty Organization (NATO), the International Council of Aeronautical Sciences, the International Academy of Astronautics, and the von Kármán Institute. In 1963 von Kármán became the first recipient of the National Medal of Science, not long before he died on May 7 of that same year, leaving a legacy as the "father of modern aerospace science."

Further Reading: Gorn, Michael. *The Universal Man: Theodore von Kármán's Life in Aeronautics*. Washington, DC: Smithsonian Institution Press, 1992; von Kármán, Theodore. *The Wind and Beyond: Theodore von Kármán Pioneer in Aviation and Pathfinder in Space*. Boston: Little, Brown, 1967.

J. A. Walwik

VONNEGUT, KURT JR. (1922–)

Author Kurt Vonnegut Jr. was born in Indianapolis, Indiana, on November 11, 1922, to an architect and a homemaker. He studied biochemistry at Cornell University beginning in 1940, but spurred by the bombing of Pearl Harbor in December 1941, he enlisted in the military. He was captured while operating as a scout in the Battle of the Bulge in 1944 and was sent to Dresden to work in a slaughterhouse, making diet supplements for pregnant women.

Vonnegut's most celebrated novel, *Slaughterhouse-Five*, arose from these experiences. Its main character, Billy Pilgrim, is witness to a fictionalized version of the horrors that the author experienced in real life as a prisoner of war. Vonnegut and four others were held in the slaughterhouse's basement refrigerator lockup while Dresden was fire bombed by English and American forces. Vonnegut witnessed the aftermath of the stupendous bombing, in which more civilians were killed that in both Japanese nuclear bombings. After the city was decimated, Vonnegut, one of the few to survive, was forced by the Germans to recover corpses until the Russians captured Dresden in 1945. *Slaughterhouse-Five or The Children's Crusade: A Duty-Dance with Death* focused on the absurdity and futility of war.

Vonnegut worked as a reporter and public relations writer for General Electric after World War II, but he also wrote short stories and novels. His writing did not receive widespread public notice until the release of *Slaughterhouse-Five* in 1969. The anti–Vietnam War movement quickly embraced his novels, and they have since been deemed classics of American literature.

Pamela Lee Gray

VON NEUMANN, JOHN LOUIS (1903–1957)

Born on December 28, 1903, in Budapest, Hungary, child prodigy John von Neumann was already internationally famous when he came to Princeton to teach mathematics in 1930. Without attending classes, he was awarded his Ph.D. in mathematics from the University of Budapest in 1926. He used that time to study chemistry at the University of Berlin and then at Zurich's Technische Hochschule, which awarded him a diploma in chemical engineering. Between 1926 and his move to Princeton, von Neumann held a Rockefeller fellowship that allowed him further study at Göttingen, and he lectured at Berlin and Hamburg. By 1932, von Neumann had determined the mathematical foundations of the new quantum mechanics.

In 1933, von Neumann joined Princeton's new Institute for Advanced Study (IAS). He was one of six new mathematics professors invited to the faculty, another having been **Albert Einstein**. Von Neumann would spend the rest of life, which was shortened by cancer on February 8, 1957, at IAS.

Von Neumann received both the President's Medal for Merit and the Distinguished Civilian Service Award for his contributions to the World War II war effort. He was on the Scientific Advisory Committee for the Ballistic Research Laboratory. In 1943 he went to Los Alamos to assist in calculations for atomic bomb detonation and remained a consultant there until 1955 to work on the hydrogen bomb. In 1944 he published his famous work on game theory, and after the war he became a pioneer of computing.

Benjamin F. Shearer

W

WALD, LILLIAN D. (1867–1940)

Already very well known by 1914 for her settlement house work in New York City, Lillian Wald actively opposed the entry of the United States into World War I. Because of her popularity, her leadership skills, and her friendship with President Woodrow Wilson, she contributed greatly to the anti-military movement. She served as the president of the executive board of the American Union Against Militarism (AUAM), for which **Crystal Eastman** was the executive secretary.

Wald was born in Cincinnati on March 10, 1867, to German immigrant parents. When she was 11, her family moved to Rochester, New York. She attended private schools and lived a privileged life. Seeking new challenges she attended nurses' training at New York Hospital School of Nursing, graduating in 1891. She studied for a year at New York Women's Medical College, but did not pursue a medical career. Instead she taught home nursing to immigrants. Through one of her students, she observed illness and poverty in the lower East Side tenement district, a turning point in her career. With financial support from wealthy friends, she established the Henry Street Nursing Service and Settlement House.

Wald supported the peace movement in opposition to the U.S. entry into World War I because she feared that warfare would divert valuable resources from social reform to military spending. On August 29, 1914 she marched down Fifth Avenue in the Women's Peace Parade led by **Helen Frances "Fanny" Garrison Villard** with 1,200 other women. In an interview with a reporter from the *New York Evening Post*, she said, "War is the doom of all that has taken years of peace to build up." She also opposed sending surgeons or nurses to the Allied front because that would be "perpetuating and in a way glorifying war and its barbarisms."

In late 1914 a group that became the American Union Against Militarism (AUAM) met at the Henry Street Settlement. Within a year, membership in this group had grown to six thousand. In 1916 Lillian Wald, **(Laura) Jane Addams**, and Ida Tarbell supported Wilson's reelection with the hope that he would keep the United States out of the war in Europe. In January 1917 Wald and a small delegation met with Wilson and congratulated him on his decision to enforce peace. However, after the Berlin blockade against Allied and neutral countries, Wilson broke off diplomatic relations with Germany and Congress approved arming ships. The AUAM opposed this, and Wald wrote a letter in behalf of the group to Wilson. Nevertheless, their drive for peace failed and the United States entered the war on April 16, 1917.

Eventually Wald withdrew from the AUAM. Later associations that grew from the AUAM were the League for Free Nations Association, a forerunner of the League of Nations and later the United Nations; the Foreign Policy Association; and the American Civil Liberties Union. Even though Wald supported the war effort by providing an office for a registration board to conscript soldiers, by helping the Red Cross formulate policy, and by helping nurses win relative rank in the army, she remained a pacifist. Within a year, **Annie Warburton Goodrich**, the director of nurses for the Henry Street Visiting Nurses Service, was named the dean of the Army School of Nursing.

Wald continued to be engaged in government policy discussions as a member of the Committee on Nothing At All that sought to reconcile democracy with militarism. She became the chair of the Committee on Home Nursing of the Section on Sanitation of the Committee on Welfare Work of the Council on National Defense. She worked on "preparedness for peace" by training visiting nurses. Recognizing the importance of civilian needs, she created the Nurses' Emergency Council in response to the 1918 influenza epidemic.

In the backlash that followed the war, Archibald E. Stevenson of the Military Intelligence Service drew up a list of people suspected of disloyalty for not supporting U.S. entry into the war. The names of Lillian Wald and Jane Addams appeared on this list, a disheartening experience for them. In 1919 the Lusk Committee investigating seditious activities targeted Lillian Wald and Jane Addams and their settlement house activities, which caused contributions to decline. In response Wald put more effort into fundraising.

She retired to the "House-on-the-Pond" in Westport, Connecticut, at the age of sixty-six and died on September 1, 1940.

Further Reading: Christy, Teresa E. "Portrait of a Leader: Lillian D. Wald." *Nursing Outlook* 18, no. 3 (1970): 50–54; Duffus, R. L. *Lillian Wald: Neighbor and Crusader.* New York: Macmillan, 1938.

Marjorie A. Baier

WALKER, ERIC ARTHUR (1910–1995)

Eric Walker left his position as head of the electrical engineering department at the University of Connecticut to help America's World War II effort at Harvard's Underwater Sound Laboratory. The laboratory, which lasted from 1943 to 1945, had been set up under the auspices of the Office of Scientific Research and Development to develop at the request of the navy methods of detecting and destroying German submarines. Walker, in charge of ordnance, was successful in making major advances in sonar and in developing effective acoustically guided torpedoes, that is, torpedoes that honed in on the sound of the propellers of enemy ships.

Walker was born in England on April 29, 1910. He came to the United States in 1923 and attained U.S. citizenship in 1937. He completed his bachelor's degree in electrical engineering in 1932, an M.B.A. in 1933, and his doctorate in electrical engineering in 1935. Walker then went to Tufts as head of the electrical engineering department and on to the University of Connecticut in the same position in 1940. When the Underwater Sound Laboratory closed its doors in 1945, the navy asked Walker to continue his research on torpedoes. Thus was born the Ordnance Research Laboratory at Pennsylvania State University in 1945. Walker became its director. After spending 1951 to 1956 as dean of the engineering school, Walker became president of Penn State until 1970. He then took the position of vice president for science and technology at Aluminum Company of America until 1976. He died on February 17, 1995.

Benjamin F. Shearer

WALKER, HILDRETH "HAL" JR. (1933–)

Hal Walker persevered through the roadblocks of racial prejudice to make important contributions to U.S. military defense systems, particularly in laser systems. Born in Alexandria, Louisiana, in 1933, Walker went to high school in Los Angeles, where he became interested in electronics. Walker's hopes to work behind the camera in the local film business were dashed because he was black, so he decided to enlist in the navy in 1951. Having qualified as an electrician's mate, he re-entered civilian life after four years.

By luck, Walker got a job with Douglas Aircraft installing radar systems in navy fighter planes and began taking electrical engineering courses. He was laid off, however, as war contracts dwindled, so he quit college and performed manual labor to pay his family's bills. He finally managed to find a contract job with RCA, which turned into a full-time job as field service engineer building a Ballistic Missile Early Warning System station in Alaska. Walker then worked on satellite-relay communications with Space Technology Laboratories, and on developing laser devices for Union Carbide's KORAD Division.

Walker operated the ruby laser used in the 1968 Lunar Ranging Experiment and in 1981 his Hughes Aircraft team introduced the first Laser Target

Designator Systems to the army's weapons arsenal. Walker retired from Hughes in 1989 and started his own laser systems consulting firm in 1990. A year later, he founded, with his wife, the non-profit organization A-MAN, Inc., to increase minority interest and employment in science and technology careers.

Benjamin F. Shearer

WALKER, MARY EDWARDS (1832–1919)

Mary Walker was born on November 26, 1832, in Oswego, New York. She was the only woman to receive the Congressional Medal of Honor. Her abolitionist and reform-minded family included her father (a doctor), mother, one brother, and four sisters. Her father believed in equality and full education for women. Mary was an early believer in women's rights and espoused dress reform and supporting reformers such as Amelia Bloomer. In June 1855 Walker became only the second woman to graduate from a medical school, Syracuse Medical College. She was twenty-one. In 1856, she married Dr. Albert Miller, but elected to keep her own name. After their medical practice in Rome, New York, floundered, they divorced in 1869.

When the Civil War erupted, Walker tried to enlist, but was denied a commission as a medical officer. She nevertheless volunteered and served as an acting assistant surgeon—the first female surgeon in the U.S. Army. Working without pay, she served in the U.S. Patent Office Hospital and on the front lines at Fredericksburg and Chattanooga. In September 1863, she was appointed assistant surgeon and assigned to the Fifty-second Ohio Infantry. Captured by Confederate troops in 1864, she was imprisoned for four months before being exchanged. On November 11, 1865, President Andrew Johnson awarded Dr. Walker the Congressional Medal of Honor for Meritorious Service. Rescinded in 1917, President Carter reinstated it in 1977. Walker wore the Medal until her death on February 21, 1919.

Jerry L. Parker

WALLACE, OLIVER (1887–1963)

Most Americans have heard composer and conductor Oliver Wallace's music. Born in London on August 6, 1887, and having received private musical education, he came to the United States in 1904. He became a U.S. citizen in 1914. Wallace made his living playing the piano for vaudeville shows and the organ for film theaters. He landed in Hollywood and composed music for various movie studios until he joined Disney in 1938. Wallace remained with Disney until his death on September 16, 1963, composing music for cartoons, features, and later, television. His music can be heard in such classics as *Dumbo, Alice in Wonderland, Lady and the Tramp, Peter Pan,* and *Jungle Cat.*

During World War II Wallace scored many of Disney's propaganda films. These included such 1943 films as *The New Spirit, Education for Death,* and

Victory through Air Power. Another 1943 film, however, proved to be the most popular. *Der Fuehrer's Face* featured Donald Duck working at an arms plant in Nutzi Land. The high point of the film was a picture of Hitler's face being drubbed with tomatoes. The original title of the cartoon was to be *Donald in Nutzi Land*, but it was changed to acknowledge the popularity of Wallace's song, which was released before the film. Spike Jones and the City Slickers had recorded "Der Fuehrer's Face" in 1942, and it became a hit as well as a proven gimmick for war bond sales. This parody of the Nazi Horst Wessell song and Donald Duck's antics won a special Academy Award.

Benjamin F. Shearer

WALSH, FRANCIS PATRICK (1864–1939)

A World War I reformer and co-chair of the War Labor Board, Frank Walsh avidly pursued social justice on the behalf of the working class. Walsh was born in 1864 in St. Louis, Missouri, and though he quit school quite early, he became qualified to practice law in Missouri by the age of twenty-five. Soon an accomplished courtroom lawyer with a thriving and progressive practice, he preferred to be known as an agitator, fighting for unions and the rights of workers.

Walsh chaired the U.S. Commission on Industrial Relations in 1913, tasked with determining the root causes of industrial violence, including leading an investigation into the Rockefellers' involvement in the massacre resulting from the Ludlow mine strike. During World War I, he and former president William Howard Taft were appointed by President Woodrow Wilson as co-chairs of the National War Labor Board, in charge of mediating labor disputes to keep war production humming. The majority of the disputes was settled in favor of labor, with the eight-hour day and collective bargaining concessions both beginning their advent into the common consciousness during the war. Walsh particularly believed that without giving workers more economic control over their workplaces, political freedom was useless to them. Even and especially during the war, he helped develop what he called "industrial democracy," which he felt was essential for workers. After the war, Walsh continued working for the working classes, arguing his last case mere months before his death on May 2, 1939.

Ellen Baier

WARREN, JOSEPH (1741–1775)

Major General Joseph Warren of the Massachusetts militia was a physician who was killed leading troops at the Battle of Bunker Hill (Breed's Hill) on June 17, 1775. He had been appointed a major general only three days before.

Two months earlier, on the night of April 18, 1775, Dr. Warren had arranged for Paul Revere and William Dawes to make a midnight ride to Lexington and Concord to warn the local militia that the British were

Major General Joseph Warren. Courtesy of the Library of Congress.

coming. Warren's participation in this daring operation was characteristic of his bravery.

In the years prior to his death Warren had been a member of the first three of the Massachusetts provincial congresses, and president of the third congress in 1774. He had played an active role in the passage of the "Suffolk Resolves," which were protests to the British Parliament's "intolerable acts."

Warren had joined the Colonial cause after the British Parliament had passed the Stamp Act in 1765. He was articulate advocate of the Patriot cause. His opposition of the royal legislation sponsored by King George III soon attracted the attention of other patriots. Warren was soon invited to join with other strong advocates of radical action.

When Warren died he was grand master of the Free Masons of the Massachusetts Provincial Grand Lodge. A monument was elected by Masons to mark his final resting place. He was born June 10, 1741, at Roxbury, Massachusetts. After graduating from Harvard College, he worked as a physician.

Andrew J. Waskey

WARREN, MERCY OTIS (1728–1814)

The sister of one prominent revolutionary and the wife of another, Mercy Otis Warren was also an important figure in the American Revolution in her own right. Her role as a writer, historian, political activist, and feminist, though largely overlooked by contemporaries, is now widely recognized.

Mercy Otis was born in Barnstable, Massachusetts, on September 14, 1728. Her brother, James Otis, was a leading voice against the royal colonial government and the British economic policies of the 1760s. Despite eighteenth-century restrictions on women's education, Mercy became extremely well versed in history, politics, and literature. In 1754 she married James Warren, speaker of the Massachusetts House of Representatives. The Warren home became a frequent meeting place for patriots throughout the course of the revolution.

In the years leading up to the outbreak of violence, Mercy Otis Warren anonymously published a number of political satires targeting specific public officials. The Colonial governor, Thomas Hutchinson, for example, was the subject of her first two plays, *Adulateur* (1772) and *The Defeat* (1773). She also wrote patriotic poetry, including "The Squabble of the Sea Nymphs" (1774), which commemorates the Boston Tea Party and criticizes the roles of the British and Colonial governments.

After the Revolution, Warren was among the minority who opposed ratification of the Constitution, in part because it did not guarantee equal rights for women. In 1805 she published a three-volume *History of the Rise, Progress, and Termination of the American Revolution*. She died on October 19, 1814, in Plymouth, Massachusetts.

Kathleen Ruppert

WATERS, AGNES (1893–?)

Agnes Waters, born in New York City on July 1, 1893, was the self-proclaimed head of Widows of World War I Veterans. She was one of numerous women who were involved is opposing American involvement in World War II, not as pacifists, but as anti-communists.

In April 1939 Waters, a Catholic, testified before House and Senate Committees on Immigration against the "Children's Rescue Bill." The bill would have allowed children from European violence easy immigrant entry into the United States. Waters, an anti-Semite, testified that the bill would turn the United States into a dumping ground for the persecuted minorities (which was undesirable to the political right). She stated that these children would damage American society and would not be easily assimilated.

In 1940 Waters published *The White Papers*. The book was mostly letters to Congress and extracts of the *Congressional Record* or hearings. Waters issued public statements about American international policy in 1941 as a representative of We, the Mothers Mobilized for America. She was aided in her goal by sympathetic members of Congress who used their franking privilege to pay for the postage for literature distributed by a coalition of the Mother's groups.

In 1942 Waters protested the lowering of the draft age. All during World War II she and others in the Mothers groups opposed the American alliance with the Soviet Union, proposing an alliance with Adolf Hitler to fight the communists as the better policy.

In 1948 Waters tried to run for president of the United States as a Democrat. However, she was ejected from the National Democratic Party Convention.

Andrew J. Waskey

WATSON, BAXTER (?–?)

When the Civil War broke out, Baxter Watson teamed up with **James McClintock** to make parts for steam engines in Louisiana. Just two weeks later, they had designed, constructed, and sold two machines that made bullets. The Confederate government paid them $1,000. By fall 1861, the partners had constructed a three-man submarine at the Leeds foundry. The submarine was named the *Hunley* after the two men formed a partnership with **Horace Lawson Hunley**. They also became members of a patriotic group of engineers formed by E. C. Singer, who had created an underwater contact mine. Watson encouraged the group, known as the Singer Submarine Corps, to invest in an underwater torpedo boat. Watson's plea was successful and he soon gained enough supporters to build the *Hunley*.

After the *Hunley* sank near Charleston, Watson tried in vain to build a better submarine. In October 1864, he corresponded with Confederate President Jefferson Davis, informing him he needed funds to construct another submarine. Watson had invested all of his capital in the *Hunley*. He said he needed $5,000 in order to travel to New York or Washington to purchase the needed electromagnetism engine. When he received no response from Davis, Watson then appealed to General Pierre Beauregard in early January 1865. Watson never secured new funding. Just four months later, on April 9, 1865, Confederate General Robert E. Lee surrendered at Appomattox Courthouse.

Further Reading: Ragan, Mark K. *The Hunley: Submarines, Sacrifice, and Success in the Civil War*. Miami: Narwhal Press, 1995.

Nicole Mitchell

WATTENBERG, ALBERT (1917–)

Albert Wattenberg worked with **Enrico Fermi** on the creation of the first nuclear chain reaction at the University of Chicago in December 1942. He later wrote one of the earliest popular accounts of this pioneering event. Wattenberg was born in New York City on April 13, 1917. He earned a B.S. in physics from City College of New York in 1938 and a masters in physics specializing in spectroscopy from Columbia in 1939. While at Columbia, he attracted Fermi's attention. In December 1941, Fermi invited Wattenberg to join his group to study nuclear chain reactions under government auspices.

At Columbia, Wattenberg experimented with using exponential uranium piles to determine the feasibility of attaining a self-sustaining nuclear chain reaction in a larger reactor to be built in Chicago. The concept of a sustained nuclear chain reaction required that the neutrons that were emitted during fission be moderated and made to collide with uranium so that more fission would result in a sustainable controlled chain reaction. Wattenberg assisted in building these piles and measuring neutron emissions.

Wattenberg and the Columbia group followed Fermi to Chicago where they continued measuring neutron emissions. Their work was instrumental in creating the first controlled chain reaction that took place at the University of Chicago on December 2, 1942.

In February 1943, Wattenberg took charge of dismantling the uranium pile (named CP-1) and loading the graphite blocks and uranium onto skids for shipment to the new Argonne laboratory outside of Chicago. At Argonne, he worked on neutron ionization chambers and on testing the purity of heavy water. From spring 1943 until the end of the war, Wattenberg was responsible for manufacturing all neutron sources that were used as standards for the Manhattan Project.

Following the war, Wattenberg was awarded a Ph.D. in physics from the University of Chicago and took a position at the University of Illinois, Urbana. Wattenberg has energetically promoted popular understanding of nuclear physics and has written extensively on the history of physics. He is presently distinguished physicist emeritus at the University of Illinois.

Further Reading: Wattenberg, Albert. "Present at the Creation." In *All in Our Time: The Reminiscences of Twelve Nuclear Pioneers.* Edited by Jane Wilson. Chicago: Bulletin of the Atomic Scientists, 1974–1975, pp. 105–125.

Walter F. Bell

WAYNE, JOHN "DUKE" (1907–1979)

John Wayne (as Sergeant John Stryker) in *The Sands of Iwo Jima.* Courtesy of Photofest.

John Wayne fought in conflicts from the Indian Wars to Vietnam on the screen. During the latter, he also became a polarizing figure politically because of his strong support for the Vietnam War.

John Wayne, born Marion Michael Morrison on May 26, 1907, in Winterset, Iowa, established himself with a starring role in John Ford's *Stagecoach* (1939). Wayne's screen persona included a cavalry officer in Ford's *Fort Apache* (1948), *She Wore a Yellow Ribbon* (1949), and *Rio Grande* (1950). Wayne's first World War II film was *Flying Tigers* (1942), in which he played a squadron leader of American flyers supporting the Chinese. Ford's *They Were Expendable* (1945) presents Wayne as a PT boat squadron officer in the Philippines.

Along with some outstanding Westerns such as *True Grit* (1969), for which he won an Academy Award for best actor, Wayne continued making war films. Among his finest roles was Sergeant Stryker, who leads with tough love, in *Sands of Iwo Jima* (1949).

The Green Berets (1968), made in support of the Vietnam War, was one of Wayne's least successful films. Although much of the intellectual elite turned against Wayne during the war, he remained enormously popular with the general public. Wayne died of cancer on June 11, 1979.

Suggested Reading: Davis, Ronald L. *Duke: The Life and Image of John Wayne.* Norman: University of Oklahoma Press, 1998; Wills, Garry. *John Wayne's America: The Politics of Celebrity.* New York: Simon and Schuster, 1997.

Edward J. Rielly

WECHSLER, DAVID (1896–1981)

David Wechsler's experiences administering the Army Alpha test led him to devise the Wechsler-Bellevue Intelligence Scale, the first assessment to recognize differences in childhood and adult intelligence. Wechsler was born on January 12, 1896, in Romania. His family immigrated to New York in 1902. After earning a master's degree in experimental psychology from Columbia University in 1917, Wechsler joined the army, where he was assigned to work under **Edwin Garrigues Boring** administering intelligence tests, including the Army Alpha test developed by **Robert Mearns Yerkes** and the Committee on the Psychological Examination of Recruits.

Wechsler was puzzled by the number of recruits who, despite leading normal civilian lives, repeatedly tested as lacking the intelligence to function in the military. He hypothesized that existing definitions of intelligence did not account for capabilities essential to handling real-life experiences. These tests also assumed, incorrectly, that adult and childhood intelligence could be measured on the same scales.

After being discharged in 1919 and earning a doctoral degree from Columbia University in 1925, Wechsler worked in industry and private practice until 1932, when he became Chief Psychologist at Bellevue Hospital, where he remained until retirement in 1967. His best-known works were *The Range of Human Capacities* (1935) and *The Measurement of Adult Intelligence* (1939). This latter book introduced the Deviation Quotient, a critical measure of adult individual differences in intelligence.

Wechsler died on May 2, 1981. The Wechsler Adult Intelligence Scale, a 1955 revision of his earlier scale, remains in use today.

Wende Vyborney Feller

WEED, LEWIS HILL (1886–1952)

Dr. Lewis Weed was a well-known anatomist and established medical administrator when he answered the call of the National Academy of Sciences to chair the Division of Medical Sciences for its National Research Council in 1939. In this position he became involved in coordinating the preparations for war among civilian and military medical scientists and services as well as British liaison officers. During the war he was appointed vice chairman of the Committee on Medical Research of the Office of Scientific Research and Development.

Weed was born in Cleveland, Ohio, on November 15, 1886. He earned a bachelor's and a master's degree from Yale University, and in 1912, an M.D.

degree from Johns Hopkins University. After a two-year fellowship in surgical research at Harvard, Weed became an anatomy professor at Johns Hopkins in 1914, where his successful studies led to clear understanding of cerebrospinal fluid. During his service as a captain in the Army Medical Corps during World War I, Weed was stationed at a lab at Johns Hopkins. He remained at Johns Hopkins, becoming dean of the Medical School in 1923 and director in 1929. He retired in 1950 and died on December 21, 1952.

During World War II, Weed tirelessly evaluated medical research in four main areas: antimalarials, antibiotics, blood substitutes and transfusions, and aviation physiology. In 1943 he also chaired the American Red Cross' Medical Advisory Committee. His service in the war garnered him the Presidential Medal for Merit and the Order of the British Empire.

Benjamin F. Shearer

WEIGL, BRUCE (1949–)

Bruce Weigl has written extensively about the Vietnam War and may be the most respected Vietnam War poet. Weigl was born in Lorain, Ohio, and served in the U.S. Army from 1967 until 1970, part of that time with the First Air Cavalry in Vietnam. His distinguished service earned him a Bronze Star. After the war, Weigl attended Oberlin College and earned a doctorate from the University of Utah (1979).

Weigl established the Vietnam War as his primary subject in his first collections of poetry, *Executioner* (1976) and *Like a Sack Full of Old Quarrels* (1977). The war continued as a major poetic focus throughout *A Romance* (1979), *The Monkey Wars* (1984), *Song of Napalm* (1988), *What Saves Us* (1992), and *Sweet Lorain* (1996).

In later poetry, Weigl expanded his subject matter, often transporting the reader to contemporary Vietnam. In *The Circle of Hanh* (2000), he turned to prose, writing of his return to Vietnam to adopt a Vietnamese daughter. He also co-edited *Poems from Captured Documents* (1994) and *Writing between the Lines: An Anthology on War and Its Social Consequences* (1997).

Bruce Weigl's poetry awards include a National Endowment for the Arts fellowship and the Academy of American Poets Prize. The Vietnam Veterans of America honored him for "Contributions to American Culture."

Further Reading: Gotera, Vince. *Radical Visions: Poetry by Vietnam Veterans.* Athens: University of Georgia Press, 1994; Rielly, Edward J. "Bruce Weigl: Out of the Landscape of His Past." *Journal of American Culture* 16, no. 3 (1993): 47–52.

Edward J. Rielly

WEIGLE, LUTHER ALLAN (1880–1976)

During World War II, Luther Allan Weigle worked to coordinate ministry to service people and civilians. He served as chairman of the Committee on

Closer Cooperation of Inter-denominational Agencies, as chairman of the Co-ordinating Committee for Wartime Service of the Churches, and as president of Federal Council of Churches. In April 1942 he sent President Franklin D. Roosevelt a letter asking him to restore civil liberties to the Japanese who had been sent to internment camps.

Weigle was born September 11, 1880, in Littlestown, Pennsylvania, the son of Hannah Maria (Bream) and Elias Daniel Weigle. He described his early life in an autobiographical article, "The Religious Education of a Protestant." He died September 2, 1976, in New Haven, Connecticut.

Weigle attended Gettysburg College and the Lutheran Theological Seminary in Gettysburg. He was ordained a Lutheran minister in 1903. From 1903 until 1915 Weigle was professor of philosophy and dean (1910–1915) at Carleton College in Northfield, Minnesota. In 1916 he was appointed Horace Bushnell Professor of Christian Nurture at Yale Divinity School in New Haven, Connecticut.

Weigle wrote a number of works dealing with Christian education. These included *Talks to Sunday School Teachers* (1920), *Training Children in a Christian Family* (1921), *We Are Able* (1937), *Jesus and the Educational Method* (1939), and *American Idealism* (1929). After World War II, Weigle was a leader in the revision of the King James Bible, which was issued in 1952 as the Revised Standard Version.

Andrew J. Waskey

WELLS, EDWARD C. (1910–1986)

Ed Wells, one of Boeing Company's most influential engineers, began his career in 1931 and worked for Boeing until his retirement in 1972. From 1972 to 1978 he served as a consultant and a member of Boeing's board of directors. Born in Boise, Idaho, on August 26, 1910, Wells attended Willamette University and then transferred to Stanford University, where he obtained an engineering degree in 1931. His first encounter with Boeing was a summer job in 1930.

Immediately after graduating, Wells joined Boeing as a draftsman and engineer. By 1937 he was chief of preliminary design engineering. In 1947 he became chief engineer. Wells is credited with playing a major role in the design of the B-17, B-29, B-47, and the famous B-52 jet bombers. He also contributed to the design of commercial aircraft from the 707 to the 767. During War World II he served as a consultant to the secretary of war.

Wells was named vice president and chief engineer in 1948. In 1961 he became vice president and general manager of the Military Aircraft Systems Division, and in 1963 he became vice president for product development. Wells was the recipient of many awards and professional distinctions including the Lawrence Sperry Award from the Institute of Aeronautical Sciences in 1942. He was elected to the National Academy of Engineering in 1967. Wells died on July 1, 1986.

Further Reading: Heinemann, Edward H. "Edward C. Wells, 1910–1986." *Memorial Tributes, National Academy of Engineering* 3 (1989): 351–353.

Nestor L. Osorio

WESSON, DANIEL (1825–1906)

Daniel Wesson developed and invented several improvements to firearms, including a pistol that he manufactured with **Horace Smith**. Born on May 1, 1825, in Worchester, Massachusetts, Wesson attended school in his hometown and initially worked in a shoe factory, which he did not like. He then did an apprenticeship with an older brother who made rifles. He worked for a number of different gun manufacturers. Wesson spent his nights studying and working on numerous ideas and eventually came up with an improvement to a bullet, replacing the primer with a steel disk, and was able to patent it.

Wesson formed a partnership with Smith in 1853 and together they developed, in principle, what would become the Winchester rifle. Instead of producing the rifle, they sold the patent to the Volcanic Arms Company, for whom Wesson then went to work. While working for Volcanic Arms, Wesson finished developing a pistol he had been working on and in 1856 partnered with Smith again to produce and sell the pistol.

Wesson and Smith built a company that not only produced and sold the pistol, but also rifles, which they sold to the United States government during the Civil War and later to other governments. Smith retired from the business in 1873, but Wesson continued on. Wesson continued to make improvements to firearms and eventually took on his two sons as partners.

Wesson was married to Cynthia Harris, and they had four children. He died on August 5, 1906.

Dallace W. Unger Jr.

WEST (WADDY), HARRIET M. (1904–1999)

Harriet M. Hardin, later West and Waddy, was born in Jefferson City, Missouri, on June 20, 1904. Having graduated from Kansas State College of Agriculture and Applied Science, she worked under **Mary McLeod Bethune** for the National Youth Administration's Division of Negro Affairs in the 1930s. She was convinced that full black participation, including military service, held the hope of ending segregation.

West joined the Women's Army Auxiliary Corps (WAAC) in 1942. Initially she supervised civilian typists who produced notes to soldiers' families, but by the end of the war she was one of two black women to rise to the rank of major. She served as an assistant to the WAC's director, Colonel **Oveta Culp Hobby**. This position allowed her to assume a role in changing the status of black women serving in the military. She became an advisor to the army on racial matters. During World War II, 3,902 black women served in the WAC, while 68 participated in the navy auxiliary. West was criticized by some blacks for serving in the military, given the discrimination they faced on the home front and in the armed services. In a radio interview in 1943, she said that by serving she felt she was contributing to the fledgling effort to ensure greater rights for blacks, and she encouraged other black women to join the military.

Promoted to the rank of lieutenant colonel in 1948, West retired from the military in 1952 and died on February 21, 1999.

Gene C. Gerard

WHARTON, EDITH (1862–1937)

Author Edith Wharton was born on January 24, 1862, in New York. She married Boston banker Edward Wharton in 1885. She traveled to France just prior to the beginning of World War I. Before America even entered the war, Wharton had become an avid champion of the Allied cause. Initially she established a sewing room for unemployed women. These women made bandages, socks, and gloves for the soldiers as well as lingerie for Americans. During the first months of the war, she committed herself to raising money for various charities. In addition to helping refugees who had escaped from France and Belgium, she also helped to establish hostels and schools for them. In 1915, Wharton founded the Children of Flanders Rescue Committee to care for orphaned and abandoned children. While in France, Wharton also wrote numerous news reports for American newspapers recounting her observations of the war. She often visited the war front, distributing medical supplies for the Red Cross.

Edith Wharton. Courtesy of the Library of Congress.

In 1923, Wharton published *A Son at the Front*, a story of an American couple whose French-born son joins the French army. The main character wrestles with the war's threat to France and the role of Americans abroad. Before her last novel, *The Buccaneers*, could be published, Wharton died in France, on August 11, 1937.

Further Reading: Dwight, Eleanor. *Edith Wharton: An Extraordinary Life*. New York: Abrams, 1994; Price, Alan. *The End of the Age of Innocence: Edith Wharton and the First World War*. New York: St. Martin's Press, 1996.

Nicole Mitchell

WHEELER, BURTON K. (1882–1975)

Burton K. Wheeler, a controversial four-term U.S. senator from Montana, began his political career as a liberal and ended it as an isolationist opposed to American entry into World War II. Elected to the Montana legislature in 1910 and the U.S. Senate in 1922 on the Democratic Party ticket, Wheeler won national recognition for his vigorous prosecution of Harding administration Teapot Dome scandals. Two years later, he joined Robert M. La Follette as the vice presidential nominee of the Progressive Party. After a crushing defeat, Wheeler returned to the Senate, where he remained until 1946, when he returned to practicing law.

Wheeler was born in Hudson, Massachusetts, on February 27, 1882, where he grew up. After graduating from the University of Michigan Law School in 1905, he moved to Montana to practice law, where he defended labor and opposed mining and oil interests.

As a liberal Democrat, Wheeler supported most of the New Deal policies until he broke with President Franklin D. Roosevelt over the "court-packing" bill. As war became imminent in Europe, Wheeler backed neutrality legislation and became a leading opponent of Lend Lease assistance to Great Britain. Along with **Charles Augustus Lindbergh**, Wheeler formed the America First Committee (AFC), an influential isolationist group that advocated a fortress-America approach and a determination to avoid any involvement in World War II. After the Japanese attack on Pearl Harbor, the AFC disbanded, and Wheeler did not oppose the American declaration of war. Wheeler died in Washington, DC, on January 6, 1975.

Burton Wheeler. Courtesy of the Library of Congress.

Arlene Lazarowitz

WHEELER, JOHN ARCHIBALD (1911–)

Physicist John A. Wheeler played a vital role theoretically and practically in the development of the atomic bomb during World War II, and the development of the hydrogen bomb after the war. Later he became interested in **Albert Einstein**'s relativity theory, began to ask cosmological questions, and dubbed the term "black hole" to describe gravitational collapse in a star.

Wheeler was born in Jacksonville, Florida, on July 8, 1911. He forsook electrical engineering for theoretical physics and completed his Ph.D. at Johns Hopkins in 1933. A post-doctoral fellowship provided him the opportunity to study with Niels Bohr in Copenhagen. Their collaboration led to an understanding of nuclear fission.

Wheeler taught at the University of North Carolina from 1935 until 1938, when he left for Princeton, retiring early to go to the University of Texas in 1976. World War II, however, found Wheeler consulting for the Manhattan Project. He worked with **Enrico Fermi** and his colleagues at the University of Chicago, where they successfully tested a controlled, sustained nuclear reaction. He went to the Hanford Engineering Works in the state of Washington, where his knowledge was critical in producing the plutonium that was being made for the bomb, and then to Los Alamos, where the bomb was tested.

Wheeler engaged in the super-secret Project Matterhorn, the project to develop the hydrogen bomb, at Princeton from 1951 to 1953. Wheeler continued public service in various government agencies. In 1971 he was awarded the National Medal of Science.

Benjamin F. Shearer

WHEELER, (JOHN) HARVEY (1918–2004)

A professor of political science and the author of several academic books, Harvey Wheeler is best known as the co-author, along with **Eugene Leonard Burdick**, of the 1962 best-selling novel *Fail-Safe*, a doomsday scenario in which a computer glitch and a fatally automated military command protocol lead the United States and the Soviet Union into an accidental nuclear war.

Born in Waco, Texas, on October 17, 1918, Wheeler served in the U.S. Army from 1941 to 1946. Wheeler's first-hand experience of World War II and his consternation over the dropping of atomic bombs on Hiroshima and Nagasaki led him to study political science. He earned a Ph.D. from Harvard in 1950 and taught first at Johns Hopkins University and subsequently at Washington and Lee, where he would eventually become chairman of the political science department. He later served as a scholar at the Center for Democratic Institutions and was an early advocate of on-line publishing.

Wheeler was at Washington and Lee when he began to collaborate on *Fail-Safe* with Burdick, who at the time was a professor at the U.S. Naval War College. Burdick brought to the partnership a technical knowledge of military procedures and armaments, while Wheeler extrapolated the political and social effects of a thermonuclear war. *Fail-Safe* was a best seller, and a film adaptation of the novel came out in 1964. Wheeler and Burdick's novel captured the national fear during the Cold War that a mutually destructive war could be triggered by accident. Wheeler died on September 6, 2004.

Matthew J. Bolton

WHITCOMB, RICHARD (1921–)

In the midst of World War II, researchers at the Langley Research Center of the National Advisory Committee for Aeronautics (later NASA) were already at work to solve the problem of reaching Mach 1, the speed of sound. Aircraft experienced so much drag as they approached Mach 1 that the jet engines of the day could not break the sound barrier, leaving supersonic travel only a dream. In 1943 Richard Holcomb went to work at Langley, just graduated from Worcester Polytechnic Institute with an engineering degree. Born in Evanston, Illinois, on February 21, 1921, Whitcomb was raised in Worcester and commuted to college there on a scholarship. While he was first assigned to work on a controlled bomb at Langley, Whitcomb insisted he wanted to work on aerodynamics.

With improvements in wind tunnel speeds, Whitcomb could study transonic airflows. He claimed in a 2002 interview that his study of airflows was intuitive—he could see the air. Calculations were used mostly as verifications. Whitcomb developed the "Area Rule," which reduced drag by lowering the effect of shock waves around the aircraft. This led to the resign of fuselages that made aircraft look like flying Coke bottles. Whitcomb's further research led to the development of the supercritical wing and winglets. All together, Whitcomb's ingenuity made supersonic flight possible.

Whitcomb remained at Langley until he retired at fifty-nine, no longer convinced that aeronautics held the hope of exciting new discoveries. He received numerous awards including the National Medal of Science in 1973.

Benjamin F. Shearer

WHITE, WALTER FRANCIS (1893–1955)

Walter F. White was a civil rights activist and a leader at the National Association for the Advancement of Colored People (NAACP). He was born in Atlanta, Georgia, on July 1, 1893, and reared there. After graduating from Atlanta University in 1916, he helped form a local NAACP chapter and fought for educational rights. In 1918, White became assistant secretary for the NAACP. He investigated lynchings in the South and supported federal anti-lynching legislation in the 1920s and 1930s. In 1931, White became executive secretary of the NAACP, and in the 1930s, he tackled the problem of segregation, which he believed always led to inadequate conditions and poor treatment of African Americans.

During World War II, White turned his attention to the War Department's plan to set up a training school for black pilots at the Tuskegee Institute. Many African Americans supported this plan, but White opposed it because it amounted to segregation. In 1943, White actually visited Britain to examine how African Americans were being treated in the armed forces. In 1948, President Harry Truman signed the order to desegregate the U.S. military, and White's agitation on behalf of the NAACP is often cited as the reason for Truman's actions. White, thus, used World War II as a venue to call attention to racial injustice and claim equal rights for African Americans. He continued to lead the NAACP until his death on March 21, 1955.

Further Reading: White, Walter. *A Man Named White: The Autobiography of Walter White*. New York: Viking Press, 1948.

Kelly J. Baker

WHITE, WILLIAM (1748–1836)

William White was a moderate Anglican priest who joined the American Revolution as a Patriot. He had been ordained an Anglican priest in England on April 25, 1772. Soon thereafter he had returned to Philadelphia where the American Revolution was about to begin.

White was appointed chaplain of the Continental Congress. He became a counselor to George Washington and many other patriots. However, he kept open his connections with many Loyalists. In 1779 White was appointed rector of the united parishes of St. Peter's and Christ Church after **Jacob Duché**, a Loyalist, left the pulpit vacant. He remained rector until his death on July 17, 1836.

After the Revolution—but before the signing of the Treaty of Paris in 1783, officially ending the Revolution—White published *The Case of the Episcopal Churches in the United States Considered* (1782), in which he proposed a revised form of government for the Anglican Church in the United States.

In 1785 he presided over the first General Convention of the Protestant Episcopal Church, which met in Philadelphia. He played a major role in adapting the Prayer Book to the new American situation. In 1786 White was consecrated a bishop by the archbishops of York and Canterbury at Lambeth palace in England.

White was born on April 4, 1748, in Philadelphia, Pennsylvania, the son of Colonel Thomas White, a prominent and prosperous lawyer. He studied at the College of Philadelphia (now University of Pennsylvania) in 1765 and later in England.

Andrew J. Waskey

William Allen White. Courtesy of the Library of Congress.

WHITE, WILLIAM ALLEN (1868–1944)

William Allen White was a journalist whose work influenced America's involvement in World Wars I and II. He was born on February 10, 1868, in Emporia, Kansas, was married in 1893, had two children, and studied at the Presbyterian College of Emporia and the University of Kansas. White worked as a journalist, editor, and reporter for Kansas newspapers and was the owner and editor of *Emporia Daily and Weekly Gazette*. His awards include a Pulitzer Prize in 1922 for "To an Anxious Friend" and posthumously in 1947 for *The Autobiography of William Allen White*.

Though he was initially an isolationist, White ultimately supported President Woodrow Wilson and America's entrance into World War I. In addition to his journalism work, he contributed to the war effort through his writing for **George Creel**'s Committee on Public Information and his investigative and publicity work for the Red Cross in Europe. At the war's end, he covered the peace conference for the Wheeler syndicate and campaigned for America's entrance into the League of Nations.

White was not in favor of the United States' entrance into World War II, but he strongly promoted aiding the allies against Hitler. He served as honorary vice chairman of the American Committee for Non-Participation in Japanese Aggression, was a member of the American Boycott against Aggressor Nations, served as chair of the Union for Concerted Peace Efforts, edited *Defense for America* in 1940, and, most notably, chaired the Committee to Defend America by Aiding the Allies.

White died in Emporia, Kansas, on January 29, 1944.

Stacy Dorgan

WHITING, RICHARD ARMSTRONG (1891–1938)

Richard Whiting was born in Peoria, Illinois, on November 12, 1891. He wrote musical scores for both film and Broadway. Whiting graduated from the Harvard Military School in Los Angeles, California, and sang for a while on the Vaudeville circuit without noted success. He got a job as a staff writer for the Jerome H. Remick Music Corporation in 1913 and also became a personal manager.

Whiting moved to Hollywood, California, in 1919 at the behest of Remick Music, and worked out of its offices for most of the 1920s. Although he did score some Broadway plays—*George White's Scandals of 1919*, *Toot Sweet*, and *Take a Chance*—Whiting's work was mostly for film. He worked for Paramount, Fox, and Warner Brothers, and wrote the film scores for *Innocents in Paris*, *Monte Carlo*, and *Cowboy from Brooklyn*, just to name a few. Working with lyricists like Gus Kahn, Ray Egan, and Johnny Mercer, Whiting created many hit songs including, "It's Tulip Time in Holland," "Breezin' along with the Breeze," and "On the Good Ship Lollipop."

One of Whiting's most noted compositions was the World War I hit song, "Till We Meet Again," which came out in 1918 and sold 5 million copies. It was a song inspired by the idea of a soldier whispering goodbye. Whiting died in Beverly Hills, California, on February 10, 1938, at the age of forty-seven and was inducted posthumously into the Songwriters Hall of Fame in 1970.

Erskine L. Levi Jr.

WHITMAN, WALT (1819–1892)

Poet Walt Whitman was born in New York on May 31, 1819, to Walter and Louisa Van Velsor Whitman. As a young man, he was apprenticed to the *Patriot*, a liberal Long Island newspaper. He later taught school in several Long Island towns, leaving this job only to begin his writing career. His first published story, "Death in the Schoolroom," developed from his teaching experiences. He eventually journeyed to New Orleans, Louisiana, where he was the editor for the *Crescent*.

When the Civil War broke out in April 1861, Whitman's younger brother George immediately enlisted in the Union Army. Whitman, like most people at the time, believed that the conflict would be over in less than three months. At the beginning of the conflict, he initially concentrated on his writing and stayed in Brooklyn. While in Brooklyn, he started visiting soldiers who had been wounded in battle and moved to hospitals in New York. From these visits, Whitman gathered various stories that he published in a series titled "City Photographs" in 1862.

Walt Whitman. Courtesy of the Library of Congress.

While visiting wounded soldiers in the Brooklyn hospitals, Whitman became an informal nurse to them, transcribing stories they told him, giving them gifts, and writing letters for them among other things. He checked the newspaper lists of wounded soldiers daily. In December 1862, he saw the name G. W. Whitmore on the casualty list from Fredericksburg, Virginia. Fearing that the name was a mangled version of his brother George Washington Whitman, he immediately traveled to Virginia to search for his brother. Whitman found his brother, who had only a slight injury. Though thankful for finding his brother safe, he was, however, horrified with what else he saw. While in Fredericksburg, he stumbled upon a mansion that had been converted into a field hospital with heaps of amputated limbs and dead bodies.

Whitman had intended to return to New York after finding his brother alive, but he chose to stay in Washington for several days first. During this time, he got to know the soldiers well. He became fast friends with a young Confederate soldier from Mississippi. He also helped to bury the dead soldiers whose bodies were still lying on the battlefield. While at the army camp, Whitman kept a journal, recording his thoughts and the sights he had witnessed. Many of these accounts were later transformed into poems in his book *Drum-Taps*.

Whitman eventually decided to remain in Washington. Through efforts from various friends, he was able to secure a job as a copyist in the Army Paymaster's office. He spent what little extra money he had to purchase small presents for the soldiers in the hospital. He continued to spend time with them, reading and writing letters for them. Whitman went back briefly to New York in late 1863, but returned to Washington a few weeks later. It was at this point that he met James Redpath, a Boston publisher, who was interested in publishing *Memoranda during the War*, Whitman's writings about the war. Redpath also arranged a fundraising campaign to raise money for Whitman's hospital work. Though Redpath ultimately chose not to publish Whitman's work, the book later formed the core of Whitman's autobiography, *Specimen Days*.

Whitman continued to compose poems about the effects of war. In early 1864, he witnessed one of his closest friends, a soldier in the hospital, having his leg amputated. For several months, Whitman also treated soldiers in a field hospital in Virginia. In the summer of 1864, he returned to his home in New York, complaining of a sore throat and dizziness. Though he was away from the most arduous fighting, he still continued to visit wounded soldiers in the New York hospitals. When his brother, George, was captured and sent to prison, Whitman began publicly advocating the exchange of prisoners between the Union and Confederacy.

Whitman returned to Washington in early 1865, this time working as a clerk in the Indian Bureau of the Department of the Interior. He continued his daily visits to the hospitals. After his brother was released from prison, Whitman went back to New York to visit with him. He was in Brooklyn when President Abraham Lincoln was assassinated. Whitman mourned the loss of the President with his poem, "When Lilacs Last in the Dooryard Bloom'd."

Whitman died of tuberculosis at his home in Camden, New Jersey, on March 26, 1892.

Further Reading: Morris, Roy. *The Better Angel: Walt Whitman in the Civil War*. New York: Oxford University Press, 2000.

Nicole Mitchell

WHITNEY, ELI (1765–1825)

Born in Massachusetts on December 8, 1765, Eli Whitney is probably best known as the inventor of the cotton gin, which removed the seeds from the rest of the plant. This 1793 invention may be Whitney's claim to fame, but it brought him very little in the way of fortune and was ultimately a financial loss for him.

Whitney, however, managed to parlay his fame into a fortune in arms manufacture. In 1798, fearing a war with France, the United States government paid Whitney $178,000 to produce 10,000 muskets for the military.

Eli Whitney. Courtesy of the Library of Congress.

Musket production in the eighteenth century was a laborious, hand-made process, requiring skilled gunsmiths of whom there were few in America, thus leaving the new nation at a serious disadvantage.

Whitney got the musket contract because he claimed that he had a system that would allow him to produce guns quickly—two years—and without the use of skilled gunsmiths. Whitney based his unprecedented claim on an idea he called the "Uniformity System." The principle was simple. If all of the various parts of a musket were made to uniform standards, then semi-skilled workers could be trained to work with only one or two parts of the guns. Thus, a group of semi-skilled workers could do the work of many skilled gunsmiths. Whitney demonstrated his system for skeptics in Washington by assembling ten muskets from a selection of parts. He argued that uniformity of parts would make production quicker, and soldiers in the field could share musket parts in the firing line.

Whitney presented his idea as radical and new. This was not entirely accurate. Clockmakers had been using a similar system of uniformity for several years. More significantly, Whitney was copying a system being used to make muskets that was pioneered by Honoré le Blanc in France. Even the demonstration Whitney presented was borrowed from le Blanc, and he even cheated in his demonstration. Each of the "uniform" parts had been carefully tooled and prepared so that they were, in fact, uniform. In the end, the 10,000 guns Whitney had contracted for took ten years to finish, not two, and most of the money was sunk into building the factory and hiring the workers who produced the guns.

Despite these facts, Whitney remains an important innovator. The factory he built in Connecticut brought all of the workers together in the same building. Whitney constructed a community for his workers, establishing a tradition of socially conscious employers. People who are working all together over a long period of time are far more likely to turn out a uniform product than people who are spread out in a variety of different locations. Uniformity largely came, however, from the use of filing jigs and lathe patterns, guides to allow workers to produce parts that were, for the most part, the same. While the guns Whitney produced could, generally speaking, interchange parts, they could not interchange ammunition. In short, while they were cheap and relatively quick to make, they were not of a particularly high quality.

In spite of previous problems Whitney received another contract for 15,000 muskets during the War of 1812. Additionally, he was granted further contracts for other small arms. Because he had already built the factory and hired the workers and created a community, the contracts in 1812 generated considerable profit for Whitney. Ironically, Whitney was one of the few people in New England to profit from the war. Most New Englanders found their businesses negatively affected by a British naval blockade. As a result, Whitney was one of the few New Englanders who was in favor of the war.

Whitney effectively severed, or rescued, America from a tradition of highly skilled workers producing individual items of very high quality. While France abandoned their mass production programs because they removed a level of government control over artisans, America embraced Whitney's system, ultimately refining it to a state in which high quality goods could be turned out at a high rate for a relatively low cost. In effect, Whitney's system began a tradition that helped to turn the United States into a world power. Whitney died on January 8, 1825.

Further Reading: Green, Constance McLaughlin. *Eli Whitney and the Birth of American Technology.* Boston: Little, Brown, 1956; Huff, Regan A. *Eli Whitney: The Cotton Gin and American Manufacturing.* New York: PowerPlus Books, 2004; Mirsky, Jeanette, and Allan Nevins. *The World of Eli Whitney.* New York: Macmillan, 1952.

Mike Timonin

WHITNEY, ELI JR. (1820–1894)

Eli Whitney Jr. was born on November 20, 1820, the son of **Eli Whitney**, the famed inventor of the cotton gin. After a year at Yale, young Whitney enrolled at Princeton. Graduating in 1841, he returned to New Haven to assume control of the Armory his father founded. After taking over in 1842, he bid successfully on the federal rifle contract of 1841. Producing over 20,000 rifles by the new percussion-cap design required not only retooling the Armory, but also employing more efficient power sources (the turbine) and the use of new metals, most notably steel.

Whitney was a successful and innovative manufacturer, and concluded a contract for production of the Whitney Colt. By 1850, the Armory was producing revolvers of its own design. In 1851, it received a major contract from the navy for 33,000 revolvers. Confronted with a shortage of waterpower on the original Armory site, Whitney opened a second plant near the center of Whitneyville to produce Colt and other handguns. He erected a foundry on the old factory site. In 1860–1861, with the raising of the dam to create Lake Whitney and, following an explosion that destroyed the old main factory building, he completely reconstructed the plant.

Whitney demonstrated entrepreneurial and civic sensibility by taking the dominant role in creating the water system for the city of Whitneyville, for which he designed and constructed a waterworks and a distribution system.

Further Reading: Fuller, Claude E. *The Whitney Firearms*. Huntington, WV: Standard Publications, 1946.

Michael L. McGregor

WIESNER, JEROME BERT (1915–1994)

Jerome Wiesner was a scientific statesman, educator, and engineer who served as presidential science advisor and advocated for arms control. Born in Detroit, Michigan, on May 30, 1915, Wiesner attended the University of Michigan at Ann Arbor, studying mathematics and electrical engineering, receiving his M.S. in 1938.

After spending two years at the Library of Congress, he went to MIT to work at the Radiation Laboratory during World War II. After the war, Wiesner worked at the University of California's Los Alamos Laboratory from 1945 to 1946, helping to develop electronic components for the Bikini Atoll atomic weapon tests. In 1946 he returned to MIT as an assistant professor of electrical engineering and worked on his Ph.D., which he completed at the University of Michigan in 1950.

Wiesner had served with **James Rhyne Killian Jr.** in the 1950s on the President's Science Advisory Committee and Wiesner had a deep respect for the group and its work. He headed a task force in 1960 that reviewed American missile and space programs and reported to president-elect John F. Kennedy in January 1961 that in both programs, the United States lagged far behind the Soviets. Wiesner urged Kennedy to consider reorganization of the programs rather than increase funding. Kennedy took Wiesner's advice and also appointed him to special assistant to the president for science and technology, a position established by President Dwight Eisenhower in 1957 in response to the Soviets' launching of *Sputnik*.

Militarization of space and arms control were the two dominant scientific issues of the 1960s. Wiesner felt passionately about arms control. He had traveled to the Soviet Union a number of times and felt that they too wished to achieve some kind of limit on the arms race. He helped to establish the U.S. Arms Control and Disarmament Agency and worked to prevent the deployment of the anti-ballistic missile (ABM) system in the early 1960s. The high point in his career in Washington came when the Soviet Union, Great Britain, and United States signed the Limited Test Ban Treaty in 1963 that limited testing of nuclear weapons in the atmosphere and underwater. Although the treaty had major limitations, it is largely considered the stepping-stone to more meaningful arms-control agreements.

Wiesner also had opinions about the American space program. Believing that the United States was unlikely to be the first to put a man in orbit, he was critical of the attention the press was giving to the Mercury program, falsely raising the hopes of the American public. However, Wiesner did believe that putting a man in orbit was the first step to moon exploration and a space station. Therefore, he recommended that the space program in NASA be reorganized so that top scientists and engineers could successfully be recruited. Kennedy agreed, and as part of that reorganization the new Office of Science and Technology (OST) was created, headed by the special assistant to the president for science and technology. Wiesner's efforts proved successful as NASA enjoyed many successes, culminating in the 1969 landing on the moon.

After briefly serving in the same two positions for Lyndon Johnson, Wiesner returned to MIT as the dean of the School of Science in 1964. He reflected upon his experience in Washington with his 1965 book *Where Science and Politics Meet*, in which he warned, "Only by agreeing to effective disarmament measures and employing the resources thus made available for constructive purposes can we have any hope of ultimate survival." He remained outspoken about arms-control issues and was a founding member of the International Foundation for the Survival and Development of Humanity, a group of Soviet and American scientists who together raised money for research on global issues. He was also a vocal critic against Johnson's policies in Vietnam. Wiesner was part of a group of scientists that met each summer since 1959 to consider defense-related issues for the Pentagon. In 1966 the "JASONs," as they were called, issued a report that advised against the use of tactical nuclear weapons in Vietnam, after hearing that the Pentagon was considering using them. The group concluded that conventional bombing was not working either, and that the North–South Vietnam network was still intact. Frustrated by the continuing war, he led a peace march of four thousand anti-war protesters between MIT and Boston Common in 1969, while provost of MIT.

In 1971, Wiesner became the thirteenth president of MIT, retiring in 1980. He died on October 21, 1994.

Further Reading: Wiesner, Jerome. *Where Science and Politics Meet*. New York: McGraw Hill, 1965.

Valerie L. Adams

WIGNER, EUGENE PAUL (1902–1995)

Born Jenó Pál Wigner on November 17, 1902, in Budapest, Hungary, Eugene Wigner finished his doctorate in chemical engineering at Berlin's Technische Hochschule in 1925. He then worked in his father's business, spent a year at the University of Göttingen, and, returned to Berlin, where by 1930 he had made a name for himself in quantum mechanics. From 1930 to 1933 he divided his time between Princeton and Berlin, but as conditions in Germany deteriorated in 1933, he left Berlin. Except for his years at the University of Wisconsin (1936–1938), Wigner spent his career at Princeton, where he held the Thomas D. Jones Chair of Mathematical Physics from 1938 until his retirement in 1971. Wigner became a U.S. citizen in 1937.

In 1942 Wigner took a leave of absence from Princeton to work in the Manhattan Project's Metallurgical Laboratory at the University of Chicago, where fellow Hungarian exile **Leo Szilard** was among the scientists attempting to build a nuclear reactor and initiate a controlled, sustained, nuclear reaction. In his three years at Chicago, Wigner acted not only as a theoretical physicist, but also as an engineer, supervising every detail of the nuclear reactors that were to produce the material needed for the nuclear bomb. He was elemental in the design of the Hanford reactors.

Wigner received the U.S. Medal for Merit in 1946 for his wartime service. In 1963 he received the Nobel Prize for physics, and in 1969, the National Medal of Science. Wigner died on New Year's Day 1995.

Benjamin F. Shearer

WILLARD, ARCHIBALD MCNEAL (1836–1918)

Born in Bedford, Ohio, on August 22, 1836, Archibald Willard taught himself the basics of art in Wellington, Ohio. He left a job with a carriage maker to enlist in the eighty-sixth Ohio Volunteers in 1861 and was mustered out in 1864 only to rejoin the army, returning home again in June 1865.

Willard continued as a carriage maker while painting local portraits of children. His 1872 humorous pair of drawings *Puck I and II*, marketed by photographer and promoter J. F. Ryder, became a successful print. Willard continued to produce variations on this theme and received his only formal training in New York under J. O. Gaton.

As the 1876 Centennial approached, Ryder suggested Willard undertake a patriotic work, which Willard based on sketches from Wellington militia picnics of veterans of the War of 1812. Finished in Cleveland, but posed with local friends, the work portrays a colonial fifer, two drummers and a dying continental soldier. It was a popular success at the Philadelphia Centennial and toured across the original thirteen colonies before being purchased for display in the Marblehead, Massachusetts, Town Hall. Willard later made several copies, while prints, photographs and lithographs were widely sold to the public.

Willard continued to produce patriotic works of a progressive and religiously charged nature. He also produced political and social cartoons. Willard parodied his *Spirit of '76* in a pro–Spanish-American War print, *On to Havana* and supported American entry into World War I by appearing in parades. He died in Cleveland on October 11, 1918.

Further Reading: Ohio Historical Society. *Archibald M. Willard and The Spirit of '76: An Ohio Artist and His Work.* Columbus: Ohio Historical Society, 1992.

Margaret D. Sankey

WILLARD, DANIEL (1861–1942)

Daniel Willard, president of the Baltimore and Ohio Railroad, claimed to have found out President Woodrow Wilson had appointed him to the

Advisory Commission of the Council of National Defense when he was reading a newspaper in a Chicago hotel room on October 30, 1916. He quickly made his way to Washington. On March 3, 1917, he was elected chair of the Advisory Commission. A month later Wilson asked Congress for a declaration of war.

Born in Vermont on January 28, 1861, Willard grew up on his father's farm, graduated from high school, and left college after a few months because of bad eyesight. Local railroad work was liberation from farming. Starting at the bottom and moving to engineer, even joining the locomotive engineers union, and finally to management, Willard became president of the B & O Railroad in 1910. He returned to that position on March 1, 1920, and remained in it until a year before his death on July 6, 1942.

Willard was known as a fair and energetic executive. He was instrumental in establishing the Railroad War Board, which was an effort by railroad executives to coordinate defense transportation priorities voluntarily. At the end of 1917, however, the government took over the railroads through the Railroad Administration, much to Willard's dislike. He remained chair of the Advisory Commission until its end and briefly the chair of the War Industries Board, resigning that position in January of 1918, thus making way for **Bernard Mannes Baruch** to take over.

Further Reading: Hungerford, Edward. *Daniel Willard Rides the Line.* 1938. Reprint. Freeport, NY: Books for Libraries Press, 1972.

Benjamin F. Shearer

WILLIAMS, JOSEPH (1918–)

Engineer Joseph Williams was a central figure in the creation of the U.S Army's World War II and Cold War–era armored forces. Between 1941 and 1976, he helped design and build combat vehicles that form the core of the army's current mobile ground warfare capabilities.

Williams was born on March 19, 1918. He started work at the Aberdeen Proving Ground in 1941 and quickly became one of the leaders in formulating the theoretical and analytical methodology for combat vehicle design and development that remains the basic framework for the production of fighting vehicles. In 1942, Williams was a designer at Aberdeen of the M-4 (Sherman) series of tanks. He spent most of the war years on the engineering staff at the Detroit Arsenal where he played a key part in designing and producing early prototypes for a heavy/medium tank, from which developed the M-26 Pershing, America's first medium tank.

After World War II at Aberdeen, beginning with the Model T37/M41 light tank, Williams was central in designing functional tanks needed for rapid deployment and flexibility. He participated in the design and development of the M-103 heavy tank, the M-48 and, later the M551 and M60A2 tanks. As Chief of the Combat Vehicle Advanced Design Branch, Research and

Engineering Division, from 1952 to 1962, he developed combat vehicles used in the Korean and Vietnam wars.

Williams retired in 1976 and is currently a part-time consultant for the Battelle Memorial Institute.

Further Reading: United States. Army. Ordnance Corps. Hall of Fame. "Mr. Joseph Williams." Accessed May 2005 at http://www.goordnance.apg.army.mil.

Walter F. Bell

WILLIAMS, R. S. (?–?)

R. S. Williams was from Covington, Kentucky, and an artillery captain in the Confederate Army. Little else is known of him other than he apparently made his living as a newspaper editor after the war. He invented a rapid-fire gun, a type of machinegun, for the Confederacy during the Civil War. Williams constructed the gun at the Tredegar Arsenal in Richmond during the winter if 1861.

Of several designs submitted to the Confederate government for a rapid-fire gun, Williams' gun was selected and produced. It became the first rapid-fire gun ever used in combat. It was first used during the Battle of Seven Pines on May 31, 1862. The exact number of the guns built is unknown, although Williams was authorized to organize at battery of six guns for the Confederate Army. The gun was a single barrel breech-loader that used a paper cartridge and fired 1.57 caliber projectiles about 2000 yards with a crank. It could fire sixty-five rounds per minute and needed a crew of three soldiers.

The Union Army finally produced a true machine gun, the Gatling gun, invented by Southerner **Richard Jordan Gatling**, very late in the Civil War. The Gatling gun employed six rotating barrels to the Williams gun's single barrel, and unlike the Williams gun, it did not heat up and jam the breech. It was the Gatling gun that became the prototype of machine guns of the future.

Further Reading: Hegsted, Lyle. "Williams Gun History." Accessed June 2005 at www.floridareenactorsonline.com/williamsgun/htm.

Dallace W. Unger Jr.

WILLIAMS, SAM B. (1921–)

Mechanical engineer Sam Williams helped to change the course of the Cold War with his invention of the small fan-jet engine, which powered America's cruise missiles. A man with 72 patents who believes that there are no horizons to the future of technological innovation, Williams was awarded the Collier Trophy in 1979, the Wright Brothers Memorial Trophy in 1988, and the prestigious National Medal of Technology in 1995. He was inducted into the Aviation Hall of Fame in 1998 and the Inventors Hall of Fame in 2003.

Williams was born in Seattle, Washington, on May 7, 1921, and raised in Columbus, Ohio. He earned his baccalaureate engineering degree at Purdue in 1942 and went to work for the Chrysler Corporation, where he helped to develop gas turbine engines for cars and received his first patents. He struck out on his own in 1954 and formed Williams Research Corporation in Birmingham, Michigan. Steadfast in his belief that large engines could be scaled down and still reach high efficiency, Williams and his colleagues undertook the research that resulted in the small fan-jet engine, which was patented in 1968. The military at once saw the application of Williams' engines to guided missiles that had to reach long distances at low trajectories. They were compact, lightweight, and produced the thrust necessary to reach desired targets. Today Williams International Corporation, the new company name chosen in 1981, continues to make small gas-turbine engines for military and general aviation customers.

Benjamin F. Shearer

WILLSON, MEREDITH (1902–1984)

Born in Mason City, Iowa on May 18, 1902, Meredith Willson was encouraged from childhood to be a musician. He left Iowa for the Damrosch Institute (now Julliard) in 1920. Willson played with the John Philip Sousa band from 1920 to 1923, then with the New York Philharmonic until 1929, when he moved to Seattle as the musical director for NBC radio.

Willson's career in radio progressed from Seattle to San Francisco, where he also conducted the San Francisco Symphony, then in 1938 he was promoted to Los Angeles as musical director of two NBC hit radio programs. While in Hollywood, Willson wrote popular music and scored the films *The Great Dictator* and *The Little Foxes*, earning Oscar nominations for both.

Willson accepted a commission as a major in the U.S. Army during the Second World War and served as the head of Armed Forces Radio, overseeing programs like *Command Performance*. Additionally, he wrote songs on the request of government agencies, including paeans to civilian truck drivers ("My Ten-Ton Baby and Me"), USO Volunteers ("Gangway, Rats, Gangway!") and the Women's Army Corps ("Yankee Doodle Girls"), as well as patriotic morale-builders like "America Calling" in 1942.

Following the war, a string of popular compositions flowed from Willson, but his largest contribution to American popular music came in 1957, when he debuted *The Music Man* on Broadway.

Willson died on June 15, 1984. He was posthumously awarded the Presidential Medal of Freedom in 1986.

Further Reading: Skipper, John C. *Meredith Willson: The Unsinkable Music Man.* Mason City, IA: Savas Publishing, 2000.

Margaret D. Sankey

WILSON, CHARLES EDWARD (1886–1972)

As the War Production Board, directed by **Donald M. Nelson**, stumbled its way in the early days of World War II through the maze of military procurement programs, civilian production facilities, supply line bottlenecks, and materiel shortages, President Franklin Roosevelt turned to an anti–New Deal Republican to take control of production. Charles Wilson, president of General Electric, was his choice.

Wilson was a production man who learned his skills largely on the job. Born in New York City on November 16, 1886, Wilson forsook his last year of grade school to go to work for the Sprague Works. By 1906 he was a production manager. He took some courses at night and by mail here and there, and continued to rise in corporate ranks. When General Electric fully integrated Sprague into its corporate structure in 1918, Wilson was made an assistant superintendent of plants in New York and Pennsylvania. Ten years later he was an assistant vice president, then a vice president, and in 1937 he joined the board of directors as an executive vice president. In January 1940 he became president.

When Wilson became vice chairman for production of the War Production Board in September 1942, he walked into a situation that hindered any future success. Statisticians had found that production, owing to conflicting, independent programs, had become unbalanced. Every branch of the military had its own procurement system. The message that war meant all-out production had in fact caused scheduling problems, with some items exceeding schedule and others woefully behind. The board had in effect abrogated true control of production to a system that took procurement out of its hands. Military authorities intently guarded what they saw as their prerogatives from civilian interference in time of war.

Wilson, not known for his political skills, had to convince the military to let the board take direct control of production, from procurement through production scheduling and further, he had to empower civilian manufacturers with military contracts to do whatever it took to maximize production. Wilson also had to find a way to coordinate the manufacture and shipment of the parts needed to produce finished items.

A compromise gave Wilson responsibility for directly scheduling war production, end products and parts, in accord with the requirements of the Chiefs of Staff. His position was strengthened by creation of a Production Executive Committee, with himself as chair. Membership also included two military representatives, the vice chairman of the Maritime Commission, and Wilson's co-equal, the vice chairman for programs, **Ferdinand Eberstadt**. Wilson's position was also strengthened by getting direct supervisory authority over the production of aircraft, radio and radar equipment, and escort ships. Coordinated production orders would go through the military bureaucracy. In February 1943 the War Production Board issued a general scheduling order and in June, a component parts scheduling plan. Both were later revised based on experience.

A problem remained. Eberstadt controlled the allocation of materials and Wilson controlled the production of parts and end products. War Production Board director Nelson tried to paper over any conflict between the two, but he continued to increase Wilson's authority at Wilson's request. By the end of February 1943, Eberstadt was gone and Wilson was the executive vice chairman of the War Production Board. Wilson directed perhaps the most intense and successful war production programs in history, but by August 1944 he, like Eberstadt, had lost the political battle, and he resigned from the board.

Wilson went back to General Electric, which flourished under him after the war. With the Korean War looming, President Harry Truman asked Wilson to serve as director of the Office of Defense Mobilization in 1950. The Republican Wilson served until he disagreed with Truman about labor relations in 1952. Wilson went back again to General Electric, but remained there only briefly because he had reached retirement age. He then joined the W. R. Grace Company as a director and consultant, retiring in 1956 as chair of the board of directors. From 1956 to 1958, Wilson was involved with the People-to-People Foundation. He died on January 3, 1972.

Further Reading: Catton, Bruce. *The War Lords of Washington*. New York: Harcourt, Brace, 1948. Reprint. Westport, CT: Greenwood Press, 1969; Sagendorph, Kent. *Charles Edward Wilson, American Industrialist: An Anniversary Biography*. Published on the fiftieth anniversary of Mr. Wilson's first employment in the General Electric family. New York: General Electric, 1949; United States Civilian Production Administration. *Industrial Mobilization for War, History of the War Production Board and Predecessor Agencies, 1940–1945*. Washington, DC, 1947.

Benjamin F. Shearer

WILSON, ROBERT RATHBUN (1914–2000)

A leading particle physicist, Robert Wilson worked on the Manhattan Project as the Cyclotron Group Leader at Los Alamos. Born March 4, 1914, to Platt Elvin and Edith (Rathbun) Wilson, in Frontier, Wyoming, Wilson attended the University of California at Berkeley. While at Berkeley, he became familiar with the cyclotron, a type of particle accelerator. When he received his doctorate in 1940, he joined the faculty at Princeton University as an instructor of physics. Despite Wilson's initial reluctance, **Julius Robert Oppenheimer** recruited him for the Manhattan Project, and Wilson spent 1943 until 1946 at Los Alamos, working on the atomic bomb. He led the Cyclotron Group, which devised ways to measure the magnitude of the test explosions. Wilson had deeply seated reservations about the use of the weaponry. He agreed, however, that the Germans posed a threat, but felt strongly that the makers of the bomb ought to have some say in its use. When he witnessed the first test, he expressed deep regret at his role in the project.

After the war ended, Wilson began designing an advanced cyclotron for Harvard University, using his knowledge of magnetic forces acting on the particles to design a new shape for the machine. He accepted a position at

Cornell University and continued his work with particle accelerators. In 1968, he even worked for the Fermi National Accelerator Laboratory, building the largest synchrotron at the world's finest particle physics laboratory. He died on January 16, 2000.

Ellen Baier

WINCHESTER, OLIVER (1810–1880)

Oliver Winchester was a businessman and small arms manufacturer. He was born in Boston, Massachusetts, on November 30, 1810. His father died young and Winchester was forced to start working at the age of seven. He worked on a farm and then as a carpenter. In 1834, he married Jane Ellen Hope. They had two children and started a men's clothing store in Baltimore, Maryland.

Winchester did well in the business, starting several clothing businesses until the early 1850s, when he was able to invest in the Volcanic Repeating Arms Company, becoming a director in 1855. The company fell on hard times, but since Winchester held the first mortgages, he received all the assets and used them to form the New Haven Arms Company with himself as president. Among the assets was a patent for a level-action loading mechanism, the rights to manufacture a metallic cartridge using a patent developed by **Horace Smith** and **Daniel Wesson**, and gunsmith **Benjamin Tyler Henry**. Henry developed the Henry repeating rifle, which would eventually be known as the Winchester repeating rifle. The Henry rifle saw limited use during the Civil War.

Winchester purchased the American Repeating Rifle Company in 1869, the Spencer Repeating Rifle Company in 1870, and the patent rights for **Benjamin Berkeley Hotchkiss'** bolt-action repeating rifle in 1876. His final purchase, in 1879, was a patent from **John Moses Browning** that was used in the Winchester single-shot rifle. Winchester died the following year, on December 11, 1880.

Dallace W. Unger Jr.

WING, HENRY EBENEZER (1840–1925)

Henry Wing was a correspondent for the New York *Tribune*, the first correspondent to defy Secretary of War Edwin M. Stanton's order that no additional civilians would be allowed at the front. Following law school, Wing enlisted in the Twenty-seventh Connecticut infantry in September 1862. He covered the early stages of the Civil War for the newspaper *New Haven Palladium*. At the Battle of Fredericksburg he was severely wounded and was discharged from the army.

Wing became a correspondent for the New York *Tribune* by defying Secretary of War Stanton's prohibition. He covered the first day of the Wilderness campaign and volunteered to deliver the pooled reports for his colleagues through Confederate territory. When Wing reached a telegraph reserved for military use, he refused to submit to Stanton's demand for turning over the report. Stanton ordered Wing's arrest, but not before Abraham Lincoln interceded, agreeing to allow him to send in his reports.

The president sent a train for Wing so he could give a more complete report in person. Arriving at the White House at 2 A.M., he was kissed by the president for the encouraging news he brought from Ulysses Grant of the Army's high morale. Wing's greatest story was the only information received from the front that day. Lincoln provided Wing an escort back to the front the following day, where he would remain throughout the war.

Further Reading: Andrews, J. Cutler. *The North Reports the Civil War*. Pittsburgh: University of Pittsburgh Press 1955.

Michael L. McGregor

WINNER, SEPTIMUS (1827–1902)

Septimus Winner wrote songs during the Civil War, including, "Give Us Back Our Old Commander," which got him into trouble with the administration. He was born on May 11, 1827, in Philadelphia, Pennsylvania. He married Hannah Jane Guyer in 1847, and they had seven children. Winner gave private music lessons, sold instruments, played in bands and orchestras, and wrote music. Before the Civil War most of his hits were published under the pseudonym Alice Hawthorne.

When the war began, Winner started publishing his songs under is own name. The song that gained him the most attention was "Give Us Back Our Old Commander." Written after seeing an 1863 demonstration in Washington, DC, by Union soldiers demanding that General George McClellan be returned to command, the song was a huge hit, selling more then eighty thousand copies in the first couple of weeks. Winner was apparently a McClellan supporter himself. However, the song was not popular with the government in Washington. In fact, it was declared treasonous and armed guards visited Winner, threatening to arrest him if he did not stop selling the music and destroy the unsold copies.

During the war Winner also wrote "Ten Little Injuns" and "Der Deitcher's Dog," with the familiar lyrics, "O where, o where, has my little dog gone?" Winner died on November 22, 1902, at his home in Philadelphia, possibly from a heart attack.

Further Reading: Remsin, Michael. *Septimus Winner: Two Lives in Music*. Lanham, MD: Scarecrow Press, 2002.

Dallace W. Unger Jr.

WINROD, GERALD BURTON (1900–1957)

Gerald Burton Winrod, a fundamentalist preacher, was one of 26 "native Fascists" indicted in 1942. The sedition charges were prompted largely by the successful mischaracterization of his ideas by his opponents. He was tried in 1944 along with twenty-nine other defendants in federal court (*United States v. Winrod*). Under oath he offered significant criticisms of Nazism as proof of his rejection of fascism, including having been jailed in Italy for publicly denouncing Mussolini during a European tour. The case ended after eight months of testimony in a mistrial when the judge in the case died.

Theologically Winrod was a Premillennialist. He published numerous articles about the last days and the role of the Jews. These ideas eventually led him to become anti-Semitic and to "prophetic" speculations on the role of the totalitarian regimes of the day.

Winrod's support for Prohibition led him into political issues. In 1925 he organized the Defenders of the Christian Faith. In 1926 he began publishing *The Defender Magazine* to spread the views of the Defenders, opposing evolution, modernism and other ideologies that fundamentalists found to be anti-Christian. *The Defender Magazine* became a vehicle for enlisting others into the fundamentalist movement. It also brought invitations to speak in fundamentalist churches and to the World Christian Fundamentalist Association.

Winrod was born in Wichita, Kansas, on March 7, 1900. He maintained his anti-Semitism until his death, on November 12, 1957.

Further Reading: Montgomery, G. H. *Gerald Burton Winrod: Defender of the Faith.* Wichita, KS: Mertmont Publishers, 1965.

Andrew J. Waskey

WINTHROP, THEODORE (1828–1861)

Theodore Winthrop was a minor novelist. His posthumously published novels, with their combination of romanticism and realism, made them extremely popular. Born in New Haven, Connecticut, Winthrop graduated from Yale University in 1848. After traveling through Europe, Winthrop worked for the Pacific Mail Steamship. After returning from a surveying expedition in Panama, he began writing poetry.

Immediately after the Civil War's outbreak, Winthrop enlisted in New York's Seventh Regiment. He and his regiment traveled to Washington, DC, and were housed in the U.S. Capitol, where they remained until May when they moved to Camp Cameron, two miles north of the Willard Hotel. While at Camp Cameron, Winthrop wrote two articles, "Our March to Washington" and "Washington as Camp," describing daily camp activities that were published in June and July 1861 in the *Atlantic Monthly*. Frustrated at not seeing action in the battlefield, Winthrop left Camp Cameron and became General Benjamin Franklin Butler's secretary and was stationed at Fort Monroe, where he found himself in the middle of the war. On the June 10, in the first engagement of the Civil War, a botched campaign at Big Bethal, Virginia, Winthrop was shot and killed.

Winthrop's fellow soldiers described him as a man of courage in the face of death. After his courageous death, Winthrop's sister Laura published three of his novels, *Cecil Dreeme* (1861), *John Brent* (1862), and *The Canoe and the Saddle* (1862).

Further Reading: Colby, Elbridge. *Theodore Winthrop*. New York: Twayne Publishers, 1965.

Michael L. McGregor

WITHERSPOON, FRANCES (1886–1973)

Frances Witherspoon, an anti-war protestor, was a co-founder of the War Resisters League in 1923. She was born in Meridian, Mississippi in 1886 to Samuel Witherspoon, a prominent lawyer and congressman, and graduated from Bryn Mawr College in 1908. She was first involved in the women's suffrage movement, when she and her lifelong friend **Tracy Mygatt** helped to organize the Women's Suffrage Party in Pennsylvania. Witherspoon and Mygatt moved to New York City in 1913 and joined the Socialist Party. Witherspoon quickly became an active member of the Woman's Peace Party. During this time, Witherspoon and Mygatt were involved with the Emergency Peace Federation and demonstrated with the American Committee Against Militarism. In 1917, Witherspoon and Charles Recht co-founded the New York Bureau of Legal Advice; Witherspoon served as Executive Secretary and Recht, as General Counsel. The organization provided the first organized legal aid for conscientious objectors.

After World War I, Witherspoon and Mygatt worked closely with the Women's Peace Union, and in 1923, the two women co-founded the War Resisters League. Witherspoon continued to work actively toward peace for more than fifty years, including writing numerous letters and petitions to Congress and authoring or co-authoring a number of anti-war books, articles and plays. Witherspoon and Mygatt were jointly awarded the WRL Peace Award in 1961 and served as Honorary Chairwomen until their deaths in 1973. In 1968, at the age of eighty-two, Witherspoon petitioned her fellow Mawrter alumnae to protest the war in Vietnam, and obtained more than a thousand signatures.

Ellen Baier

WITHERSPOON, JOHN (1723–1794)

Born on February 5, 1723, at Yester, Scotland, and educated at the University of Edinburgh, John Witherspoon served as a Presbyterian pastor until 1768, when he left his parish at Paisley for the presidency of the College of New Jersey. Under his leadership, the college flourished, but the American Revolution halted its advance. Although Witherspoon did not approve of pastors entering politics, colonial circumstances changed his position.

Beginning in 1774, Witherspoon served as a county delegate, member of the Somerset County Committee of Correspondence, attended political conventions, and led the movement to arrest the Tory governor, William Franklin. In June 1776, when chosen as delegate to the Continental Congress, he urged that body not to delay in declaring independence. Witherspoon was the only clergyman to sign the Declaration of Independence. His sermon, preached at Princeton in May 1776 and titled, *Dominion of Providence over the Passions of Men*, was the first of many such discourses Witherspoon wrote in defense of American liberty.

Witherspoon held a seat in Congress almost continually from 1776 to 1782, served on over one hundred committees, and took an active part in the debates on the Articles of Confederation. In addition, he helped to organize the executive branch and to form alliances with foreign governments. He also played a role in drawing up instructions for the peace commissioners responsible for negotiating terms with Great Britain. Indeed, Witherspoon earned the title of the "political parson." He spent his remaining years rebuilding the College of New Jersey and died on November 15, 1794.

James S. Baugess

WOLFF, IRVING (1894–1988)

Irving Wolff, the holder of nearly eighty patents, was one of the pioneers of radar. Born in New York City in 1894, he received his undergraduate degree in physics from Dartmouth in 1916 and his doctorate in physics from Cornell in 1923. After a one-year fellowship at Cornell, Wolff went to work for the Radio Corporation of America (RCA). Beginning in the acoustics department, he officially retired from RCA as a vice president for research in 1959. He died on September 5, 1988.

After having worked on the development of loudspeakers, sound systems for theaters, and high-fidelity sound, Wolff became bored with acoustics and decided in the early 1930s to work with microwaves. In 1934 he conducted his first continuous wave experiment, which successfully indicated the direction of an object and in 1937, he had developed a pulse radar system that indicated both direction and distance, which meant that radar could be used for navigational purposes. Wolff called this "radio-vision." He proceeded to build a low-frequency system for use on airplanes so that pilots could see obstacles in front of them. Navy trials in 1939 showed the CXAM (what became the SK or "flying bedspring") radar to be superior to the RCA system, but Wolff's radar was installed on flying boats at the beginning of World War II. Wolff's wartime contributions also included an accurate radio-reflection altimeter meant to improve bombing results and an infrared "sniperscope" that was first used effectively on Okinawa.

Benjamin F. Shearer

WOLFF, TOBIAS (1945–)

Tobias Wolff was born on June 19, 1945, in Birmingham, Alabama. His father abandoned the family when he was young, and the family moved around the country seeking economic survival. After high school, Wolff enlisted, and from 1964 to 1968 served in Vietnam as a lieutenant with the Army Special Forces, often as a translator.

After Vietnam, Wolff worked briefly for the *Washington Post* before earning B.A. and M.A. degrees from Oxford University (1972 and 1975). In 1978, he earned another master's degree, from Stanford University. He has taught writing and English at Goddard College, Arizona State University, Temple University, Syracuse University, and Stanford.

His first collection of short stories, *In the Garden of the North American Martyrs*, was published in 1981. Three years later, Wolff received the P.E.N./ Faulkner Award in fiction for his novella *The Barracks Thief*, which focused on the failure of young men to find solace and family within the military. Wolff's second collection of stories, *Back in the World* (1985), addressed the struggles of Vietnam veterans, as well as other estranged individuals, to forge a sense of community. *This Boy's Life: A Memoir* (1989) drew on Wolff's personal development up to his Vietnam enlistment.

In 1994, Wolff was finally able to write directly about his Vietnam experiences. *In Pharaoh's Army: Memories of the Lost War* describes Wolff's disillusionment with the military and the Vietnam War, experiences that failed to provide the sense of male camaraderie he had sought.

Further Reading: Wolff, Tobias. *In Pharaoh's Army: Memories of the Lost War*. New York: Houghton Mifflin, 1994.

Ron Briley

WOOD, CHARLES ERSKINE SCOTT (1852–1944)

Poet and writer Erskine Wood, born on February 20, 1852, in Erie, Pennsylvania, graduated from West Point in 1874 and was sent out west as a young officer to fight in the Indian wars. He would later write about his experiences. He convinced the army to let him pursue a law degree, and he graduated from Columbia in 1882 with a bachelor's degree and the next year with his law degree. One year later Wood resigned his commission, moved to Portland, Oregon, and set up what became a very lucrative law practice and successful writing career.

Wood perceived America's westward expansion from the Rockies as a history of the common man's having been shut out of the American promise of freedom by wealth, power and legalities. This made him philosophically an anarchist. He came to the defense of Wobblies (members of the radical International Workers of the World) and others who fought vainly for change in the American system. Wood was also against American imperialism abroad.

In 1899 he published the poem, "Battle Hymn of the Republic," which expressed a far different sentiment from that which caused **Julia Ward Howe** to pen her "Battle Hymn of the Republic" during the Civil War. Oozing sarcasm, Wood encouraged Filipino rebels to take up their guns against the Americans "conquerors, by God."

Writing in *The Masses* for **Max Forrester Eastman** before World War I, Wood continued to criticize patriotic religion and war in his satirical "Heavenly Discourses." He died on January 22, 1944.

Benjamin F. Shearer

WOOD, ROBERT ELKINGTON (1879–1969)

The unorthodox and effective head of Sears during the Great Depression, Robert Wood served as chair of the America First Committee (AFC), which opposed U.S. entry into World War II. Born on June 13, 1869, Wood graduated from West Point in 1900. His army service took him to the Panama Canal, where he was recognized for service in managing the canal project's supplies and equipment, then in 1917, to France. Wood became Acting Quartermaster General for the American Expeditionary Force, earning a Distinguished Service Medal.

Upon retiring from the army in 1919, Wood joined mail-order giant Montgomery Ward, which fired him for championing expansion into retail stores. He took his idea to competitor Sears, Roebuck, with dramatic success. Wood became president of Sears in 1928 and reshaped the company into a retail giant.

In 1939, about the time Wood retired as president of Sears, but remained chair of the board, he was tapped to be head of the AFC. This group, which included famed aviator **Charles Augustus Lindbergh** and other notables, argued that the United States should concentrate on becoming impregnable, stay out of the war in Europe, and avoid being sucked into the war by providing non-military aid. Always troubled by association with radicals and American Nazis, the AFC disbanded after Japan attacked Pearl Harbor in December 1941.

During the war, Wood served as a civilian supply advisor to the military, earning a Legion of Merit award. He presided over Sears' vast expansion after the war, involved on the board until his death on November 6, 1969.

Wende Vyborney Feller

WOODBRIDGE, RICHARD GEORGE JR. (1886–1946)

Improved Military Rifle (IMR) Powder helped the Allies win World War I. Richard Woodbridge and his assistant, Alfred Broadbent, had developed and patented a process that improved the ballistics of smokeless powder used in rifles and cannons.

Woodbridge was born on March 18, 1886, in Iowa City. After he received his undergraduate degree in chemistry at MIT in 1907, he spent another year there with a fellowship to study cellulose. Woodbridge then put this knowledge to work for DuPont's new Smokeless Powder Division. IMR Powder was in production and being used successfully by the British before America entered the war. However, even with Woodbridge's engineering know-how, DuPont's production was not enough. General Pershing was begging the government to get powder to France at the rate of 200 tons per day in August of 1917 before disaster occurred. Powder was also in short supply in the United States. Estimates were for a shortfall of 350 million pounds in 1918 alone.

This activated the Army Ordnance Department to award a contract to DuPont for a government-owned plant to produce 1 million pounds of smokeless powder per day. The contract was held up and eventually met with opposition from the War Industries Board, but DuPont did finally get another contract on January 29, 1918, and produced over 25 million pounds of powder by the armistice. Woodbridge's even further improved powders were produced in billions of pounds during World War II. He died on November 7, 1946, after thirty-eight years with DuPont.

Benjamin F. Shearer

WOODS, HELEN HAMILTON (?–?)

In 1941, before Pearl Harbor, Congresswoman Edith Nourse Rogers proposed creation of the Women's Army Auxiliary Corp (WAAC), a quasimilitary organization to serve the army by filling clerical positions with women so that enlisted men were free for combat. In 1942, Rogers proposed another to make the WAAC part of the army, allowing women to serve in noncombat situations. After initial strong resistance the WAAC became part of the regular army in 1943, and was named the Women's Army Corps (WAC).

Helen Hamilton Woods was instrumental in the creation of the WAAC, and its transition to the WAC. Starting as a third officer in the first recruitment of the WAAC, she rose to the rank of lieutenant colonel (and deputy director of the corps) by the end of the war. Woods was subsequently promoted to colonel.

In addition to assisting with the initial creation of the WAAC, Colonel Woods was highly influential in discussing what would happen to the WAC following the end of the war. While dissolution of the corps was a popular option, Colonel Woods argued for maintaining it and folding it into the army. With the testimony of regular army personnel who had seen WACs at the frontline, and with the example of European women, especially Russians, who fought along side their male counterparts, Colonel Woods was successful in maintaining a female presence in the post–World War II army.

Further Reading: Treadwell, Mattie E. *The Women's Army.* Washington, DC: U.S. Army, Center of Military History, 1991. Accessed May 20, 2005, at http://www.army.mil/cmh/books/wwii/Wac.

Mike Timonin

WOUK, HERMAN (1915–)

Herman Wouk's powerful novels brought World War II to life for generations of readers. A prolific novelist, Wouk was born on May 27, 1915, in the Bronx, New York, to a family of Jewish immigrants from Russia. His career as a radio scriptwriter was interrupted by service on a destroyer in the Pacific during World War II.

Wouk returned a changed man and became a full-time writer the following year. His first bestseller was *The Caine Mutiny,* in which he created a rundown minesweeper commanded by a mentally unbalanced captain. Queeg demands every perquisite of his rank, but when the ship sails into a typhoon, he cannot act decisively. When the executive officer relieves him of duty, he calls it mutiny. The lawyer who gets the officers acquitted then condemns them for putting their efforts into breaking Queeg instead of supporting him, turning the usual intellectual distaste for the military on its head. The novel won the 1952 Pulitzer Prize and became required reading at the U.S. Naval Academy.

Wouk returned to World War II in 1971 with *The Winds of War,* the first volume of his sweeping story of a career navy family caught up in the war. It deals with the war before the U.S. joins and ends with the bombing of Pearl Harbor. The second volume, *War and Remembrance,* published in 1978, takes the war to its end. Throughout both volumes, which have been compared to Leo Tolstoy's *War and Peace* in their scope, Wouk's admiration for the American military shines through.

Leigh Husband Kimmel

WRIGHT, ORVILLE AND WILBUR (1871–1948; 1867–1912)

Orville and Wilbur Wright are famous for being the first people to pilot a heavier-than-air airship (on December 17, 1903, at Kitty Hawk, North Carolina). Despite that successful day in 1903, the Wright brothers kept their achievement quiet, perfecting their craft in Dayton, Ohio, and actually deciding at the end of 1905 to not fly anymore. After taking a year off, the Wright brothers got back into the business and worked toward securing contracts with the U.S. Army and European governments. It was these endeavors that brought heavier-than-air aviation to the military.

Born to Milton and Susan Wright, Wilbur was born on April 16, 1867, in Indiana and Orville on August 19, 1871, in Ohio. Wilbur was a bright kid and loved school, wishing to pursue a degree at Yale to prepare for a career as a teacher. Orville, equally as bright but less inclined to apply himself at school, was more of the inventor—a quick mind and abundant enthusiasm compared to his brother's more contemplative nature. Wilbur's dreams of Yale vanished when he became ill after high school, and eventually the brothers opened up a rental and repair shop for bicycles in 1893. A craze in the 1890s, bicycling gave the brothers an opportunity to look seriously into building a heavier-than-air machine because bicycles, like airplanes, required propulsion, balance, and control.

Meticulous researchers, the two developed a series of gliders that they perfected on the Outer Banks of North Carolina between 1900 and 1902. The Outer Banks afforded them privacy and good winds. Each year they perfected their glider while also becoming expert pilots. In 1903 they returned to the Outer Banks—Kitty Hawk—with their first airplane. Charlie Taylor had helped them build a 12 horsepower, 4-cylinder engine and, after many delays, Wilbur and Orville were ready to flip a coin on December 17 to decide who would fly first. Wilbur won the coin toss, but his flight was too short to count as a success. Orville took his turn and made history

Orville and Wilbur Wright. Courtesy of the Library of Congress.

with his 12-second, 120-foot flight. After a few more flights, each one longer in duration and ground covered, the men called it a day. That evening a gust of wind smashed their craft, *The Flyer*, and their flying was done for the season.

The inherent problem for the Wright brothers for the next few years was that they did not wish to fly their plane for the public, fearing that someone might be able to copy their design, getting around the patents that the Wright brothers felt they owned outright. Without flying their machine, no reasonable businessman or government would sign a contract with them. The technology was too new to be trusted and perhaps, conventional wisdom stated, the Wrights were fakes. So the Wrights would not fly until they had a contract, and no one would sign a contract until seeing the craft fly.

In 1907 a French business seemed interested in the Wrights' plane and Wilbur set sail with their mechanic, Charlie Taylor. Frustratingly, they returned home without a contract and without having demonstrated their flying machine. However, they did leave the plane in France, hopeful that they would return soon. An offer did come, and Wilbur returned to France in May

1908. The French crowds were not so sure about the Wright brothers and greeted Wilbur with suspicion. The French had already begun their entry into aviation with the success of Brazilian Alberto Santos-Dumont, who flew in October 1906, leaving many to claim him as the first man to make a successful heavier-than-air flight. Succeeding him were French greats like Louis Bleriot and Henri Farman, who were flying around Europe by 1908. Yet, after months of labor to put his flyer back together from its transatlantic journey, in August Wilbur delighted a crowd of spectators, proving that his plane was far superior than anyone had imagined, certainly far superior to what the French were flying. He demonstrated a level of control that had not been seen by the Europeans, completing a tight figure eight that stunned the crowd. After convincing the French that he was the king of aviation, he toured Europe, stopping in Italy to train its first military pilots. He and his brother, who had joined him in Europe, left Europe in 1909 having signed business contracts with France and England. More important, they left Europe heroes.

Also in 1908 Orville was in Virginia trying to convince the U.S. Army that his plane was a worthwhile investment. The army, interested in a craft if it could meet certain specifications, published a set of criteria that reflected the performance claims made by the Wrights. The army wanted a two-seater plane that could fly 40 miles per hour for 125 miles. It also had to have control at all times and be able to be transported on an army wagon. Once published, the Wrights knew they could sell their plane to the military. Modifying a 1905 plane, making it a two-seater, Orville set off to Ft. Myer, Virginia, to demonstrate the Military Flyer for the army. On September 3, 1908, Orville piloted his first test flight for the army before a crowd of 10,000. Records were broken and the army was impressed. On September 17, Lt. Thomas Selfridge went up as a passenger with Orville. Tragically the plane crashed. A crack in one of the two propellers was split, causing the crash. Orville suffered serious injuries, but Selfridge was killed—the first heavier-than-air fatality. As a testament to his skill as a pilot, in a letter to his brother explaining what had happened, Orville commented if he had had just a few more feet he believed that he would have recovered control of the plane. Orville had to take a year off to recover, joining his brother in Europe, but returned to Ft. Myer in the spring of 1909 to complete the trials. For over a month, Orville delighted crowds, including one young boy, **Donald Wills Douglas**, who was there witnessing history. The Military Flyer exceeded all of the army's specifications and the army signed a contract with the Wrights in 1909. One flyer, complete with flying lessons for two officers, was $30,000.

Wilbur died young, at the age of forty-five, on May 30, 1912. His father had written in his journal that his son's life was "a short life, but full of consequences." Indeed it was. Typhoid fever took his life, but Orville blamed the patent wars with **Glenn Hammond Curtiss** as the reason for his brother's death, claiming the litigation had worn Wilbur out, preventing him from being able to stave off the typhoid fever. Orville felt the loss the most, losing his best friend, business partner and brother in one stroke. Orville went on to live to the age of seventy-six, dying from a heart attack on January 30, 1948. After Wilbur's death,

Orville withdrew from their business by 1915 and stopped flying by 1918. A shy and quiet man, he remained more or less out of the spotlight, but never lost interest in aviation, serving on the National Advisory Committee on Aeronautics from 1920 until his death. Together, these two brilliant men gave the world flight and with that, launched a new era for the militaries of the world. Only eleven years after the first flight at Kitty Hawk, the airplane was being flown in the skies of a war-torn Europe in the British, French, German, Russian, and Italian forces. A new day had dawned.

Further Reading: Crouch, Tom. *The Bishop's Boys: A Life of Wilbur and Orville Wright.* New York: W. W. Norton, 2003; Tobin, James. *To Conquer the Air: The Wright Brothers and the Great Race for Flight.* New York: Free Press, 2003.

Valerie L. Adams

WRIGHT, THEODORE PAUL (1895–1970)

Going against the grain of his pacifist family and his own socialist sympathies, Theodore Wright (no relation to **Orville and Wilbur Wright**) attended the United States Naval Reserve Flying Corps at MIT in 1917, where he received a few weeks of aeronautical engineering instruction and then became a naval aircraft inspector until he left the navy in 1921. Born in Galesburg, Illinois, on May 25, 1895, Wright finished his undergraduate degree at Lombard College in his hometown in 1915 and three years later got another bachelor's degree in architectural engineering at MIT. This preparation somewhat surprisingly led Wright into a successful twenty-year career as an aeronautical engineer for the Curtiss Aeroplane and Motor Company and then the merged Wright-Curtiss Corporation after 1928.

Wright had already joined the National Defense Advisory Committee in 1940, but he resigned his position as vice president and chief engineer at Curtiss-Wright in 1941 and moved to Washington, DC, to assist in the war effort. He became assistant chief in the Office of Production Management's Aircraft Section and then chair of the Joint Aircraft Committee. He also became a director of the Aircraft Resources Control Office and a member of the War Production Board's Aircraft production Board. Wright was instrumental in increasing and measuring aircraft production during World War II. He was appointed administrator of the Civil Aeronautics Administration in 1944 and left that position in 1948 to serve as vice president for research at Cornell. Wright died on August 21, 1970.

Benjamin F. Shearer

WRUBEL, ALLIE (1905–1973)

Allie Wrubel was born on January 15, 1905, in Middleton, Connecticut. He grew up in the field of music, and attended both Wesleyan University and Columbia University in the state of New York. He played with several dance orchestras, including the Whiteman Orchestra starting with the saxophone. Wrubel eventually traveled throughout Europe, including England with his own band. This is when he started writing his own music. Soon after this tour, he worked as a manager in the film industry and was eventually hired by the Warner Brothers Film Studio in Hollywood in 1934.

Wrubel worked for Warner Brothers from 1934 to 1946 and during the World War II years. He wrote songs for film musicals including: *Happiness Ahead, Alibi Ike, We're in the Money, The Lady in Red, Private Buckaroo, Sing Your Way Home*, and many others.

Disney Studios hired Wrubel in the late 1940s. He contributed to the films *Song of the South, Make Mine Music, Tulsa, Melody Time, I Walk Alone, Duel in the Sun, Midnight Lace*, and *Never Steal Anything Small*.

Wrubel wrote a number of popular songs: "Zip A Dee Doo Dah," "Everybody's got a Laughing Place," "Gone with the Wind," and "Good Night Angel." His musical contributions to World War II included "Farewell to Arms," " My Own America," "A Boy in Khaki, a Girl in Lace," and "Cleanin' My Rifle and Dreamin' of You."

Wrubel died in Twentynine Palms, California, on December 13, 1973, at the age of sixty-eight.

Erskine L. Levi Jr.

Y

YARDLEY, HERBERT OSBORNE (1889–1958)

Herbert Yardley was a cryptanalyst who organized and directed the U.S.'s first code-breaking efforts. Born in Worthington, Indiana, on April 13, 1889, Yardley learned to use the telegraph from his father. In 1912, he began his career as a code clerk in the U.S. State Department.

Yardley's "Solution of American Diplomatic Codes" initiated a complete change in the U.S. code system. He convinced the head of military intelligence that he could also break other country's codes and in June 1917 became head of the newly created eighth section of military intelligence (MI-8). While MI-8 had no real successes in World War I, the U.S. Army and the State Department continued to fund MI-8 after the war.

Code-named "The Cipher Bureau" and disguised as a company that produced codes for businesses, MI-8's mission was breaking the diplomatic codes of several countries. In 1921–1922, Yardley and his staff decrypted codes used by Japanese negotiators at the Washington Naval Conference, thus helping the United States succeed in the negotiations.

In 1929, the State Department stopped operation of MI-8 because Secretary of State Henry Stimson absolutely disliked the covert operation of breaking other nation's codes. In 1931, Yardley dealt with his sudden unemployment by writing his memoirs. During World War II he did cryptanalysis work for the Chinese and Canadian governments. Despite never being trusted by the U.S. government again, Yardley obtained a place in the National Security Agency Hall of Honor in 1999. He died on August 7, 1958, and was buried at Arlington National Cemetery.

Charlene T. Overturf

YARMOLINSKY, ADAM (1922–2000)

One of the early critics of American policies in the Vietnam War, Adam Yarmolinsky was born on November 17, 1922, in New York City. He graduated from Harvard in 1943, spent three years in the military, and got his law degree at Yale in 1948, when he began his legal career, which included clerking for Supreme Court Justice Stanley Reed.

Having sifted through various jobs, Yarmolinsky joined the Kennedy administration in 1961 as special assistant to Secretary of Defense Robert McNamara. He continued as McNamara's special assistant when Lyndon B. Johnson became president, but in 1964, he was moved to the position of deputy director of the President's Task Force on the War against Poverty. After serving as chief of the U.S. Emergency Relief Mission to the Dominican Republic in 1965, Yarmolinsky became principal deputy assistant secretary of defense for International Security Affairs.

By this time the war was going badly and Yarmolinsky like other of the administration's intellectuals, people whom Secretary McNamara admired, had become dovish on the war in Vietnam, wondering if it could be won. In fact in 1966, Yarmolinsky co-authored an influential study that showed that the bombing campaigns had not been effective. McNamara himself wanted to change policy, but found an easier out by becoming president of the World Bank. Yarmolinsky, left to teach law at Harvard. He moved to the Institute of Politics in 1972, and then to a professorship at the University of Massachusetts. The author of several books, Yarmolinsky died on January 5, 2000.

Jitendra Uttam

YERKES, ROBERT MEARNS (1876–1956)

Robert Yerkes led development of the Army Alpha and Army Beta tests, the first intelligence tests administered to large groups of subjects. Born on May 26, 1876, on a farm outside Philadelphia, Yerkes studied biology at nearby Ursinus College, but shifted to comparative psychology during his studies at Harvard, on the advice of his mentor Josiah Royce. After earning his doctorate from Harvard in 1902, Yerkes remained there as a professor of comparative psychology until 1917.

When the United States entered World War I, Yerkes, who was president of the American Psychological Association (APA), mobilized psychologists to join the war effort and became chair of the National Research Council's Psychology Committee. He also chaired the APA's Committee on the Psychological Examination of Recruits, a group of prominent psychologists working to replace informal screening of military recruits with systematic mass intelligence testing that could route soldiers into the most appropriate roles. Their Army Alpha (for literate recruits) and Army Beta (for illiterates and non-English-speakers) tests were ultimately administered to about 2 million soldiers.

These tests established the average mental age of Americans as a "moronic" thirteen. Made inexpensively available after the armistice, the Army Alpha became the most popular intelligence test at colleges.

Yerkes left the National Research Council in 1924 to become a professor of psychobiology at Yale, where he founded the Yale Laboratories of Primate Biology in 1929 and directed it until 1941. With his wife, Ada, he pioneered research on ape intelligence. Yerkes died on February 3, 1956.

Wende Vyborney Feller

YLVISAKER, NILS MARTIN (1882–1972)

After the beginning of World War II, but before the entry of the United States, Nils Martin Ylvisaker published *A Service Prayer Book with Bible Readings, Hymns, and Orders of Worship: Dedicated to the Army, Navy, and Air Corps of the United States and to the Canadian Armed Forces* (1940). It was re-issued in 1941. This was the second songbook that he published. The first, *Convention Song Book*, had been published in 1922.

Ylvisaker was a member of the Luther College Board of Trustees during World War II and for close to two years afterward (1942–1947). From 1930 to 1947 Ylvisaker served on the National Lutheran Service Commission (NLC). The NLC had been established on September 8, 1918, as a coordinating agency for participating Lutheran Churches to administer domestic programs, publicize Lutheran programs and doctrine, and to provide emergency relief to areas devastated by World War I.

During World War II, the NLC expanded its operations. The Service Commission, at first referred to as the Service Men's Division, sought to spiritually minister to service men and women, especially Lutherans. Ylvisaker was in charge of publishing the NLC files beginning in 1940.

Ylvisaker was born in 1882. He was of Norwegian immigrant stock. In 1901 he graduated from Luther College. He was a prolific writer. In 1933 he published *The Glory Road* (1933), *Faces toward God* (1936), and *No Other Way* (1938). Other works include *Trumpets of God* (1945), *Tomorrow's Lutheran Church*, and *The Ylvisaker Story* (1962).

Andrew J. Waskey

YOUNG, ARTHUR HENRY (1866–1943)

During World War I, Art Young, an anti-war cartoonist, was accused of violating the Espionage Act and undermining the war effort. Born on January 14, 1866, in Orangeville, Illinois, Young studied at Chicago's Academy of Design as well as the Art Student League in New York. He sold his cartoons to magazines such as *Life*, and illustrated stories for several newspapers. Though he was once engaged to draw a commission that contradicted his political views, he felt that doing so was hypocritical, and he swore to produce only work that was consistent with his beliefs.

A Socialist and noted activist, he drew cartoons and wrote articles in support of woman suffrage, labor organization, and racial equality, and against child labor and war. In particular, his satires in *The Masses* between 1911 and 1917 were well known, if not well received—though the criminal libel suit that the Associated Press brought against him in 1913 was eventually dropped. He frequently attacked the war in Europe, convinced that its only cause was imperialism, and that the United States should remain neutral. He even went so far as to imply that American industrialists were milking the conflict for profit. Several contributors to *The Masses*, including Young, were accused of violating the Espionage Act, but were not convicted. The newspaper failed, however, under the force of the legal action.

After the war, Young contributed cartoons to **Max Forrester Eastman**'s socialist newspaper, *The Liberator*, among other, more mainstream, papers. He died on December 29, 1943.

Ellen Baier

YOUNG, LEO CLIFFORD (1890–1981)

Radio engineer Leo Young was a pioneer in radio detection and ranging or radar. He and **Albert Hoyt Taylor**, both employed at the U.S. Naval Aircraft Radio Laboratory, discovered in September 1922 that ships passing by on a river disturbed the continuous high-frequency radio waves they were testing. This began the search for a military application that would permit American ships to detect enemy ships and planes. It was Young's idea in 1934 to use radio pulses rather than waves and his colleague **Robert Morris Page** built the very first pulse radar system, which was widely used in World War II.

Born in Ohio in 1890, Young was an early radio enthusiast who built his own radio sets as a teenager. He joined the naval reserve when the United States entered World War I and worked with Taylor at the Great Lakes Naval Radio Station before going to the Radio Aircraft Laboratory. Young remained at the Naval Research Laboratory when it was created in 1923, and his work eventually led him into research on the ionosphere with **Gregory Breit** and **Merle Antony Tuve** at the Carnegie Institution. He died in 1981.

The use of pulses rather than continuous radio waves was an elemental leap forward in early radar development. By mounting sending, receiving, and display equipment closely together the echo could indicate the range, bearing, and detection of a target. Most important, all this equipment could be placed on one ship.

Benjamin F. Shearer

YOUNG, LORETTA (1914–2000)

Hollywood screen diva Loretta Young was born Gretchen Young in Salt Lake City, Utah, on January 6, 1914. She and her two older sisters all became actresses. Young's entry into Hollywood was a fluke. In 1926, she answered a call for one of her sisters and went for the audition of what was to be her first film, *Naughty, But Nice*. With the film's release, Gretchen, to her surprise, was suddenly Loretta.

There was no looking back from then on even as she continued her schooling privately. Young worked with Warner Brothers for seven years and then with 20th Century Fox before she started free-lancing in 1940. A fashion icon, she also modeled for such magazines as *Vogue* and *Cosmopolitan*.

In 1942, the U.S. government established a War Finance Committee, which urged the citizens, especially those unable to directly contribute to the war effort, to support the fight by purchasing war bonds. While war bonds could be purchased through payroll deduction, they were not marketed as cuts in salaries, but as interest-bearing investments that would be paid back after the war ended. As a prominent celebrity of her time, Young joined other patriotic celebrities like **Ruth Elizabeth "Betty" Grable** and **Leslie Townes "Bob" Hope** in promoting the war bond campaigns through personal appearances, movie shorts, and radio programs.

After a long and successful career in film, radio, and television, which included Academy and Emmy Awards, and a retirement doing charitable work, Young died on August 12, 2000.

Jitendra Uttam

YOUNG, ROBERT RALPH (1897–1958)

"The daring young man of Wall Street," Robert Ralph Young opposed American involvement in World War II even after the Japanese attack on Pearl Harbor.

Born in a Texas cow town on February 14, 1897, Young graduated first in his class at Culver Military Academy in 1914. He dropped out of the University of Virginia before the end of his sophomore year. Bored with a subsequent string of jobs where advancement seemed slow, Young tried the stock market. There, he gained his reputation for daring and insight by selling short in the crash of 1929, thus walking away with a fortune. He used his resulting wealth to buy shares in the Alleghany Corporation, a railroad holding company. From 1930 into the mid-1950s, Young battled for control of first the Chesapeake and Ohio, then the New York Central railroads, championing reforms in how readily banks could control railroads.

Shortly after Germany invaded Poland in 1939, a number of prominent Americans including **Charles Augustus Lindbergh** and **Burton K. Wheeler** joined the America First Committee (AFC), to speak out against U.S. involvement in a war in Europe. Young was one of the founders and directors of this organization. When the AFC voted to disband after Pearl Harbor, Young opposed the decision, arguing that U.S. misconduct and mistakes, including using economic pressure against Japanese expansionism, caused the attack.

Young continued his battles with the "damned bankers" until his death January 25, 1958.

Wende Vyborney Feller

Z

ZINN, WALTER HENRY (1906–2000)

Born in Kitchener, Ontario, Canada, on December 10, 1906, Walter Zinn majored in mathematics at Queen's University and left the insurance business in 1930 to pursue physics at Columbia University. He earned his Ph.D. in 1934 and taught at City College of New York. In 1928 he became an American citizen. While at City College, Zinn and **Leo Szilard** collaborated on uranium fission experiments, concluding by 1939 that fission was indeed possible. In 1942 **Enrico Fermi** brought Zinn to the Metallurgical Laboratory at the University of Chicago to be his right-hand man. As a member of the Manhattan Project there, Zinn made elemental contributions to the construction of the atomic bomb.

It was Zinn who supervised the building of CP-1, Chicago Pile No. 1, the first atomic pile or nuclear reactor on a squash court at the University of Chicago. And it was Zinn who pulled the ZIP, a weighted control rod he invented, to begin the first self-sustained nuclear reaction and to end it after twenty-eight minutes on December 2, 1942. With this proof of controlled atomic chain reaction, the nuclear age was born, and the use of the atomic bomb against the Japanese ended World War II in the Pacific.

Zinn stayed at the Metallurgical Lab when it became the Argonne National Laboratory and was its director from 1946 until 1956, where he pioneered in developing breeder reactors and applying atomic energy to electricity generation. He died on February 14, 2000.

Benjamin F. Shearer

ZWORYKIN, VLADIMIR (1889–1982)

Vladimir Zworykin's research toward inventing an all-electronic television also led to contributions to military navigation and targeting, nighttime combat, electric eyes, text readers and the electron microscope.

Zworykin was born on July 30, 1889, in Murom, Russia and studied at the St. Petersburg Institute of Technology, where he worked with Boris Rosing on an early electromechanical version of television. Although Zworykin studied briefly at the College de France, World War I interrupted his work. Throughout the war, he was an officer in the Russian signal corps. Following the Bolshevik Revolution, he toured the world before moving to the United States in 1919 and obtaining a job at Westinghouse. He became a U.S. citizen in 1924 and completed his doctorate at the University of Pittsburgh in 1926, writing his dissertation on improvements to photoelectric cells.

Throughout the 1920s, Zworykin tried to convince Westinghouse to invest in developing television. His first patented system, in 1923, did not impress Westinghouse decision makers. Working on his own time, Zworykin developed the electric camera tube, called the iconoscope, and the electric picture tube, the kinescope. A 1929 demonstration of this technology convinced **David Sarnoff** of RCA that the system was worth developing. Zworykin was recruited to head an RCA research laboratory that would focus on this technology. This research culminated in Sarnoff's demonstration of television at the 1939 World's Fair.

The lag between Zworykin's first patent and this demonstration was the result of difficulties in developing a system that provided a clear, steady image. Throughout the 1930s, RCA funded work in this area, insisting that it should perform research and development for the entire industry. Though Zworykin had estimated that perfecting television would cost about $100,000, Sarnoff later told the *New York Times*, "RCA spent $50 million before we ever got a penny back from TV." The company spent money not only on research in the laboratory, but also on legal disputes and royalties, as rival inventor **Philo Taylor Farnsworth** successfully sued RCA when Zworykin's technology used elements similar to his own inventions. Farnsworth had demonstrated a working television system in 1927, four years after Zworykin's 1923 patent; but Farnsworth's system was closer to being ready for commercial use.

Both the iconoscope and the kinescope were based on the cathode ray tube (CRT). The iconoscope starts with projecting an image onto a photosensitive plate. This plate has an insulating layer of oxidized aluminum, which is coated with tiny drops of potassium hydride. When light falls on the drops of potassium hydride, it knocks out the electrons, leaving those drops with a positive charge. Thus, if an image is projected onto the plate, the potassium hydride drops will reproduce the light and dark areas of the image in a pattern of electrical charges. By scanning the beam with an electron gun, the charges on the plate are converted to electrical signals that convey the same information. These signals can then be transmitted to another device. Bright lights were required if the camera was to yield an accurate image.

The kinescope essentially reverses the process. As the electrical signals are sent to an electron gun, the electron gun sweeps the fluorescent picture tube, reproducing the original image in the picture tube's pixels. A key issue in this technology was therefore how quickly the kinescope could build and refresh an entire image. By the time RCA was ready to field test this technology in 1933, the scanning pattern was 240 lines, sufficient to produce a clear image on a small screen, but the frame frequency was just twenty-four cycles, leading to noticeable flicker. Early versions of Zworykin's television were also too bulky for widespread use and created only an inch-square image.

Although the television set has made successors to the iconoscope ubiquitous in American homes, the first widespread use of this technology was to guide bombs in the later years of World War II. The GB-4 guided bomb, which was affixed to a glider and dropped from a B-17, included a model 1846 iconoscope camera. A crew in an accompanying plane controlled the bomb, using data from the camera to guide it to its target. Although RCA had succeeded in miniaturizing cameras sufficiently for this use, the guidance systems were rarely capable of making the bombs hit their targets. By the end of the war cameras were mounted on derelict B-17s, which were filled with explosives and guided to hit an enemy target. This bomb was the result of Zworykin's 1934 proposal for a bomb guided by an electric eye.

Military applications of television were so top-secret that in a 1975 oral history interview sponsored by the IEEE, Zworykin refused to disclose any details. However, RCA's in-house history of the war, made available by the David Sarnoff Library at Princeton, explains that RCA obtained military contracts for three major classes of device. The BLOCK system consisted of suitcase-sized cameras used in drone missiles. The more compact and lighter MIMO system was used in glide bombs. The RING system involved non-expendable cameras used for reconnaissance. While the BLOCK and MIMO systems saw relatively little combat use, scientists in the Manhattan Project used the BLOCK system to observe processes related to making the atomic bomb safely.

The more advanced systems were based on an improvement over the original iconoscope: the Image Orthicon tube, which was ten times more sensitive than the iconoscope. While this tube, developed around 1942, was not actually used in military applications until after World War II, its lightness and compactness, as well as its superior image quality and ability to function in more normal lighting conditions, also contributed to making consumer television more appealing after the war.

Zworykin's lab also worked on other projects related to vision. These included a sniperscope, in which the processes of the iconoscope and the kinescope were modified to work with infrared radiation rather than with visible light. A 4½-inch tube mounted to a standard carbine, this sniperscope allowed marksmen to see their targets in the dark. American military in the Pacific used the sniperscope for night combat; a modified version, mounted on a pole, was used for reconnaissance. A third variant, an infrared telescope used on ships and planes, was critical to accurate bombardment in the Pacific theater. This technology has since been developed into the basis for electric eyes and text readers.

After the war, Zworykin remained with RCA until his retirement in 1954. His management style is credited with recruiting James Hillier, who invented the electron microscope. As Hillier told the story, he chose RCA because Zworykin was willing to move the project forward quickly; in fact, it was completed within four months. Zworykin also assisted **John Louis von Neumann** in creating computer applications for forecasting weather accurately.

In 1951, Zworykin married fellow scientist Katherine Polevitsky. On retirement from RCA, he became director of the Rockefeller Institute's Medical Electronics Center. He held more than 120 patents and was elected to the National Inventor's Hall of Fame in 1977. His twenty-seven major awards included a Presidential Certificate of Merit and the French Legion of Honor, both awarded in the late 1940s; the American Institute of Electrical Engineers' Edison Medal, awarded in 1952; and the National Medal of Science, awarded in 1966.

Zworykin died on July 29, 1982. His most famous work was his 1940 book, *Television: The Electronics of Image Transmission.* He was not happy with what had become of television by the end of his life.

Wende Vyborney Feller

Bibliography

Note: This selective bibliography includes general sources used in the compilation of biographical entries for this work.

Aaseng, Nathan. *Business Builders in Computers*. Minneapolis: Oliver Press, 2000.

Albaugh, William A., III, and Richard D. Steuart. *The Original Confederate Colt: The Story of the Leech & Rigdon and Rigdon-Ansley Revolvers*. New York: Greenberg, 1953.

"The American Revolution." Accessed online 1/5/2005, at www.americanrevolution .com.

Andrews, J. Cutler. *The North Reports the Civil War*. Pittsburgh: University of Pittsburgh Press, 1955.

Andrews, J. Cutler. *The South Reports the Civil War*. Princeton, NJ: Princeton University Press, 1970.

Ashmore, Harry S., and William C. Baggs. *Mission to Hanoi; A Chronicle of Double-Dealing in High Places: A Special Report From the Center for the Study of Democratic Institutions*. With a chronology of American involvement in Vietnam by Elaine H. Burnell. New York: Putnam, 1968.

Bankert, Marianne. *Watchful Care: A History of America's Nurse Anesthetists*. New York: Continuum, 2002.

Baruch, Bernard. *American Industry in the War: A Report of the War Industries Board*. New York: Prentice-Hall, 1941.

Bates, David Homer. *Lincoln in the Telegraph Office*. Lincoln: University of Nebraska Press, 1995.

Bauer, Eugene E. *Boeing in Peace and War*. Enumclaw, WA: TABA Publishing, 1991.

Beidler, Philip D. *Re-Writing America: Vietnam Authors in Their Generation*. Athens: University of Georgia Press, 1991.

Bennett, Scott H. *Radical Pacifism: The War Resisters League and Gandhian Nonviolence in America, 1915–1963*. Syracuse, NY: Syracuse University Press, 2003.

Boyne, Walter J. *Beyond the Horizons—The Lockheed Story*. New York: St. Martin's Press, 1998.

Brockett, Linus P., and Mary C. Vaughan. *Woman's Work in the Civil War: A Record of Heroism, Patriotism and Patience*. Philadelphia: Zeigler, McCurdy, and Co., 1867.

Brodie, James Michael. *Created Equal: The Lives and Ideas of Black American Innovators*. New York: William Morrow and Company, 1993.

Brooke, George M., Jr., Ed. *Ironclads and Big Guns of the Confederacy: The Journal and Letters of John M. Brooke*. Columbia: University of South Carolina Press, 2002.

Brown, Charles H. *The Correspondents' War: Journalists in the Spanish-American War*. New York: Charles Scribner's Sons, 1967.

Brown, Louis. *Radar History of World War II: Technical and Military Imperatives*. Washington, DC: Institute of Physics Publishing, 2000.

Bull, Stephen. *Encyclopedia of Military Technology and Innovation*. Westport, CT: Greenwood Press, 2004.

Burchard, J. E. *Q.E.D.: M.I.T. in World War II*. New York: John Wiley and Sons, 1948.

Burns, Stewart. *To the Mountaintop: Martin Luther King Jr.'s Sacred Mission to Save America: 1955–1968*. San Francisco: Harper, 2004.

Cassidy, David C. *J. Robert Oppenheimer and the American Century*. New York: Pi Press, 2005.

Catton, Bruce. *The War Lords of Washington*. New York: Harcourt, Brace, 1948. Reprint, New York: Greenwood Press, 1969.

Cimbala, Paula A., and Randall M. Miller. *An Uncommon Time: The Civil War and the Northern Homefront*. New York: Fordham University Press, 2002.

Clarkson, Grosvenor B. *Industrial America in the World War: The Strategy behind the Line, 1917–1918*. Boston: Houghton Mifflin, 1923.

Compton, Arthur H. *Atomic Quest: A Personal Narrative*. New York: Oxford University Press, 1956.

Conant, Jennet. *Tuxedo Park: A Wall Street Tycoon and the Secret Palace of Science That Changed the Course of World War II*. Waterville, ME: Thorndike Press, 2002.

Copeland, David A., general ed. *The Greenwood Library of War Reporting*. 8 Vols. Westport, CT: Greenwood Press, 2005.

Cornebise, Alfred E. *Art from the Trenches: America's Uniformed Artists in World War I*. College Station: Texas A&M University Press, 1991.

Crowell, Benedict, and Robert Forrest Wilson. *The Armies of Industry*. 2 vols. New Haven: Yale University Press, 1921.

Curran, Thomas F. *Civil War Pacifism and the Postwar Radical Peace Movement*. New York: Fordham University Press, 2003.

DeBenedetti, Charles. *Peace Heroes in Twentieth-Century America*. Bloomington: Indiana University Press, 1986.

DeJong, Russell N. *A History of American Neurology*. New York: Raven Press, 1982.

DeNoon, Christopher. *Posters of the WPA*. Los Angeles: Wheatley Press, 1987.

Dickey, Thomas S., and Peter C. George. *Field Artillery Projectiles of the American Civil War*. Atlanta, GA: Arsenal Press, 1980.

Dodd, Loring H. *Generation of Illustrators and Etchers*. Boston: Chapman and Grimes, 1960.

Dubovsky, Melvyn and Warren Van Tine, eds. *Labor Leaders in America*. Urbana: University of Illinois Press, 1987.

Eastman, Max. *Love and Revolution: My Journey through an Epoch*. New York: Random House, 1964.

Ehrhart, W. D., ed. *Unaccustomed Mercy: Soldier-Poets of the Vietnam War*. Lubbock: Texas Tech University Press, 1989.

Ellsberg, Daniel. *Secrets: A Memoir of Vietnam and the Pentagon Papers*. New York: Viking, 2002.

Elshtain, Jean Bethke. *Jane Addams and the Dream of American Democracy*. New York: Basic Books, 2002.

Emerson, Gloria. *Winners and Losers: Battles, Retreats, Gains, Losses, and Ruins from the Vietnam War*. New York: Penguin Books, 1985.

Federici, Gary. *From the Sea to the Stars: A History of U.S. Navy Space and Space-Related Activities*. Washington, DC: Department of the Navy, Naval Historical Center, June 1977. Accessed online 9/12/2005, at www.history.navy.mil/books/space.

"FirstWorldWar.Com: The War to End All Wars." Accessed online 1/10/2005, at www.firstworldwar.com.

Fitzgerald, Richard. *Art and Politics: Cartoonists of the* Masses *and* Liberator. Westport, CT: Greenwood Press, 1973.

Flexner, J. T. *Steamboats Come True*. 2nd ed. Boston: Little, Brown, 1978.

Foner, Eric. *Tom Paine and Revolutionary America*. New York: Oxford University Press, 1976.

Friedman, Norman. *U.S. Naval Weapons*. Annapolis: Naval Institute Press, 1982.

Fuller, Claude E. *The Whitney Firearms*. Huntington, WV: Standard Publications, 1946.

Gavin, Lettie. *American Women in World War I: They Also Served*. Niwot: University Press of Colorado, 1997.

Gies, Joseph, and Frances Gies. *The Ingenious Yankees*. New York: Thomas Y. Cromwell Company, 1976.

Giesberg, Judith Ann. *Civil War Sisterhood: The U.S. Sanitary Commission and Women's Politics in Transition*. Boston: Northeastern University Press, 2000.

Gilman, Owen W. Jr. *Vietnam and the Southern Imagination*. Jackson: University Press of Mississippi, 1992.

Gitlin, Todd. *The Sixties: Years of Hope, Days of Rage*. New York: Bantam Books, 1987.

Gluckman, Arcadi. *United States Muskets, Rifles, and Carbines*. Buffalo, NY: Otto Ulbrich Co., 1948.

Gotera, Vince. *Radical Visions: Poetry by Vietnam Veterans*. Athens: University of Georgia Press, 1994.

Green, Constance McLaughlin. *Eli Whitney and the Birth of American Technology*. Boston: Little, Brown, 1956.

Green, Constance McLaughlin, Harry C. Thomson, and Peter C. Roots. *The Ordnance Department: Planning Munitions for War*. Washington, DC: Department of the Army, Office of the Chief of Military History, 1955.

Grubbs, Frank L. *Samuel Gompers and the Great War: Protecting Labor's Standards.* Wake Forest, NC: Meridional Publications, 1982.

Guerlac, Henry. *Radar in World War II.* Los Angeles: Tomash Publishers; New York: American Institute of Physics, 1987.

Hallahan, William H. *Misfire: The History of How America's Small Arms Have Failed Our Military.* New York: Charles Scribner's Sons, 1994.

Hallin, Daniel C. *The "Uncensored War": The Media and Vietnam.* Berkeley: University of California Press, 1989.

Harris, Brayton. *Blue and Gray in Black and White.* Washington, DC: Brassey's, 1999.

Hecht, Jeff. *City of Light: The Story of Fiber Optics.* New York: Oxford University Press, 1999.

Herken, Gregg. *Brotherhood of the Bomb: The Tangled Lives and Loyalties of Robert Oppenheimer, Ernest Lawrence, and Edward Teller.* New York: Henry Holt & Co., 2002.

Hoffman, Abbie, et al. *The Conspiracy.* New York: Dell Publishing Co., 1969.

Hughan, Jessie Wallace. *Three Decades of War Resistance.* New York: War Resistors League, 1942.

Ingham, John N. *Biographical Dictionary of American Business Leaders.* 4 Vols. Westport, CT: Greenwood Press, 1983.

Irons, Peter. *Justice at War: The Story of the Japanese American Internment Cases.* Berkeley: University of California Press, 1983.

Jason, Philip K., and Mark A. Graves, eds. *Encyclopedia of American War Literature.* Westport, CT: Greenwood Press, 2001.

Jeansonne, Glen. *Women of the Far Right.* Chicago: University of Chicago Press, 1996.

Kennedy, David M. *Over Here: The First World War and American Society.* 25th Anniversary Ed. New York: Oxford University Press, 2004.

Killian, James R. Jr. *Sputnik, Scientists, and Eisenhower.* Cambridge, MA: MIT Press, 1977.

Klejment, Anne, and Nancy L. Roberts. *American Catholic Pacifism: The Influence of Dorothy Day and the Catholic Worker Movement.* Westport, CT: Praeger, 1996.

Langguth, A. J. *Patriots: The Men Who Started the American Revolution.* New York: Simon and Schuster, 1988.

Lanker, Brian, and Nicole Newnham. *They Drew Fire: Combat Artists of World War II.* New York: TV Books, 2000.

Leeman, Richard. *African-American Orators: A Bio-Critical Sourcebook.* Westport, CT: Praeger, 1996.

Letterman, Jonathan. *Medical Recollections of the Army of the Potomac.* New York: D. Appleton and Company, 1866.

Lewis, Tom. *Empire of the Air: The Men Who Made Radio.* New York: E. Burlingame Books, 1991.

Library of Congress. "Women Come to the Front: Journalists, Photographers, and Broadcasters during World War II." Accessed online 9/12/2005, at www.loc.gov/exhibits/wcf/wcf0014.html.

Library of Congress, Hispanic Division. "The World of 1898: The Spanish-American War." Accessed online 1/3/2005, at www.loc.gov/rr/hispanic/1898.

Malone, Michael S. *The Microprocessor: A Biography.* Santa Clara, CA: TELOS, 1995.

McAulay, John D. *Civil War Breech Loading Rifles.* Lincoln, RI: A. Mowbray, 1987.

Melton, Jack W., Jr., and Lawrence E. Pawl. *Introduction to Field Artillery Ordnance 1861–1865*. Kennesaw, GA: Kennesaw Mountain Press, 1994.

Miles, Wyndham D., ed. *American Chemists and Chemical Engineers*. Washington, DC: American Chemical Society, 1976.

National Inventors Hall of Fame Foundation, Inc. "Hall of Fame." Accessed online 12/8/2004, at www.invent.org.

Nelan, Charles. *Cartoons of Our War with Spain*. New York: F. A. Stokes Company, 1898.

Nelson, Donald M. *Arsenal of Democracy*. New York: Harcourt, Brace, 1946.

Northrup, Mary. *American Computer Pioneers*. Springfield, NJ: Enslow Publishers, 1998.

Pilcher, J. E. *The Surgeon Generals of the Army*. Carlysle, PA: Association of Military Surgeons, 1905.

Plum, William Rattle. *The Military Telegraph during the Civil War in the United States*. Chicago: Jansen, McLurg & Co., 1882. Reprint, New York: Arno Press, 1974.

Price, Alfred. *Instruments of Darkness: The History of Electronic Warfare*. Mechanicsburg, PA: Stackpole Books, 2005.

Rall, Ted. *Attitude 2: The New Subversive Alternative Cartoonists*. New York: Nantier Beall/Minoustchine Publishing, 2004.

Rawls, Walton. *Wake Up, America! World War I and the American Poster*. New York: Abbeville Press, 1988.

Reed, Walt. *The Illustrator in America: 1860–2000*. New York: Watson-Guptill, 2001.

Reporting Vietnam: Part One: American Journalism 1959–1969. New York: Library of America, 1998.

Rhodes, Richard. *The Making of the Atomic Bomb*. New York: Simon & Schuster, 1986.

Rosenblum, Naomi. *A History of Women Photographers*. New York: Abbeville Press, 2000.

Rywell, Martin. *The Gun That Shaped American Destiny*. Harriman, TN: Pioneer Press, 1957.

Sarnecky, Mary T. *A History of the U.S. Army Nurse Corps*. Philadelphia: University of Pennsylvania Press, 1999.

Schwarz, Jordan A. *The New Dealers: Power Politics in the Age of Roosevelt*. New York: Alfred A. Knopf, 1993.

Schweber, Silvan S. *In the Shadow of the Bomb: Bethe, Oppenheimer, and the Moral Responsibility of the Scientist*. Princeton, NJ: Princeton University Press, 2000.

Sears, Richard S. *V-Discs: A History and Discography*. Westport, CT: Greenwood Press, 1980.

Sheehan, John C. *The Enchanted Ring; The Untold Story of Penicillin*. Cambridge, MA: MIT Press, 1982.

Shulman, Seth. *Unlocking the Sky: Glenn Hammond Curtiss and the Race to Invent the Airplane*. New York: Perennial, 2003.

Silber, John. *Songs of the Civil War*. New York: Columbia University Press, 1960.

Smith, Anthony. *Machine Gun: The Story of the Men and the Weapon That Changed the Face of War*. New York: St. Martin's Press, 2002.

Smith, R. Elberton. *The Army and Economic Mobilization*. Washington, DC: Department of the Army, Office of the Chief of Military History, 1959.

Spann, Edward K. *Democracy's Children: The Young Rebels of the 1960s and the Power of Ideals*. Wilmington, DE: SR Books, 2003.

Stewart, Irvin. *Organizing Scientific Research for War*. Boston: Little Brown, 1948.

Straubing, Harold Elk, comp. *In Hospital and Camp: The Civil War through the Eyes of Its Doctors and Nurses*. Harrisburg, PA: Stackpole Books, 1993.

Sundiata, Ibrahim. *Brothers and Strangers: Black Zion, Black Slavery, 1914–1940*. Durham, NC: Duke University Press, 2003.

Taylor, Nick. *Laser: The Inventor, the Nobel Laureate, and the Thirty-Year Patent War*. New York: Simon & Schuster, 2000.

Treadwell, Mattie E. *The Women's Army Corps*. Washington, DC: Department of the Army, Office of the Chief of Military History, 1954.

United States Army Ordnance Corps. "U.S. Army Ordnance Hall of Fame." Accessed online 3/4/2005, at www.goordnance.apg.army.mil.

United States Civilian Production Administration. *Industrial Mobilization for War, History of the War Production Board and Predecessor Agencies, 1940–1945*. Washington, DC, 1947.

Weil, David, Ed. *Leaders of the Information Age*. New York: H. W. Wilson, 2003.

Wicks, Frank. "Trial by Flyer." In "100 Years of Flight." *ME Magazine Online*, 2003. Accessed online 11/15/2005, at http://www.memagazine.org/supparch/flight03/trialby/trialby.html.

Williams, Eugene Frank. *Soldiers of God—The Chaplains of the Revolutionary War*. New York: Carlton Press, 1975.

Wilson, Edmund. *Patriotic Gore*. New York: W. W. Norton, 1994.

Winkler, Allan M. *Politics of Propaganda*. New Haven: Yale University Press, 1978.

Yenne, Bill. *100 Inventions That Shaped World History*. San Francisco: Bluewood Books, 1983.

Index

Note: Single page numbers called out within a bold number or range indicate a photograph. Bold-faced numbers indicate main entry.

Morrison, Harry Steele, **605**
Morrison, Norman, **605–6**
Morrison, Philip, **606**
Morse code, 222
Morse, Philip M., 178, **607–9**
Morse, Samuel Finley Breese, 112, 171, 333, 607, **607–9**
Moses, Robert, 549
Moss, Sanford Alexander, **609–10**
motion picture industry, 224; pioneers, 264–65; soundtracks introduced in, 224
Mott, John R., 43
Mott, Lucretia Coffin, 540, **610**
Moulton, Forest Ray, **610–11**
movement: anti-war, 544–45, 572; civil rights, 40, 166, 481–84; isolationist, 675, 822, 847, 851; labor, 216, 390, 407–8; men's, 97–98; open source, 12; Pan-Africanist, 331; peace, 79, 430; protest, 774; women's, 259, 405, 408, 428, 430
MoveOn, 143, 657
movie industry, 727–28
Moyer, Andrew J., 270, **611–12,** 750
Moynier, Gustave, 56
Muhlenberg, John Peter Gabriel, **612**
Mulliken, Robert Sanderson, **612–13**
multiplexing, 23
Munroe, Charles Edward, 266, 613, **613–14**
murals, 85
Murphy, Audie Leon, 614, **614**; Medal of Honor awarded to, 614; Purple Heart awarded to, **614**
Murray, Henry Alexander, **614–15**
Murray, John Courtney, **615**
Murray, Philip, 521, **616**
Murrow, Edward Roscoe, 209, **616–18,** 617, 662, 748
musical compositions, 83, 89, 132–33, 142, 166, 198, 385, 440, 475
musket(s), 229; production, 853–54; rifles, 15; used during War of 1812, 855
Musser, C. Walton, 493, **618**
mustard gas, 5
Muste, Abraham Johannes, **618–21**
Myer, Dillon Seymour, 269, 492, **621–23**
Myers, Isabel Briggs, 584, **623–24**

Mygatt, Tracy, 42, **624,** 867
My Life So Far (Fonda, Jane Seymour), 306

NAACP. *See* National Association of Colored People
Nader, Ralph, 20
Nakayama, Jimmy, 325
The Naked and the Dead (Mailer, Norman Kingsley), 552
napalm, 293–94, 726; used in Vietnam War, 605
NASA, 684
Nash, John Forbes, **625–27**; Nobel Prize awarded to, 627
Nast, Thomas, **627–28,** 628
Nathan, Robert Roy, 496–97, **628–29**
Nation of Islam, 14
The Nation, 42, 227, 350, 519, 804
National Academy of Sciences, 2
National American Women's Suffrage Organization, 152
National Association of Colored People (NAACP), 407, 691, 849
National Cash Register Company, 219
National Defense Research Committee, 5, 137–38, 173, 175, 247, 288, 350, 383, 392, 443, 534, 561, 641, 685, 809, 815, 830
National Geographic Society, 68
National Medal of Science: awarded to Baker, William Oliver, 41; awarded to Eckert, John Presper Jr., 263; awarded to Edgerton, Harold Eugene, 264; awarded to Goldmark, Peter Carl, 350
National Portrait Gallery, 4
National Reconnaissance Organization, 671
National Research Defense Council, 486
National Review, 260
National Rifle Association, 404
Native Americans: activists, 48–49, 226; in military, 597; during World War I, 597. *See also* assimilation; Hopi(s)
Native American veterans, 598, 703–5; citizenship and, 704; World War II, 758
naval aircraft, 433–34
Naval Research Library, 1–2
navy: medicine practiced in, 57; ships, 432–33

About the Editor
and the Contributors

BENJAMIN F. SHEARER received his Ph.D. in the history of ideas from St. Louis University and his M.S.L.S. from the University of Illinois–Urbana–Champaign. He has written and edited several reference works including *The Uniting States* (Greenwood, 2004) and *State Names, Seals, Flags, and Symbols* (Third Edition, Greenwood Publishing Group, 2002).

VALERIE L. ADAMS, Ph.D., is Assistant Professor of History at Embry-Riddle Aeronautical University in Prescott, Arizona. Her main interests are in twentieth-century American history and diplomatic history. She is the author of several pieces on the Cold War and on science and technology.

REBECCA A. ADELMAN is a Ph.D. student in the Department of Comparative Studies at the Ohio State University, where she recently completed her M.A. in women's studies. Her research interests lie primarily in the study of American nationalism and the militarization of popular culture. She teaches a course on the role of television spectacles in American politics.

MADALYN ARD earned her B.A. in both English and History in 2002 from Texas A&M University–Corpus Christi. She is currently a graduate student at Texas A&M University in the history department.

ELLEN BAIER is an independent scholar and writer who is also active in theater and national tour productions. In 2004 Franklin & Marshall College awarded her its Williamson Medal.

MARJORIE A. BAIER earned a B.S. in nursing in 1972 from the University of Illinois in Chicago, an M.S. from Southern Illinois University–Edwardsville in 1977, and a Ph.D. from Saint Louis University in 1995. She is an associate professor at Southern Illinois University–Edwardsville in the School of Nursing.

KELLY J. BAKER holds a B.A. in American and Florida studies and an M.A. in religion (American religious history), both from Florida State University. She is assistant to the editors of *Church History: Studies in Christianity and Culture*.

BALA JAMES BAPTISTE, Ph.D., is an Assistant Professor of Communications at Miles College.

JOHN H. BARNHILL received his Ph.D. in twentieth-century American history from Oklahoma State University, Stillwater, Oklahoma. Retired from the Defense Information Systems Agency, he is currently an independent scholar in Houston, Texas. His publications are in civil rights and liberties, immigration, labor, and military history.

JAMES S. BAUGESS is an instructor in the humanities department at Columbus State Community College in Columbus, Ohio, where he has taught since 1991. He has published entries in *The Encyclopedia of the American Civil War, The Chronology of World Slavery*, and *Amazons to Fighter Pilots: A Biographical Dictionary of Women in the Military*. He also has in print two dozen book reviews, and recently finished a term as a coordinator for the United States Department of Education's Teaching American History Grant Project.

WALTER F. BELL is retired Assistant Reference Librarian at the University of North Texas, Denton and Lamar University, Beaumont, Texas. He completed his Ph.D. in history at the University of Iowa in 1983 and his M.L.S., also from Iowa, in 1986.

CHRISTOPHER BERKELEY, independent scholar, has taught history at the University of Wisconsin–Madison, Lassell College, and Framingham State College and contributed to numerous reference works including *The Oxford Companion to United States History, The Encyclopedia of New England*, and *The Encyclopedia of History and Historians*.

MATTHEW J. BOLTON, Ph.D., completed his doctoral work in English at the Graduate Center of the City University of New York. He is the Dean of Students at the Loyola School in New York City, an Adjunct Professor in English at the College of Mount Saint Vincent, and the author of numerous articles and reviews.

RON BRILEY is a history teacher and Assistant Headmaster at Sandia Preparatory School in Albuquerque, New Mexico, where he has taught for twenty-seven years. He is also an Adjunct Professor of History at the University of New Mexico, Valencia Campus. His academic specialties are film, sports history, and popular culture. In addition to articles in numerous scholarly journals, anthologies, and reference works, Ron is the author of *Class at Bat*, *Gender on Deck*, and *Race in the Hole: A Line Up of Essays on Twentieth-Century Culture and America's National Game* (2003).

DAVID M. CARLETTA holds two M.A. degrees, one in history, from Sonoma State University, and another in international affairs, from Ohio University. A doctoral student in history at Michigan State University, he is currently writing a dissertation on twentieth-century U.S.–Latin American relations.

AL CARROLL recently completed his Ph.D. in history at Arizona State University. His primary research interest is in Native American veterans.

XIMENA CHRISAGIS is a Health Sciences Librarian at the Fordham Health Sciences Library at Wright State University in Dayton, Ohio. She earned her M.S. in Library and Information Science from the University of Illinois at Urbana-Champaign (1995) and her M.A. in Public History from Wright State University (2003). She also achieved senior status in the Medical Library Association's Academy of Health Information Professionals in 2003.

MARGARET DENNY is a Ph.D. candidate in art history and the history of photography at the University of Illinois at Chicago. She has taught a number of courses in art history as an adjunct member of the faculty.

KERRY DEXTER is a writer, producer, and photographer who specializes in heritage music, including folk, country, Celtic, Native American, bluegrass, Americana, and Hispanic. She is Senior Contributing Editor at *FolkWax* and Senior Contributing Writer to the roots/world music magazine *Dirty Linen*. She has also been Folk Music Editor at VH1.com. She is a contributor to *The MusicHound Guide to World Music*, *The MusicHound Guide to Classical Music*, and *The Encyclopedia of Counter Culture*, as well as other reference works. She holds degrees in visual arts and history. Currently she is researching a book on Irish American musicians and contributing chapters to a work on career strategies for musicians.

DAVID DIEHL is pursuing a Doctor of Arts degree in music at Ball State University in Muncie, Indiana. He has taught instrumental music in the public school system in Nashville, Tennessee, and music history, music education, and instrumental music at his alma mater, Trevecca Nazarene University, also in Nashville.

STACY DORGAN is a graduate student in American Studies at the City University of New York, Graduate Center. Her research uses comparative analysis and the development of a transnational perspective to work beyond a nation-based frame of analysis. Her master's thesis is entitled, "The Promotion of American Literature in Postwar Germany: Reflecting Changing Notions of American Culture."

JÉRÔME DORVIDAL, Ph.D., D.E.A., M.A., is Associate Researcher, CRE-SOI (University of La Réunion). In parallel with a Ph.D. dissertation on pacifism and nuclear deterrence in Australia, he participated in several academic projects, including the *Dictionary of Modern Myths* (2000). He is the author of several articles in the field of contemporary military history. Most of his papers have a focus on the Australasian strategic area during the Cold War.

JACQUELINE E. ENGLERT received her M.A. degree from Georgia Southern University. She is the author of an article titled, "Hell's Angel: Eleanor Kinzie Gordon's Summer at Camp Miami." She is very interested in women's unexpected roles in war. She also teaches various history courses at colleges in the Savannah, Georgia, area.

LISA A. ENNIS, B.A., M.S., is Reference Librarian and School of Nursing liaison at the University of Alabama–Birmingham Lister Hill Library of the Health Sciences. She received her M.A in history from Georgia College (1994) and her M.S. in Information Science from the University of Tennessee (1997). Among her research interests are medical history, women's basketball, and library leadership.

WENDE VYBORNEY FELLER, Ph.D., is a corporate consultant and freelance writer. A graduate of the University of Minnesota, she has taught at a variety of universities, including most recently the Executive MBA program at the College of St. Mary in Moraga, California. Among her academic presentations are papers on changes in Japanese and American war rhetoric at the conclusion of World War II. She lives in Phoenix and is working on her first novel.

WILLIAM M. FERRARO holds a Ph.D. in American Civilization from Brown University and is a Documentary Editor with the Ulysses S. Grant Association, Southern Illinois University—Carbondale. His research and publications focus on nineteenth-century U.S. history, with an emphasis on the family and lives of John Sherman and William Tecumseh Sherman.

DONALD C. FORCE is a native of western Pennsylvania who graduated from Southern Illinois University Carbondale in December 2004 with an M.A. in history, concentrating on World War I and American History. Currently, he is at Indiana University working on M.S. degrees in library science and library information science and studying to become an archivist.

DIANE FOSTER received her M.S. in library and information studies from Florida State University in 1995. She is a Reference Librarian at Florida State's Dirac Science Library. She is also active in national and local library organizations and is working toward certification as a Certified Genealogical Records Specialist.

GENE C. GERARD is an Adjunct Instructor in History at Tarrant County College in Arlington, Texas. He attended the University of Oklahoma, receiving a B.A. with distinction in ethics and religion in 1990, and an M.A. in history in 1992. He is the Book Review Editor for nineteenth-century American history with the History News Network. He has been a contributing author to several reference works, including *Encyclopedia of the Great Black Migration* and *Women in the American Civil War: An Encyclopedia.*

AGNES HOOPER GOTTLIEB is the Dean of Freshman Studies at Seton Hall University. She was a Professor of Journalism History in the Communication Department at the university and is the author of two books, *Women Journalists and the Municipal Housekeeping Movement* and *1,000 Years, 1,000 People: Ranking the Men and Women Who Shaped the Millennium*, which she co-authored with her husband and another couple. She has written dozens of articles to journalism history journals, books, and newspapers.

PAMELA LEE GRAY is an independent scholar who holds a Ph.D. in American History from the University of Southern California. Her written work includes over one hundred academic articles and several books on local history. Her curriculum design work teaches history using ethnography and historical visual images.

MICHAEL R. HALL is Associate Professor in the History Department at Armstrong Atlantic State University. He did his undergraduate work at Gettysburg College and his M.A. and Ph.D. at Ohio University. He is the author of *Sugar and Power in the Dominican Republic: Eisenhower, Kennedy, and the Trujillos* (Greenwood Press, 2000).

RALPH HARTSOCK, Senior Music Catalog Librarian for the University of North Texas Libraries, is author of two Greenwood biobibliographies in music: *Otto Luening* (1991), and *Vladimir Ussachevsky* (2000), the latter in collaboration with Carl Rahkonen. He has published numerous articles on American composers and musicians, including Jacob Estey, Francesco Fanciulli, Milton Babbitt, and Edgard Varese.

ANN M. HICKS recently completed a Masters of Music degree in clarinet performance and music education from Ball State University. She is an active performer and next year will be on faculty in the Music Education Department at the University. Prior to her studies at Ball State, Ann taught band for six years in Iowa and earned her B.A. degree in instrumental music from Iowa State University.

MARTIN KICH, Ph.D., completed his doctoral work at Lehigh University and is professor of English at Wright State University–Lake Campus. He has authored numerous articles and reviews.

LEIGH HUSBAND KIMMEL, the author of numerous articles, is an independent scholar who holds an M.A. in history from Illinois State University.

ARLENE LAZAROWITZ is an Associate Professor of History at California State University, Long Beach. She holds a Ph.D. in U.S. political history and foreign policy from the University of California, Los Angeles. Her research interests include the politics and foreign relations of the Cold War. She also directs the Jewish Studies Program and coordinates the Social Science Credential Program at California State University, Long Beach.

ERSKINE L. LEVI JR., M.Ed., is a former captain in the U.S. Army. Currently, he teaches U.S. history at the Baldwin Park Unified School District and is an Adjunct Professor of History, Humanities, and Teacher Education at the University of Phoenix, Southern California.

RONALD S. MARMARELLI received his M.A. in journalism from Temple University and has over thirty years of experience as a writer, editor, and educator.

MELISSA A. MARSH received her B.A. in history from Chadron State College in 1997 and her M.A. in history from the University of Nebraska–Lincoln in 2004. She is an independent historian and writer and lives with her family in Lincoln, Nebraska.

PATRICIA MARTON holds a Ph.D. in education from the University of Illinois–Urbana-Champaign, with a concentration in history. She is currently a Road Scholar for the Illinois Humanities Council, lecturing on family history, and also lectures at conferences throughout the country on the same subject.

MICHAEL L. MCGREGOR is an independent scholar who studied history at the University of Northern Iowa and George Mason University. His research is focused on German-American relations in the second half of the nineteenth century.

PATIT PABAN MISHRA is Professor of History at Sambalpur University, Orissa, India. His articles have been published in various international journals, and he is author of a number of books. He regularly attends international conferences and has presented papers and chaired sessions around the world.

He has contributed many articles in encyclopedias published in the United States. He was president of the Indian History Congress, Countries Other Than India, in 2004.

NICOLE MITCHELL, a former archivist, is currently pursuing a Ph.D. in library science at the University of Alabama. She received her M.A. in history from Georgia College and State University.

NESTOR L. OSORIO received an undergraduate degree in mathematics and physics from the Universidad del Atlantico, Colombia, and M.S. degrees in physics and in library and information science from the State University of New York. He is a Professor and Subject Specialist for Science and Engineering at Northern Illinois University, DeKalb. An author of numerous scholarly papers and bibliographies, his areas of interest include technical information, the use and development of digital collections, content analysis, and bibliometrics.

CHARLENE T. OVERTURF is an Instructor at Armstrong Atlantic State University in the Department of History. She received her M.A. degree in history in May 2005 and planned to begin work on her Ph.D. in 2006. She specializes in U.S. Diplomatic History, Latin American History, and Third World Studies.

JERRY L. PARKER received his M.A. in history from California State University–Chico. He currently lives in Reno, Nevada, and is on the adjunct faculty of Truckee Meadows Community College. He has contributed to *The Detective as Historian: History and Art in Historical Crime Fiction*, *The Louisiana Purchase: An Encyclopedia*, and the third edition of the *Dictionary of American History*.

MARGUERITE R. PLUMMER is Associate Professor of History and Director of the Pioneer Heritage Center at Louisiana State University in Shreveport. She received her Ph.D. in Humanities–History of Ideas from the University of Texas at Dallas.

LINDA POHLY earned her Ph.D. from Ohio State University and is a Professor of Music History at Ball State University. Her primary research area is American music of the late nineteenth and early twentieth centuries. She teaches music history for non–music majors and undergraduate music majors as well as a variety of graduate-level music history courses, including a special topic seminar, "Music and War." In 2005 she was a Summer Research Visiting Scholar at Oxford University.

EDWARD J. RIELLY chairs the English Department at Saint Joseph's College of Maine. He has taught and written extensively about the Vietnam War and the 1960s, including *The 1960s* in the Greenwood American Popular Culture through History series. Other books include ten collections of his own poetry, *Baseball: An Encyclopedia of Popular Culture*, and *Baseball and American Culture: Across the Diamond*. He is working on a biography of F. Scott Fitzgerald for Greenwood Press and another book, to be titled, *Baseball in the Classroom: Teaching America's National Pastime*.

KATHLEEN RUPPERT is an independent scholar who holds a Ph.D. in history from the Catholic University of America. She specializes in British and Irish history, but has written on a wide array of topics in American and Continental European history as well. She lives in Rochester, New York, where she spends her time teaching, writing, and raising three young children.

KELLY BOYER SAGERT is a freelance writer who has published more than a thousand pieces of her writing in magazines, newspapers, encyclopedias, and online venues. She has also published four books, the most recent of which is *Joe Jackson: A Biography* (Greenwood Publishing Group, 2004).

MARGARET D. SANKEY earned her Ph.D. in history at Auburn University and is an assistant professor at Minnesota State University–Moorhead.

MARC L. SCHWARZ received his Ph.D. from University of California at Los Angeles and is Associate Professor of history at the University of New Hampshire.

CARLA ROSE SHAPIRO received her D.Phil. in Media and Cultural Studies from the University of Sussex. She is currently a Research Fellow at the Department of History, University of Toronto. She is also an independent curator whose research focuses on artistic and museological approaches to visualizing the experiences of Holocaust and genocide survivors. She has recently applied approaches to exploring historical events through the prism of photographic portraiture, biography, and autobiography in a broadened context.

DAVID J. STEELE, Ph.D., is Associate Dean for Curriculum and Evaluation and Director, Office of Medical Education, at the Florida State University College of Medicine.

ILENE STEELE, J.D., retired from the practice of law to become a Master Gardener and a popular actor in the Tallahassee, Florida, area community theater.

CORY JOE STEWART received his B.A. degree from Appalachian State University in Boone, North Carolina, and then completed his M.A. degree in history there. He is currently working on a Ph.D. in American history at the University of North Carolina at Greensboro.

MIKE TIMONIN holds a B.A. in English from the University of Ottawa and an M.A. in American history from James Madison University. He has contributed to several publications and conferences and served as a research assistant at the George C. Marshall Memorial Library.

WILLIAM P. TOTH teaches writing at Heidelberg College and has been published in both the United States and England. His history and literary writing have appeared in *African American National Biography*, *Back Home in Kentucky*, *Bend in the River*, *Chronicles of the Old West*, *Encyclopedia of African American History*, *SuperReal: The British Journal of Surrealism*, and others.

DALLACE W. UNGER JR. received his M.A. degree in military history from Colorado State University. He is a freelance writer living in Colorado who has written on a number of different topics dealing with military history.

JITENDRA UTTAM earned his Ph.D. in international political economy from Seoul National University. He is a Research Associate at the Center for East Asian Studies in the School of International Studies at Jawaharlal Nehru University.

J. A. WALWIK holds a Ph.D. in history from American University and is currently an assistant professor in the Department of History at the American University in Cairo.

ANDREW J. WASKEY, Ph.D., has degrees from Georgia Institute of Technology, the University of Southern Mississippi, and Austin Presbyterian Theological Seminary. He is now an associate professor of social science at Dalton State College, where he teaches philosophy, world religion and government. His specialties are Calvinism, political theory, world history and world religions.

LINDA S. WATTS is Professor of Interdisciplinary Arts and Sciences at the University of Washington, Bothell. She earned her B.A. at the University of Delaware and her Ph.D. in American Studies at Yale University. She is the author of *Rapture Untold: Gender, Mysticism, and the "Moment of Recognition" in Writings by Gertrude Stein* (1996) and *Gertrude Stein: A Study of the Short Fiction* (1999). She is currently writing a book to be titled, *An Encyclopedia of American Folklore*.